Chapter 21: Blood Flower

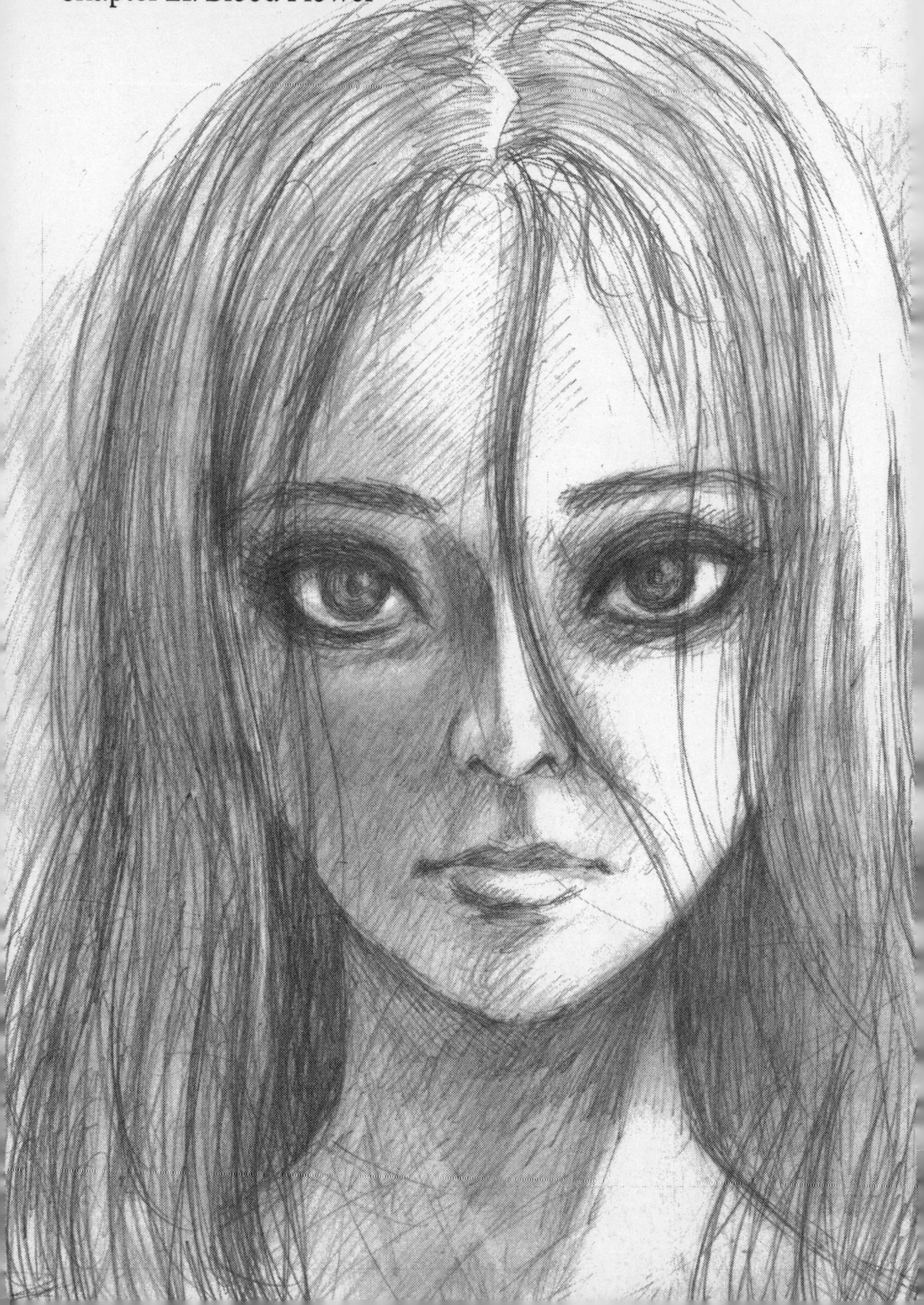

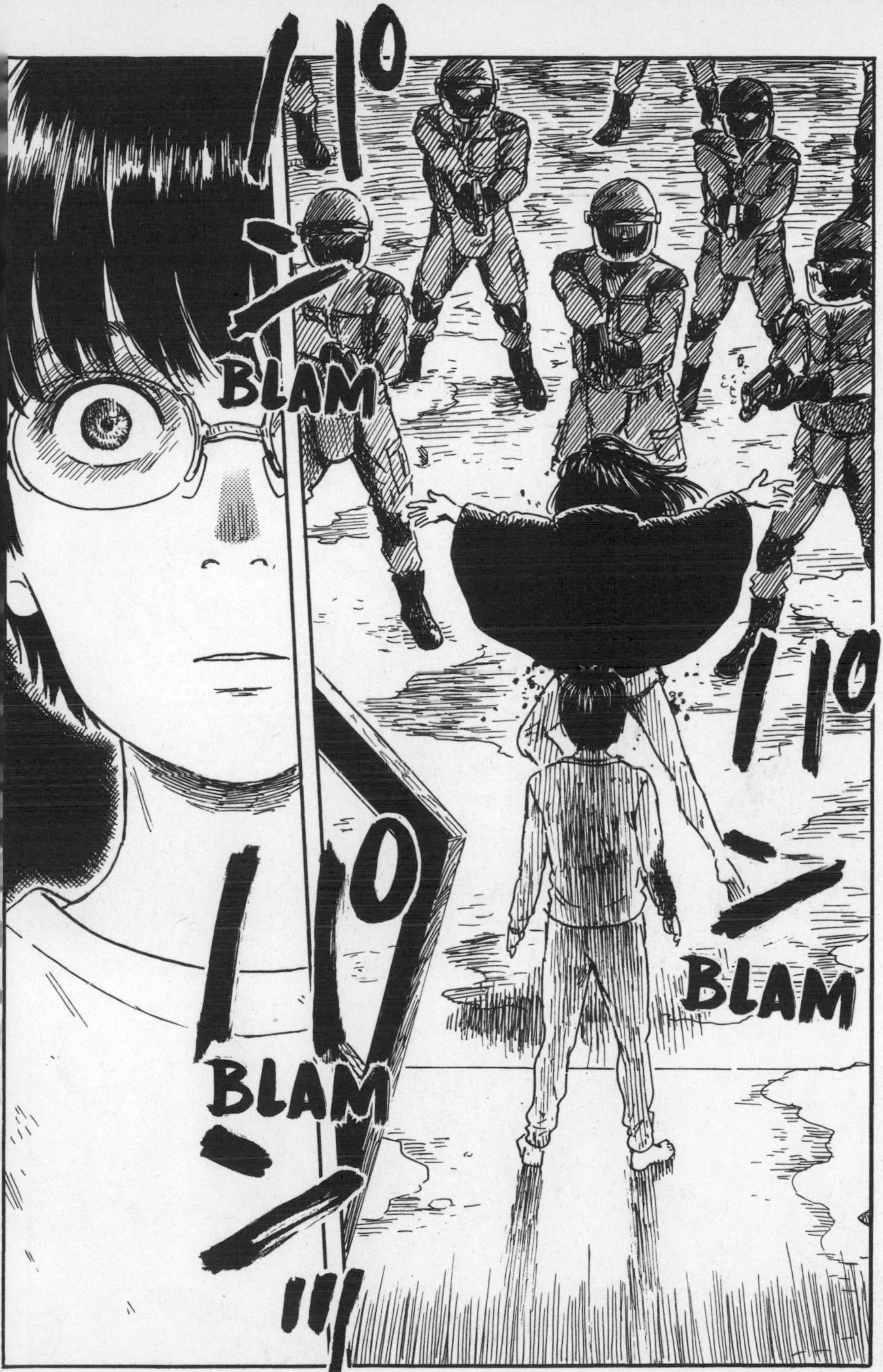
BLAM
BLAM
BLAM

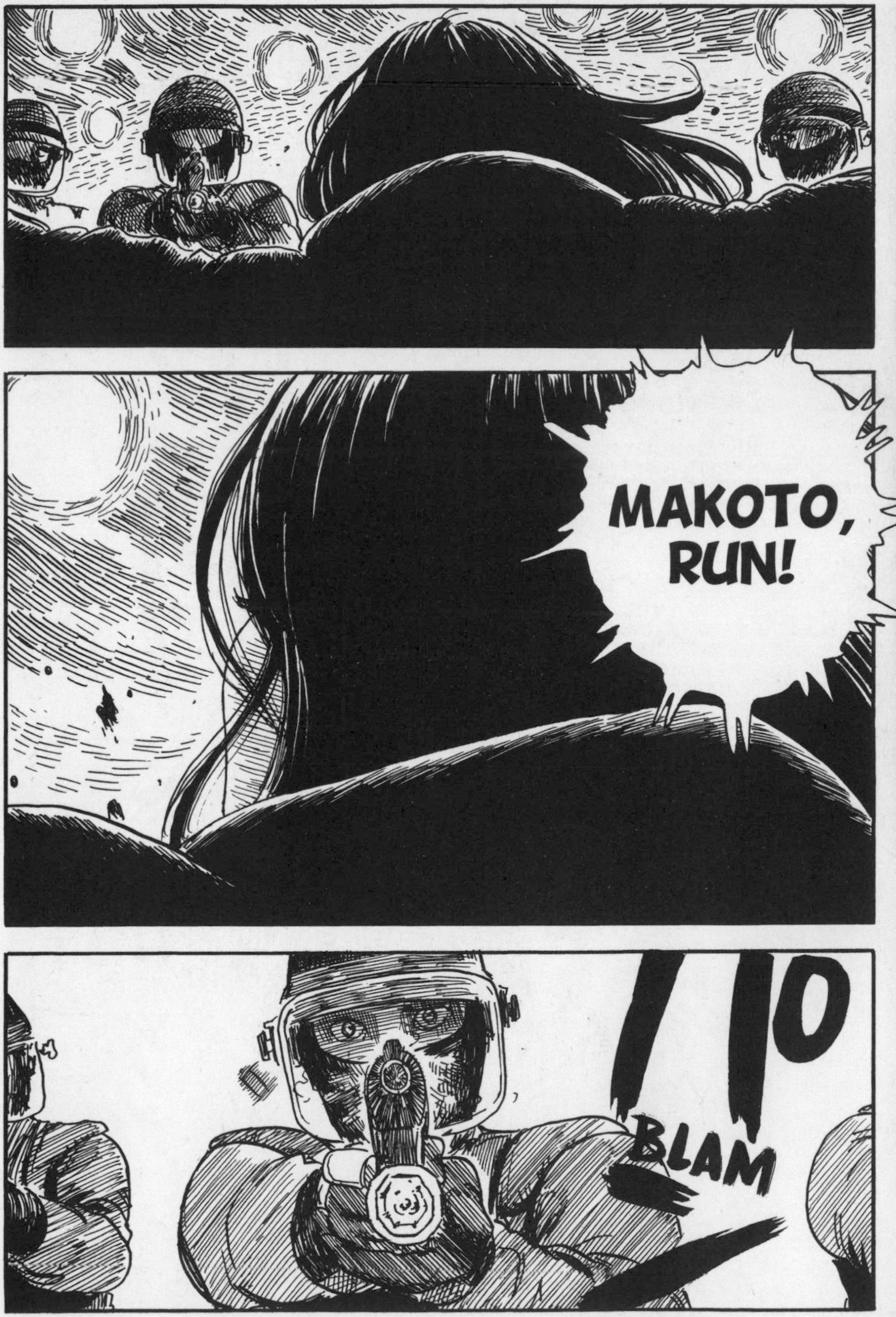
MAKOTO, RUN!
BLAM

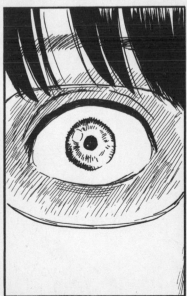

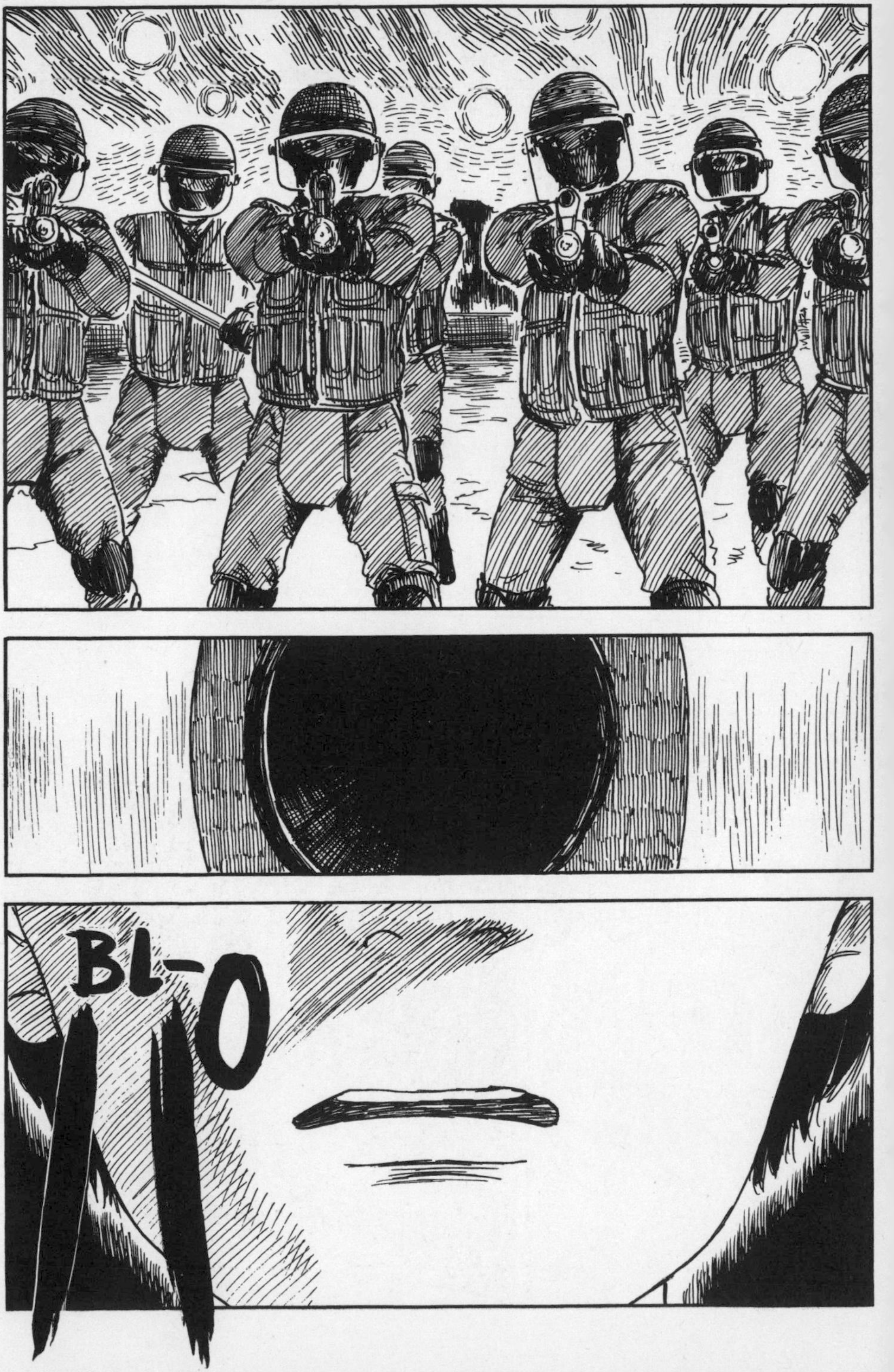
BL-O

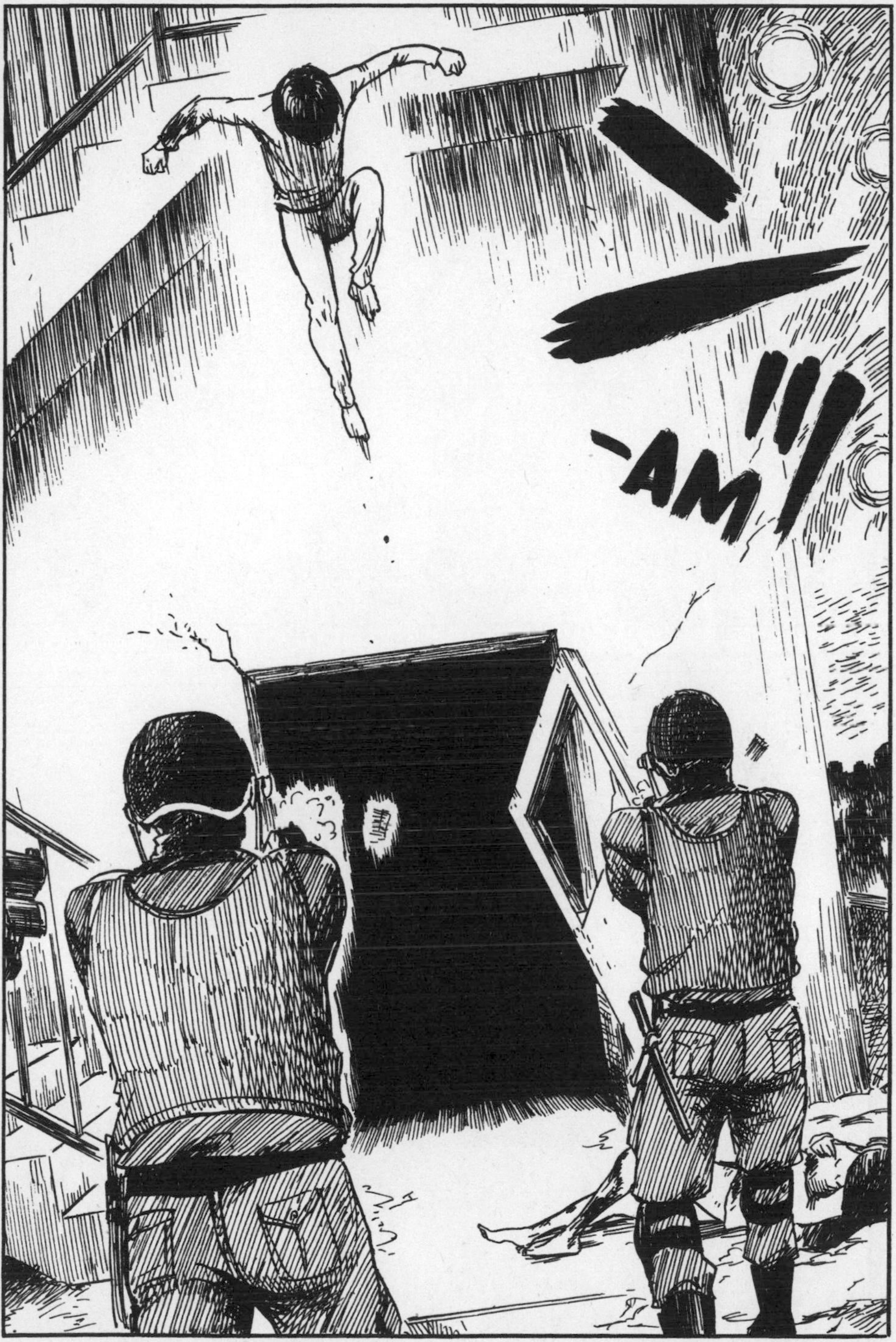
-AM!!!

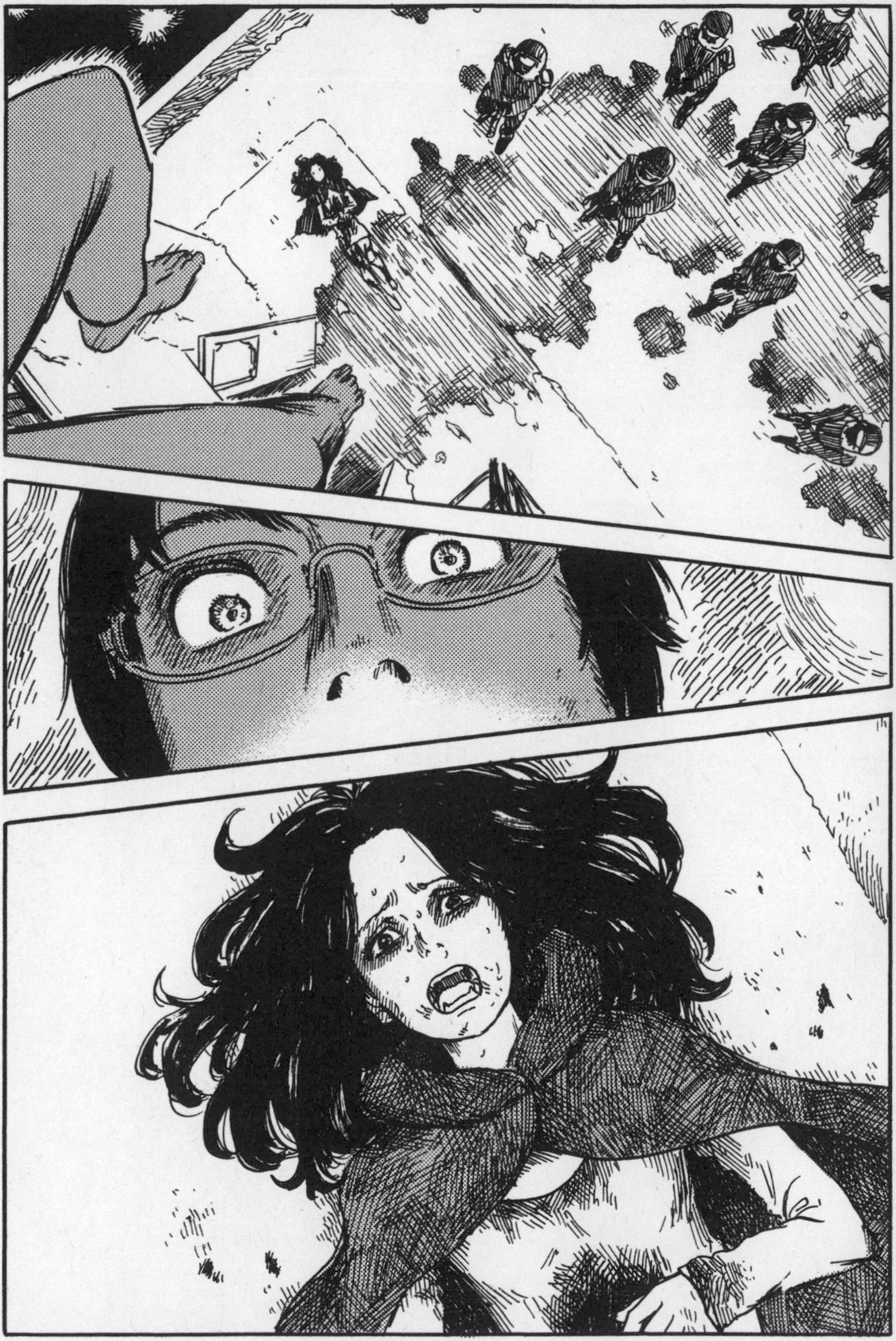

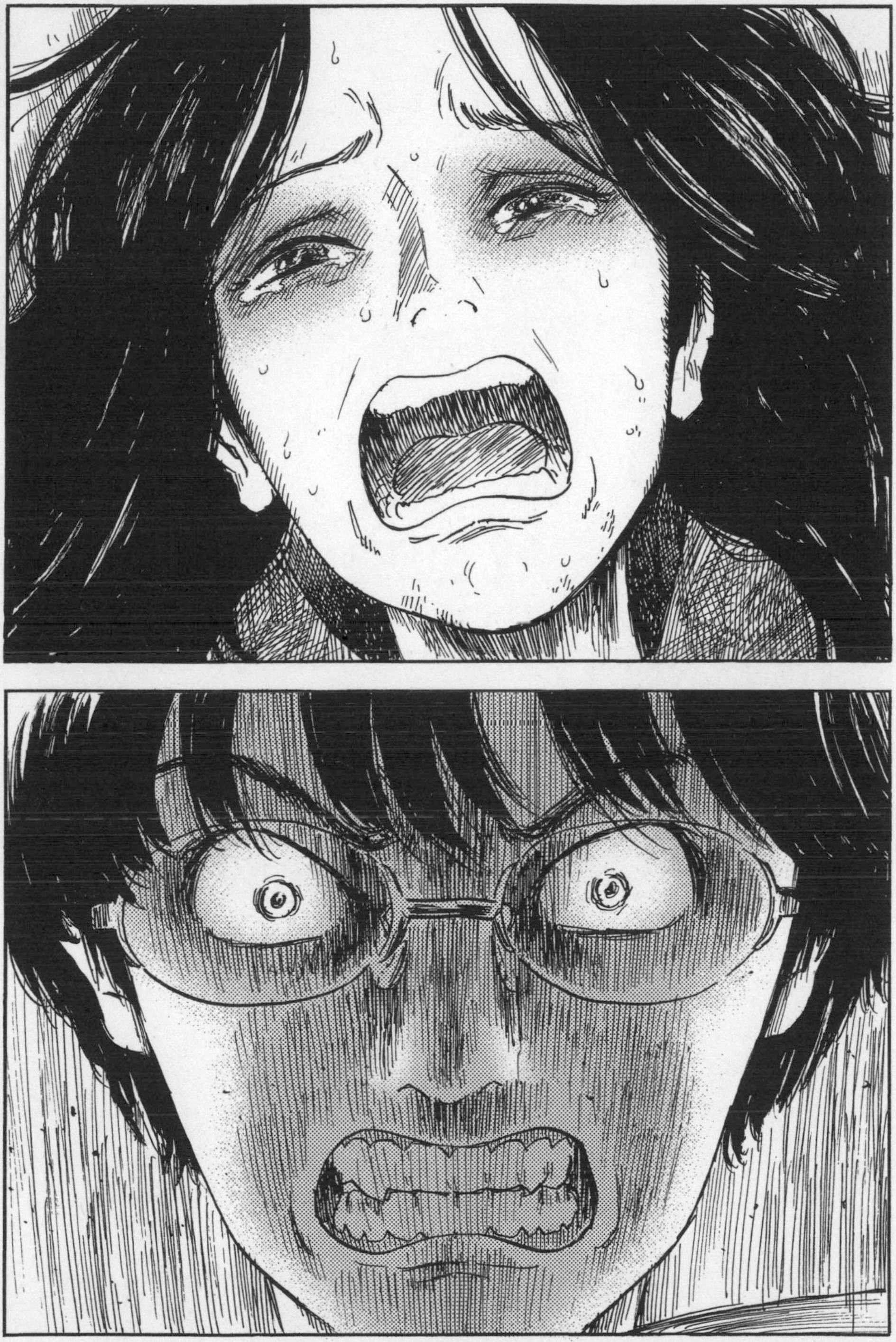

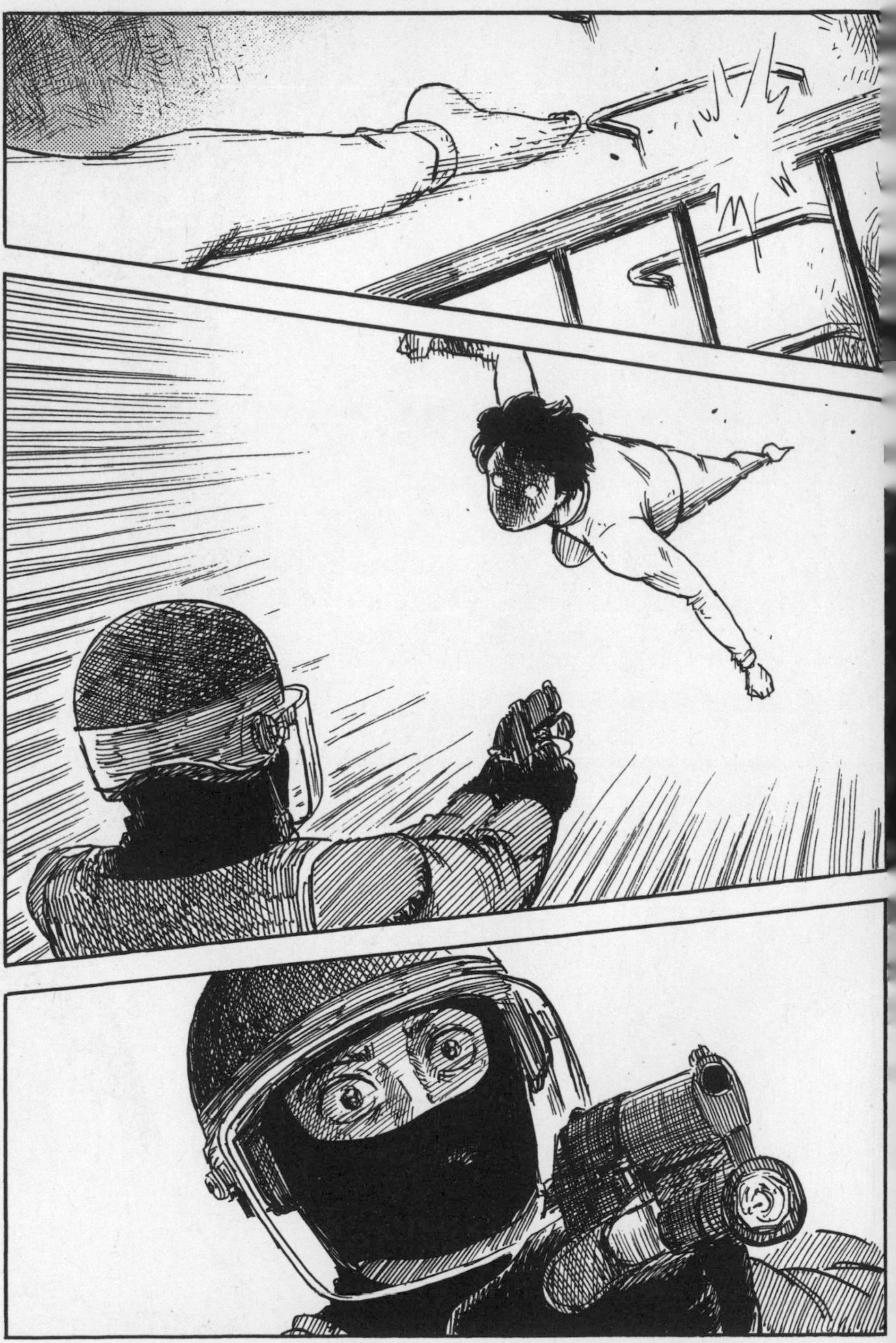

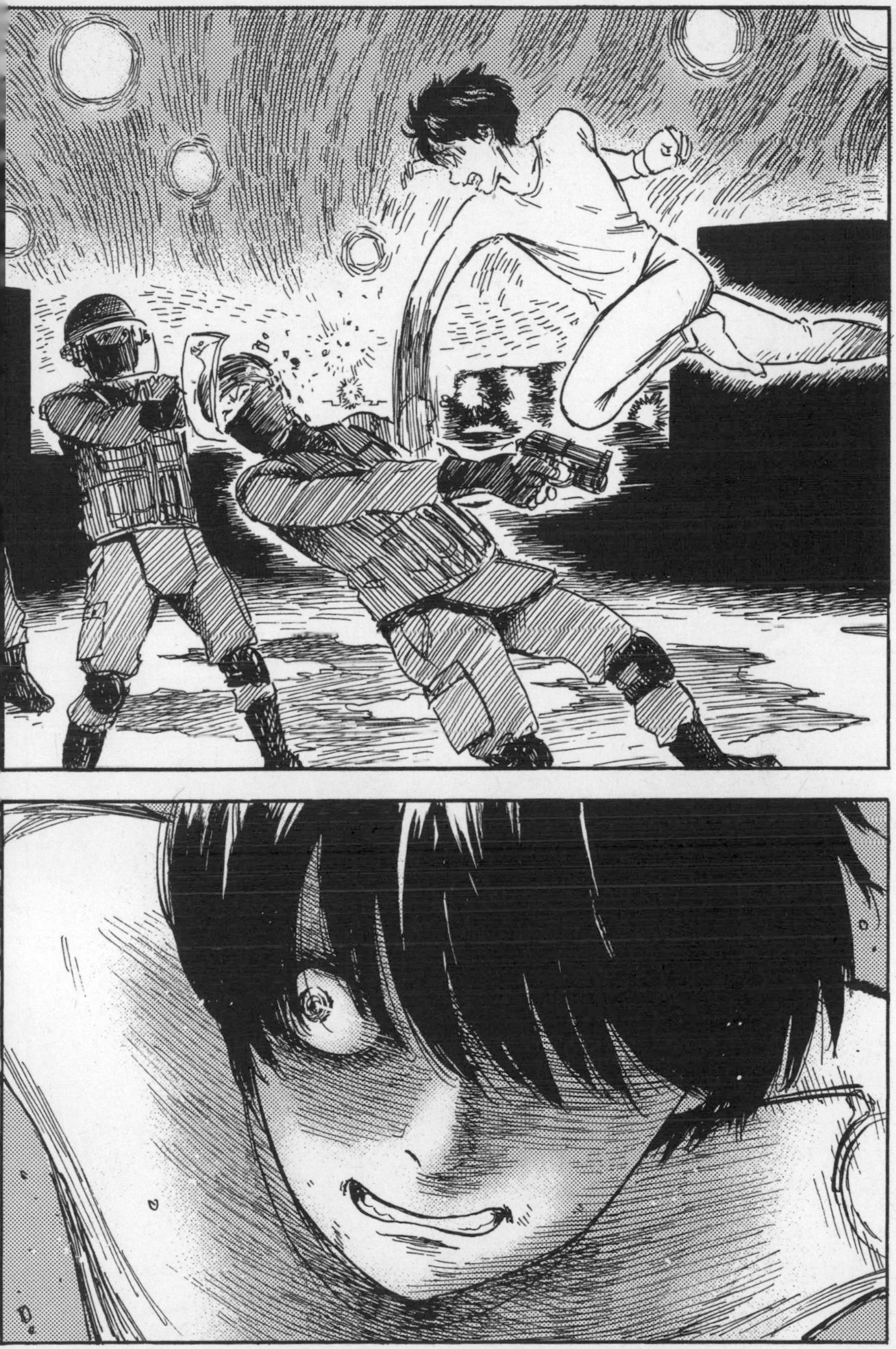

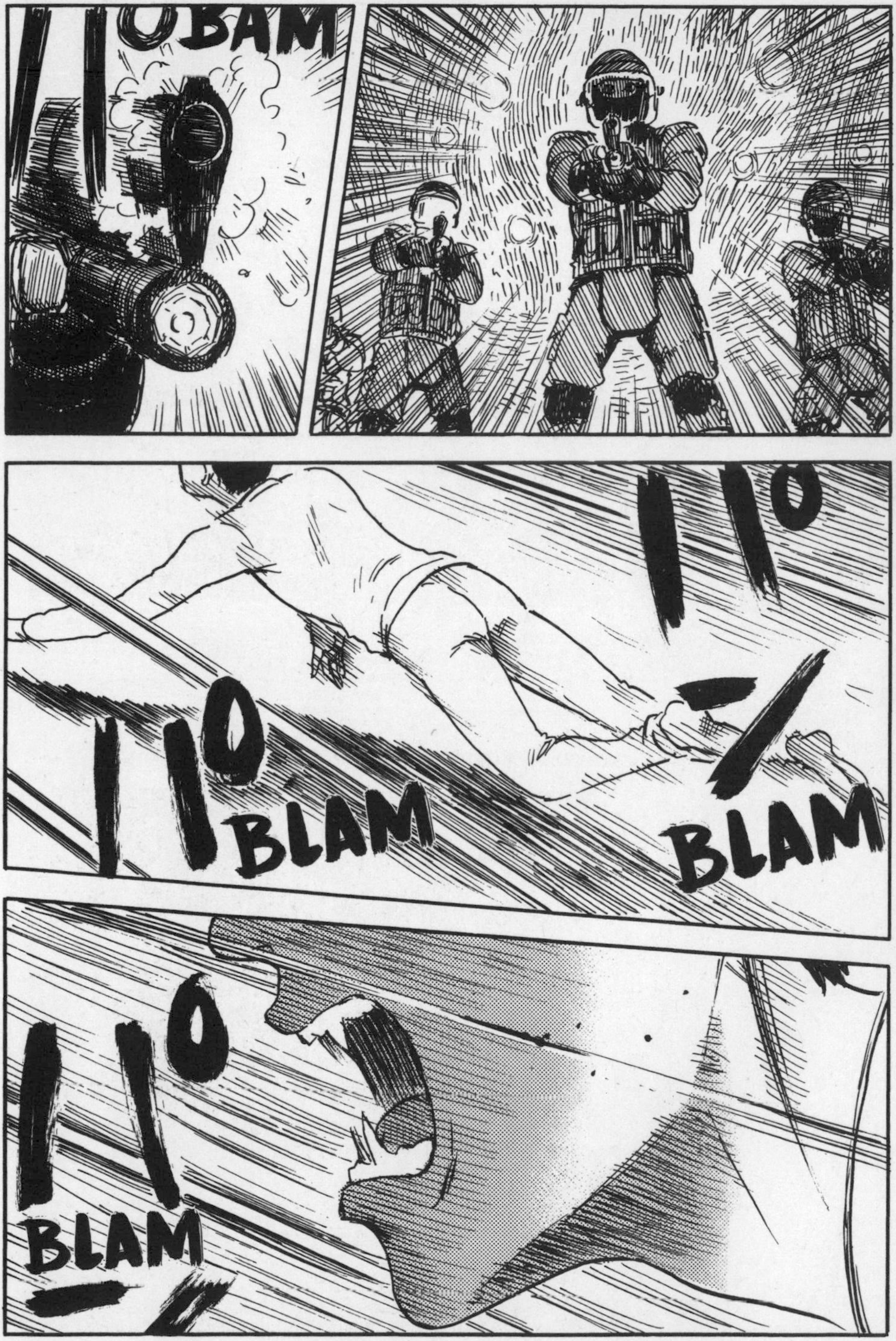
BAM
BLAM
BLAM
BLAM

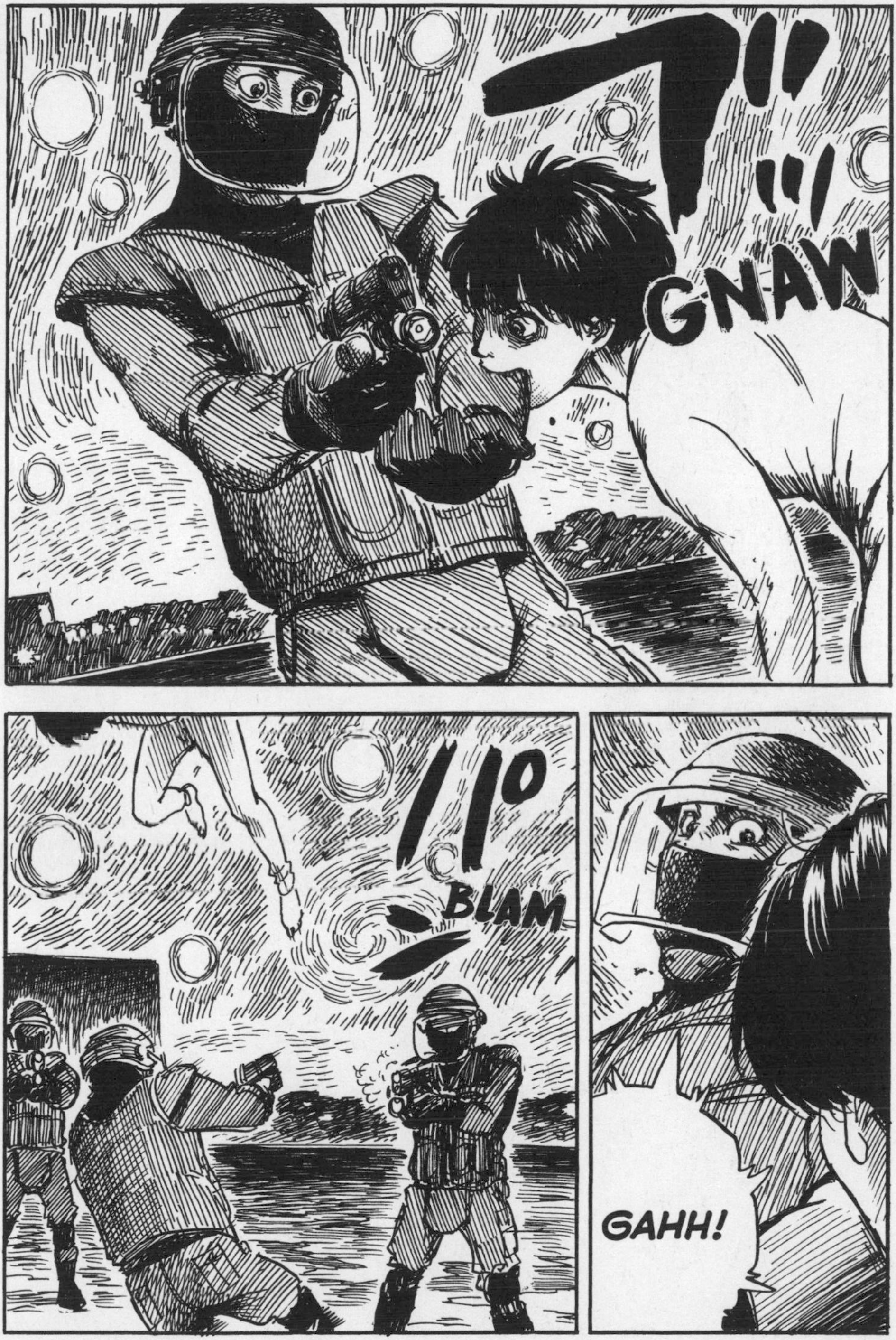
GNAW
GAHH!
BLAM

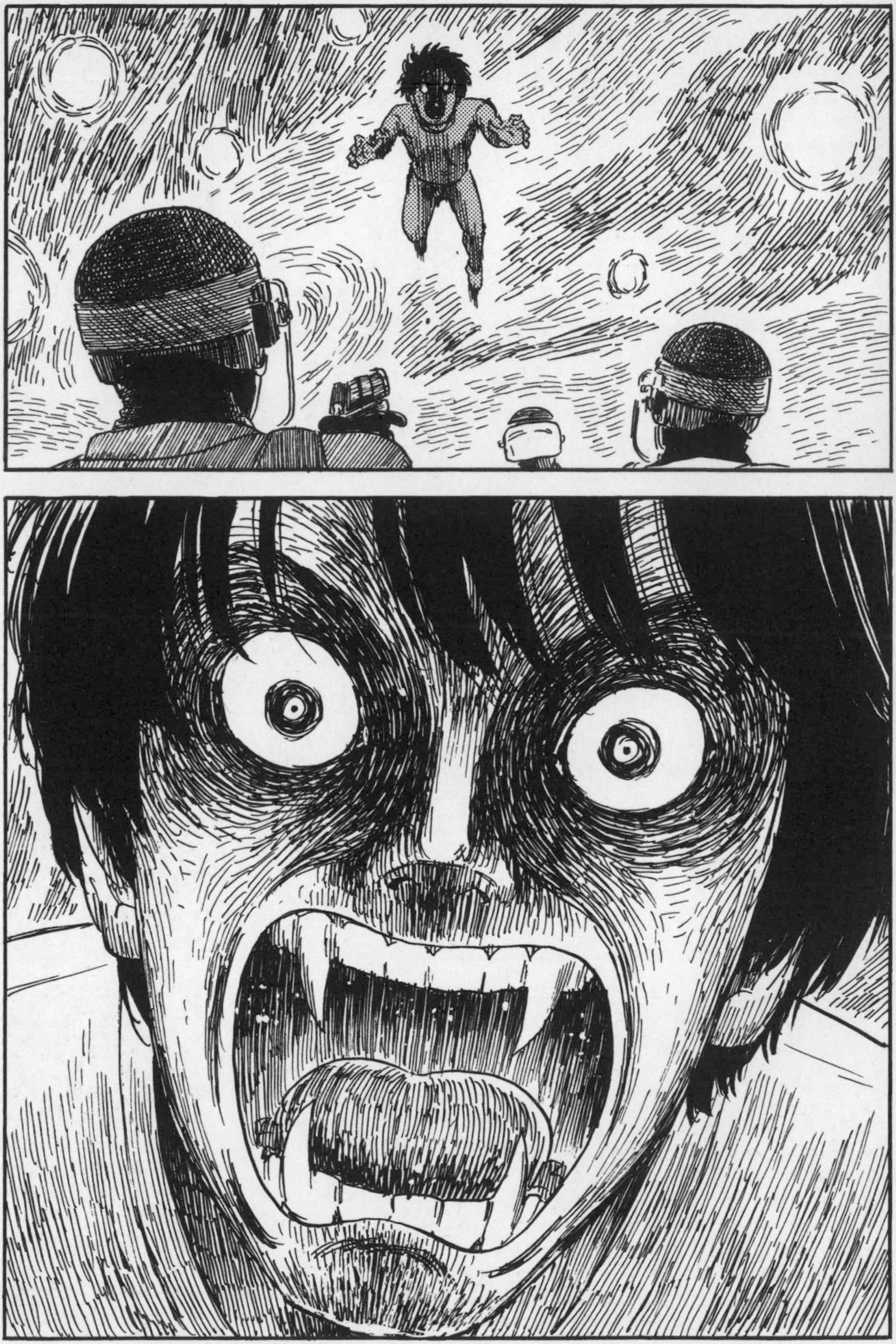

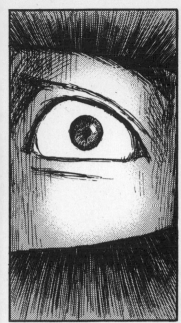
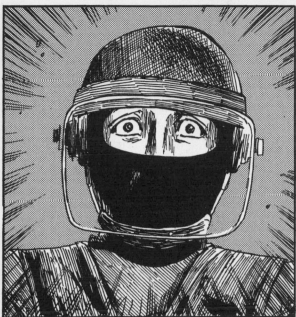
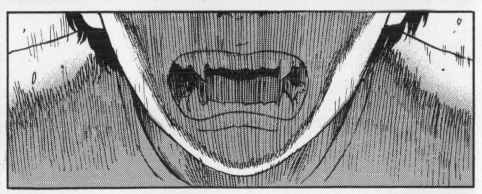
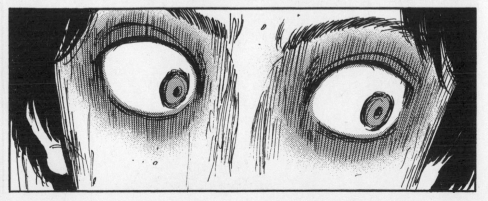

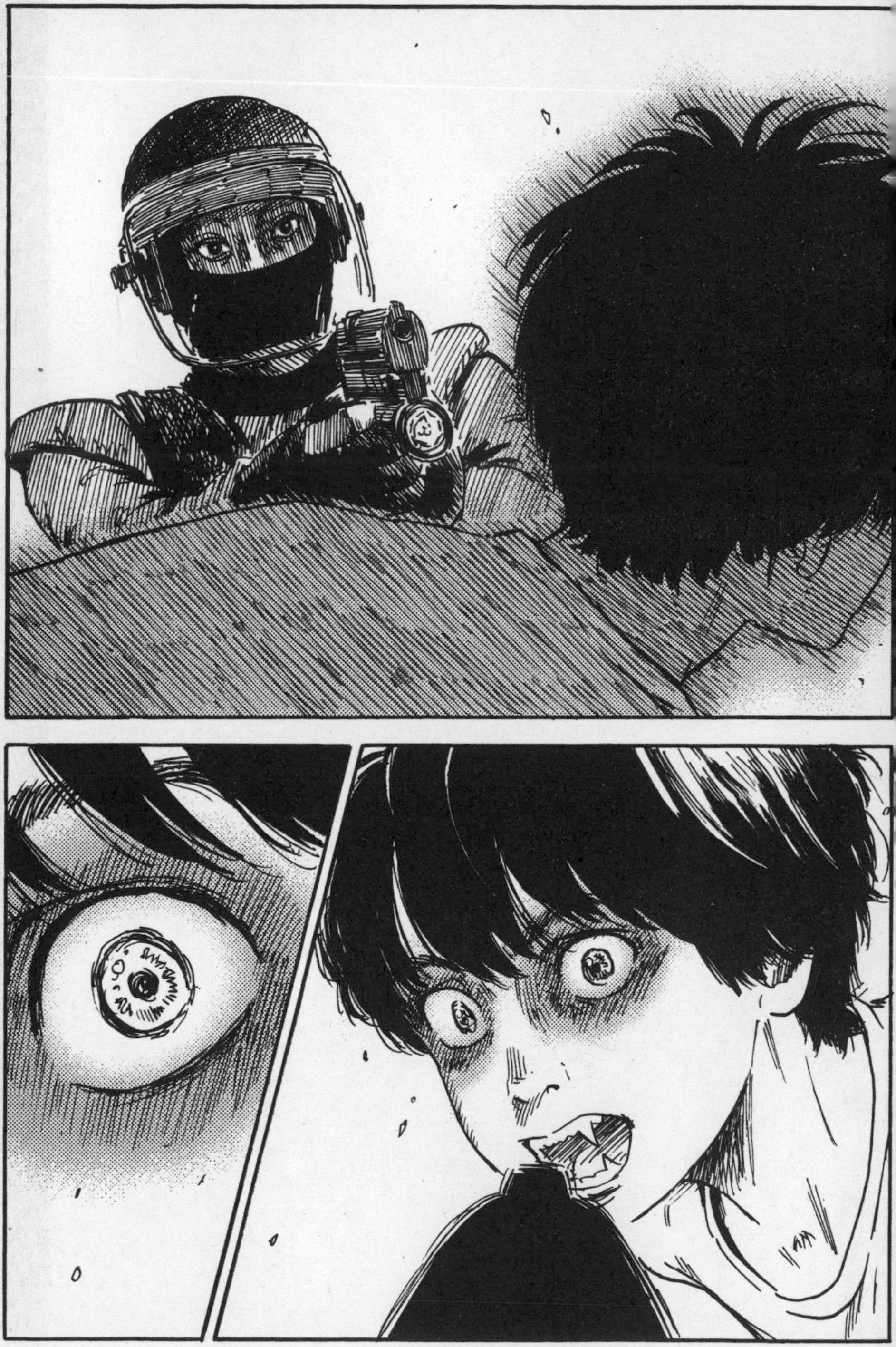

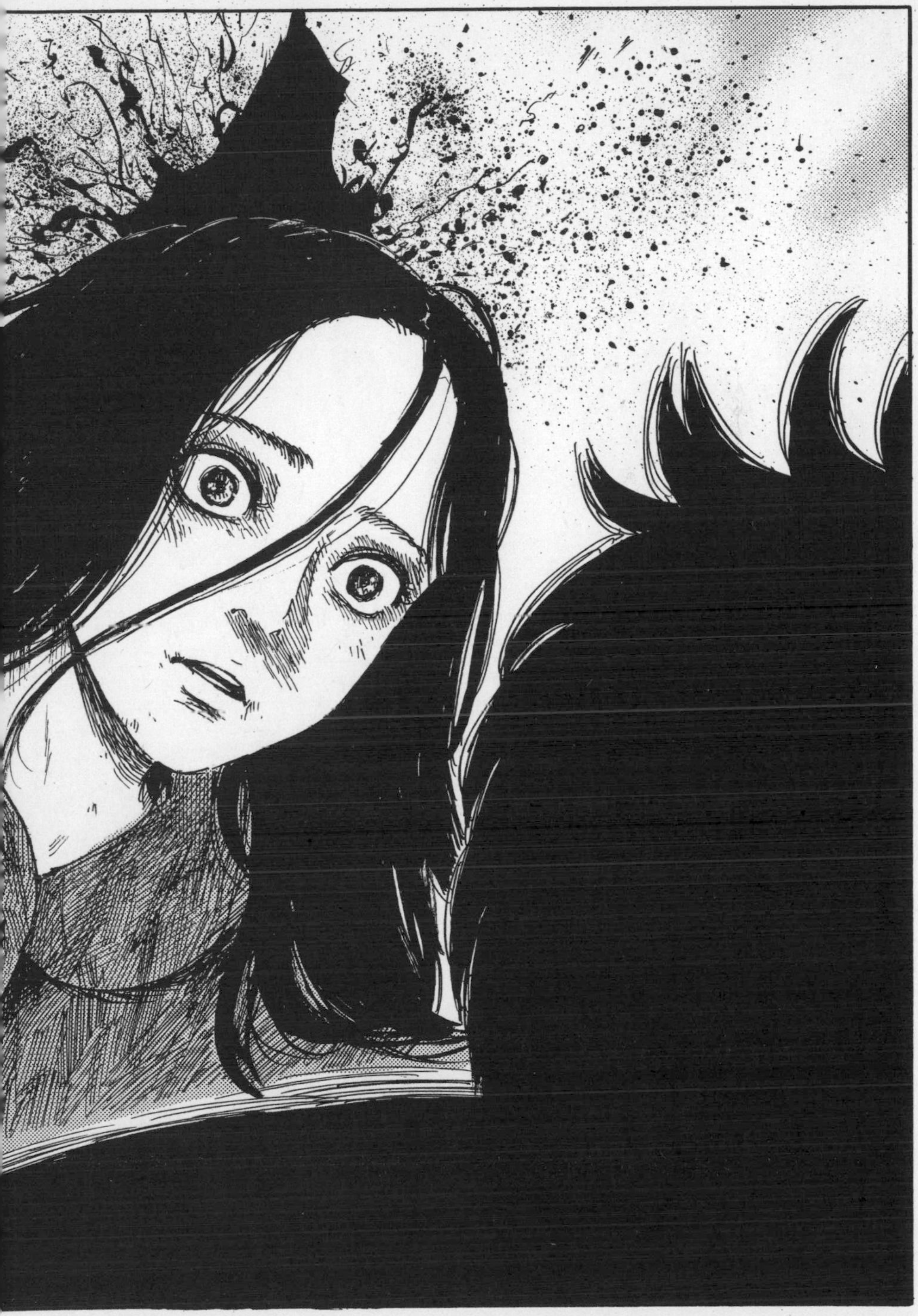

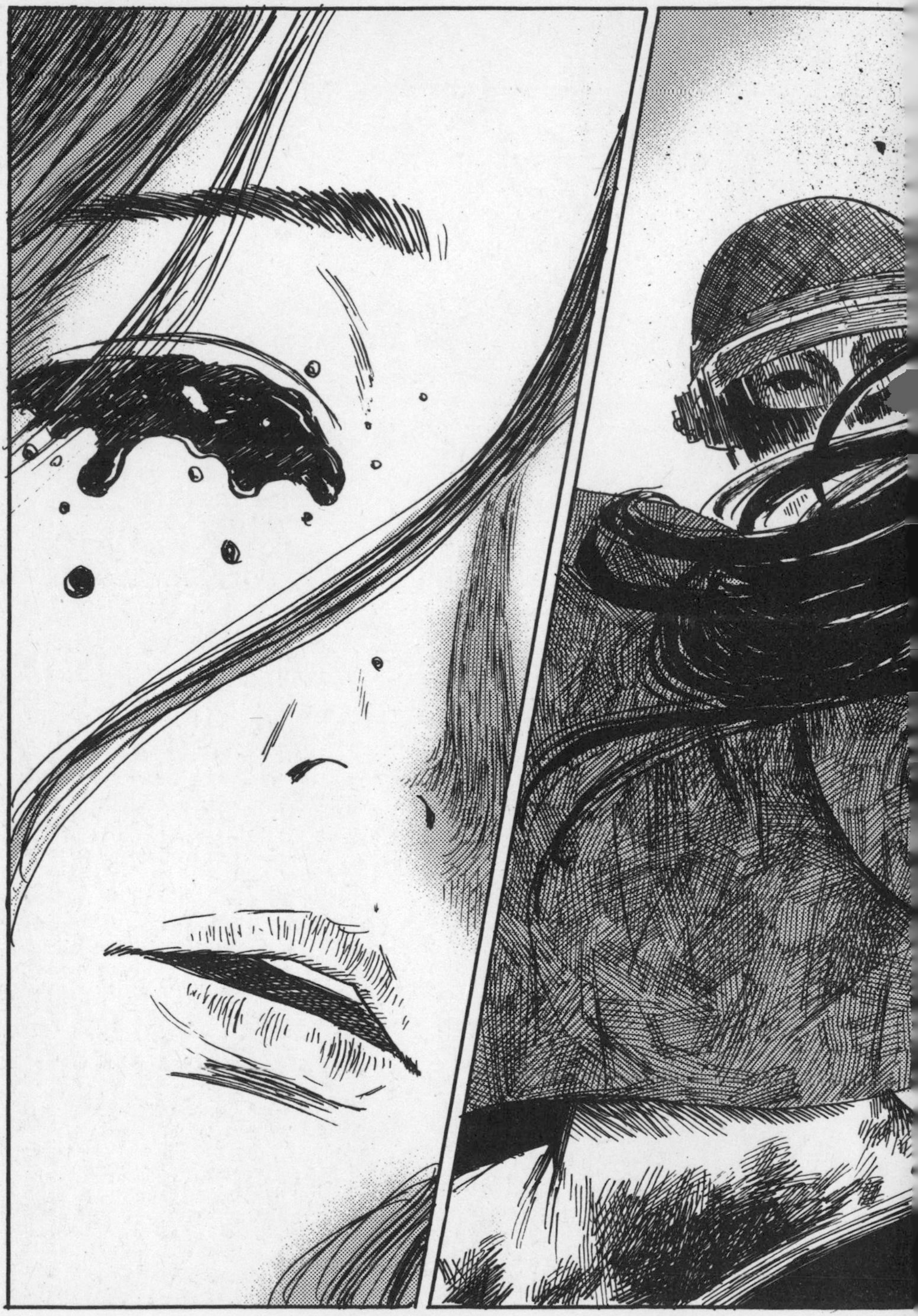

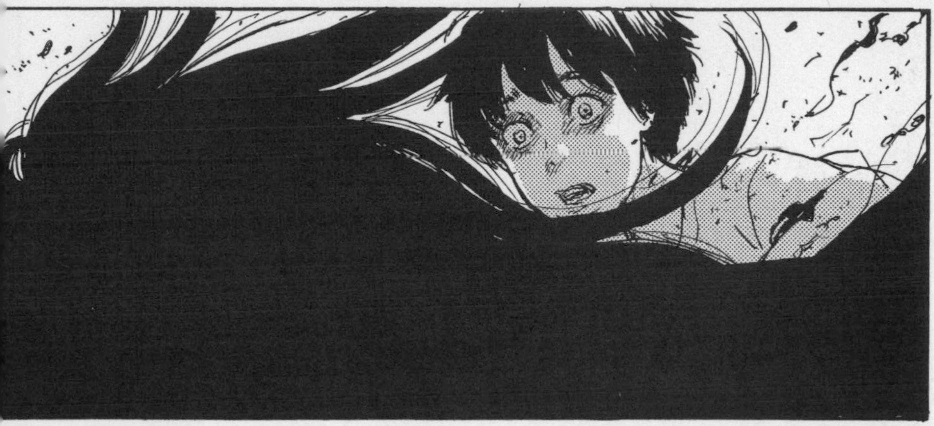

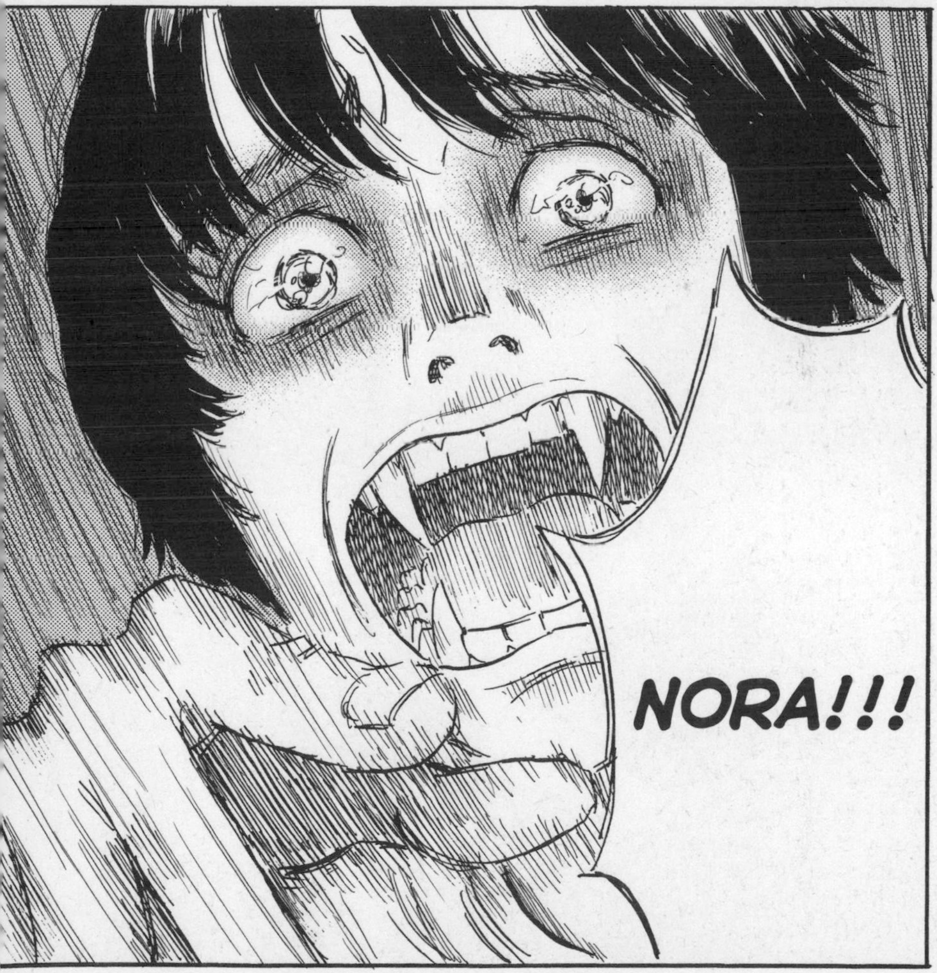
NORA!!!

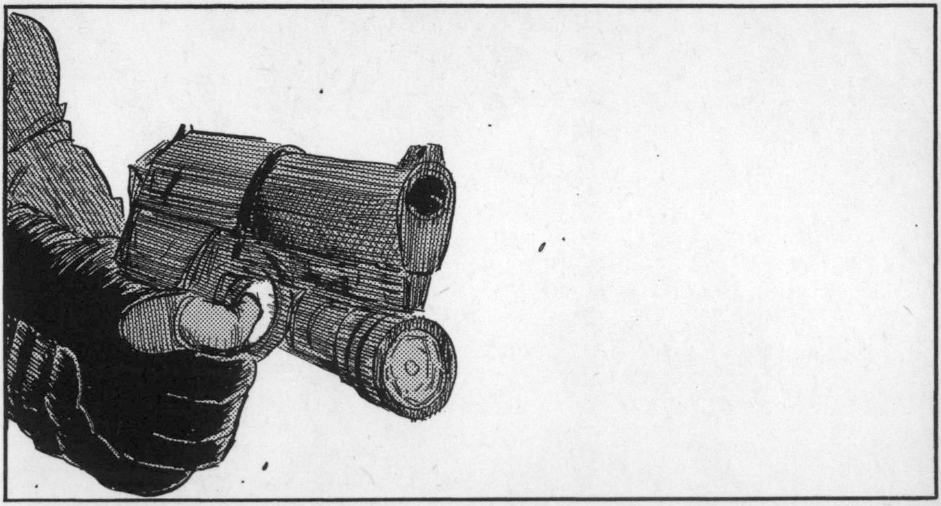

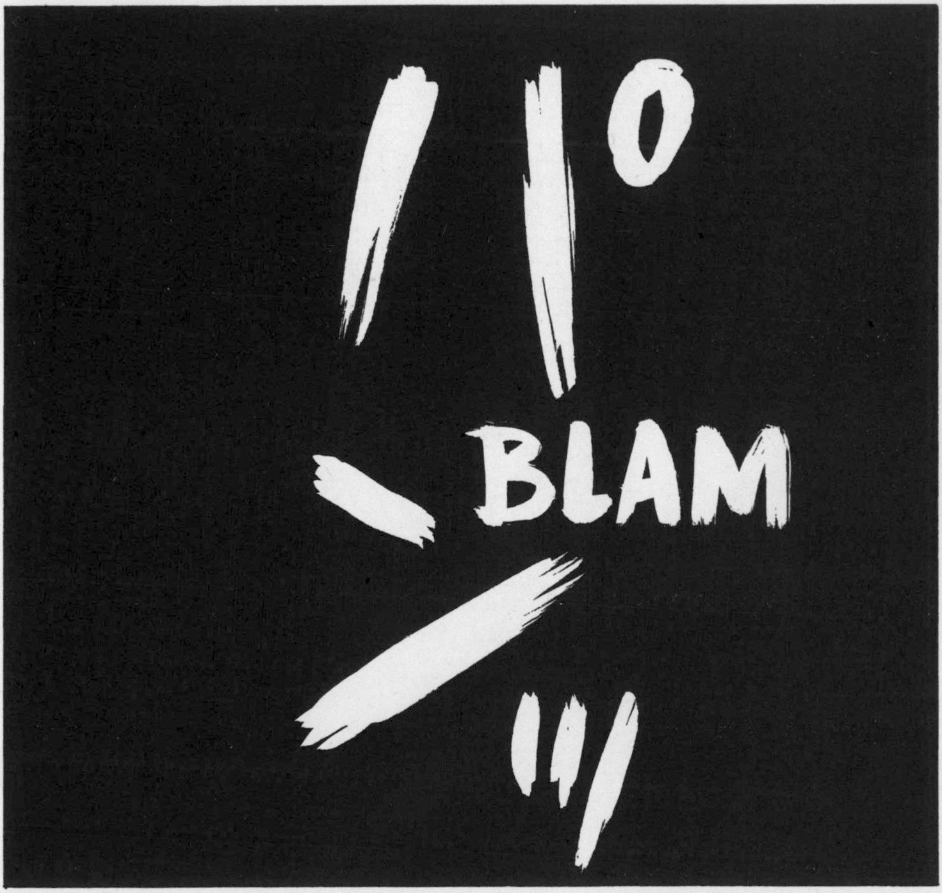

BLAM

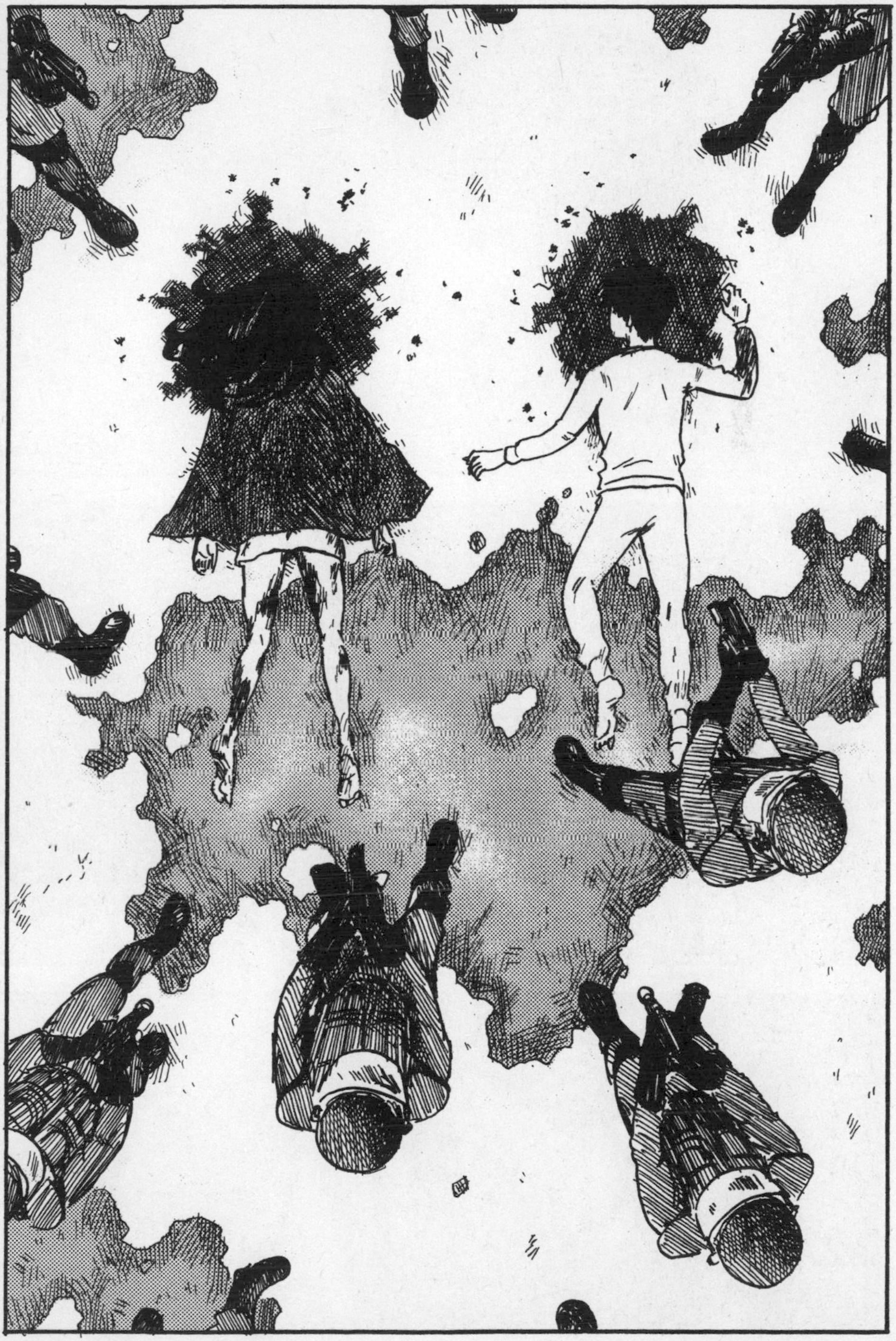

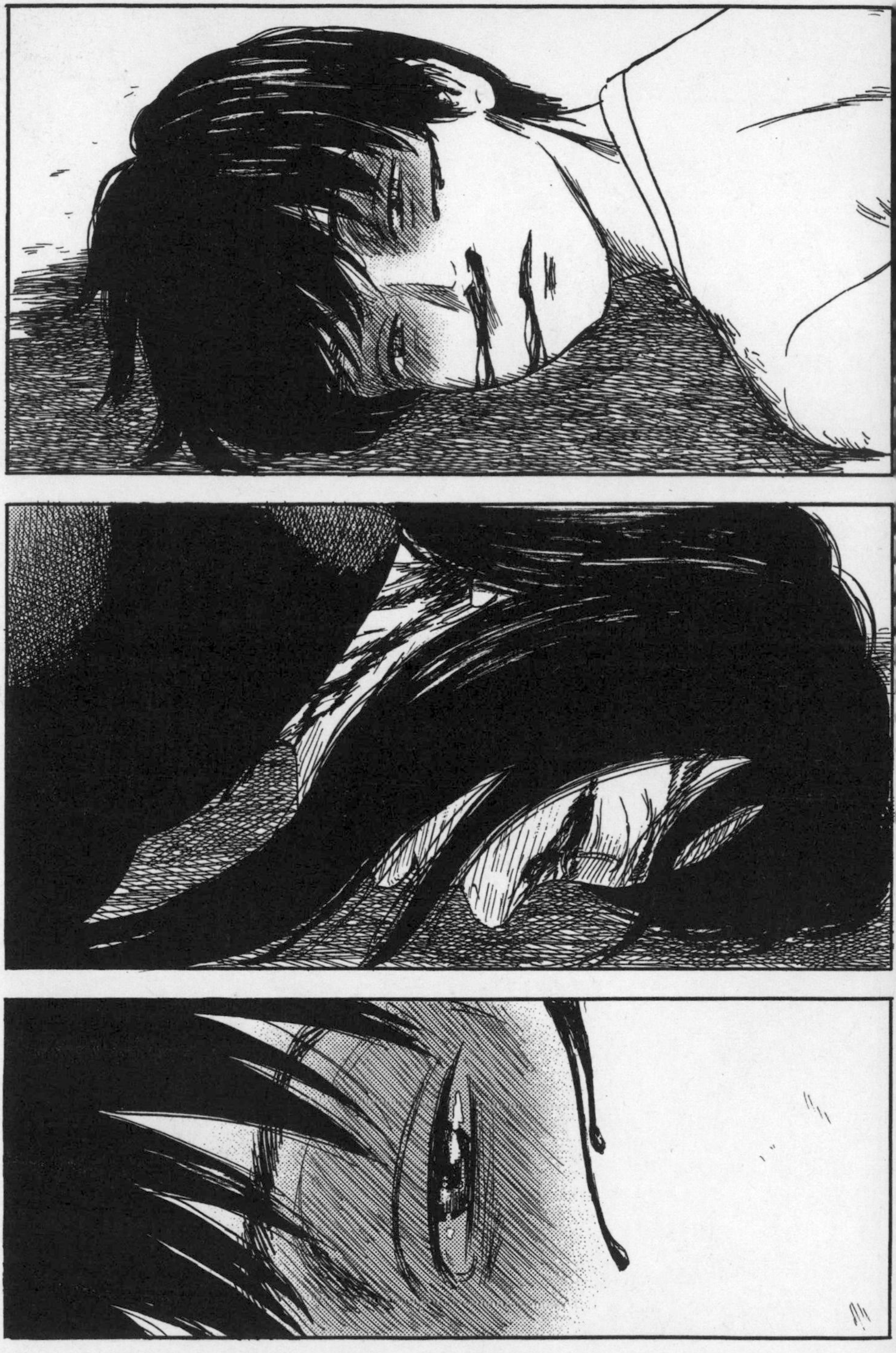

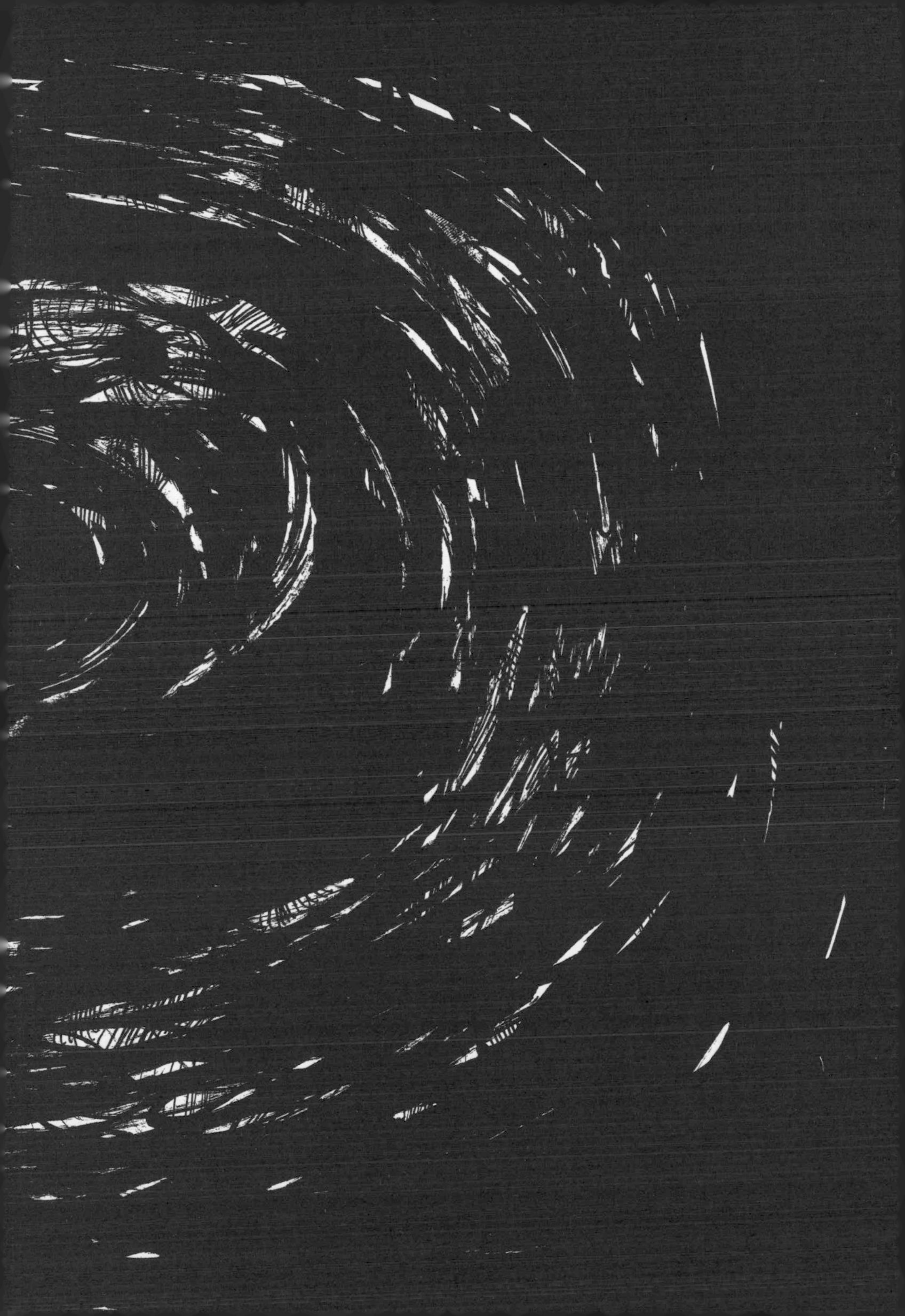

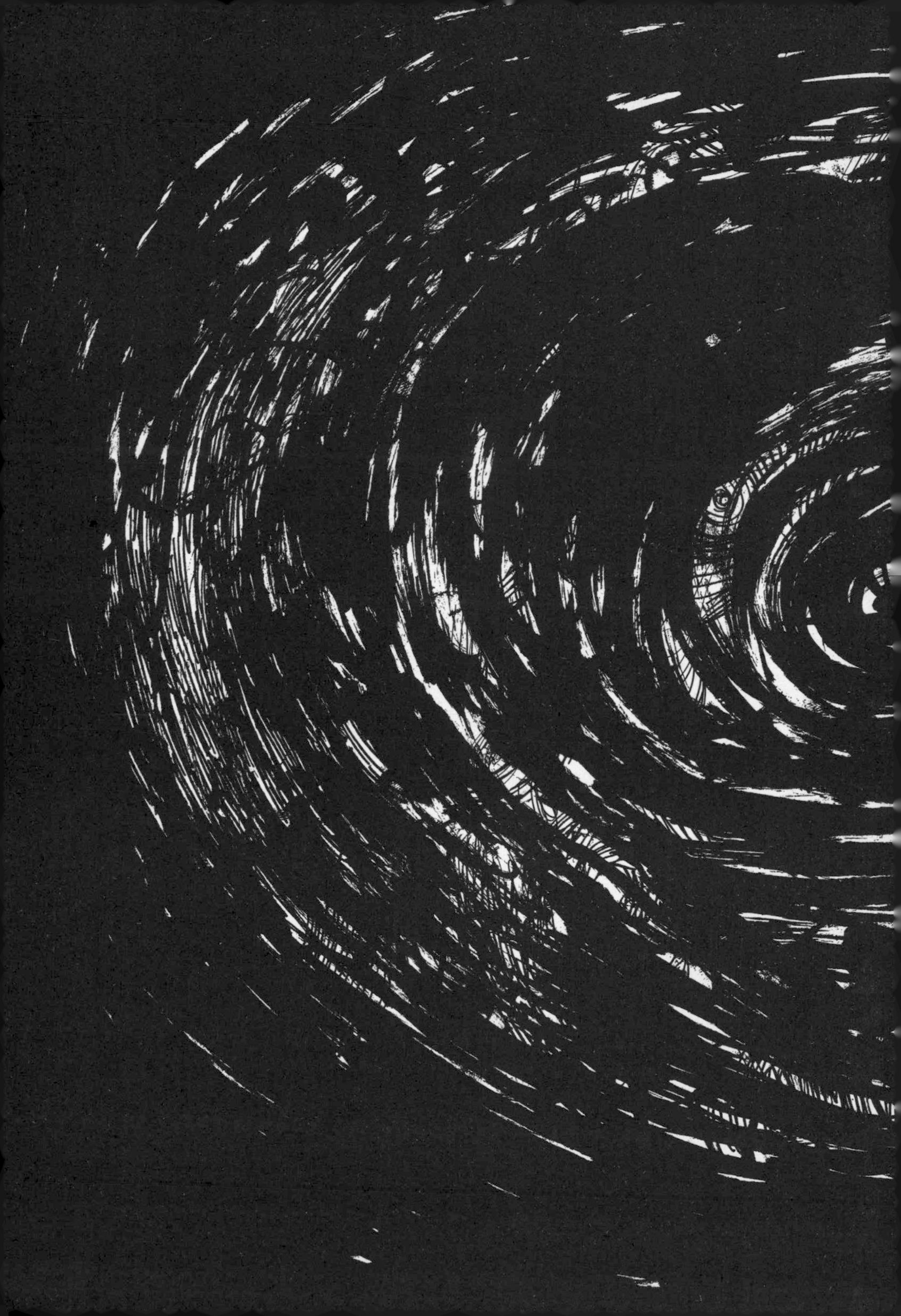

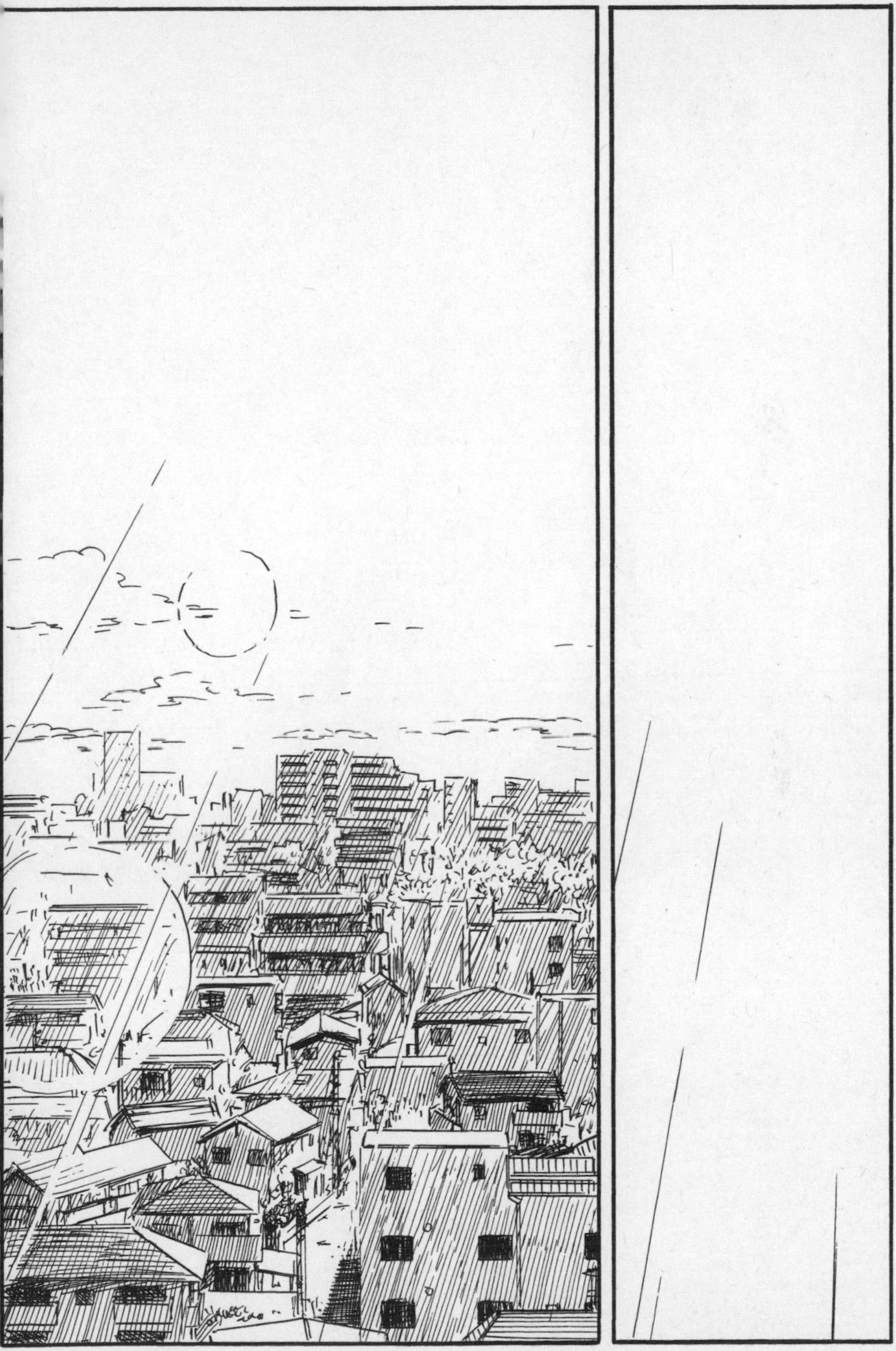

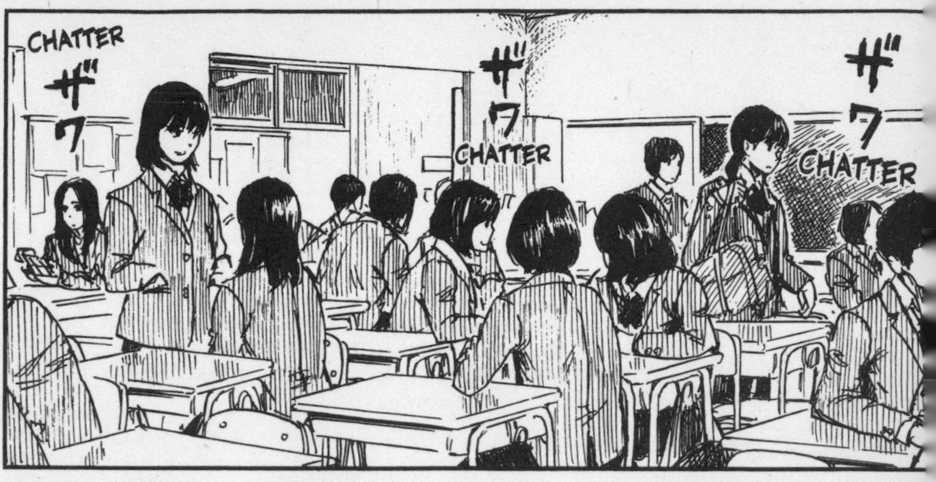
ザワ
CHATTER
ザワ
CHATTER
CHATTER
ザワ

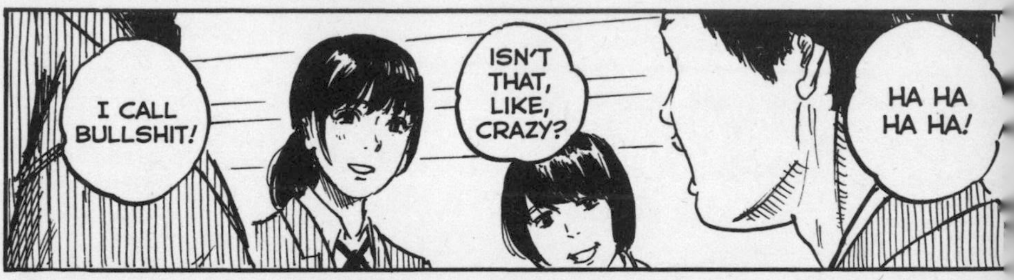
HA HA HA HA!
ISN'T THAT, LIKE, CRAZY?
I CALL BULLSHIT!

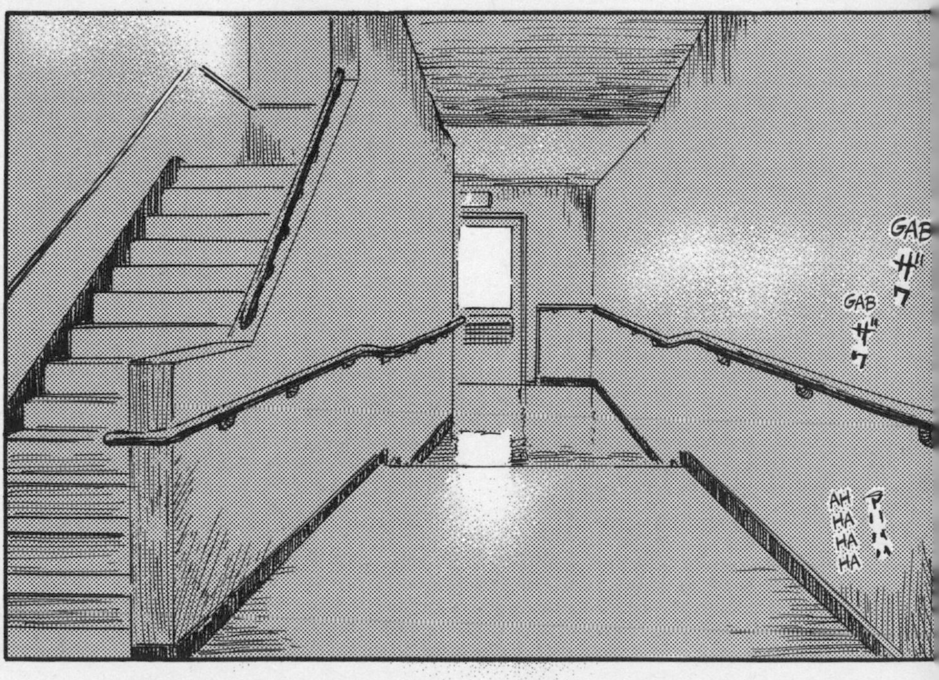
GAB
ザワ
GAB
ザワ
アハハ
AH HA HA HA

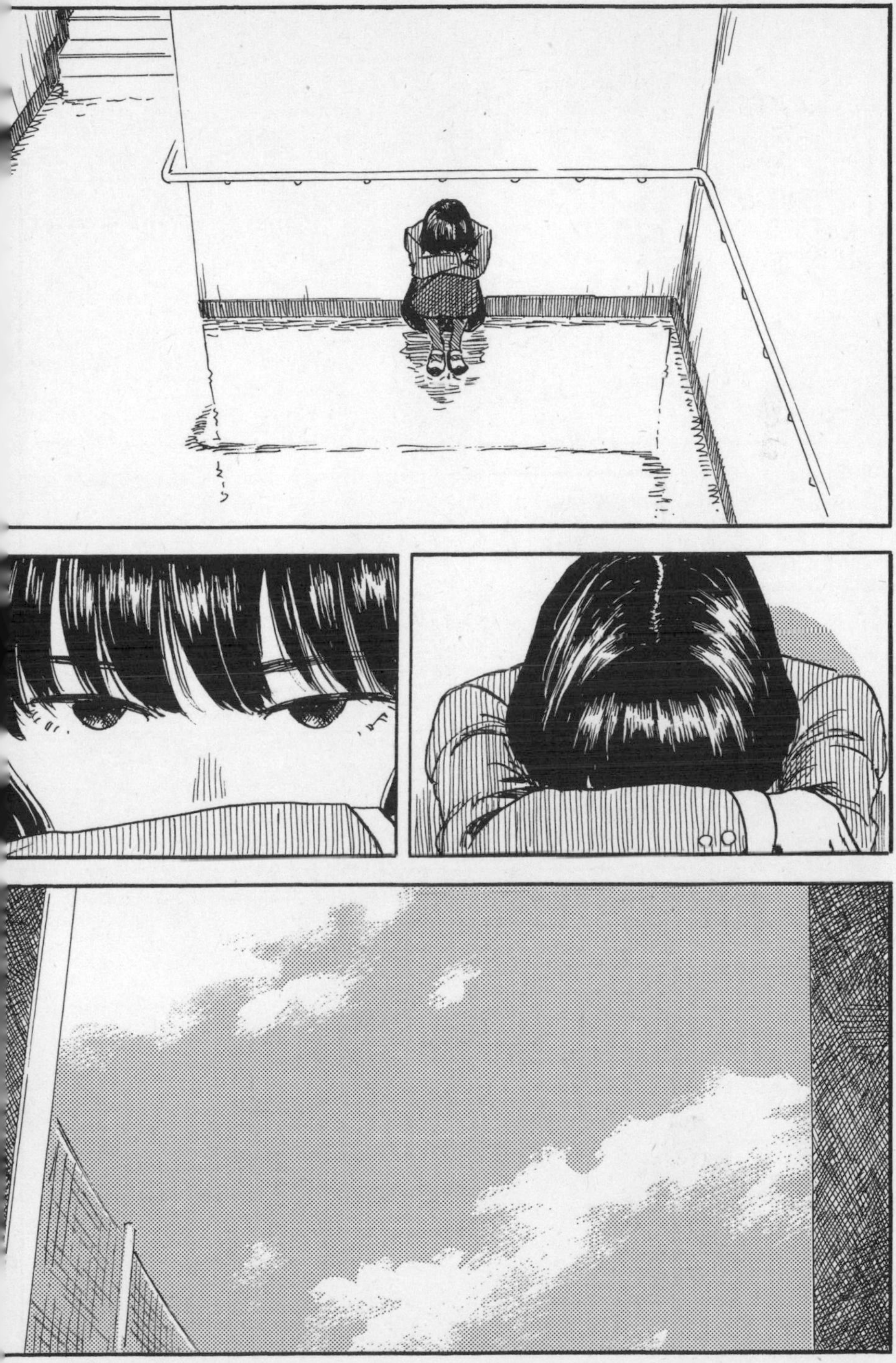

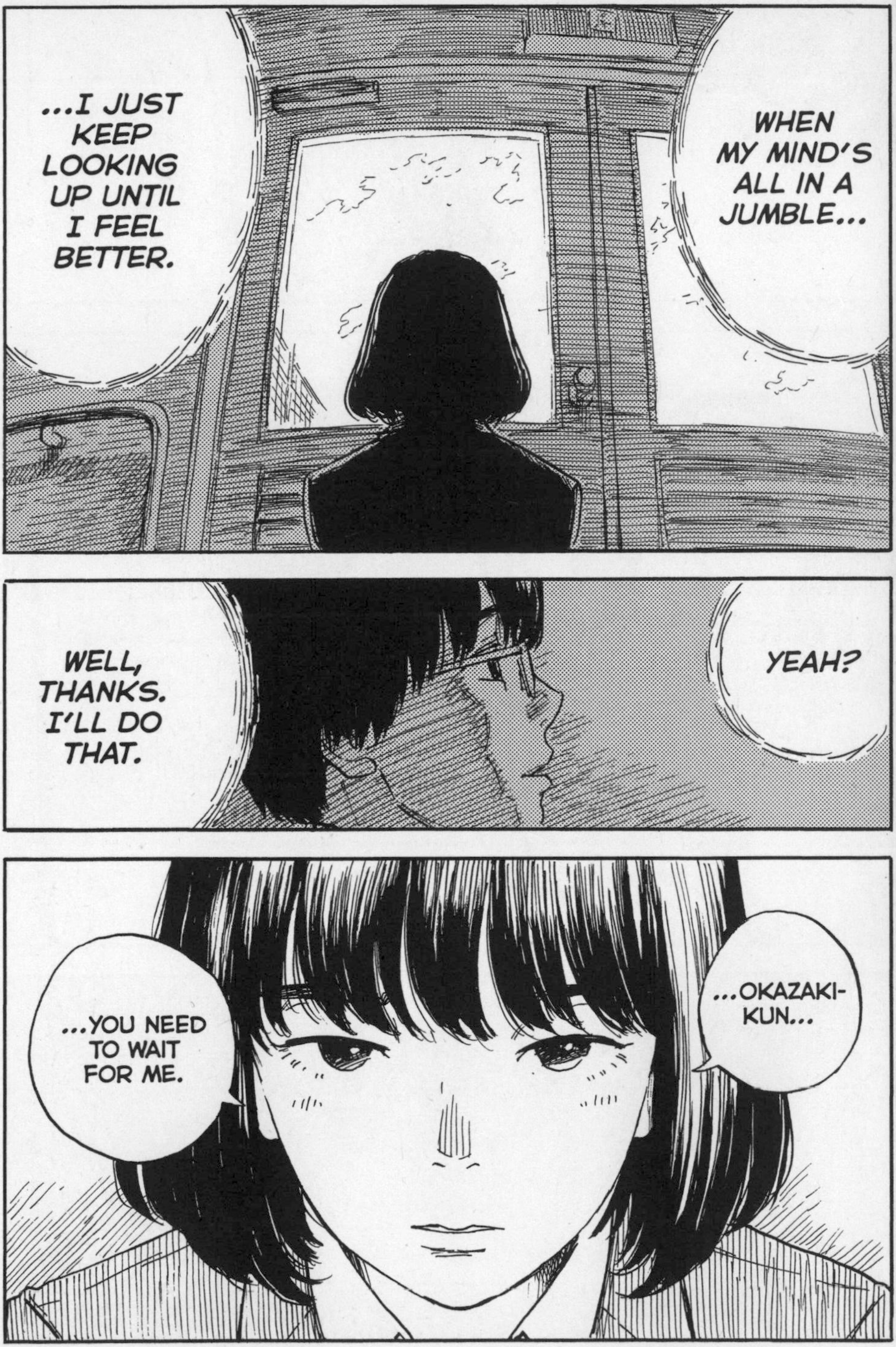
WHEN MY MIND'S ALL IN A JUMBLE...
...I JUST KEEP LOOKING UP UNTIL I FEEL BETTER.
YEAH?
WELL, THANKS. I'LL DO THAT.
...OKAZAKI-KUN...
...YOU NEED TO WAIT FOR ME.

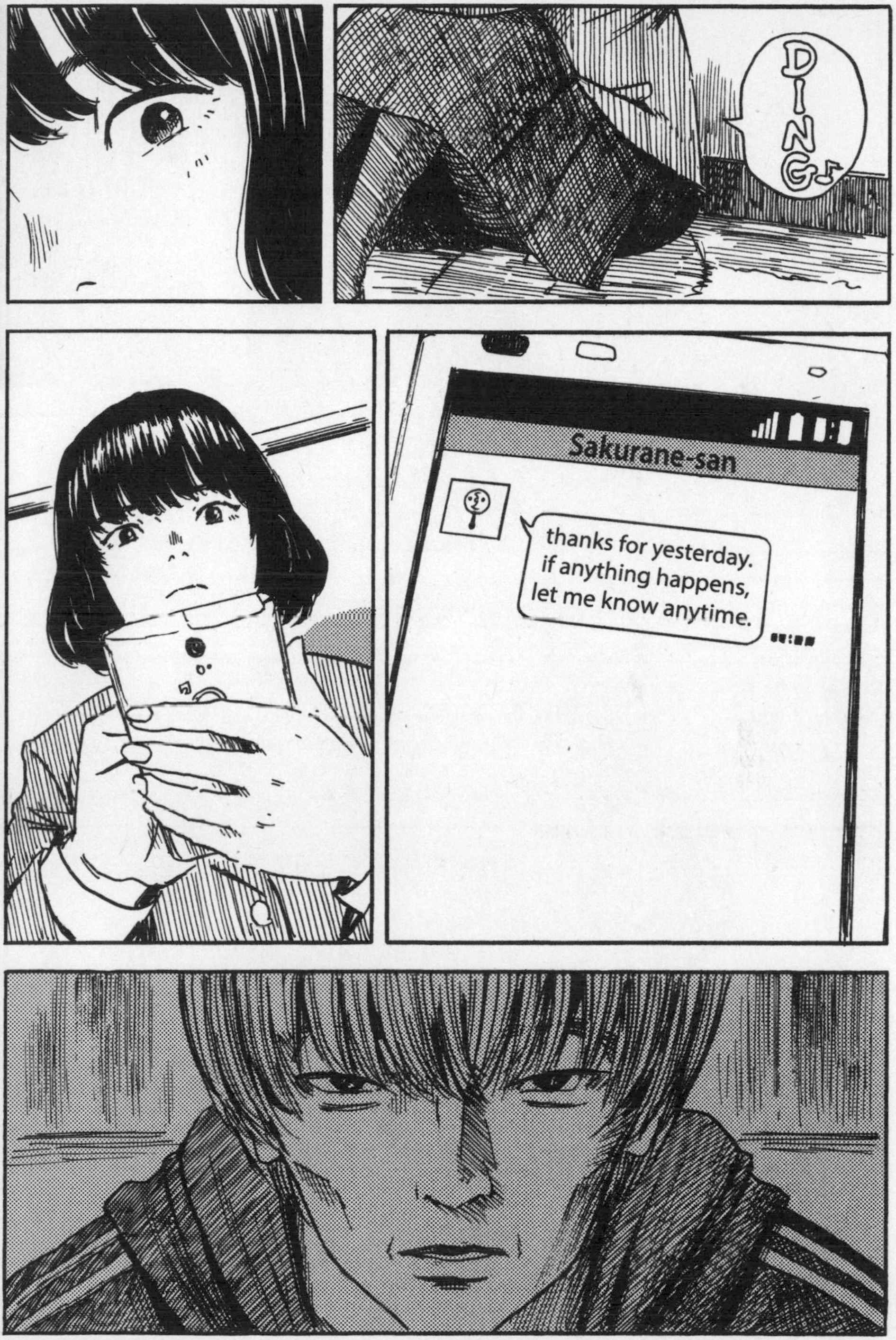
DING
Sakurane-san
thanks for yesterday. if anything happens, let me know anytime.

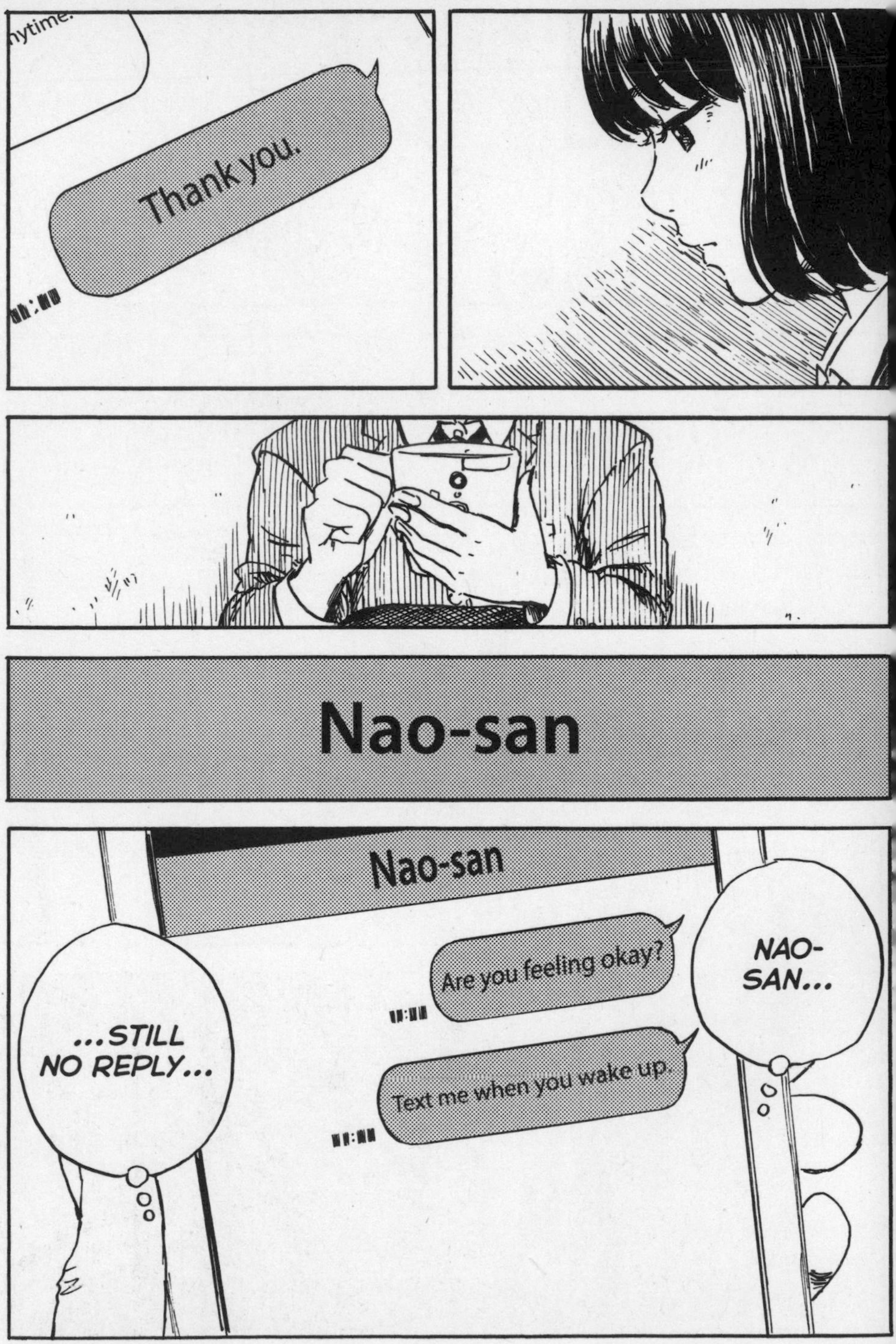
Thank you.
Nao-san
NAO-SAN...
Nao-san
Are you feeling okay?
Text me when you wake up.
...STILL NO REPLY...

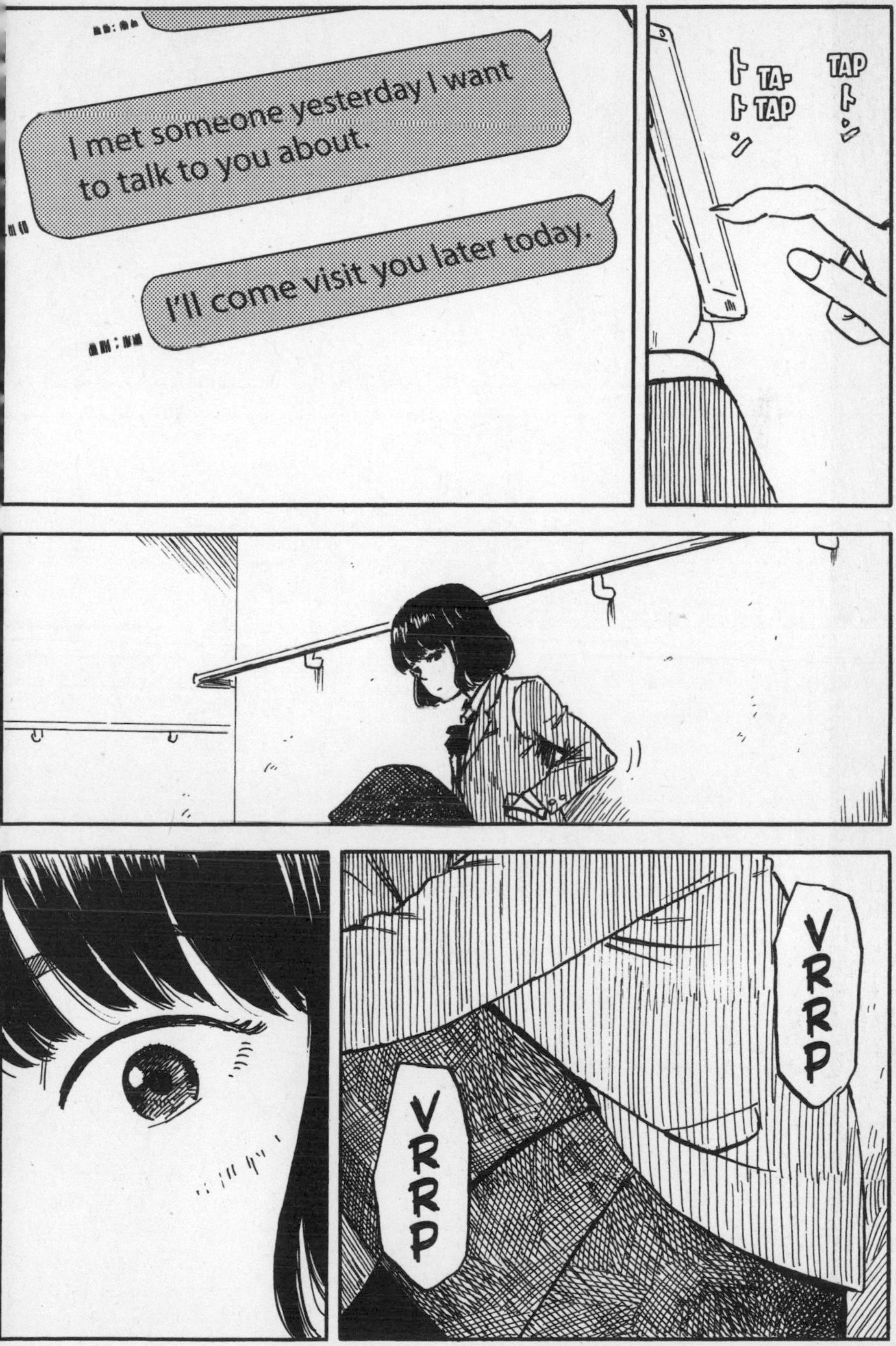

TAP
トン
TA-TAP
トトン
I met someone yesterday I want to talk to you about.
I'll come visit you later today.
VRRP
VRRP

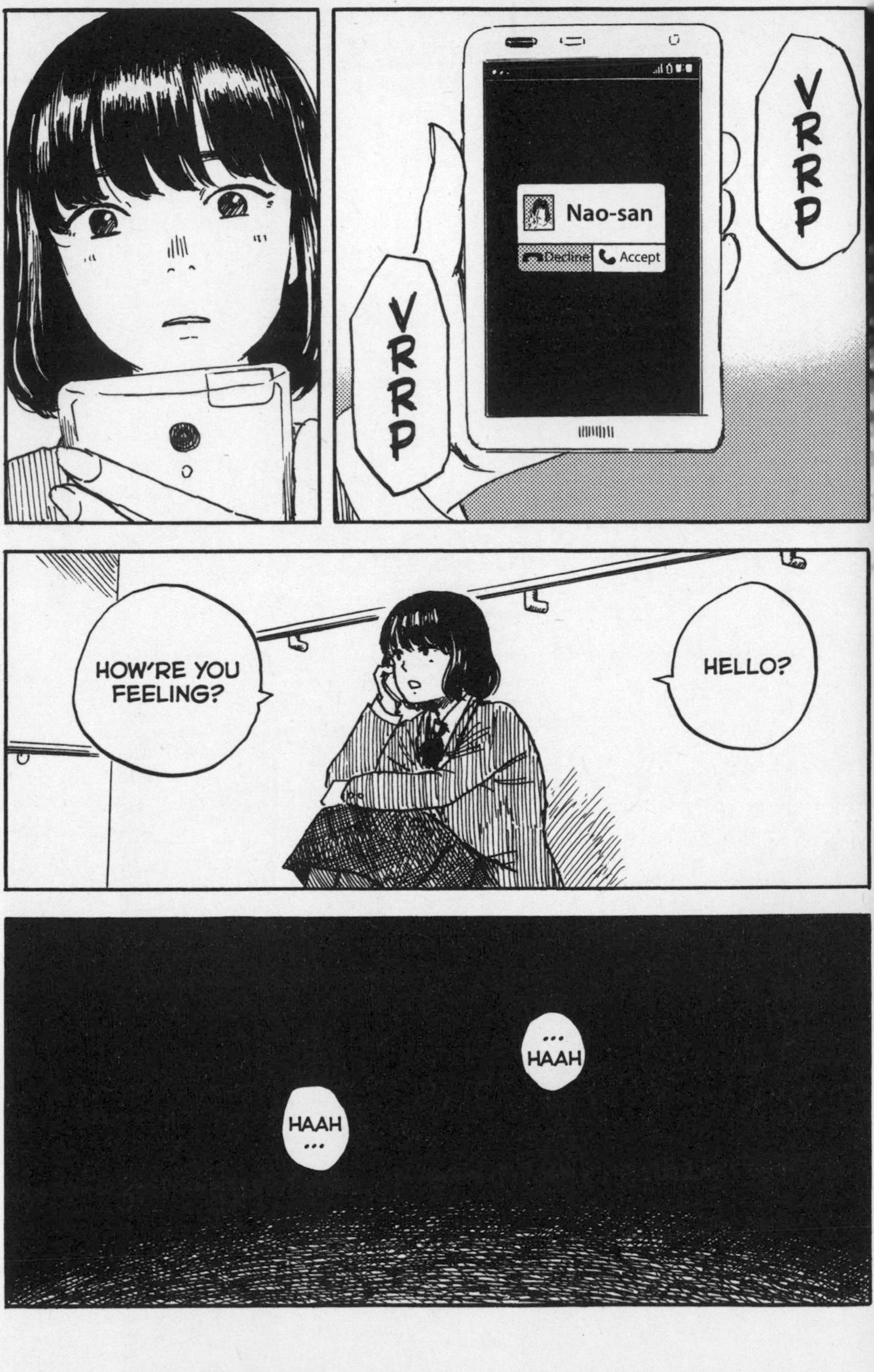
VRRP
VRRP
Nao-san
Decline
Accept
HELLO?
HOW'RE YOU FEELING?
...HAAH
HAAH...

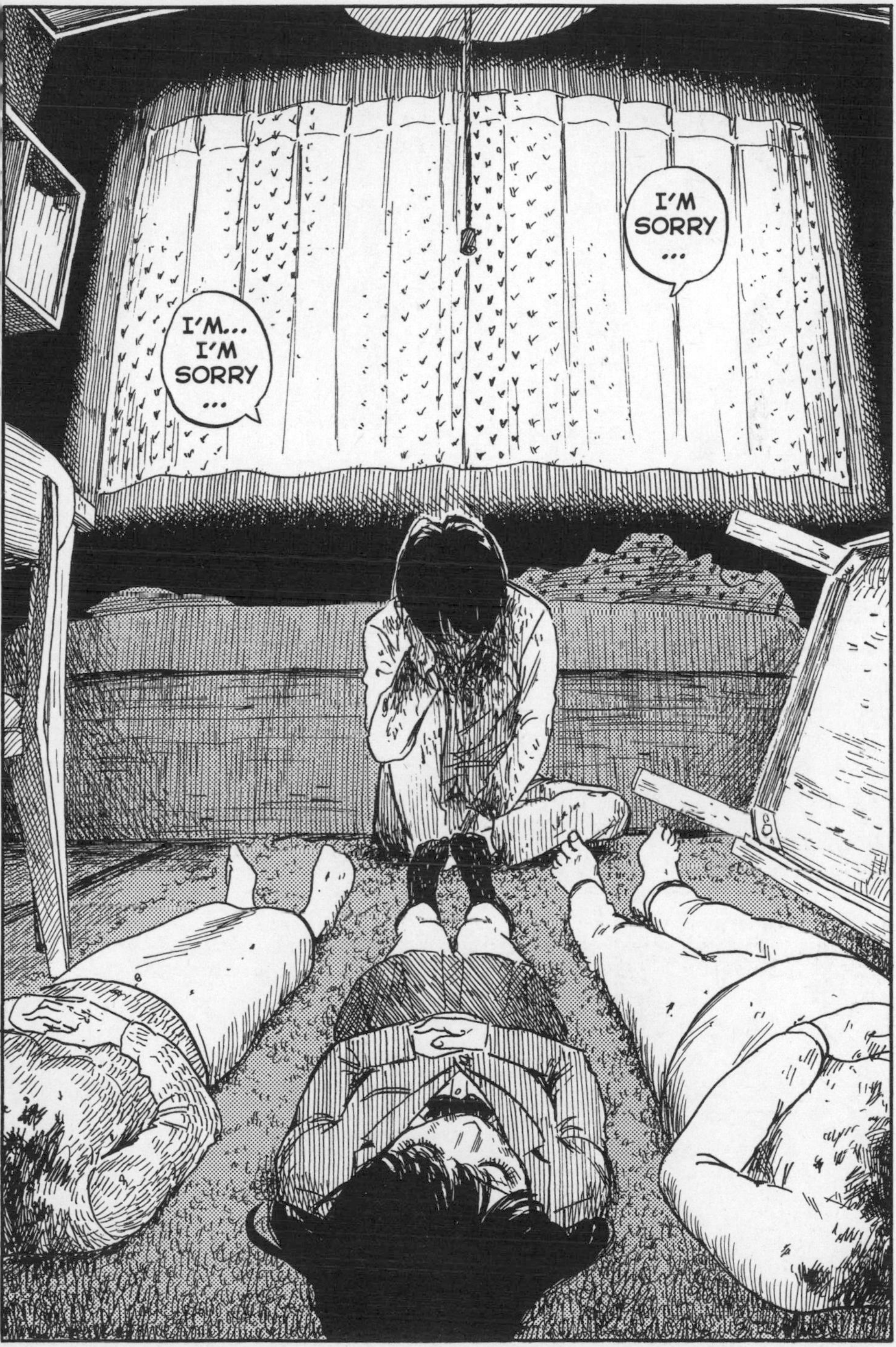
I'M SORRY ...
I'M... I'M SORRY ...

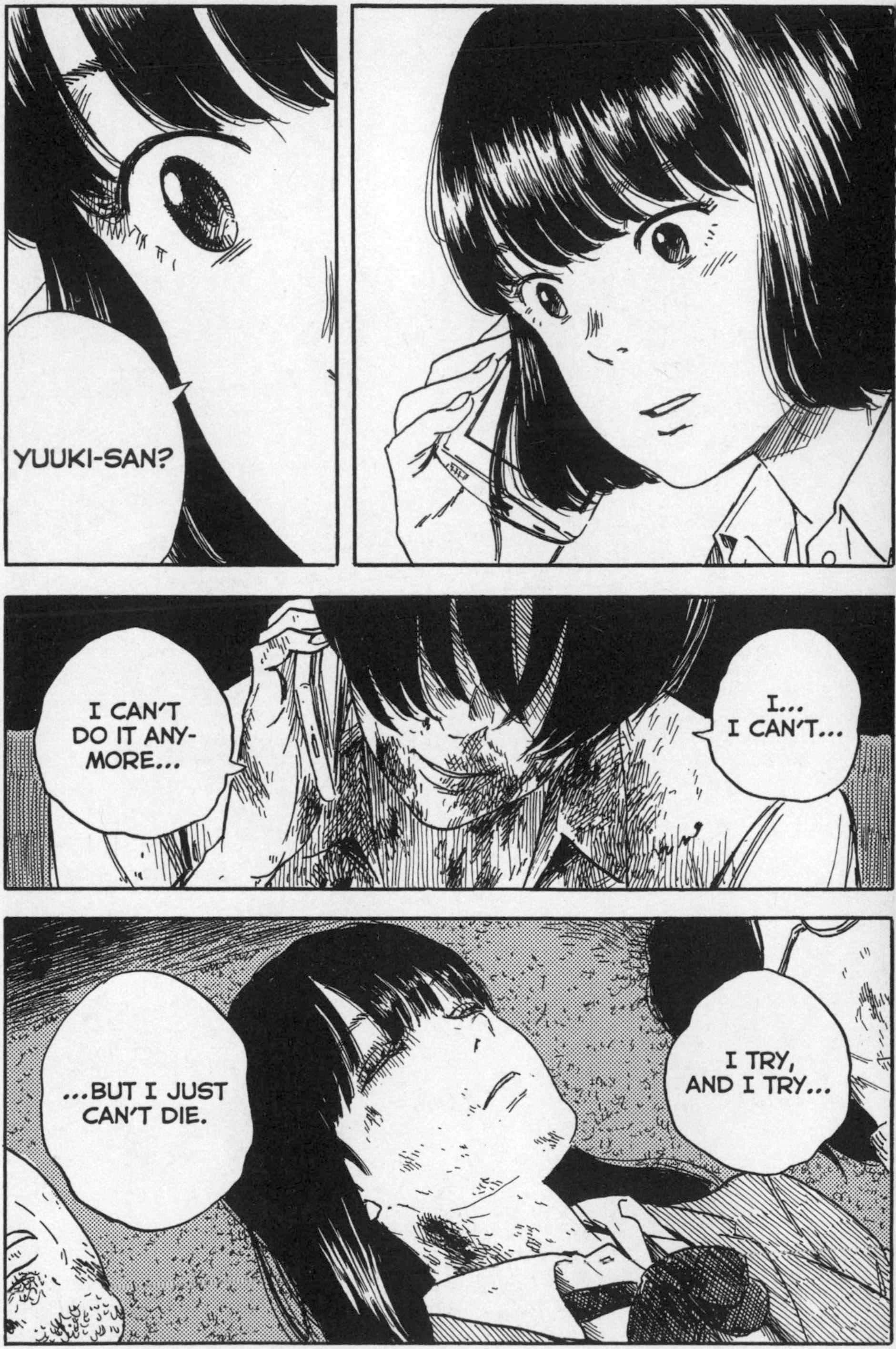

YUUKI-SAN?
I... I CAN'T...
I CAN'T DO IT ANY-MORE...
I TRY, AND I TRY...
...BUT I JUST CAN'T DIE.

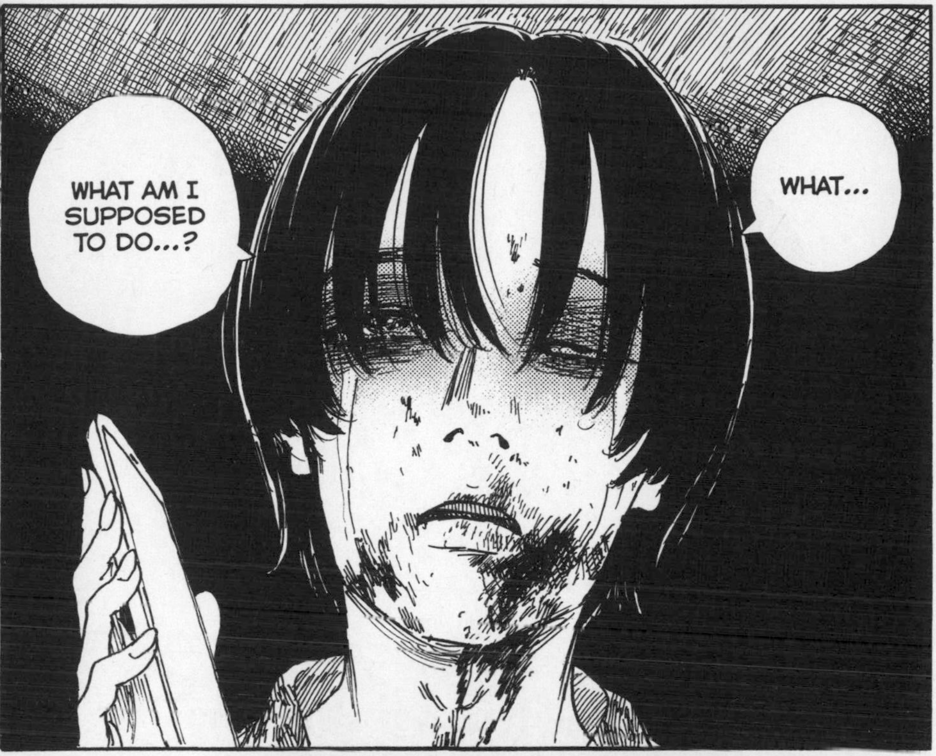
WHAT...
WHAT AM I SUPPOSED TO DO...?

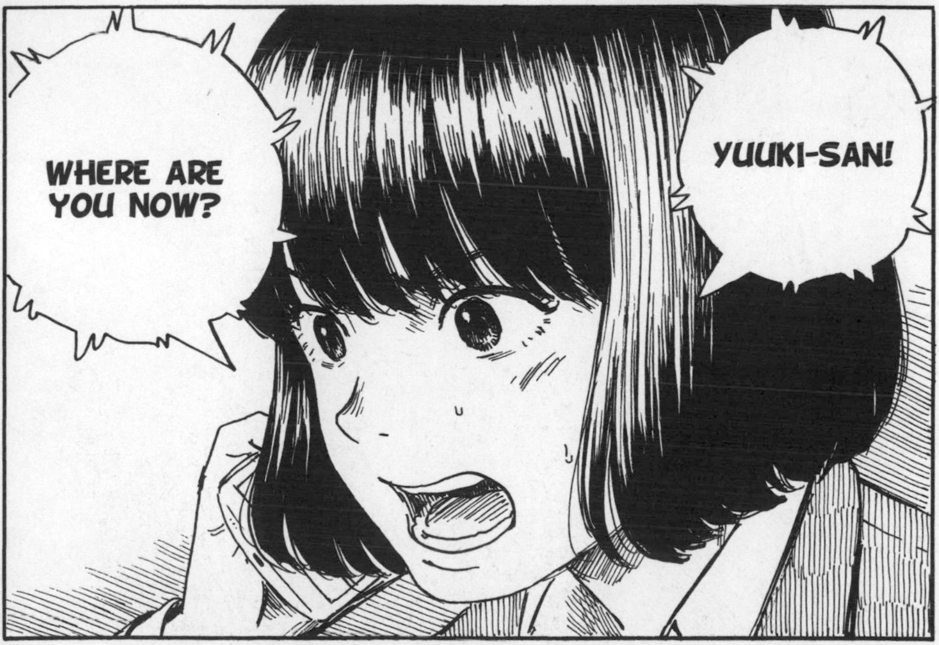
YUUKI-SAN!
WHERE ARE YOU NOW?

Chapter 22: Allies

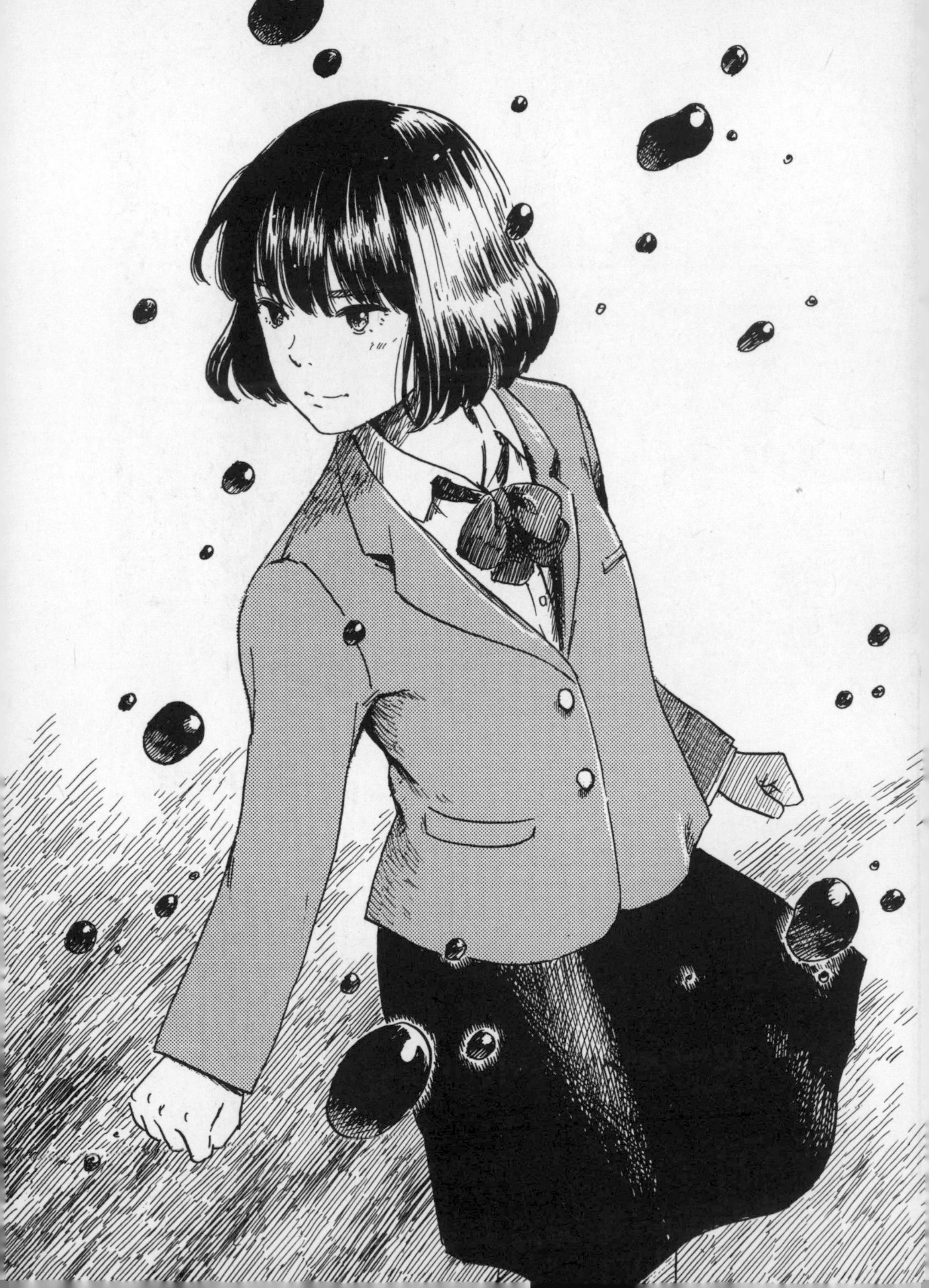

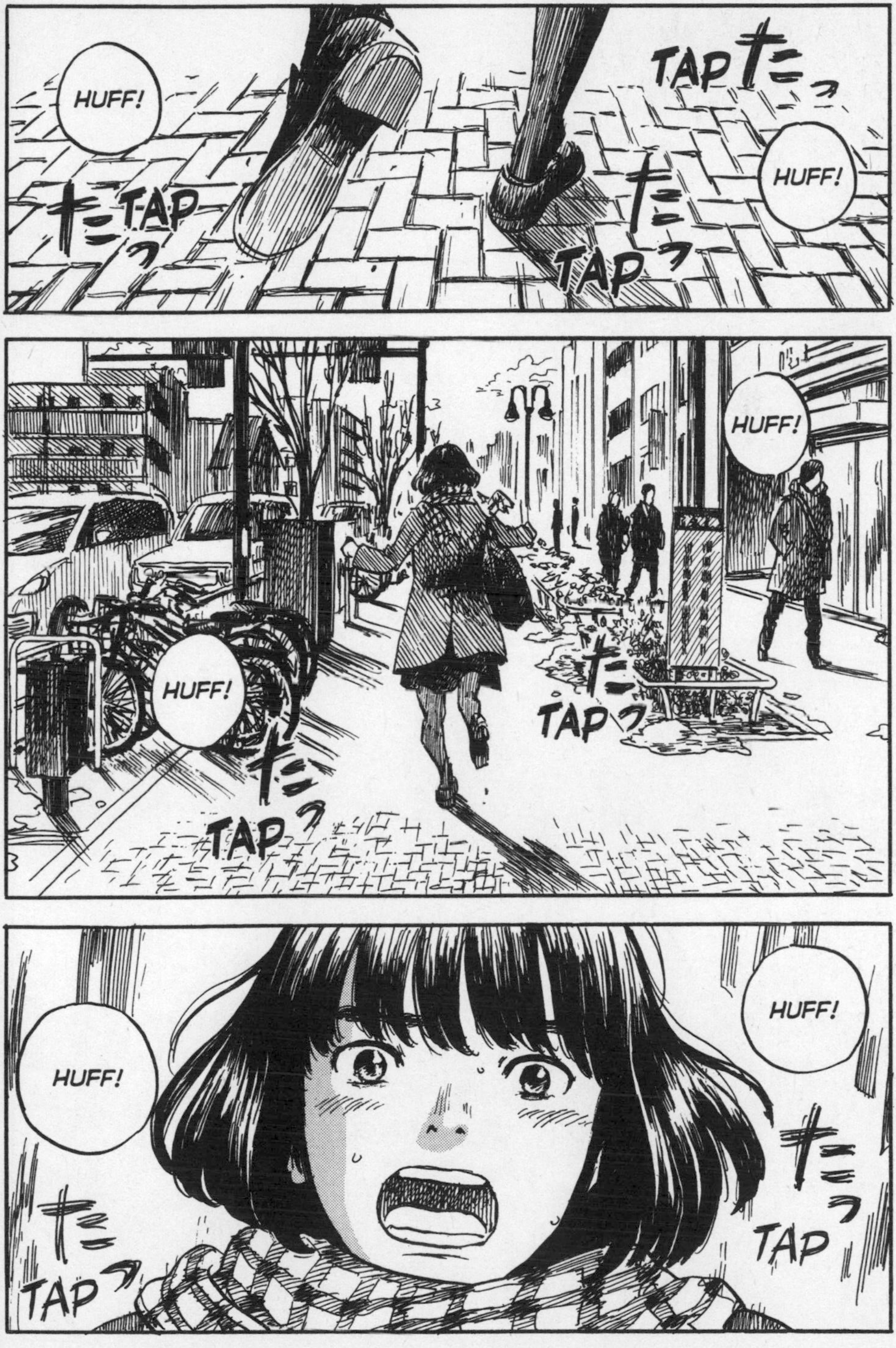
TAP たっ
HUFF!
たっ TAP
HUFF!
たっ TAP
HUFF!
たっ TAP
HUFF!
たっ TAP
HUFF!
たっ TAP
HUFF!
たっ TAP

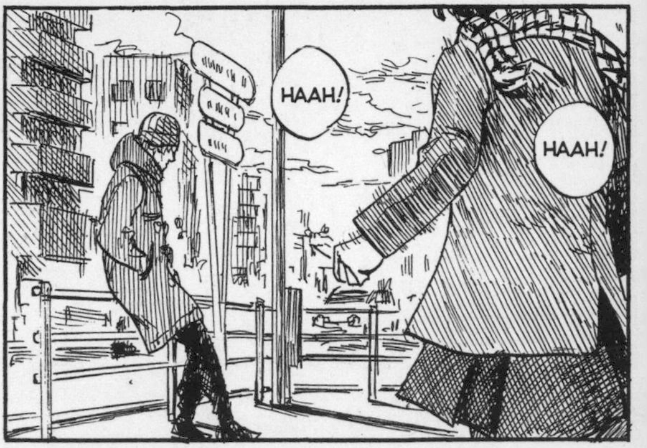
HAAH!
HAAH!
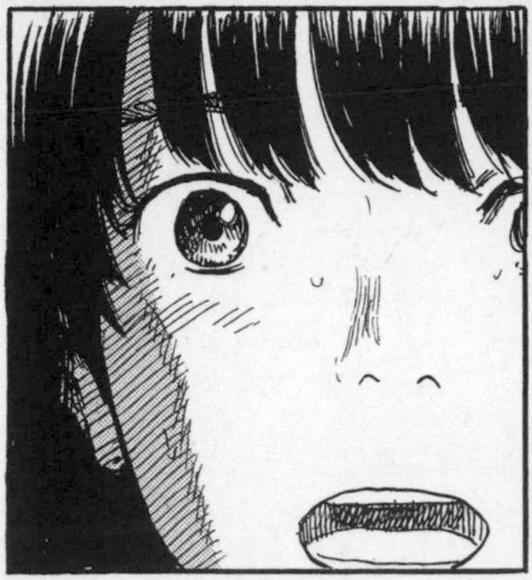
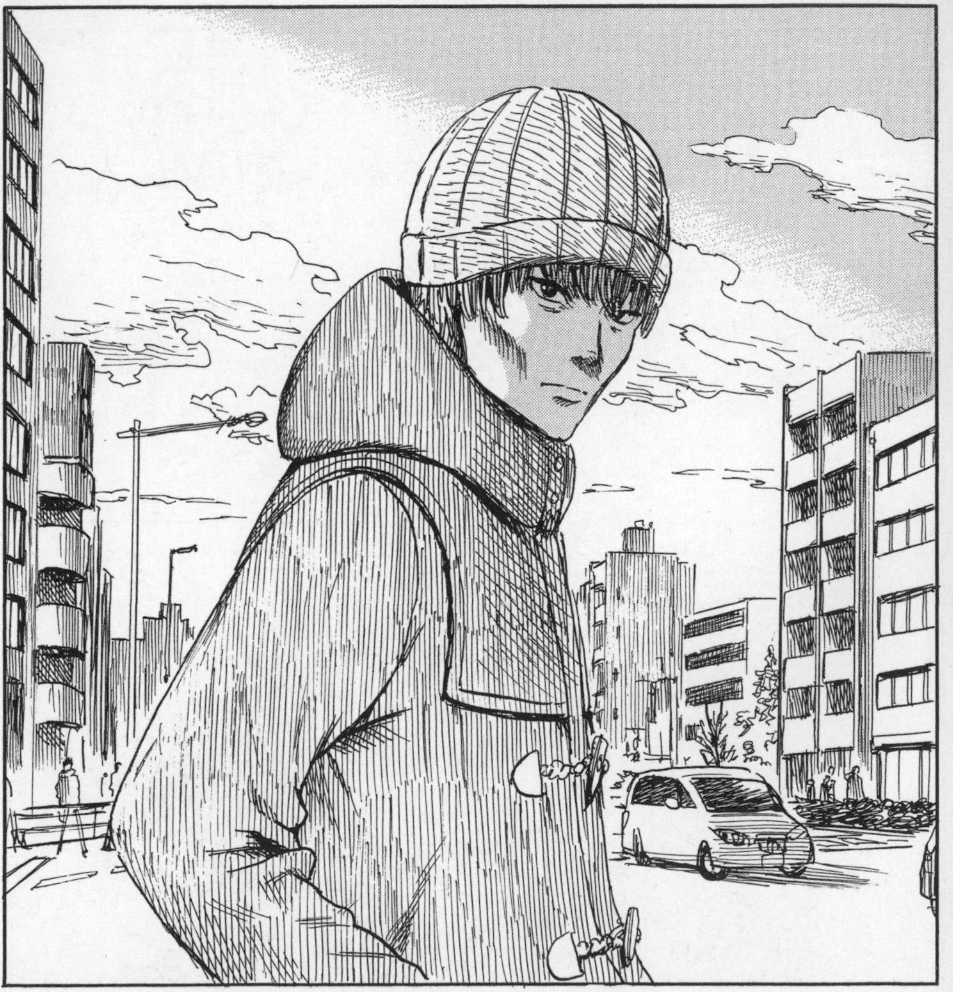

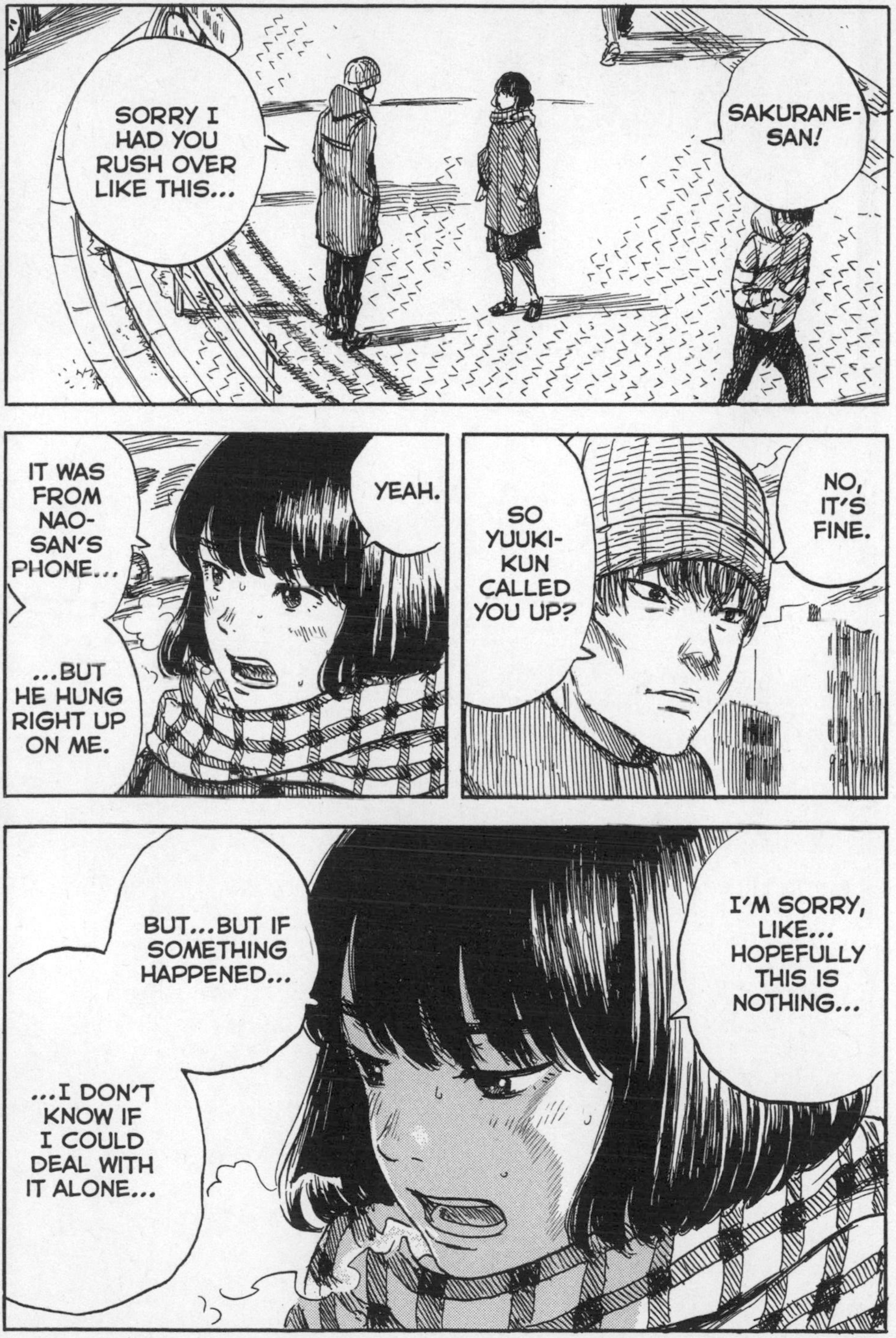
SAKURANE-SAN!
SORRY I HAD YOU RUSH OVER LIKE THIS...
NO, IT'S FINE.
SO YUUKI-KUN CALLED YOU UP?
YEAH.
IT WAS FROM NAO-SAN'S PHONE...
...BUT HE HUNG RIGHT UP ON ME.
I'M SORRY, LIKE... HOPEFULLY THIS IS NOTHING...
BUT...BUT IF SOMETHING HAPPENED...
...I DON'T KNOW IF I COULD DEAL WITH IT ALONE...

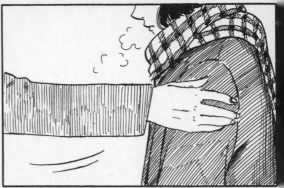

IT'S ALL RIGHT.

CALM DOWN.

BUT FOR NOW...

...WE SHOULD GO TO NAO-SAN'S PLACE...!

...

...THANK YOU...

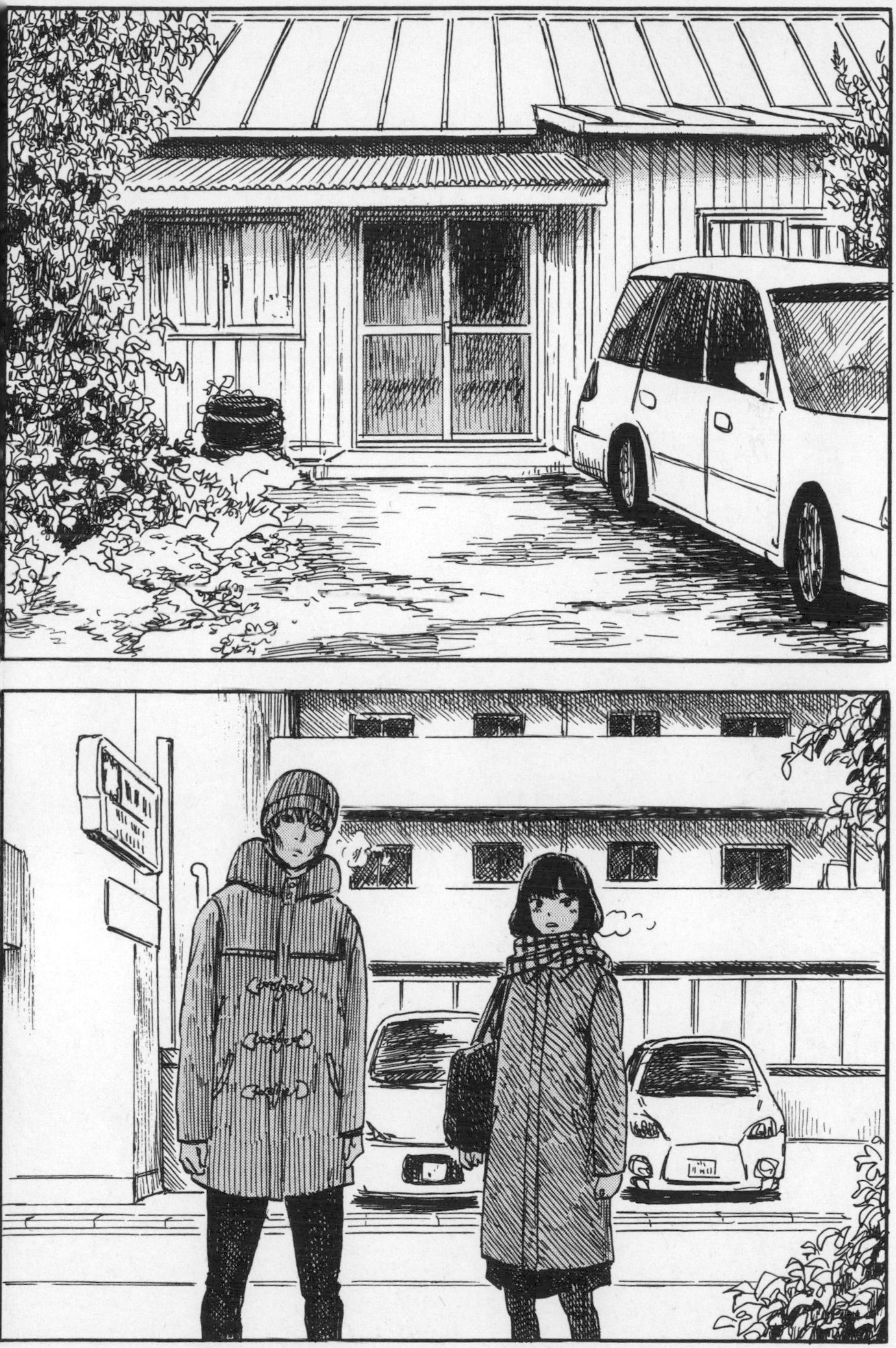

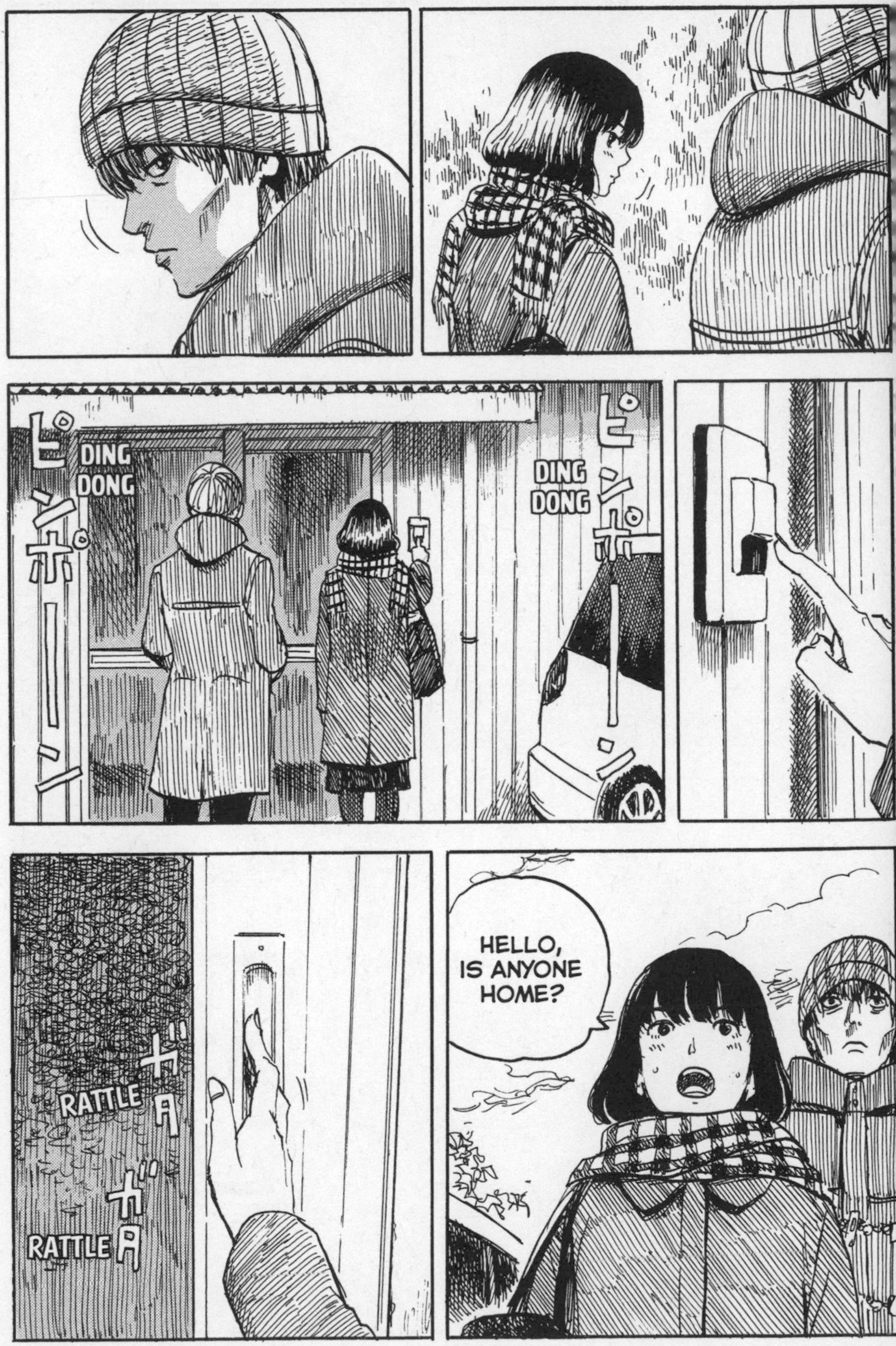
DING DONG
ピンポーン
DING DONG
ピンポーン
HELLO, IS ANYONE HOME?
ガタ
RATTLE
ガタ
RATTLE

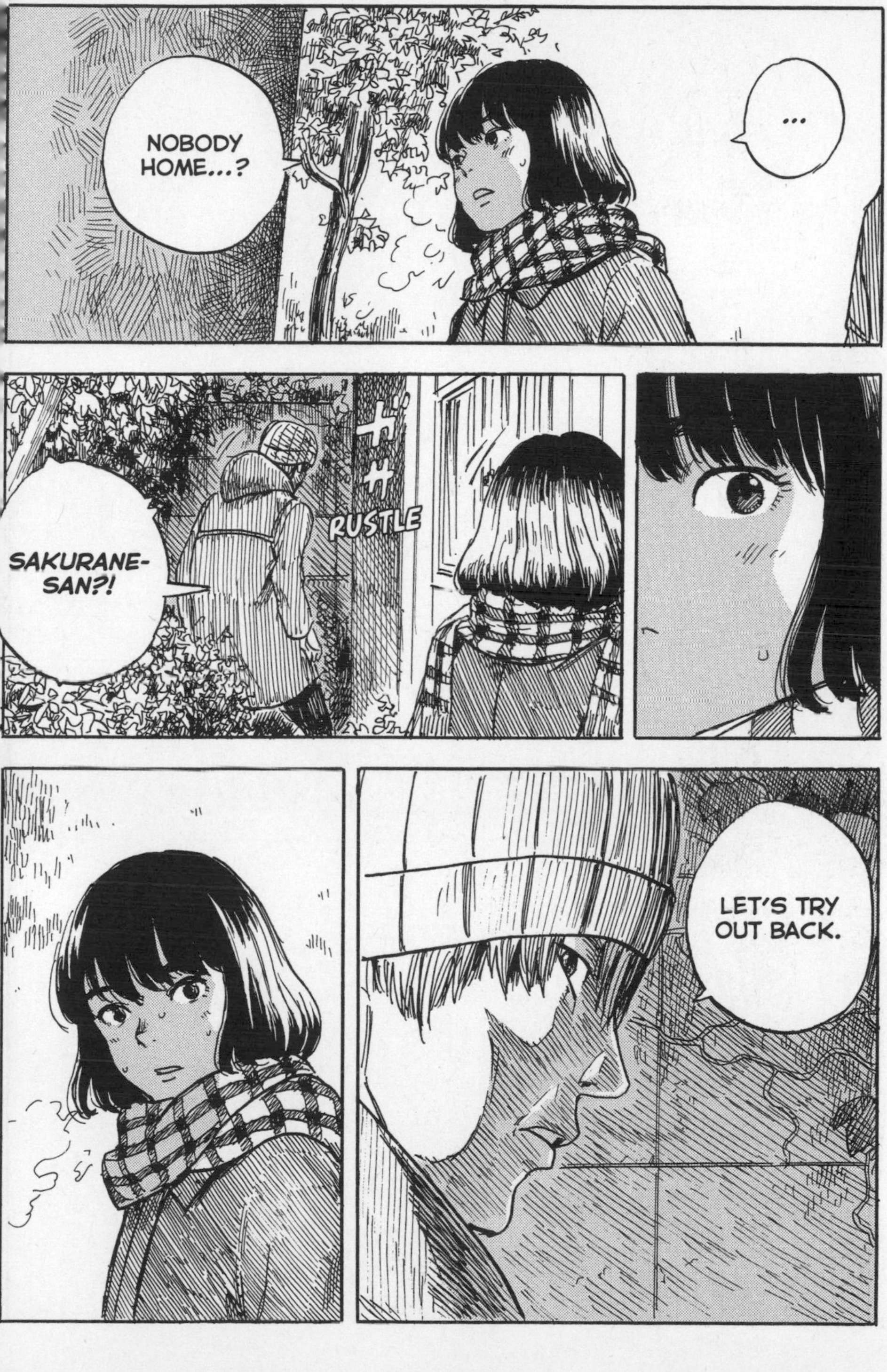
...
NOBODY HOME...?
RUSTLE
SAKURANE-SAN?!
LET'S TRY OUT BACK.

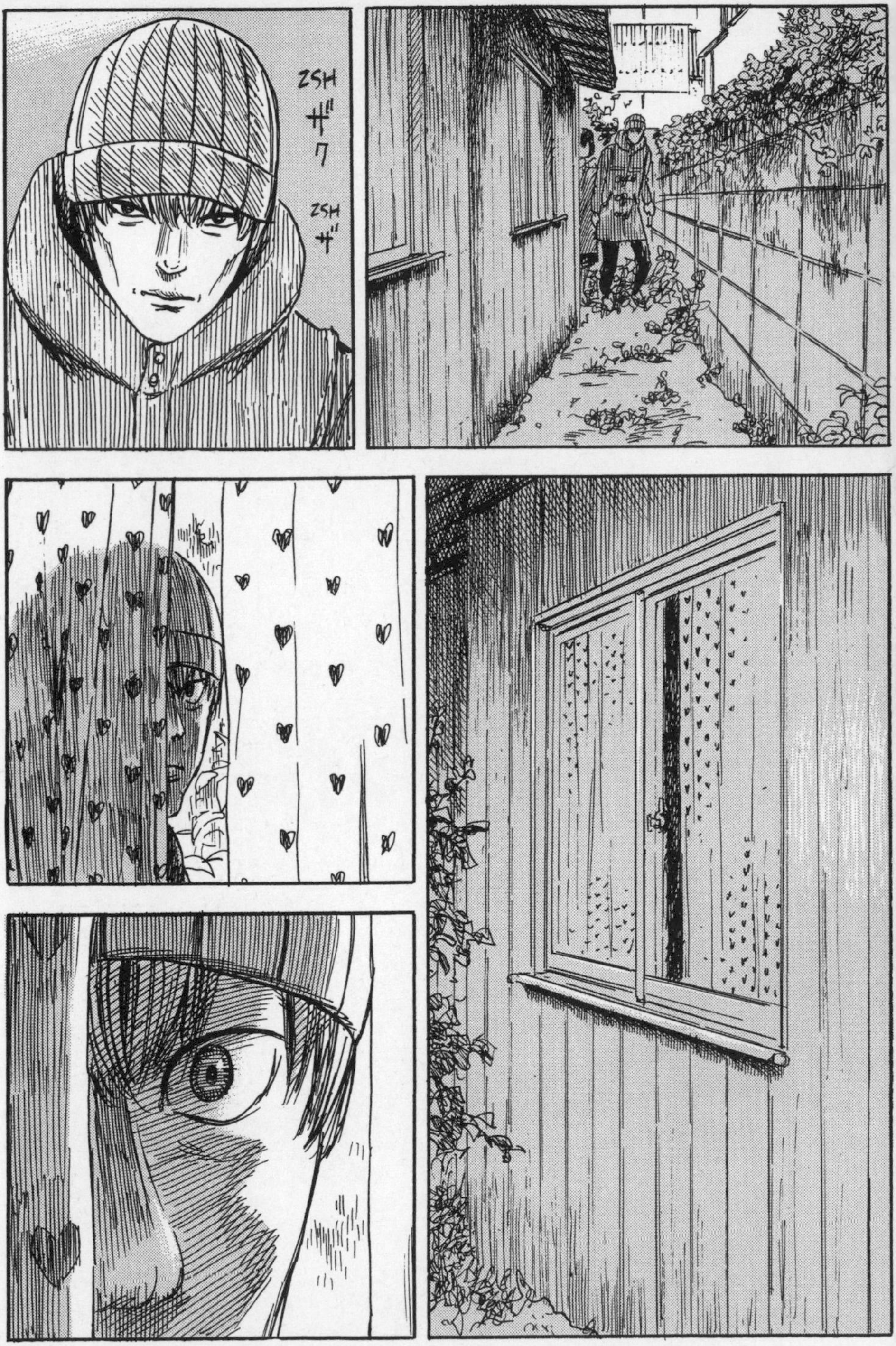
ZSH
ザッ
ZSH
ザ

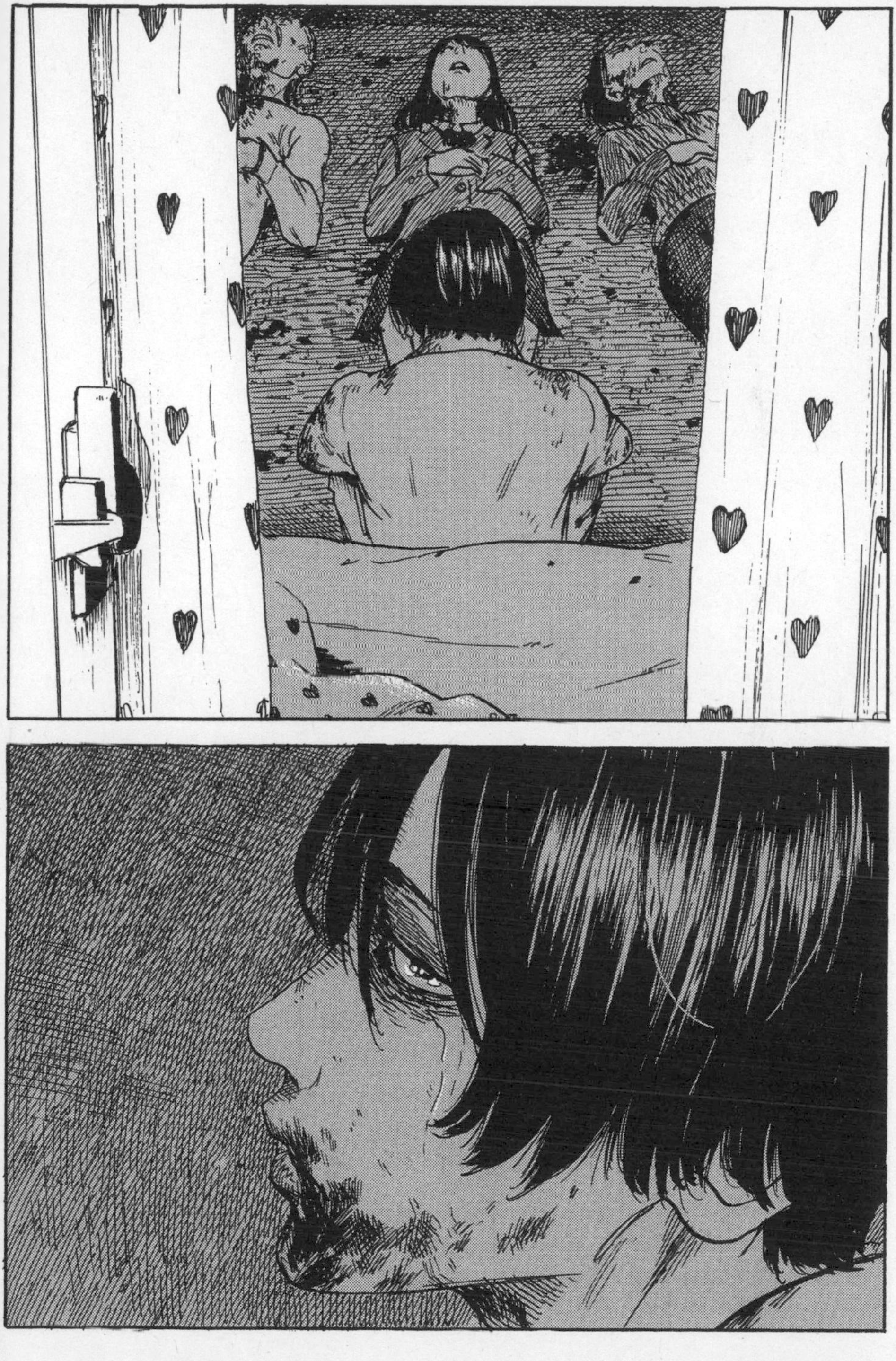

SAKU-RANE-SAN...?

IS *THAT* YUUKI-KUN?

IS...

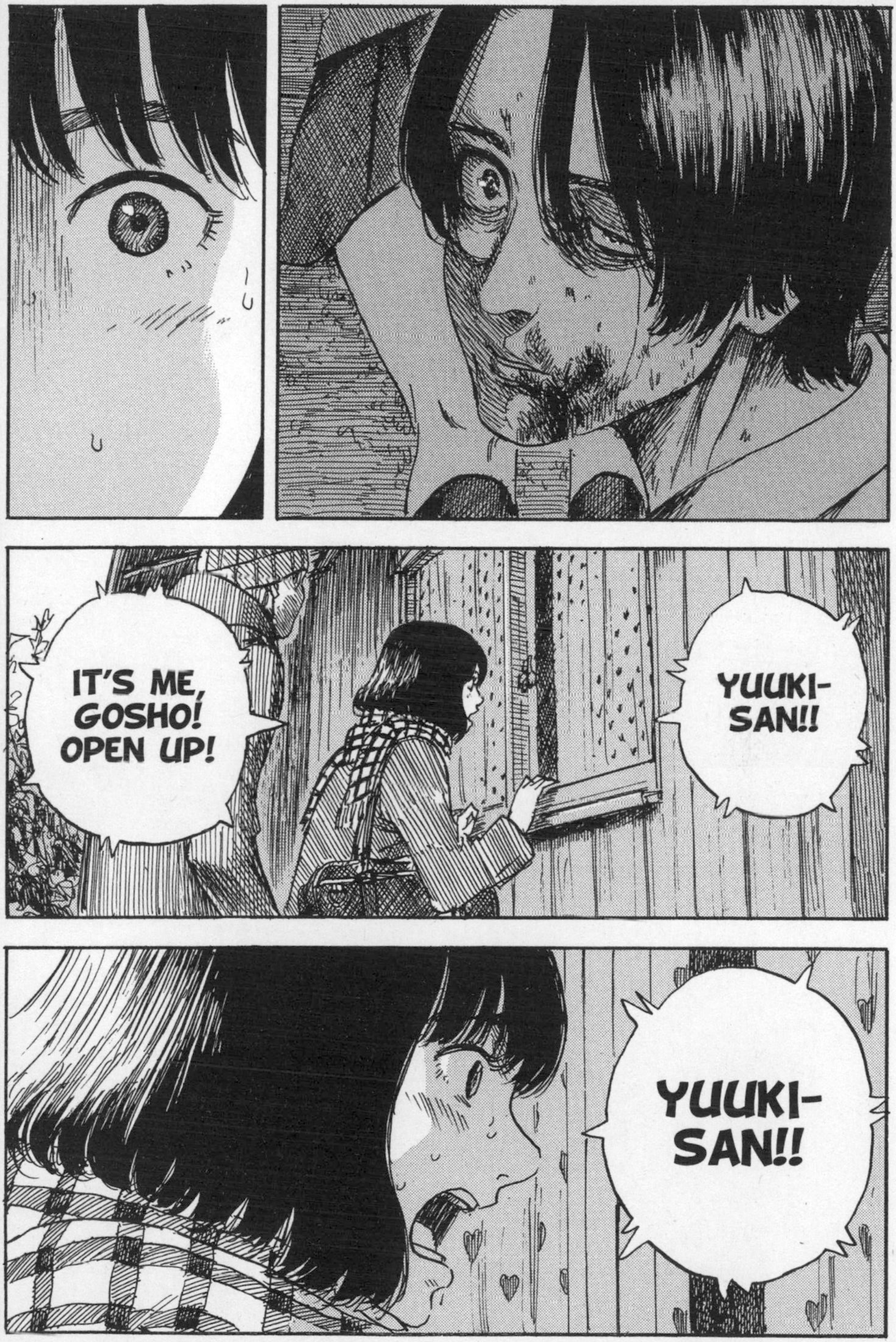
YUUKI-SAN!!
IT'S ME, GOSHO! OPEN UP!
YUUKI-SAN!!

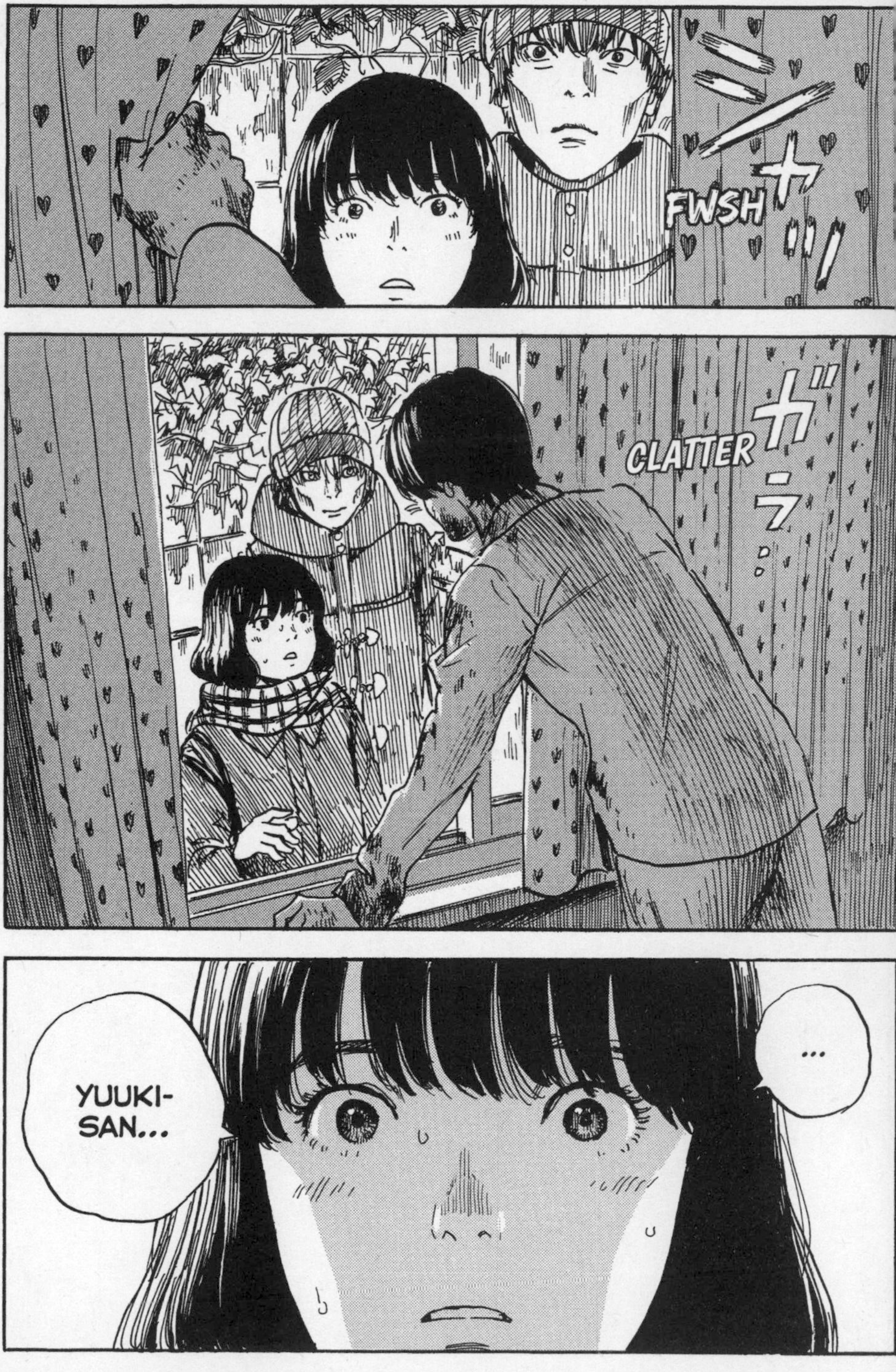
FWSH
CLATTER
...
YUUKI-SAN...

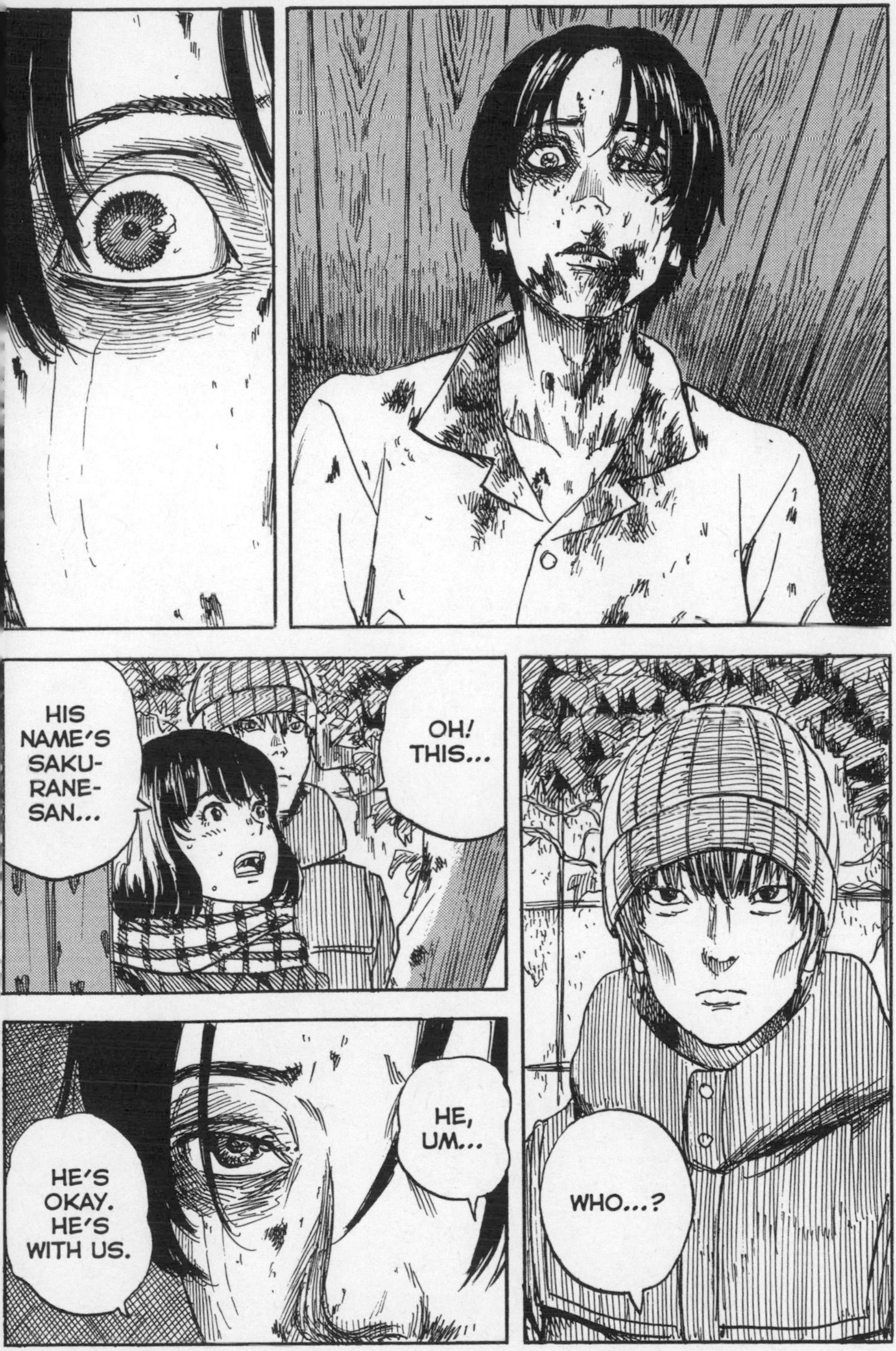
WHO...?
OH! THIS...
HIS NAME'S SAKURANE-SAN...
HE, UM...
HE'S OKAY. HE'S WITH US.

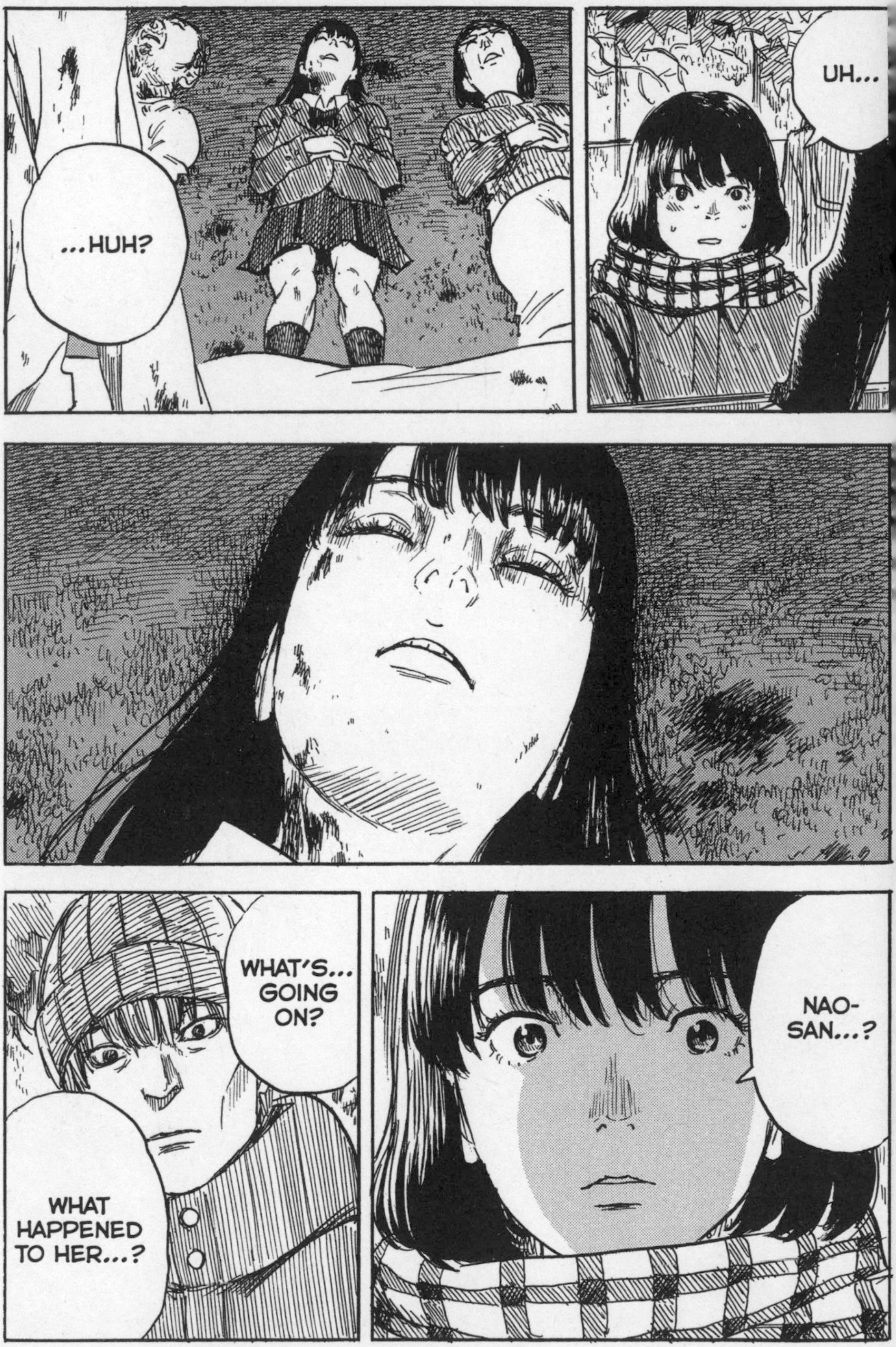
UH...
...HUH?
NAO-SAN...?
WHAT'S... GOING ON?
WHAT HAPPENED TO HER...?

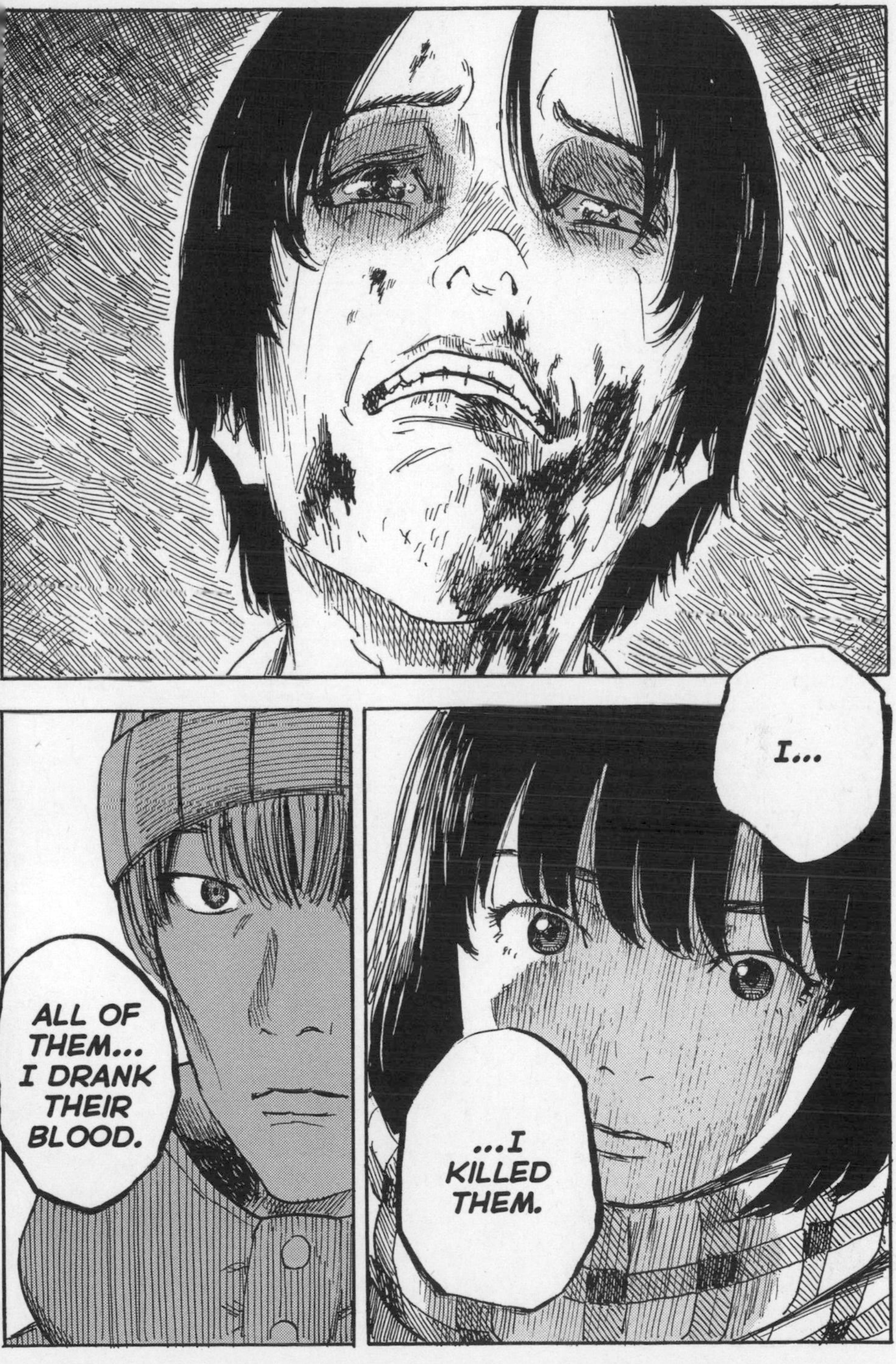
I...
...I KILLED THEM.
ALL OF THEM... I DRANK THEIR BLOOD.

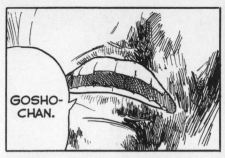

WHAT ...?
GOSHO-CHAN.
YOU HAVE TO KILL ME, TOO.
I CAN'T KILL MYSELF.
I...I'M SCREWED.
IT'S ALL OVER.
AHHH, WHY...
WHY...?

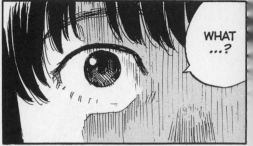

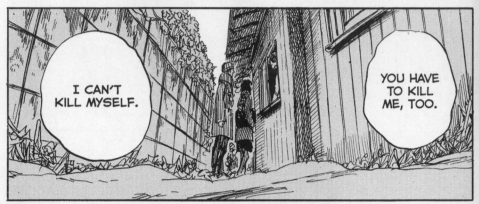

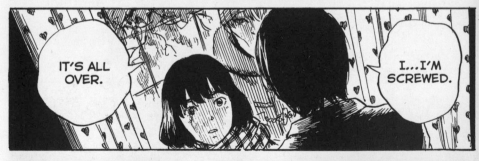

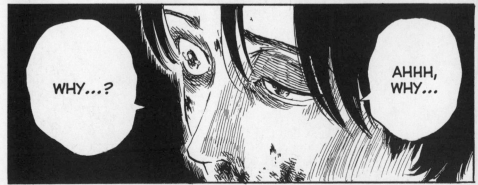

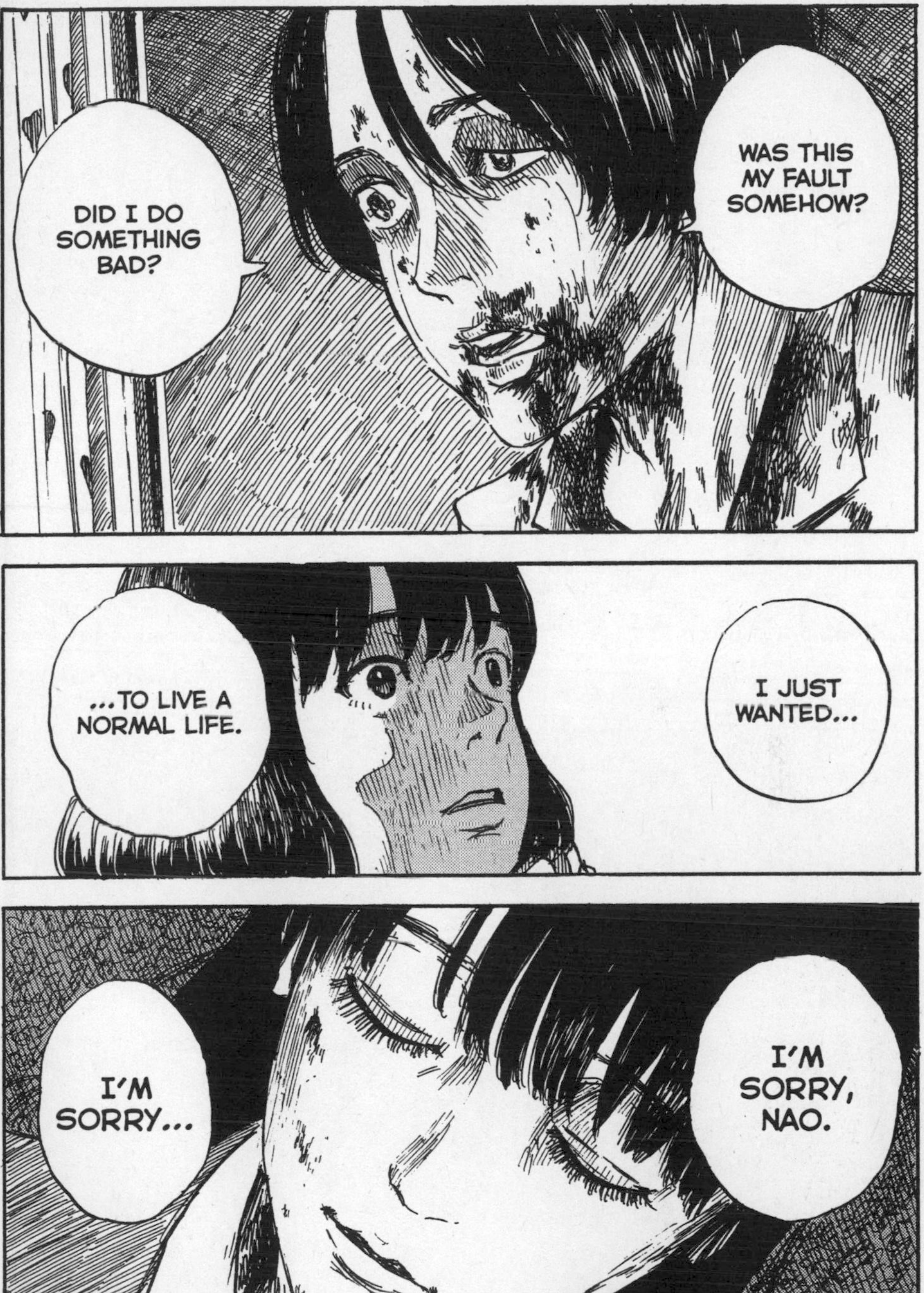
WAS THIS MY FAULT SOMEHOW?
DID I DO SOMETHING BAD?
I JUST WANTED...
...TO LIVE A NORMAL LIFE.
I'M SORRY, NAO.
I'M SORRY...

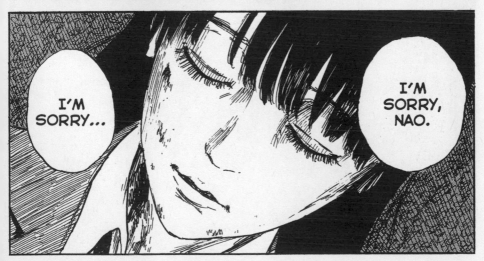

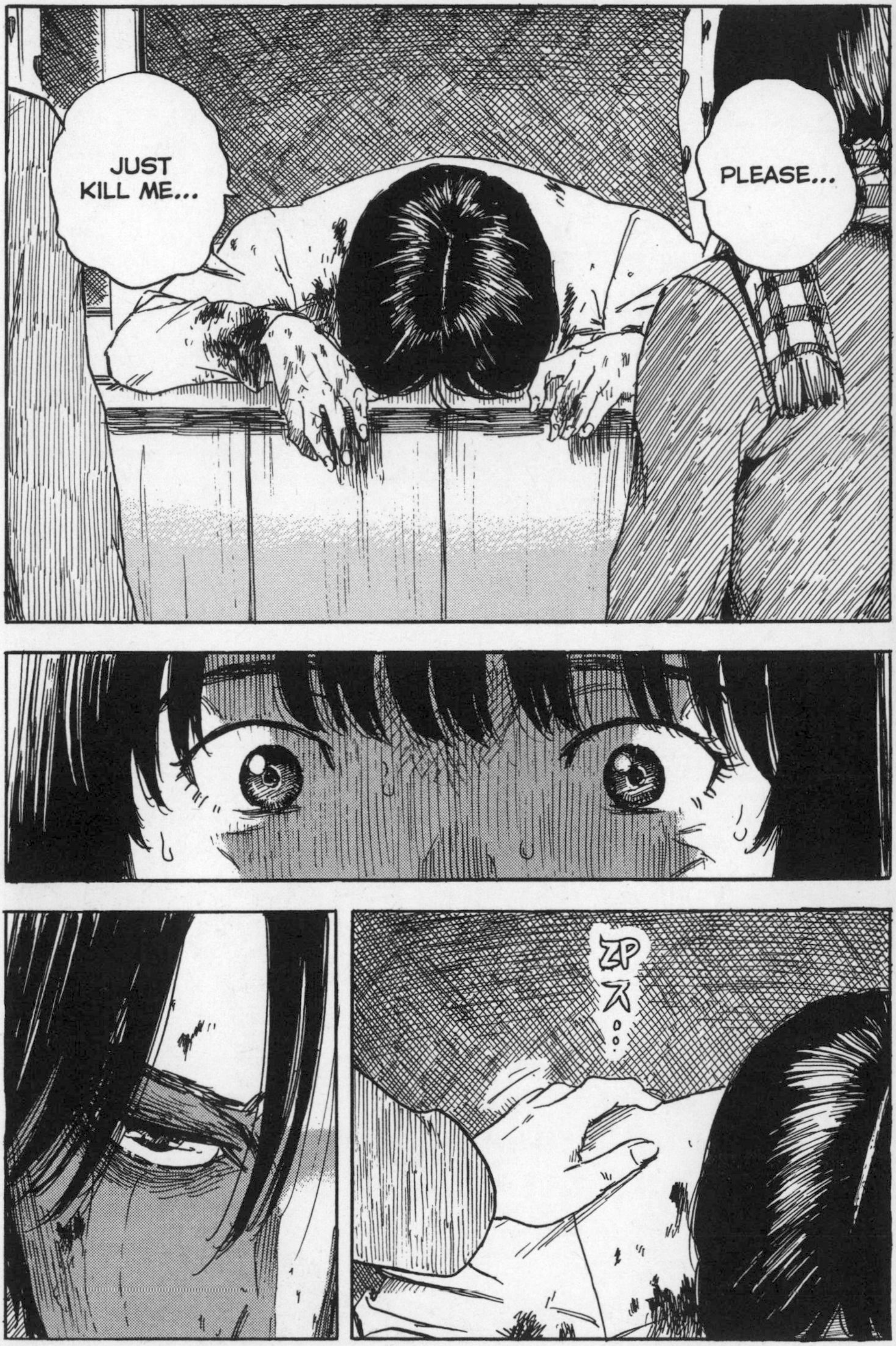
PLEASE...
JUST KILL ME...
ZP
ス..

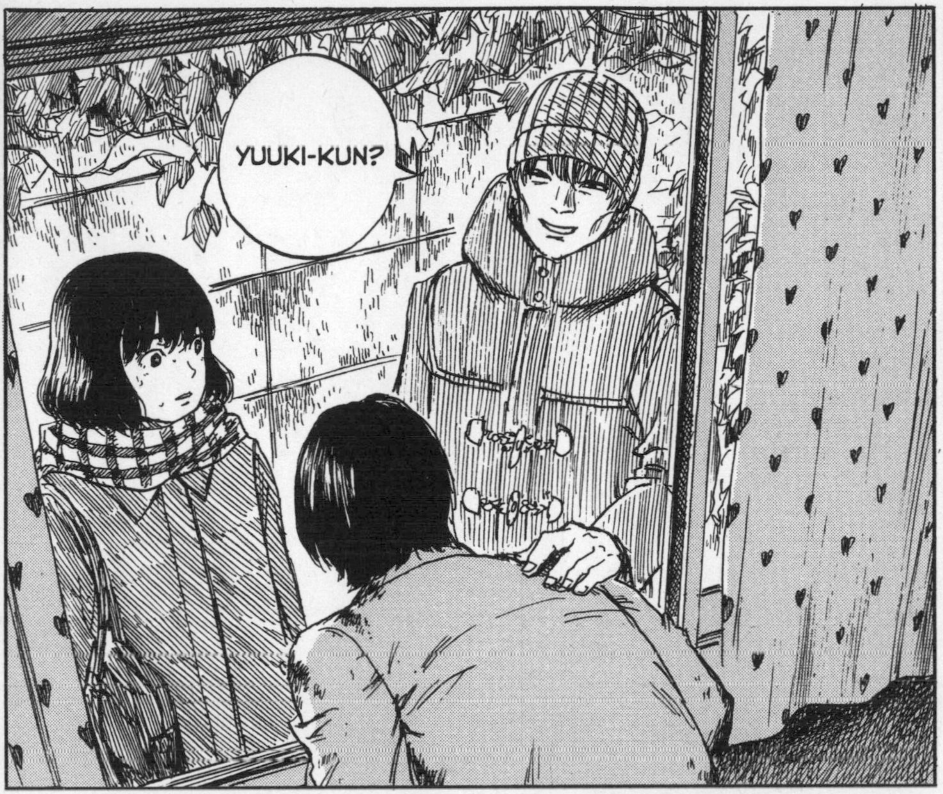
YUUKI-KUN?

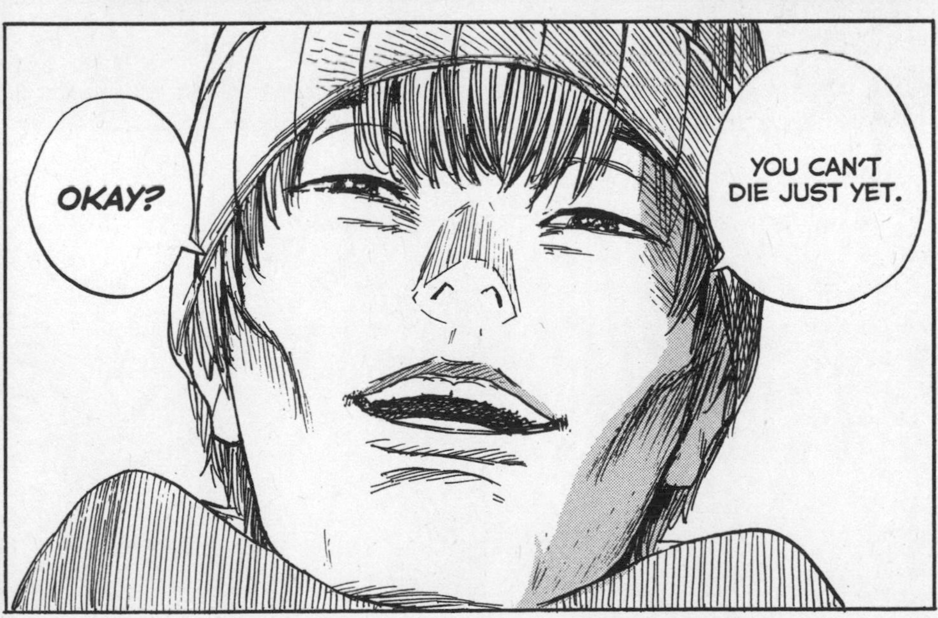
YOU CAN'T DIE JUST YET.
OKAY?

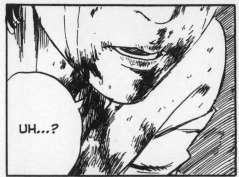

UH...?
WHO THE HELL ARE YOU?
WHAT WOULD *YOU* KNOW ABOUT ME?

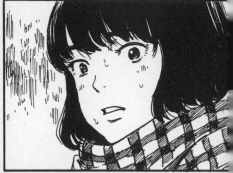

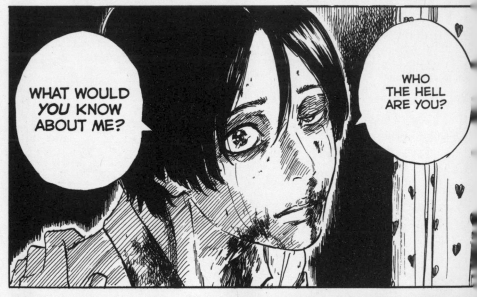

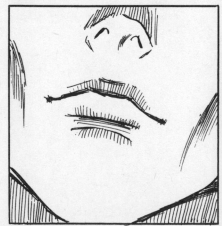

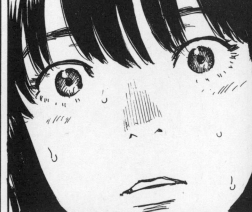

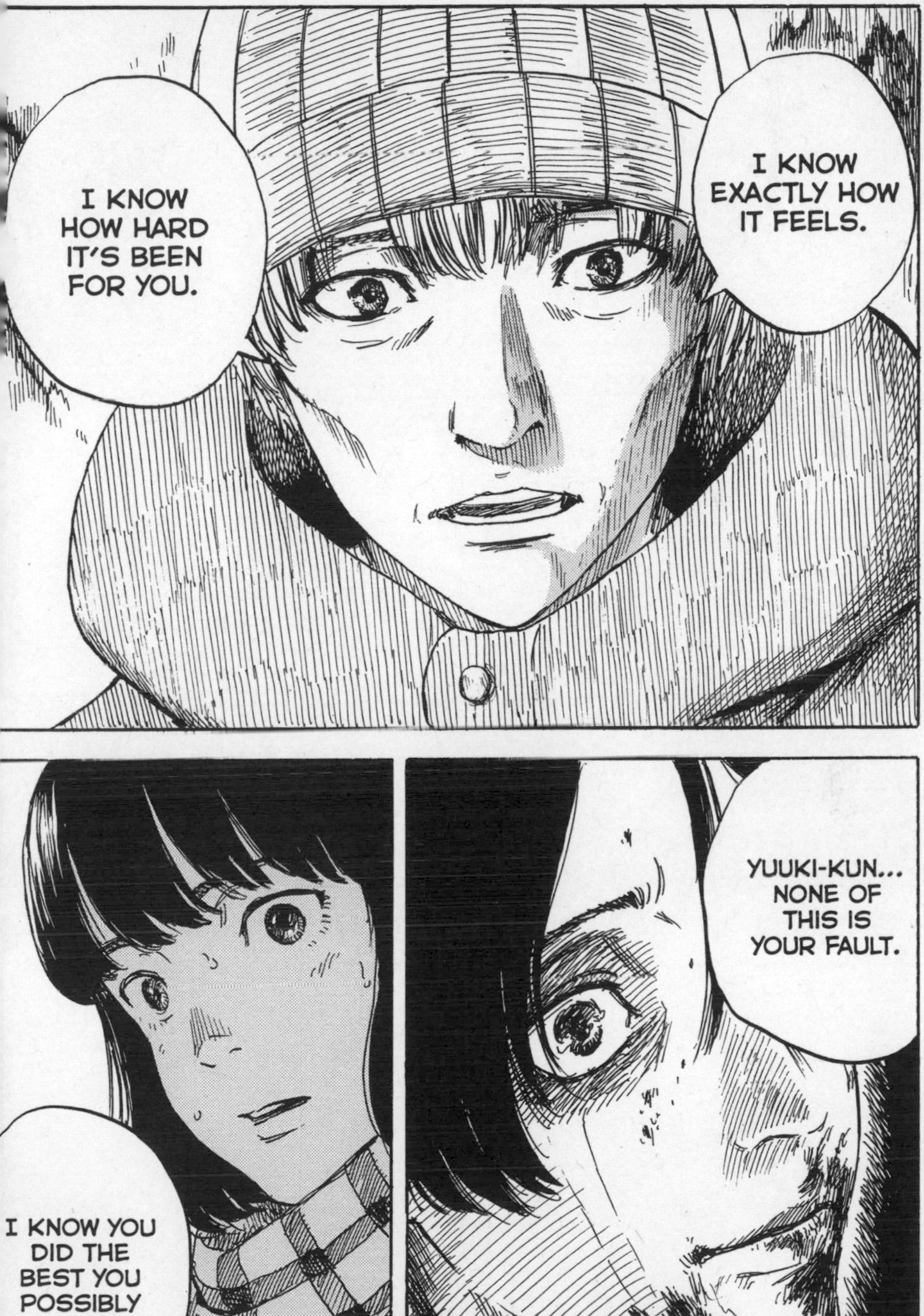
I KNOW EXACTLY HOW IT FEELS.
I KNOW HOW HARD IT'S BEEN FOR YOU.
YUUKI-KUN... NONE OF THIS IS YOUR FAULT.
I KNOW YOU DID THE BEST YOU POSSIBLY COULD.

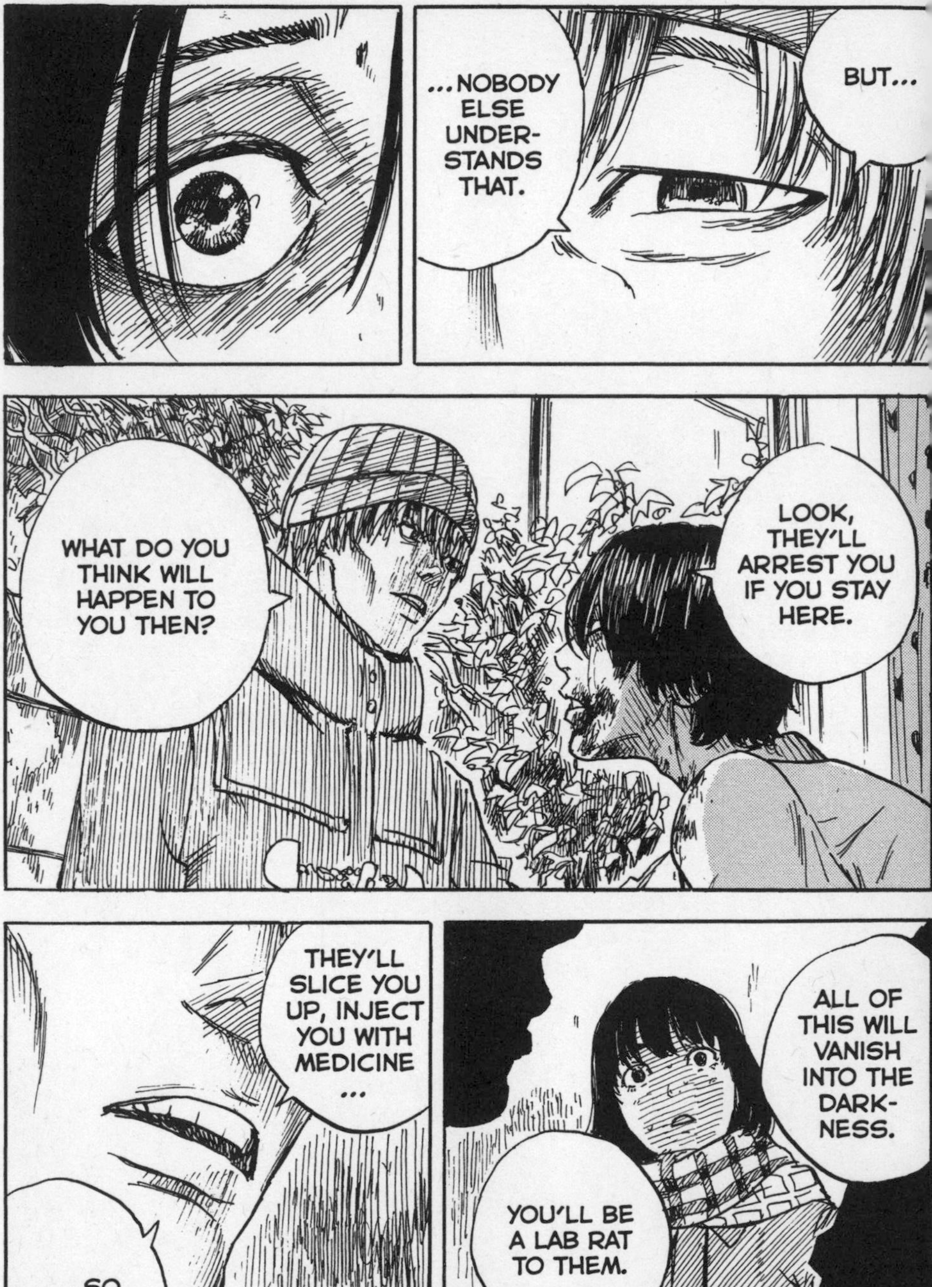
BUT...
...NOBODY ELSE UNDER-STANDS THAT.
LOOK, THEY'LL ARREST YOU IF YOU STAY HERE.
WHAT DO YOU THINK WILL HAPPEN TO YOU THEN?
ALL OF THIS WILL VANISH INTO THE DARK-NESS.
YOU'LL BE A LAB RAT TO THEM.
THEY'LL SLICE YOU UP, INJECT YOU WITH MEDICINE ...
...SO LISTEN, YUUKI-KUN.

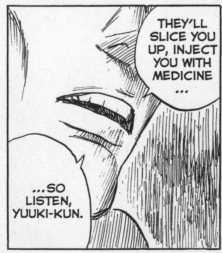

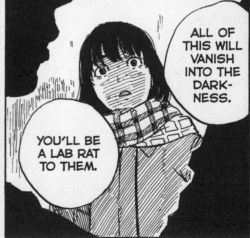

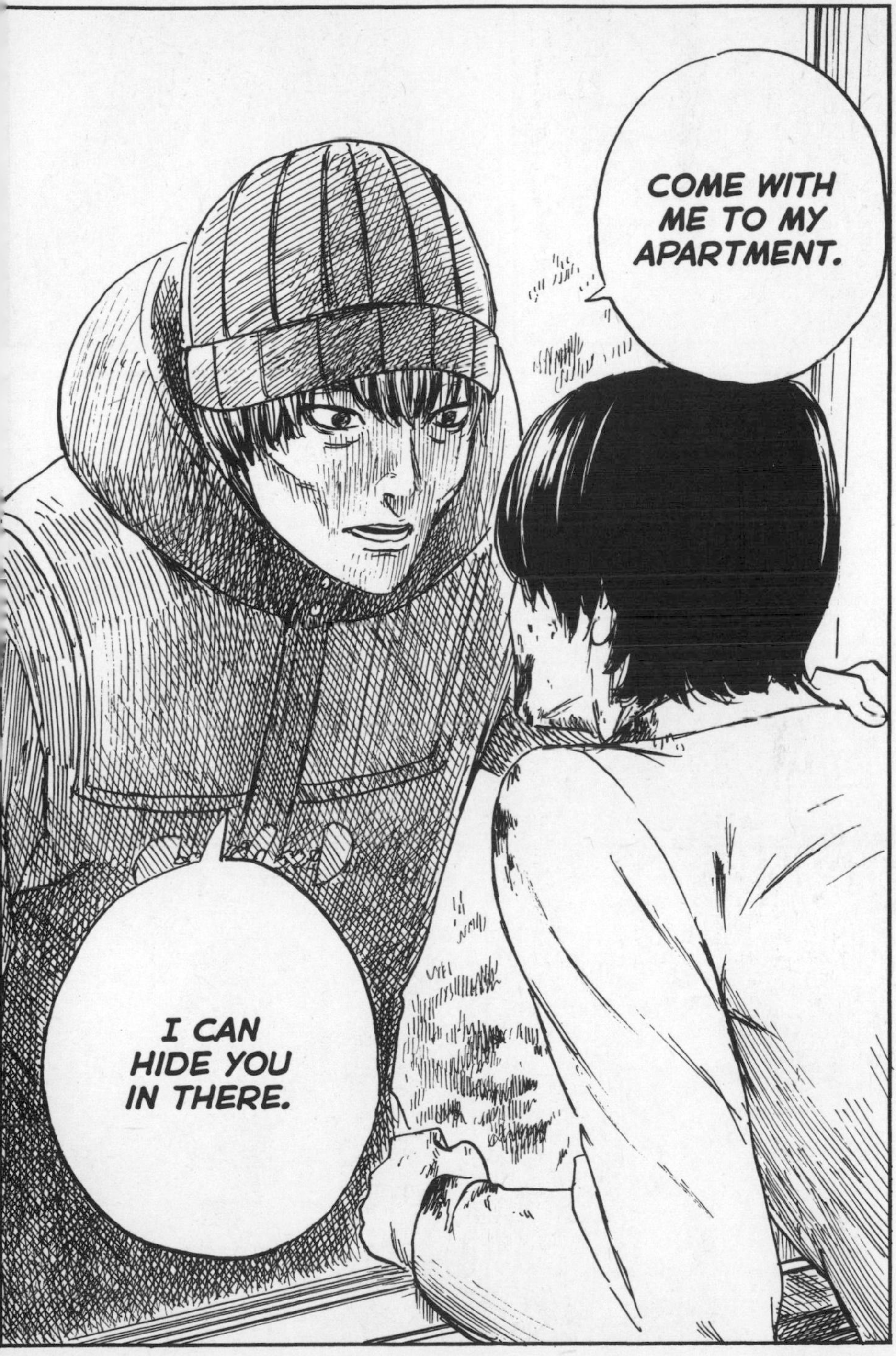
COME WITH ME TO MY APARTMENT.
I CAN HIDE YOU IN THERE.

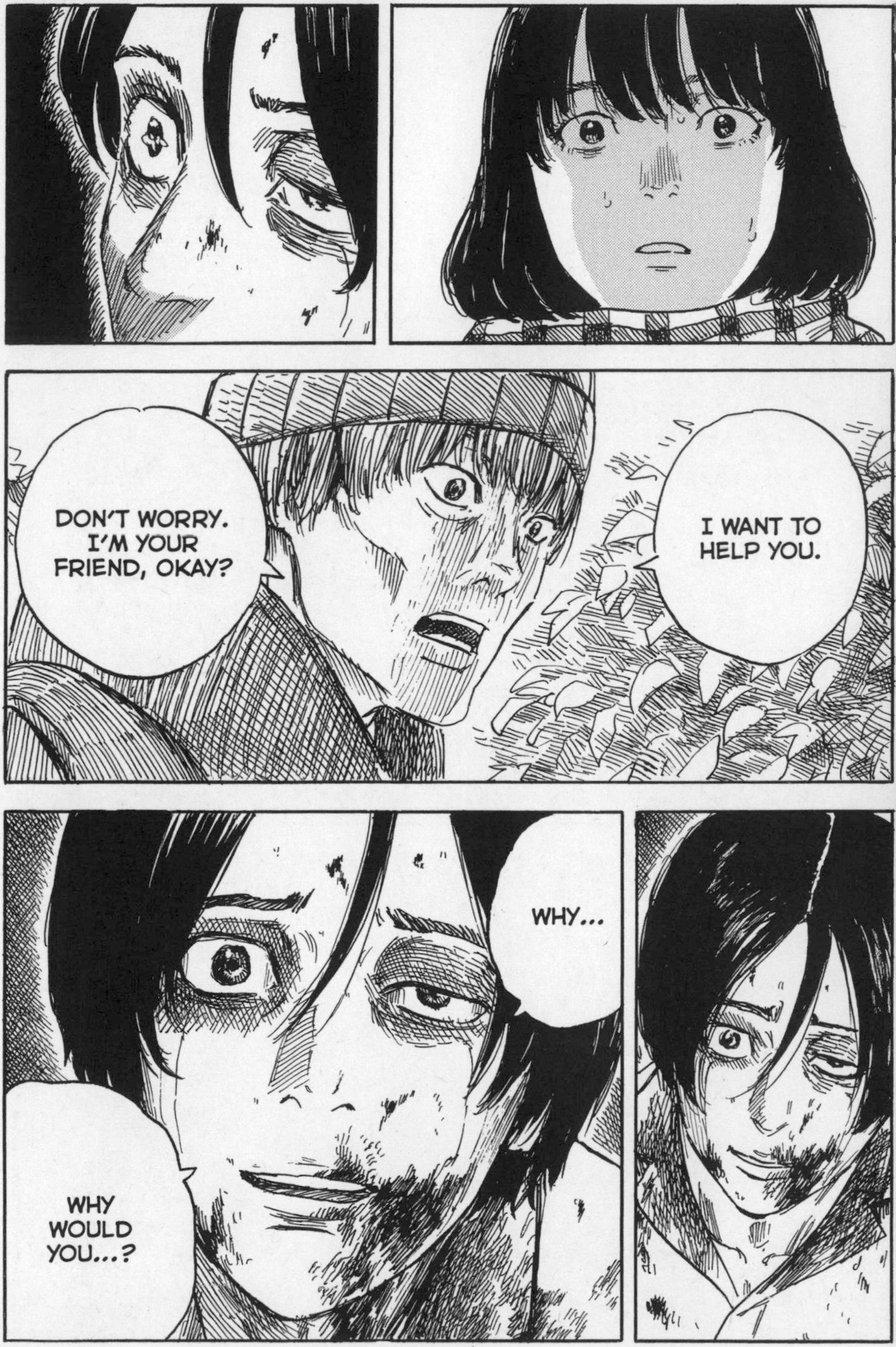
I WANT TO HELP YOU.
DON'T WORRY. I'M YOUR FRIEND, OKAY?
WHY...
WHY WOULD YOU...?

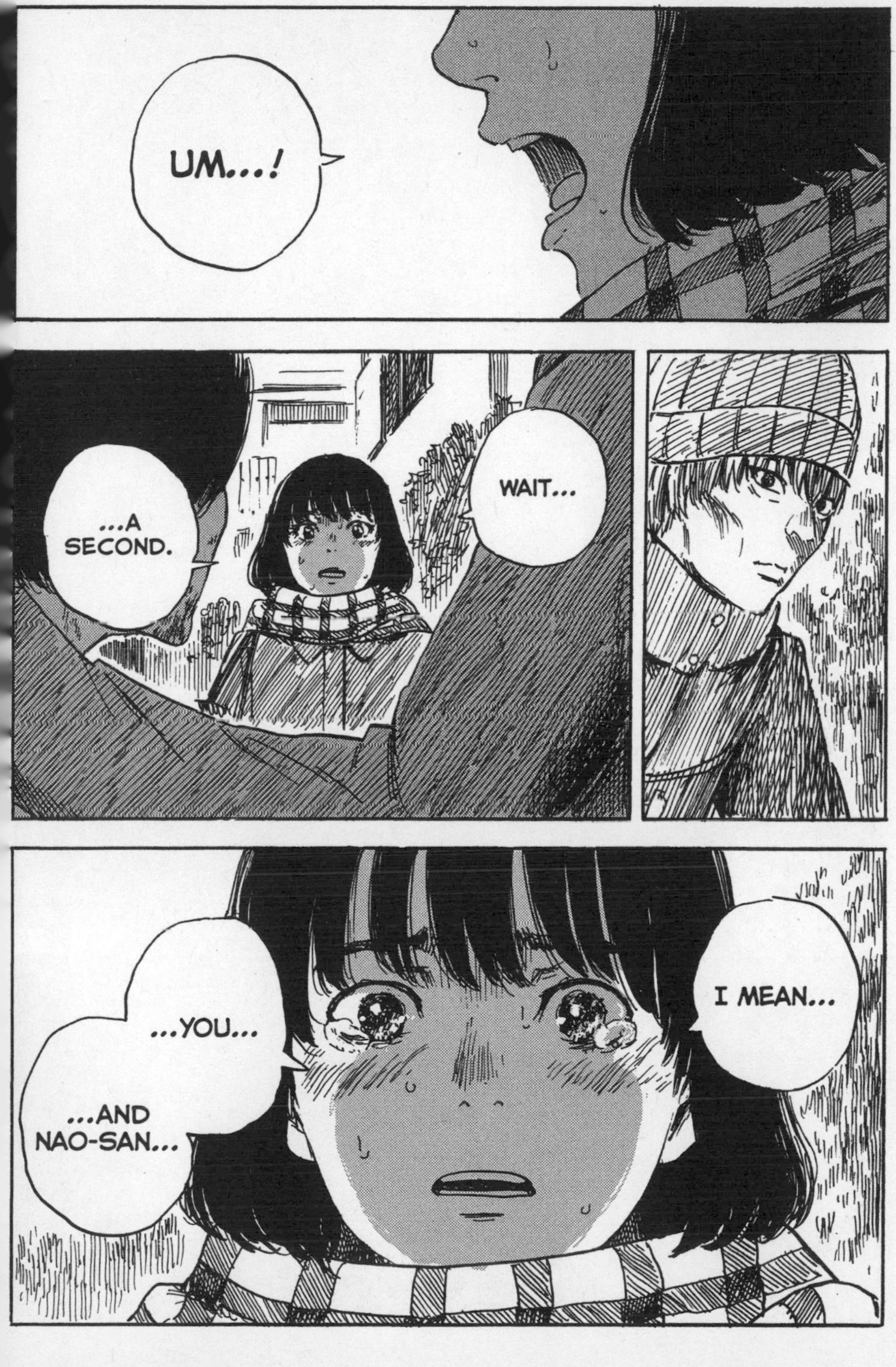
UM...!
WAIT...
...A SECOND.
I MEAN...
...YOU...
...AND NAO-SAN...

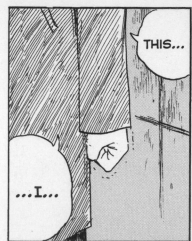

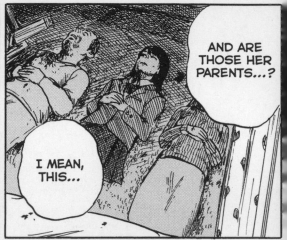

AND ARE THOSE HER PARENTS...?
I MEAN, THIS...
THIS...
...I...
YOU'RE JUST GONNA RUN AWAY...?
YOU CAN'T JUST... I MEAN...
GOSHO-SAN.

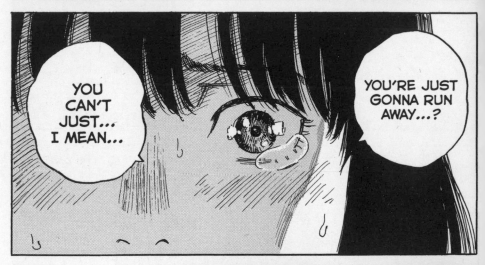

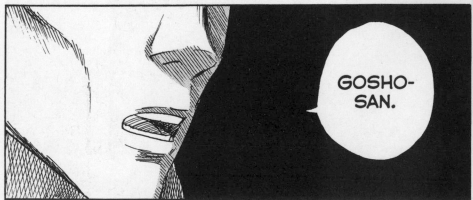

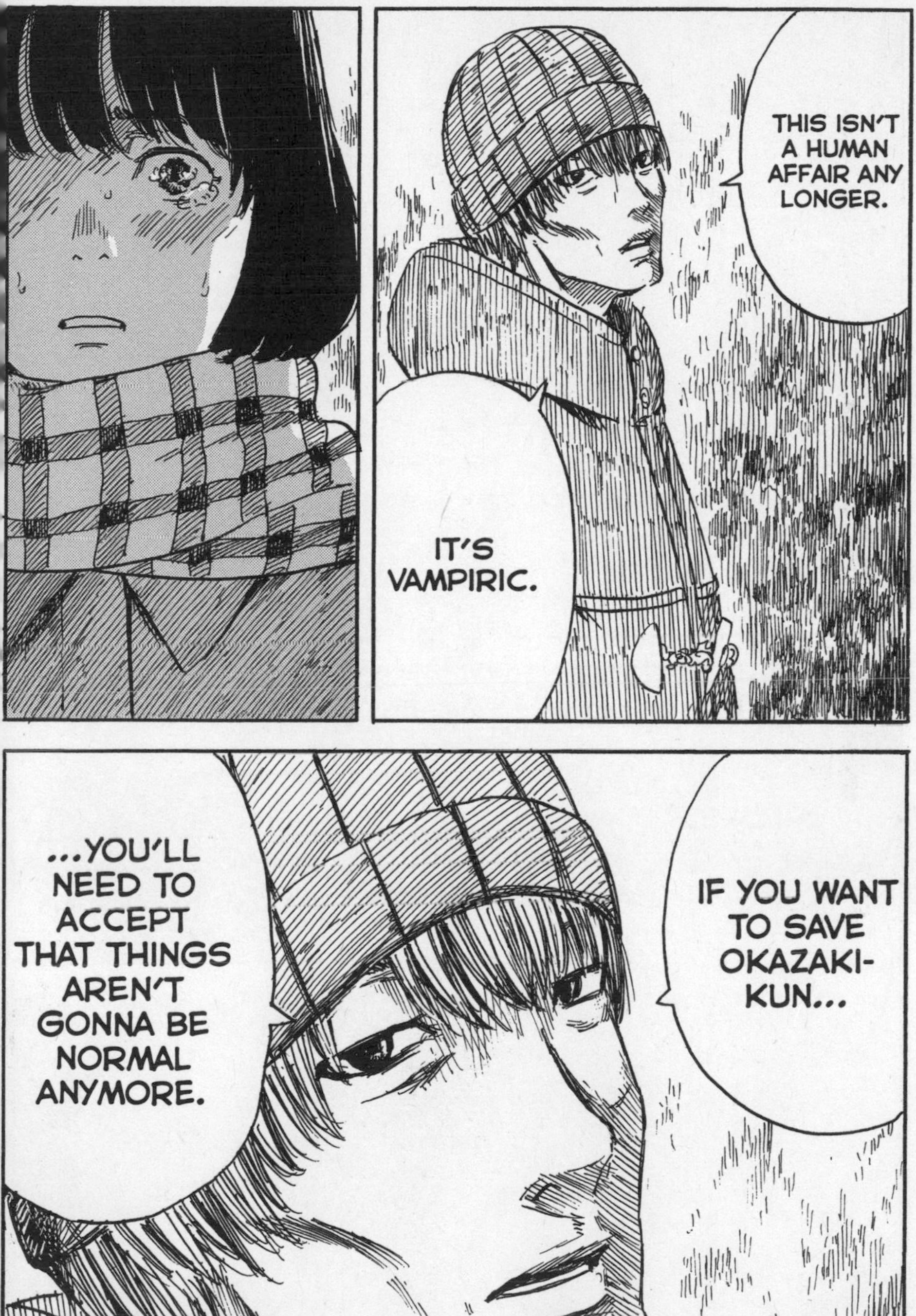
THIS ISN'T A HUMAN AFFAIR ANY LONGER.
IT'S VAMPIRIC.
IF YOU WANT TO SAVE OKAZAKI-KUN...
...YOU'LL NEED TO ACCEPT THAT THINGS AREN'T GONNA BE NORMAL ANYMORE.

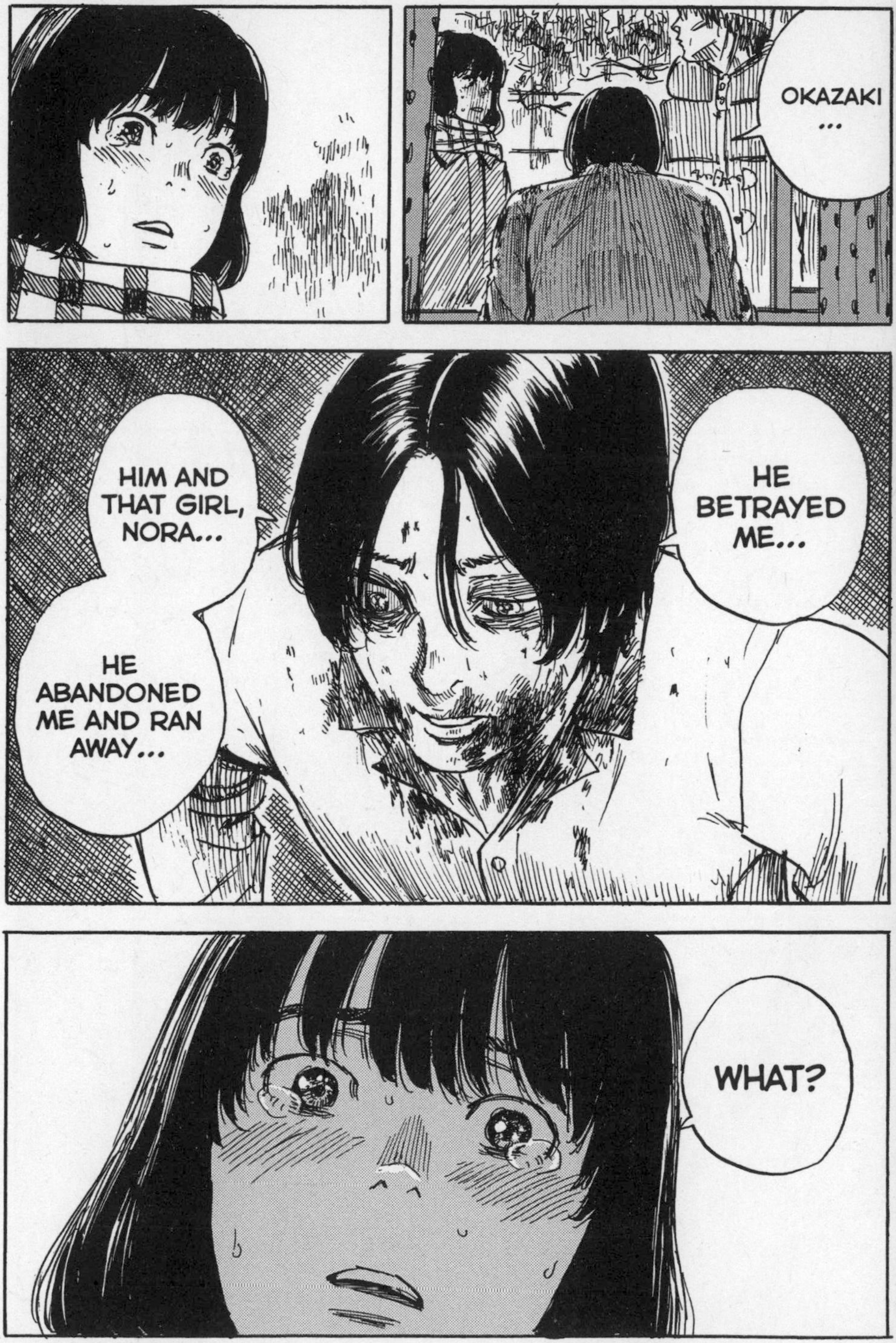
OKAZAKI ...
HE BETRAYED ME...
HIM AND THAT GIRL, NORA...
HE ABANDONED ME AND RAN AWAY...
WHAT?

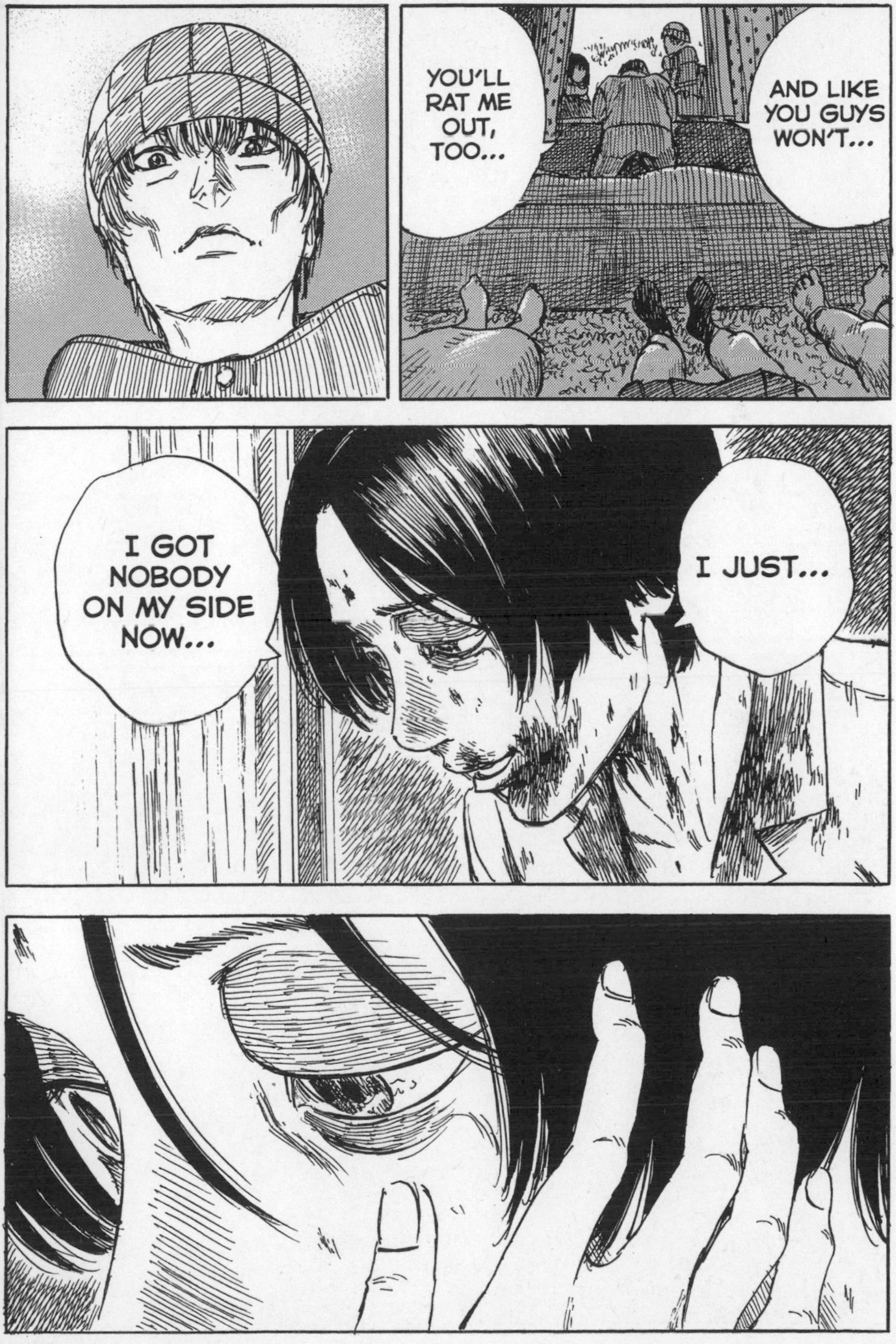
AND LIKE YOU GUYS WON'T...
YOU'LL RAT ME OUT, TOO...
I JUST...
I GOT NOBODY ON MY SIDE NOW...

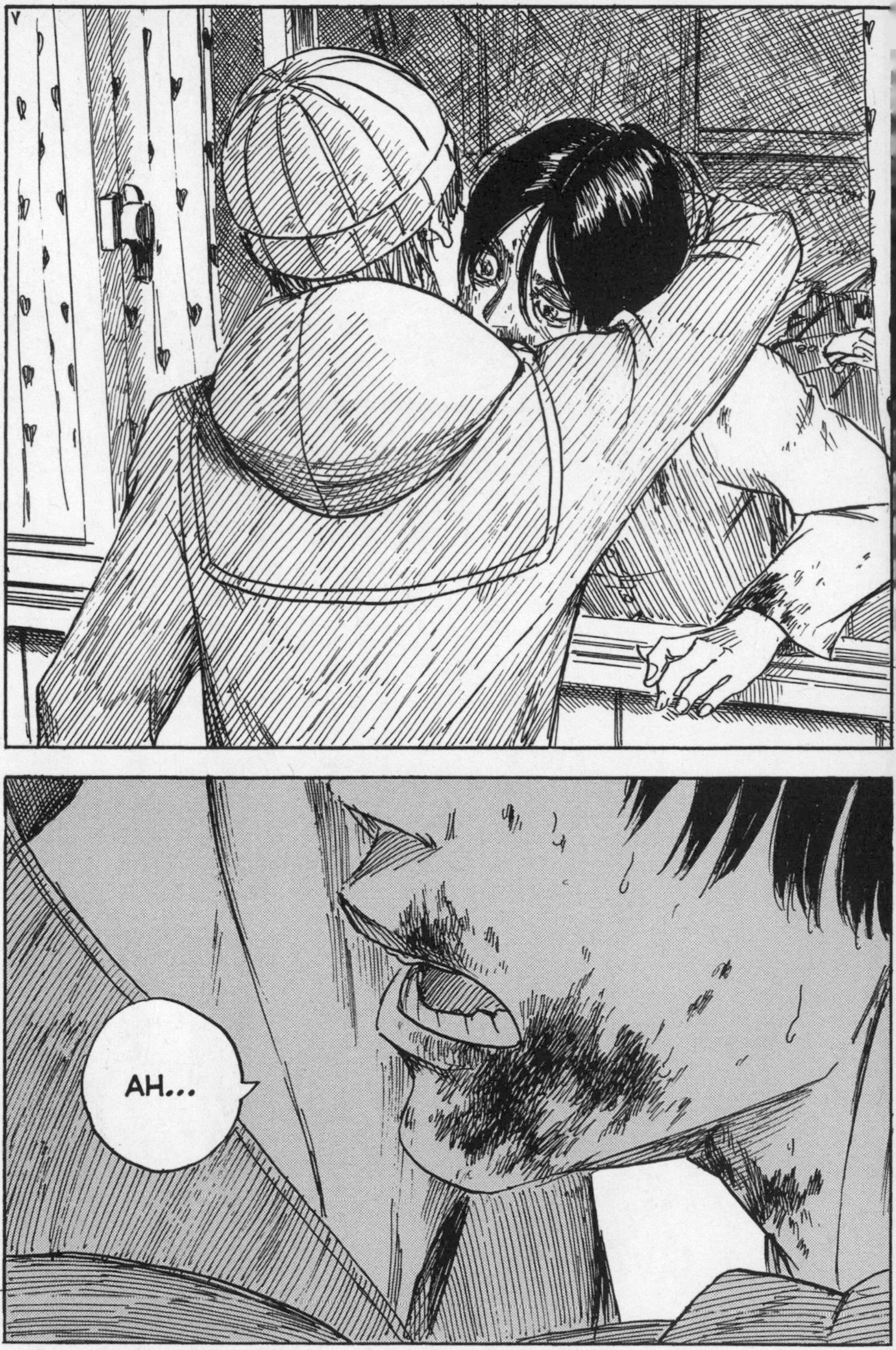
AH...

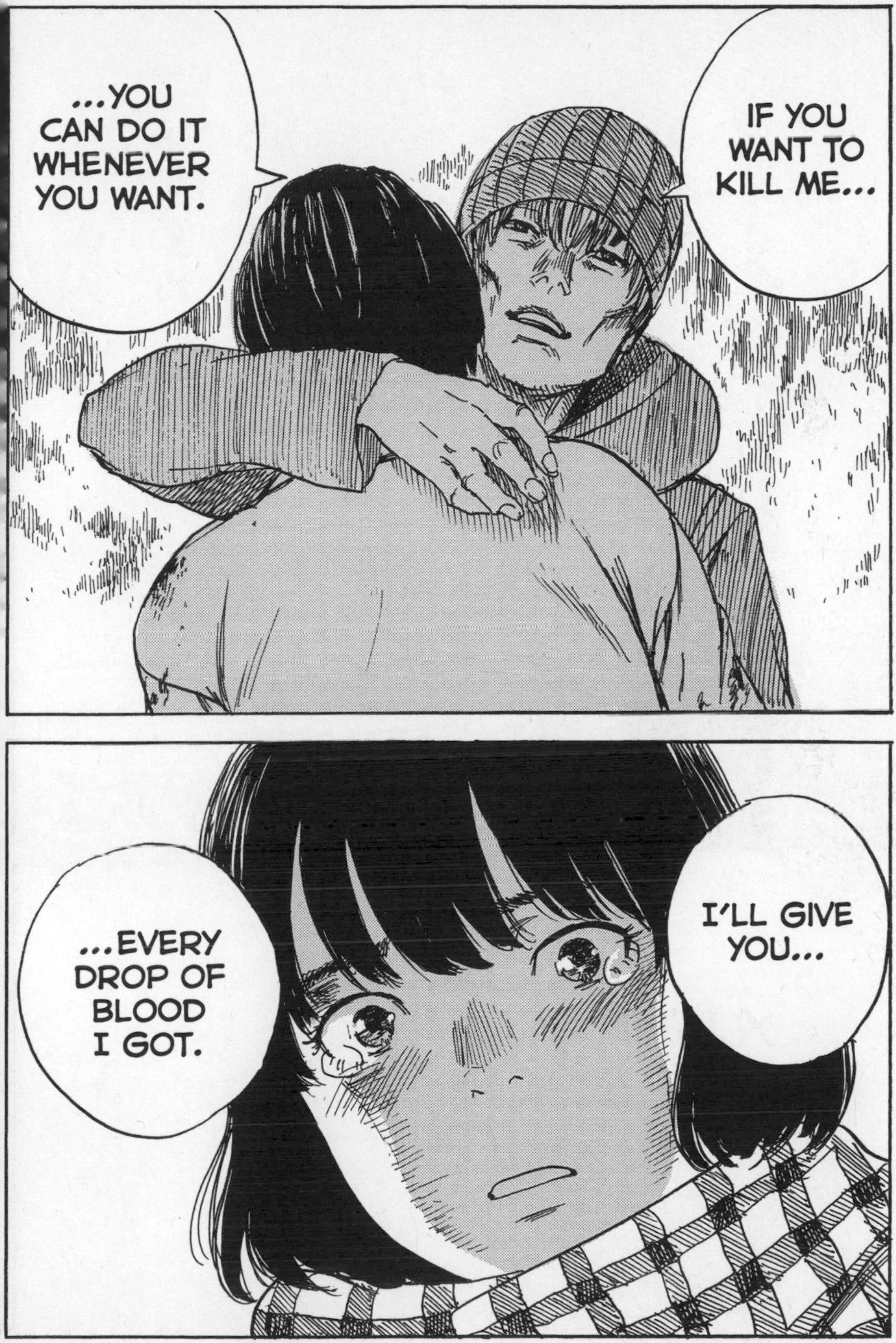
IF YOU WANT TO KILL ME...
...YOU CAN DO IT WHENEVER YOU WANT.
I'LL GIVE YOU...
...EVERY DROP OF BLOOD I GOT.

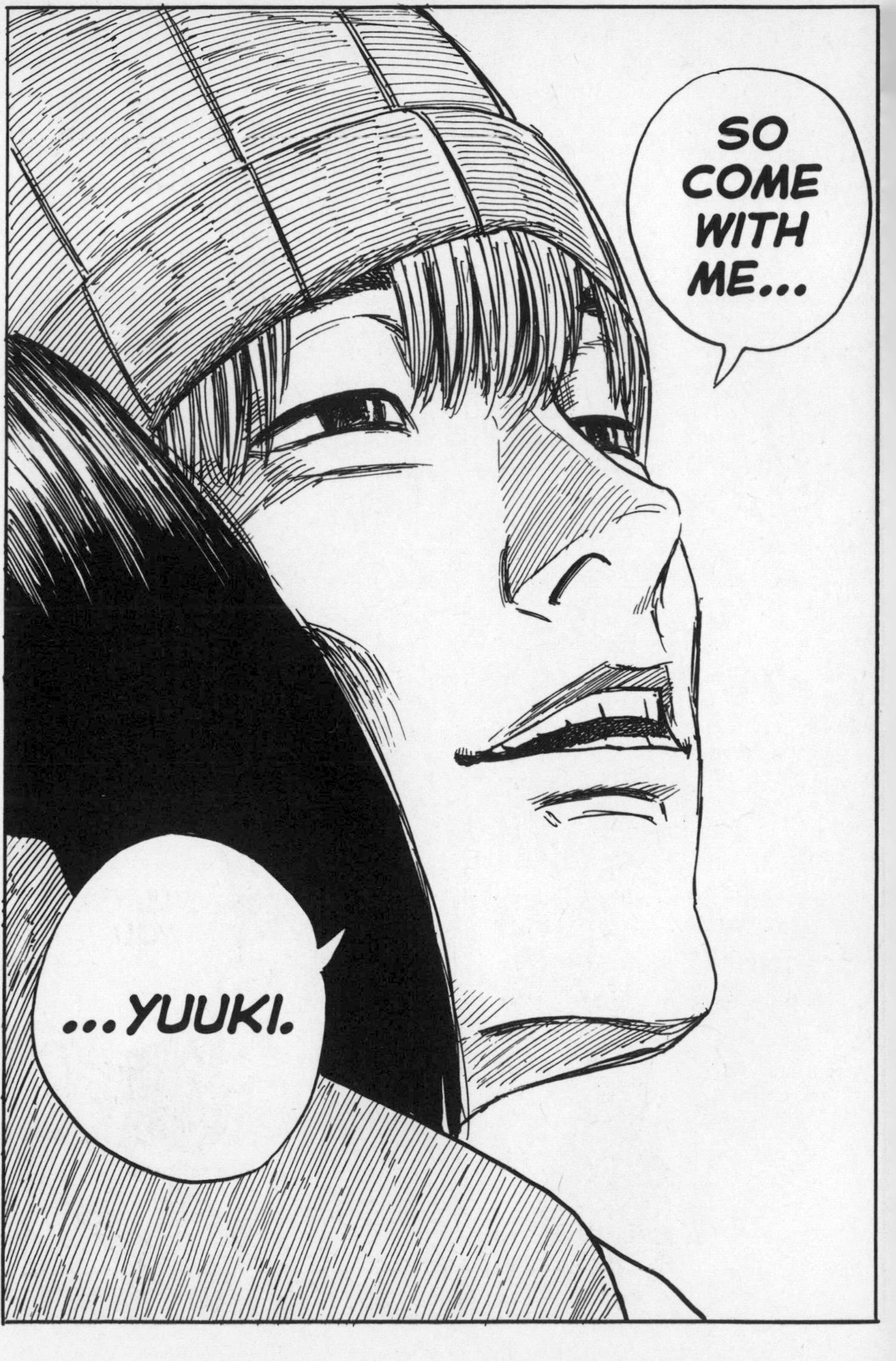
SO COME WITH ME...
...YUUKI.

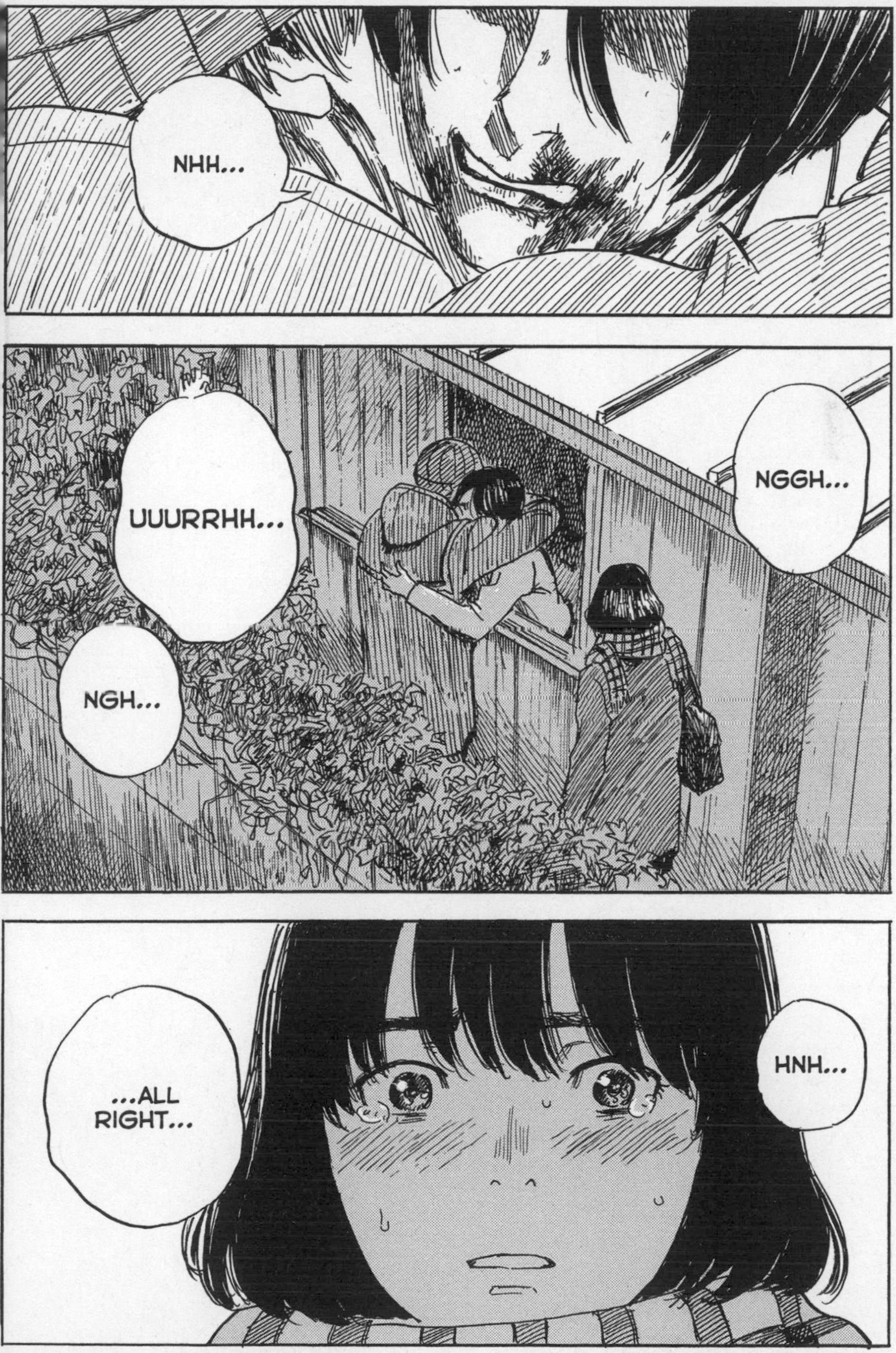
NHH...
NGGH...
UUURRHH...
NGH...
HNH...
...ALL RIGHT...

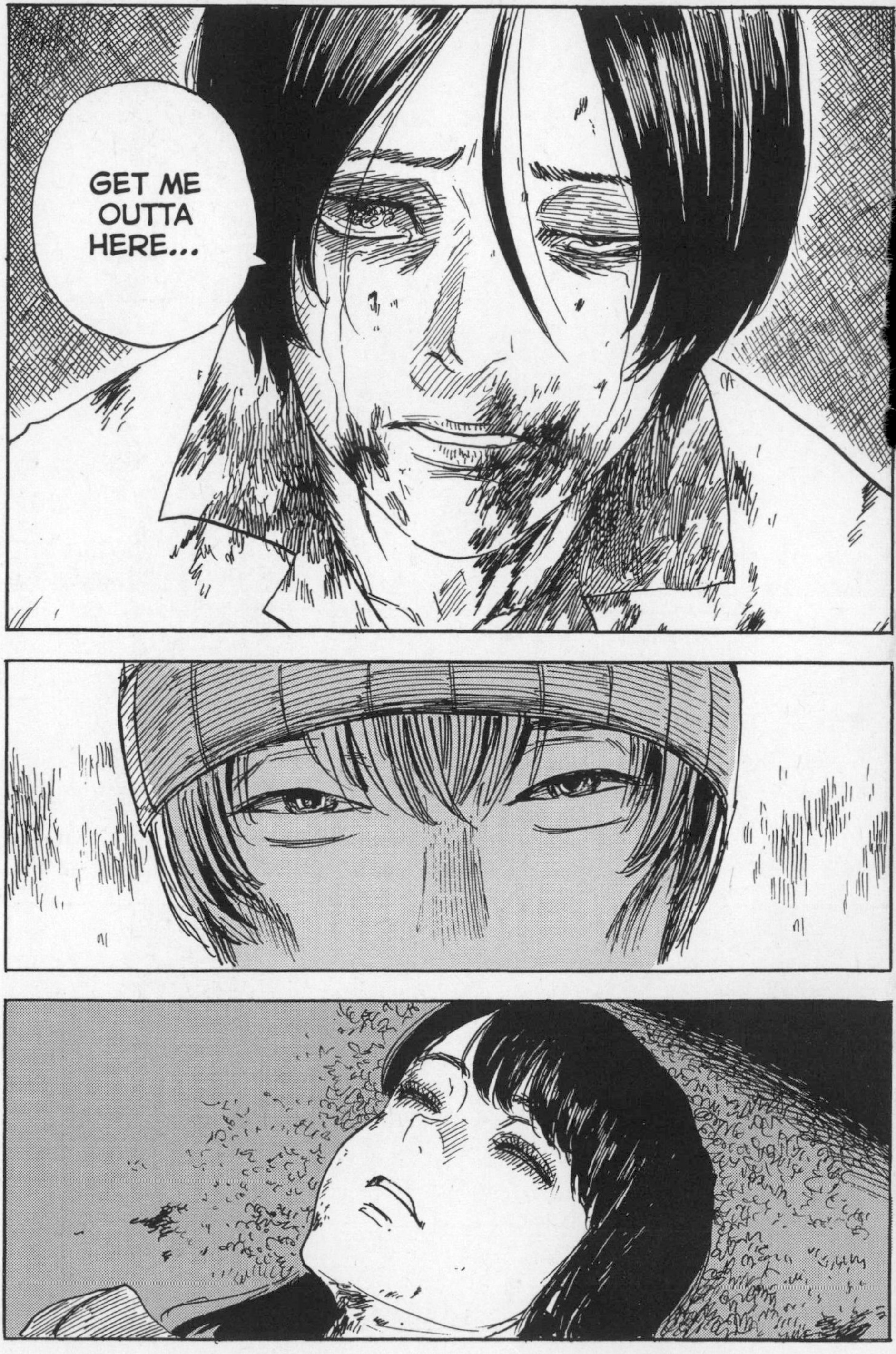
GET ME OUTTA HERE...

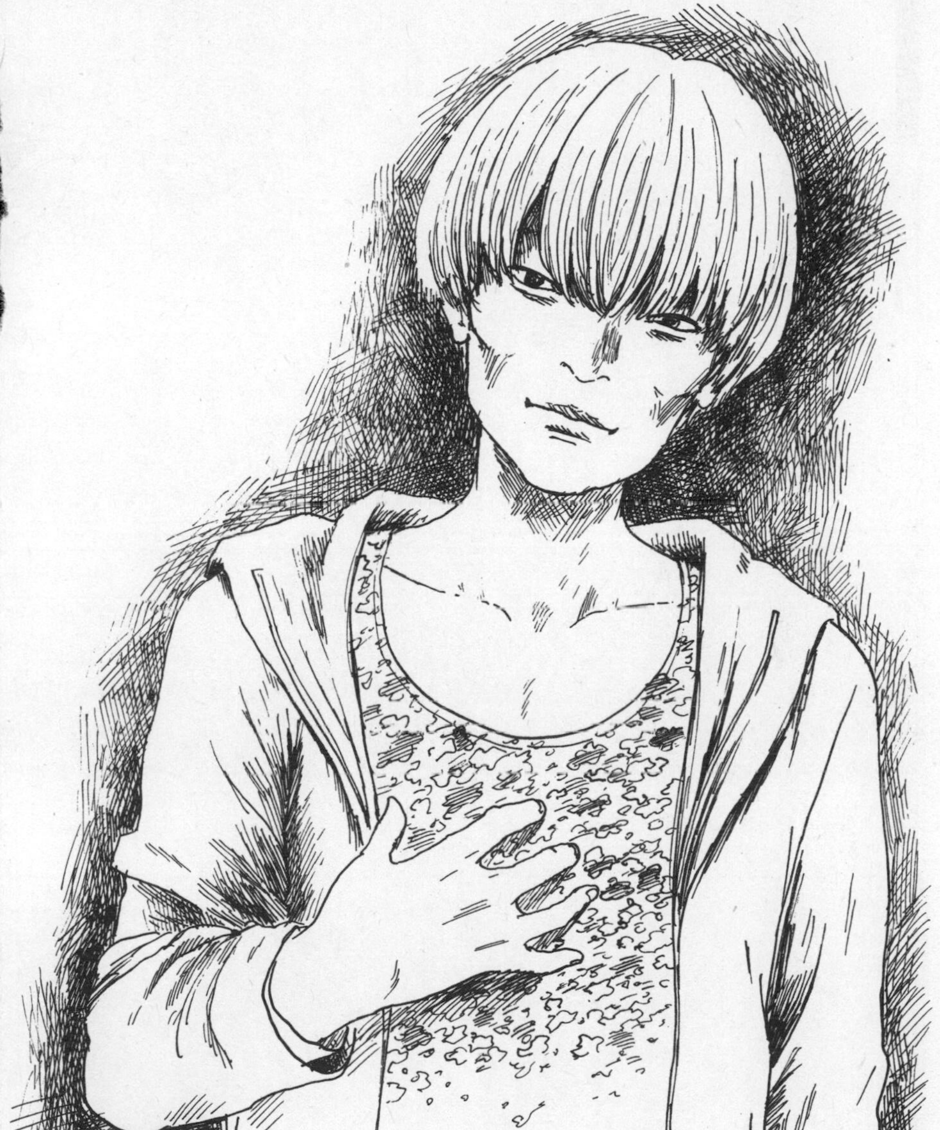

Chapter 23: The Two of Them

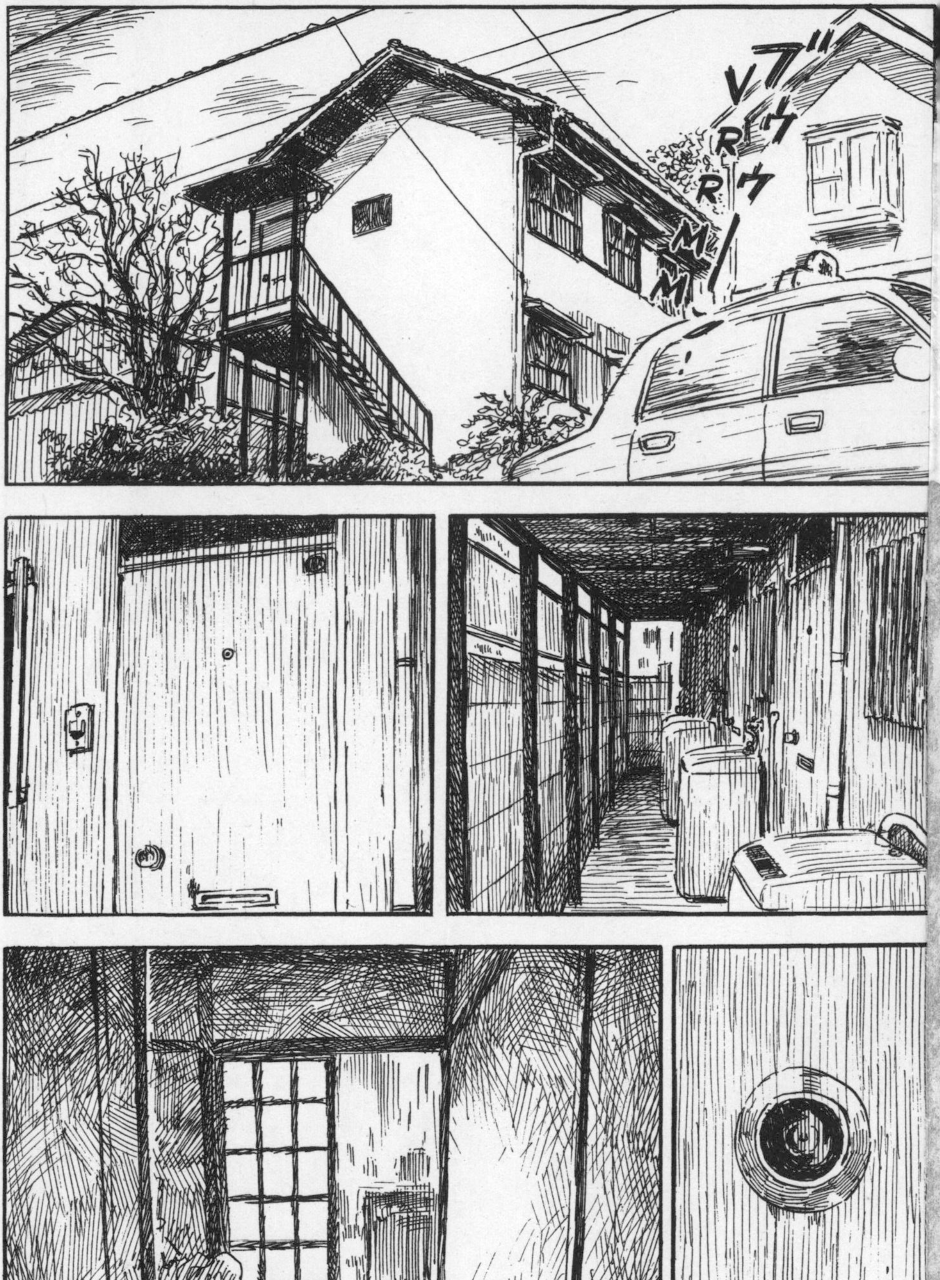
ブウウ
VRRMM

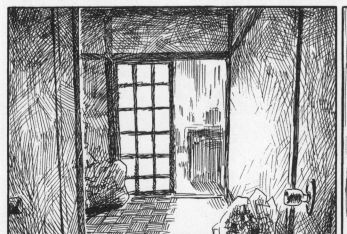

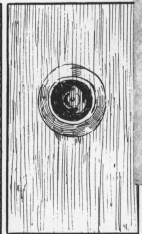

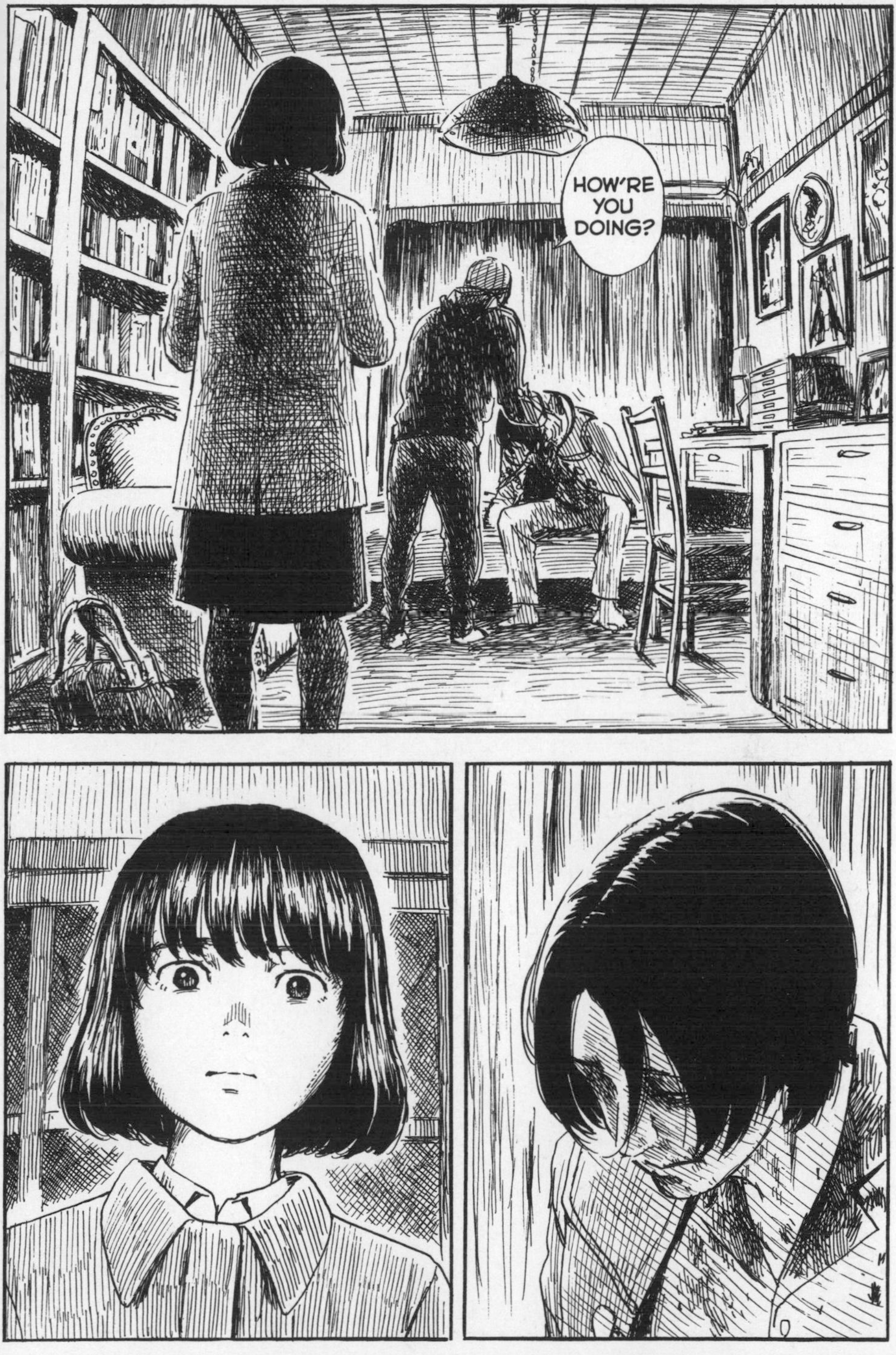
HOW'RE YOU DOING?

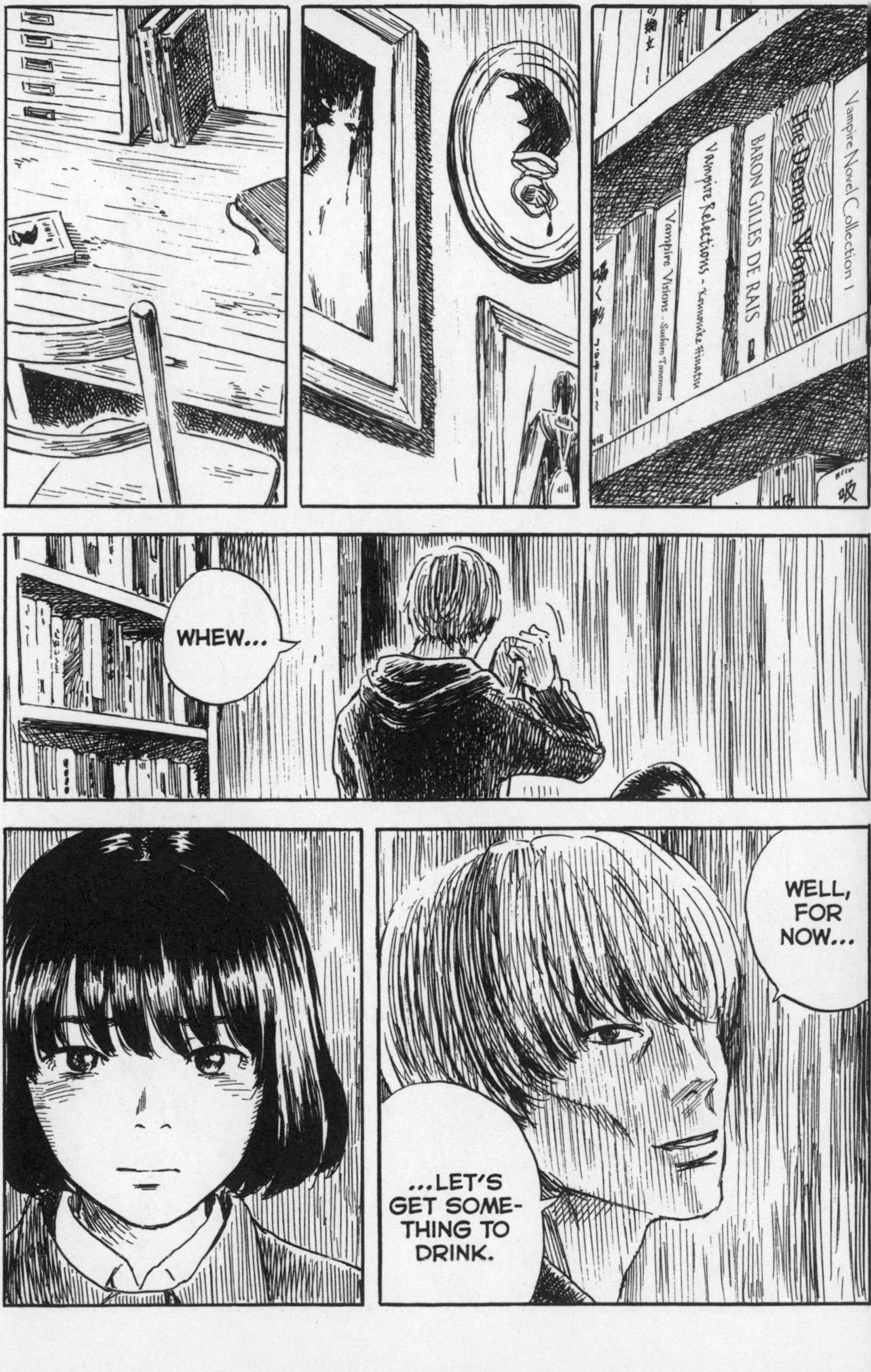
Vampire Novel Collection 1
The Demon Woman
BARON GILLES DE RAIS
Vampire Relections - Kounosuke Hinatsu
Vampire Visions - Suehiro Tanemura
WHEW...
WELL, FOR NOW...
...LET'S GET SOME-THING TO DRINK.

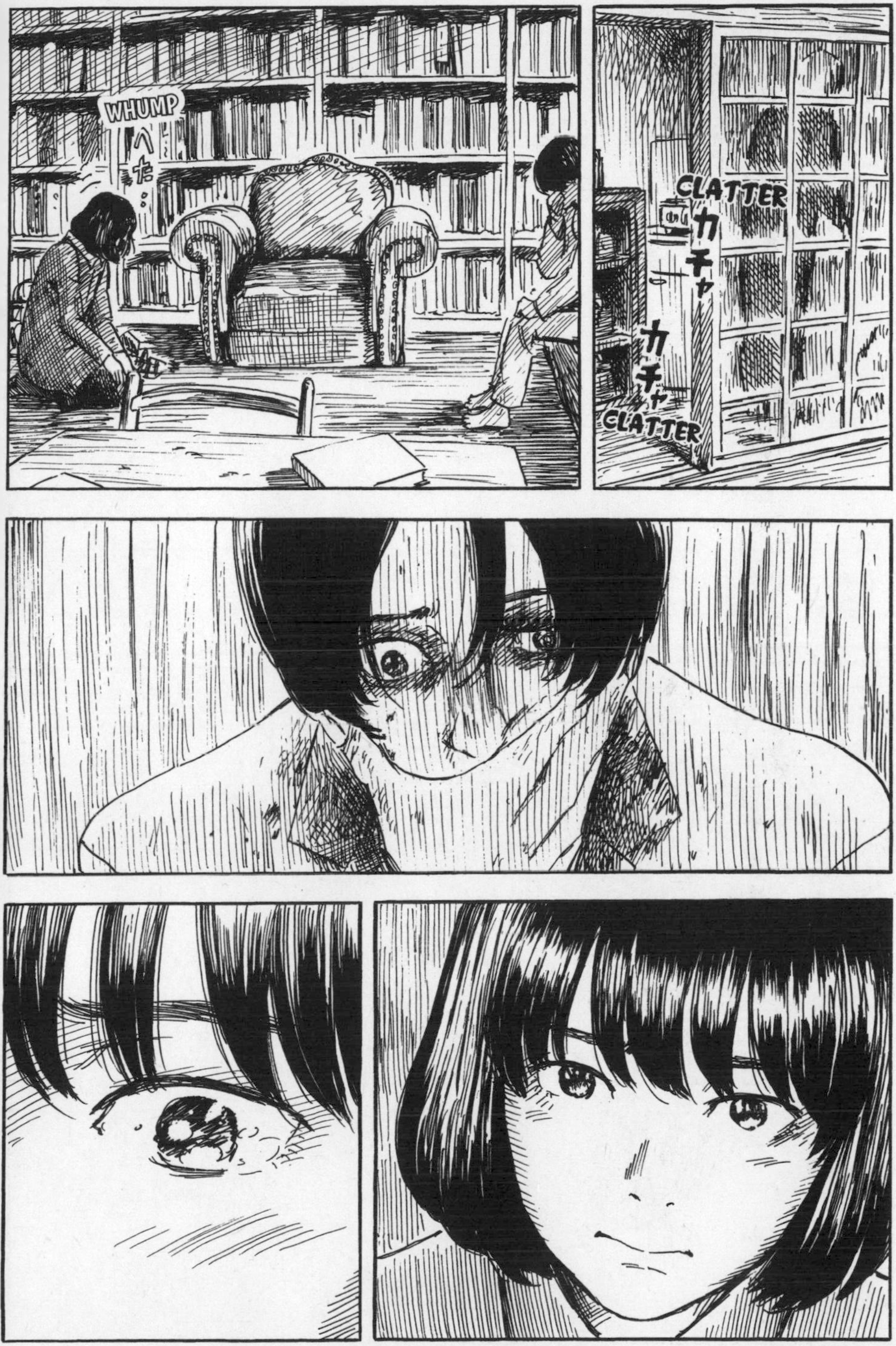
CLATTER
カチャ
カチャ
CLATTER
WHUMP
へた‥

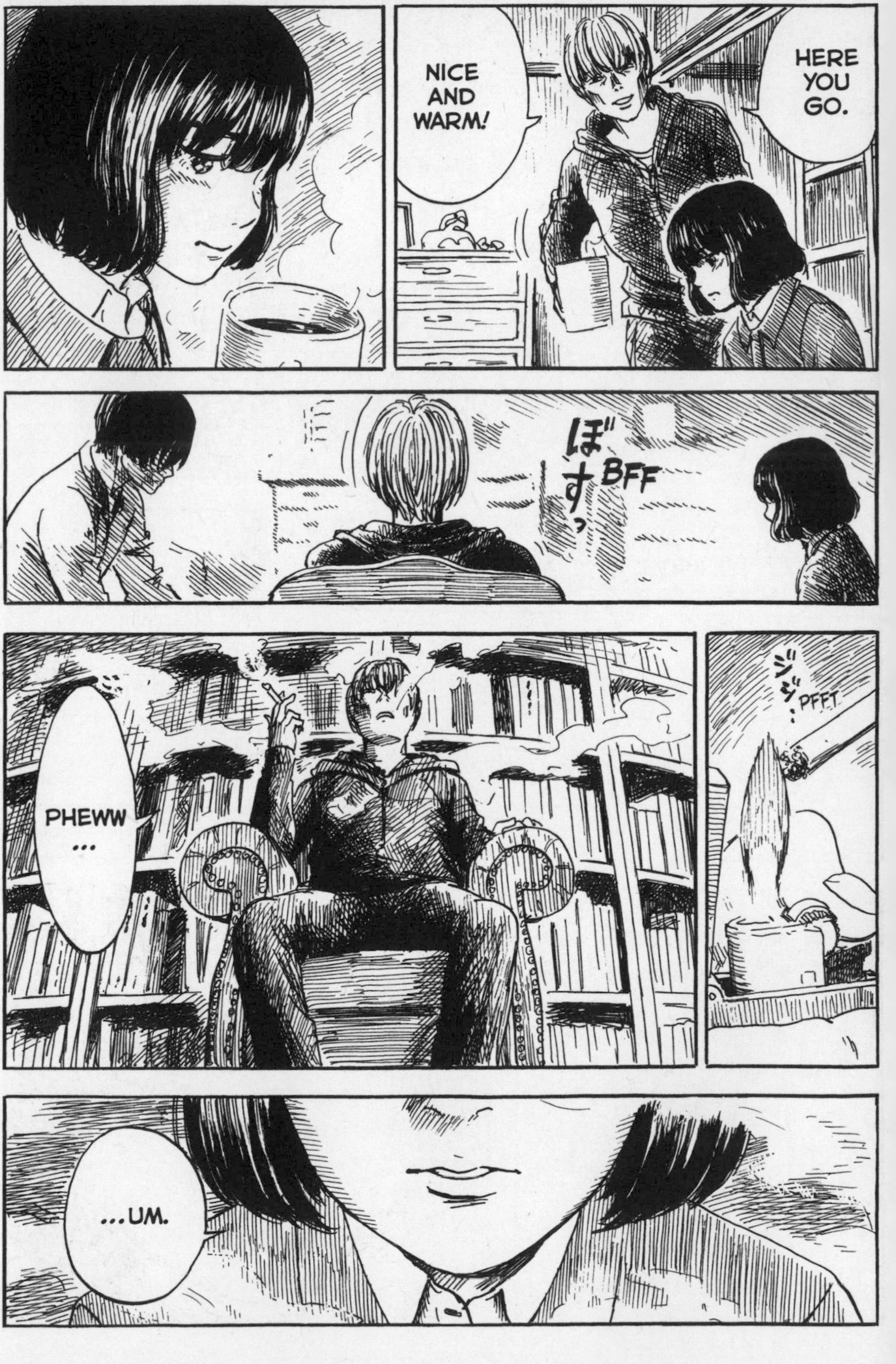
HERE YOU GO.
NICE AND WARM!
ぼすっ
BFF
ジジ…
PFFT
PHEWW...
...UM.

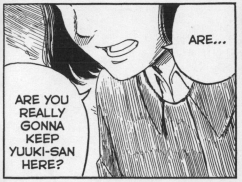

ARE...
ARE YOU REALLY GONNA KEEP YUUKI-SAN HERE?
BE... BECAUSE I REALLY DON'T THINK THIS IS GOOD.
HOW LONG IS HE GONNA HAVE TO HIDE FROM PEOPLE LIKE THIS?
I MEAN... THEY'RE DEAD.
NAO-SAN... EVERYONE...
YUUKI-SAN...

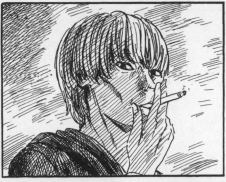

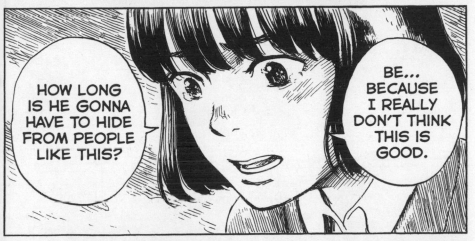

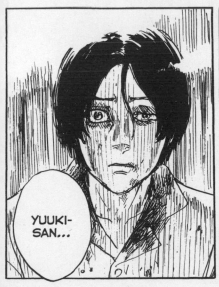

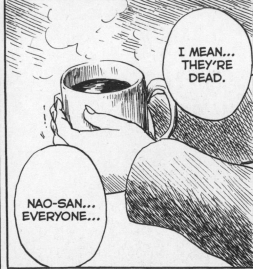

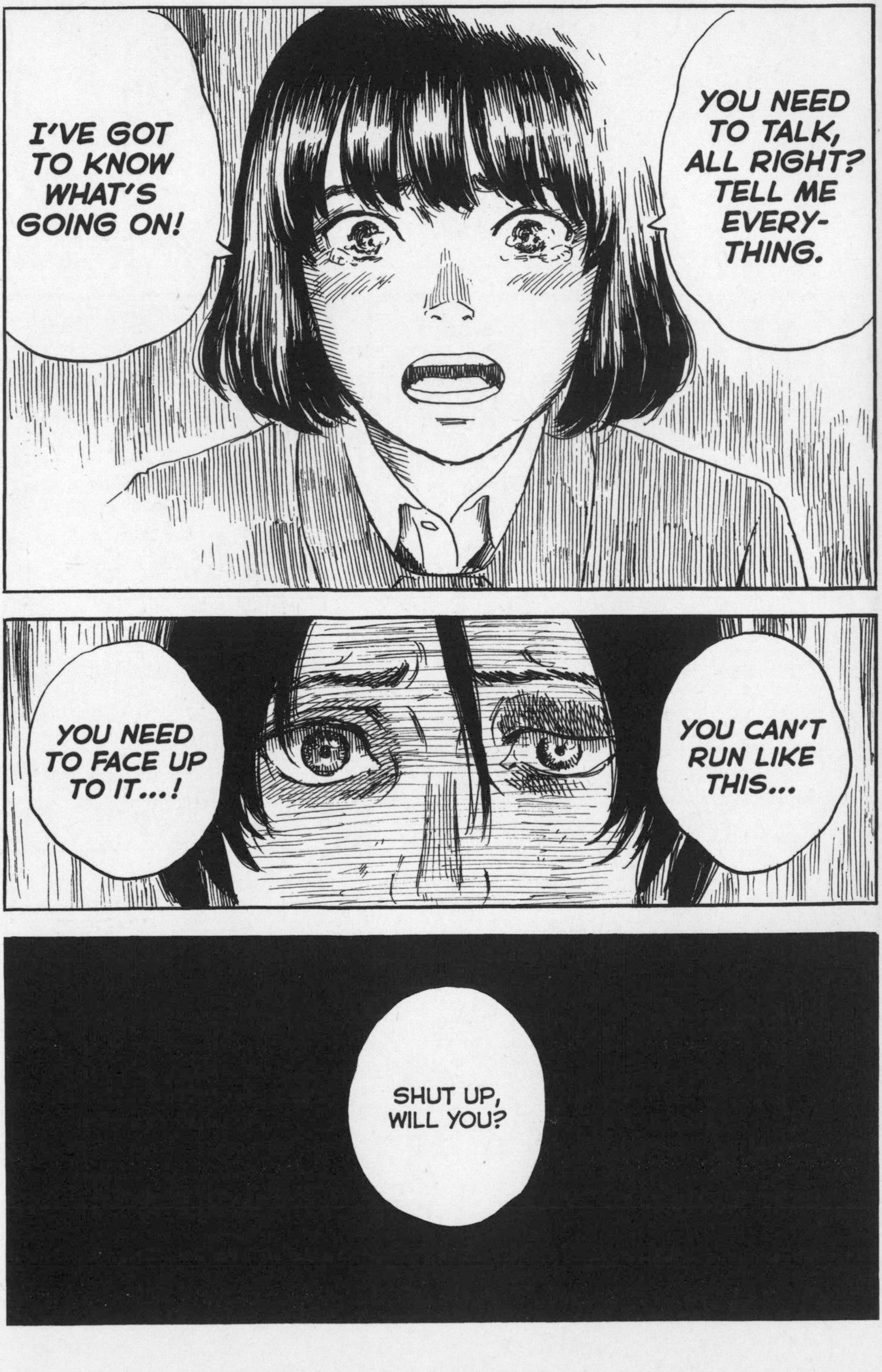
YOU NEED TO TALK, ALL RIGHT? TELL ME EVERY-THING.
I'VE GOT TO KNOW WHAT'S GOING ON!
YOU CAN'T RUN LIKE THIS...
YOU NEED TO FACE UP TO IT...!
SHUT UP, WILL YOU?

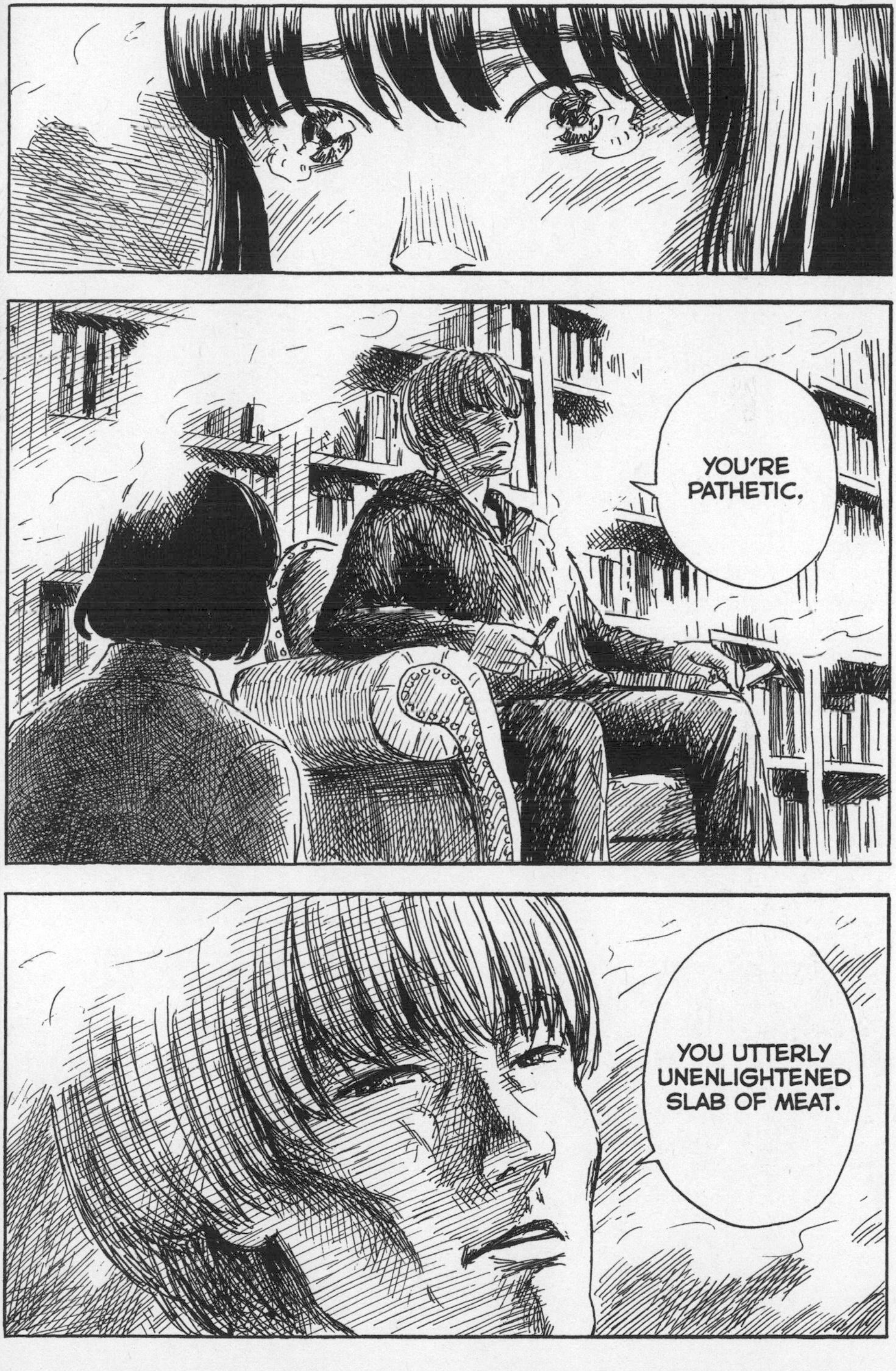
YOU'RE PATHETIC.
YOU UTTERLY UNENLIGHTENED SLAB OF MEAT.

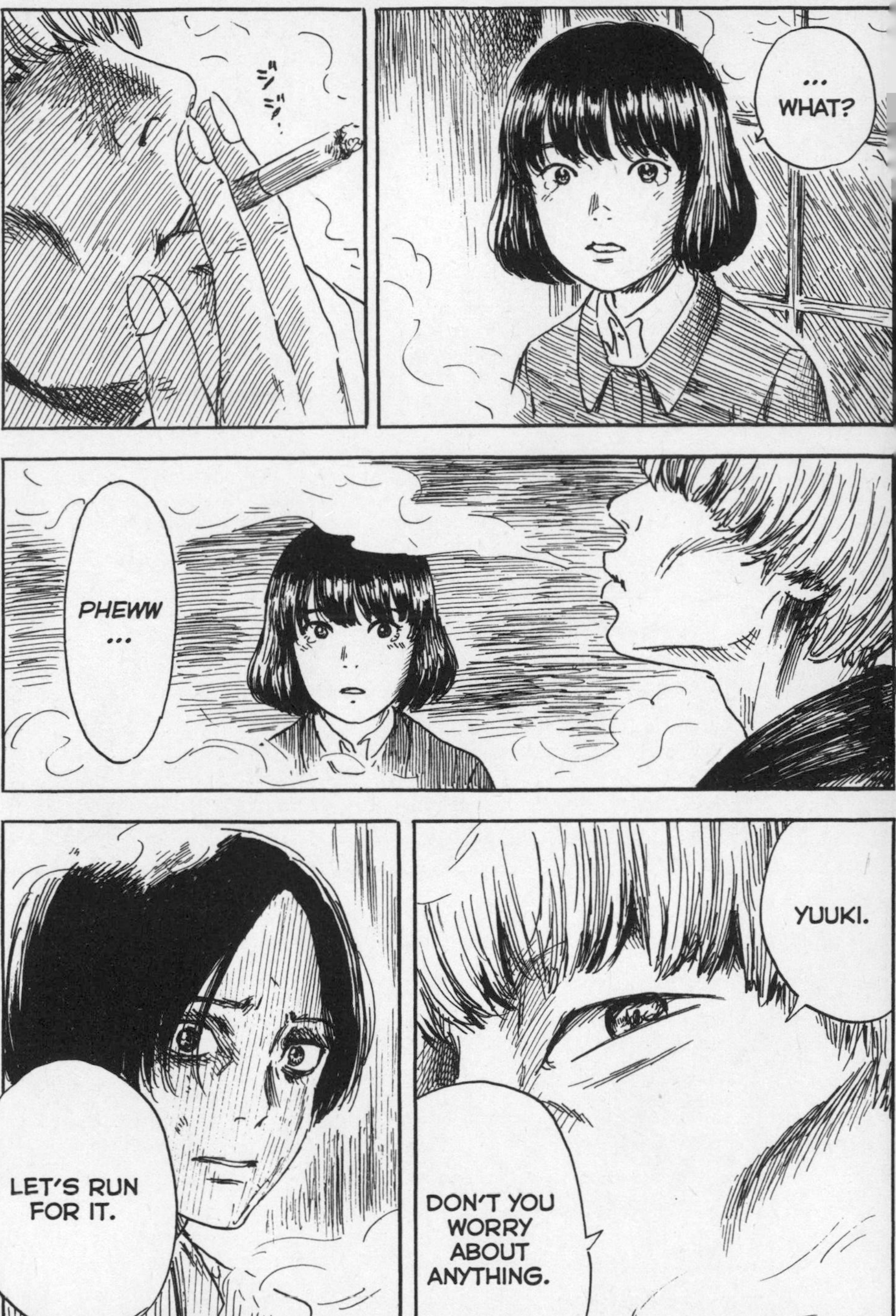

... WHAT?
PHEWW ...
YUUKI.
DON'T YOU WORRY ABOUT ANYTHING.
LET'S RUN FOR IT.

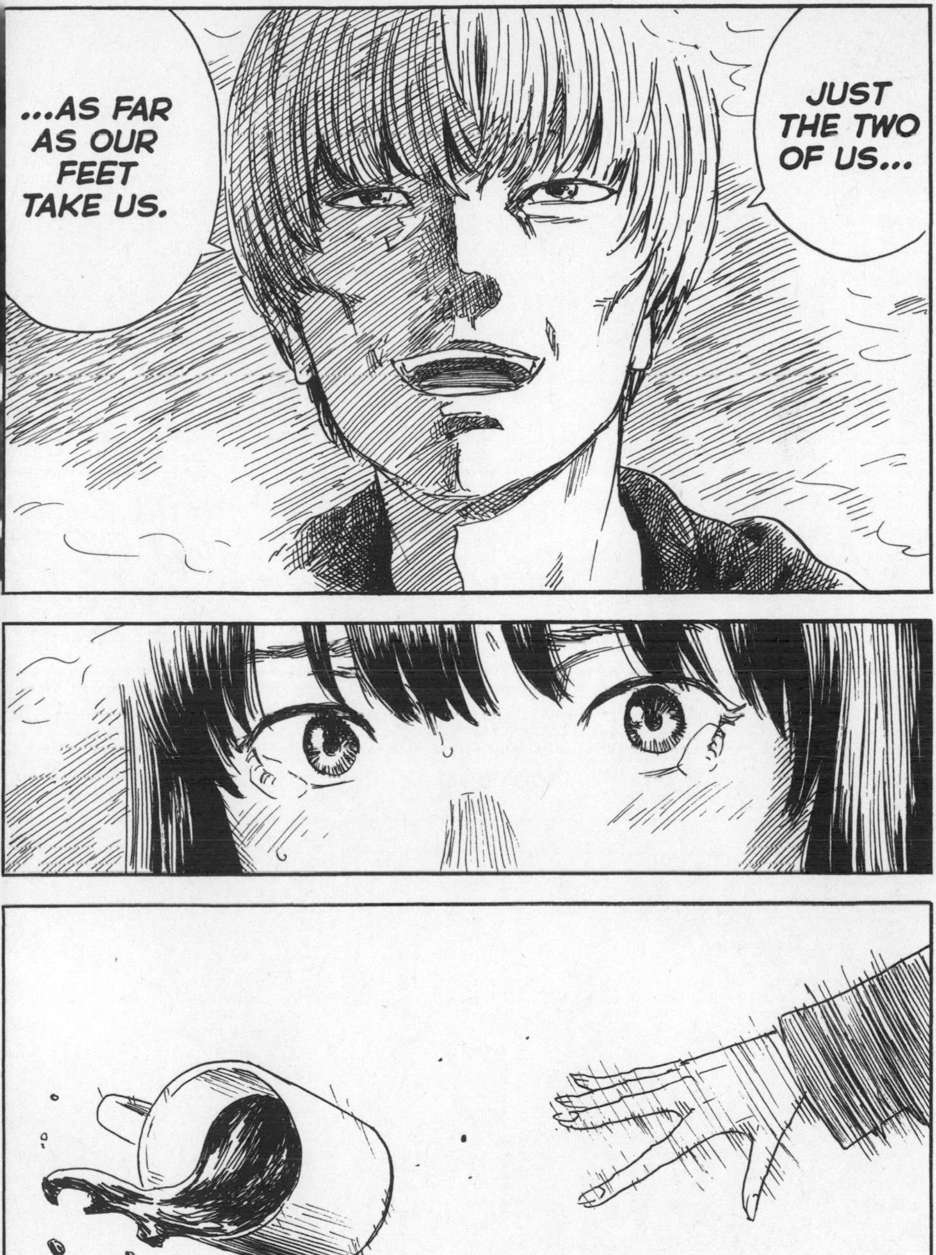
JUST THE TWO OF US...
...AS FAR AS OUR FEET TAKE US.

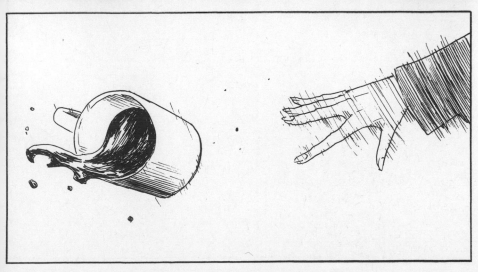

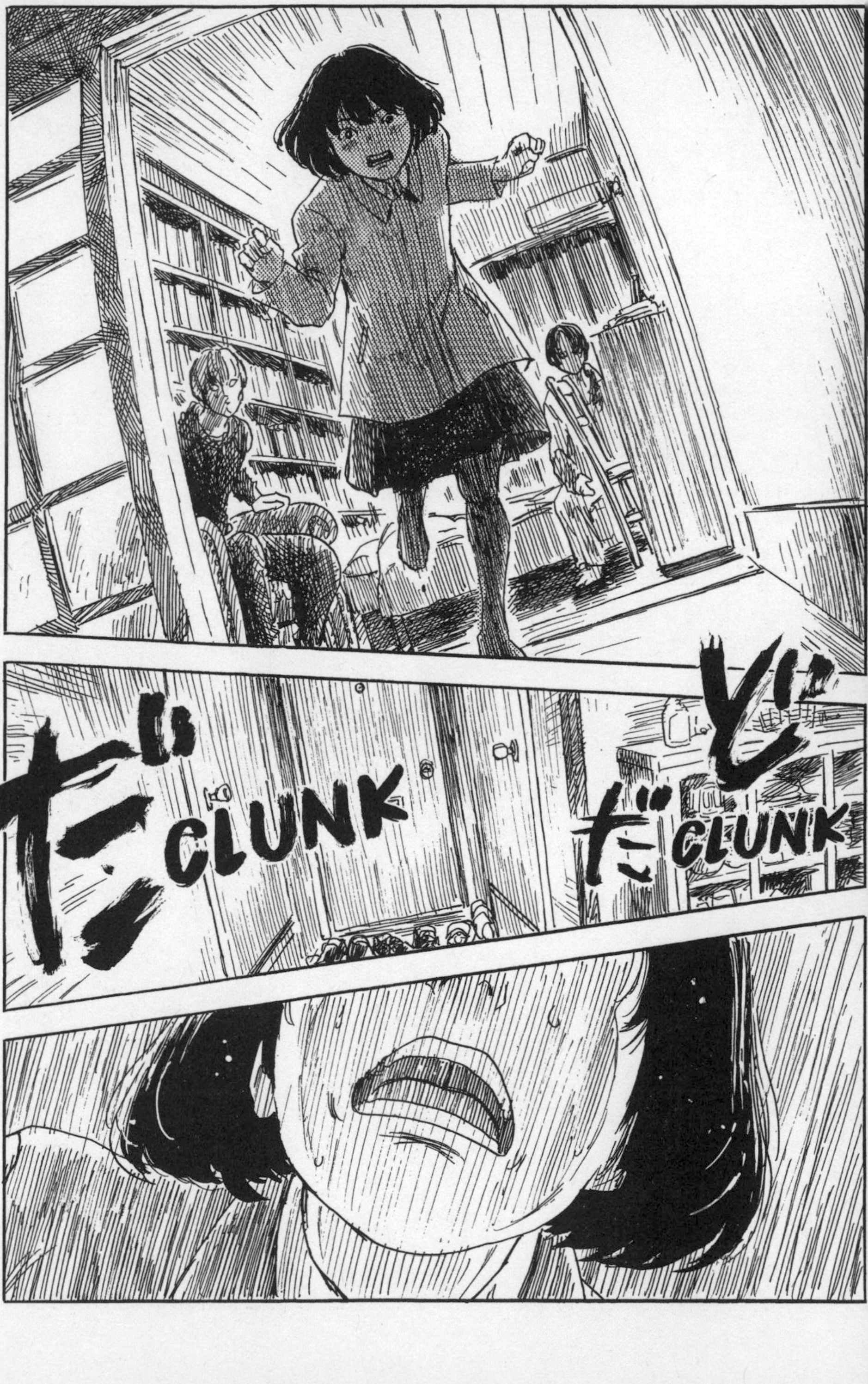
ど
だ
CLUNK
だ
CLUNK

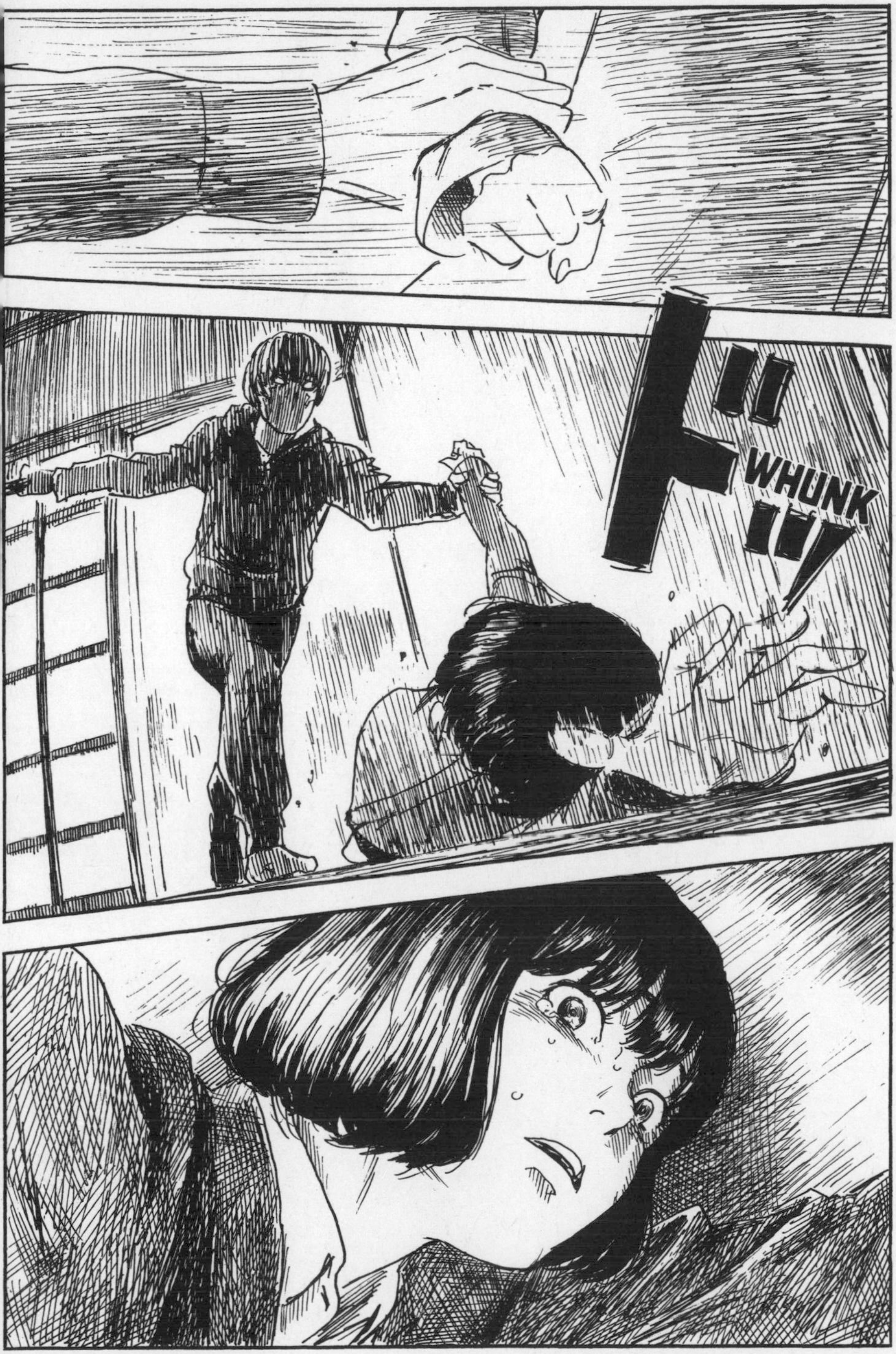
ドッ
WHUNK

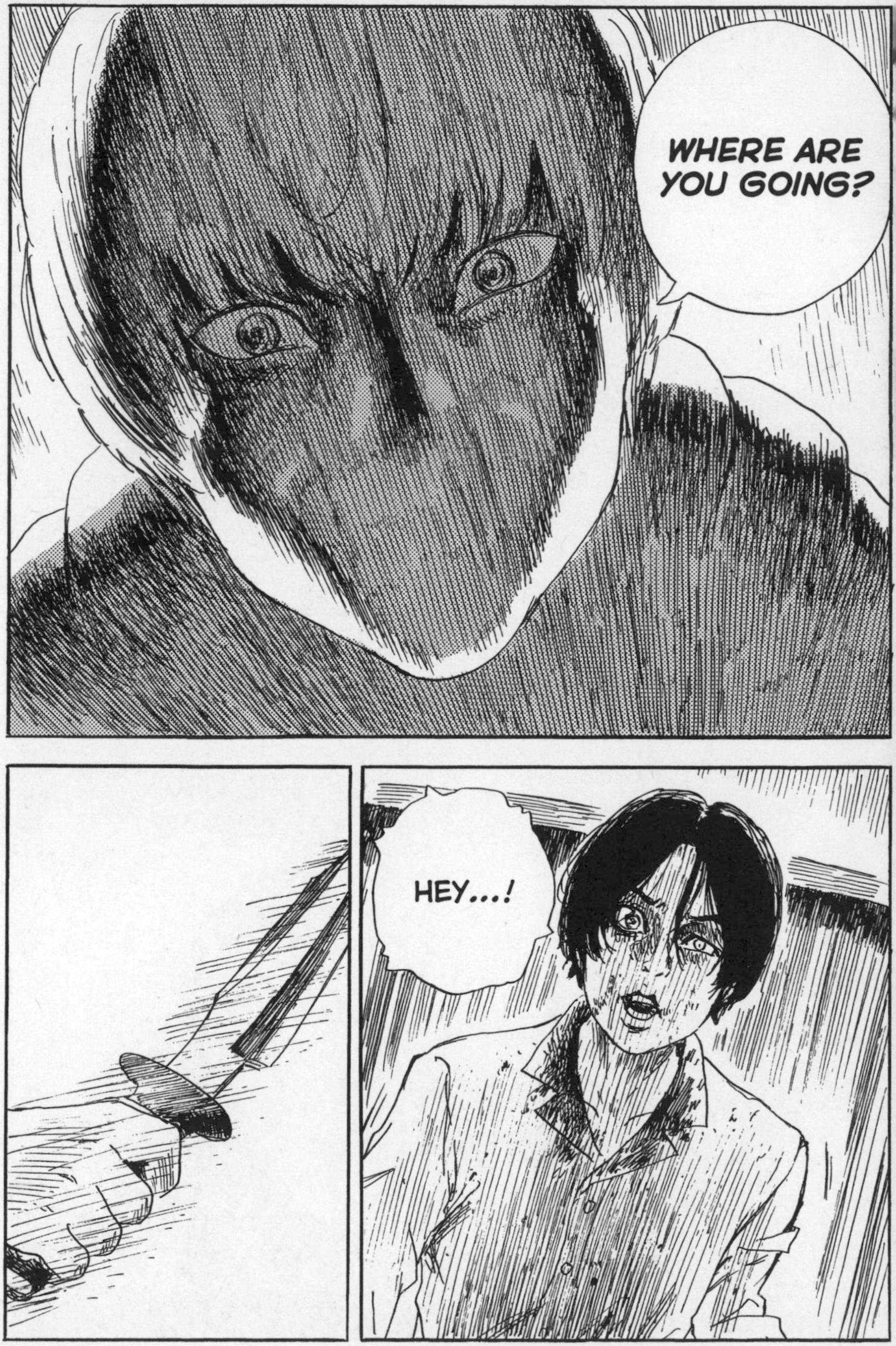

WHERE ARE YOU GOING?
HEY...!

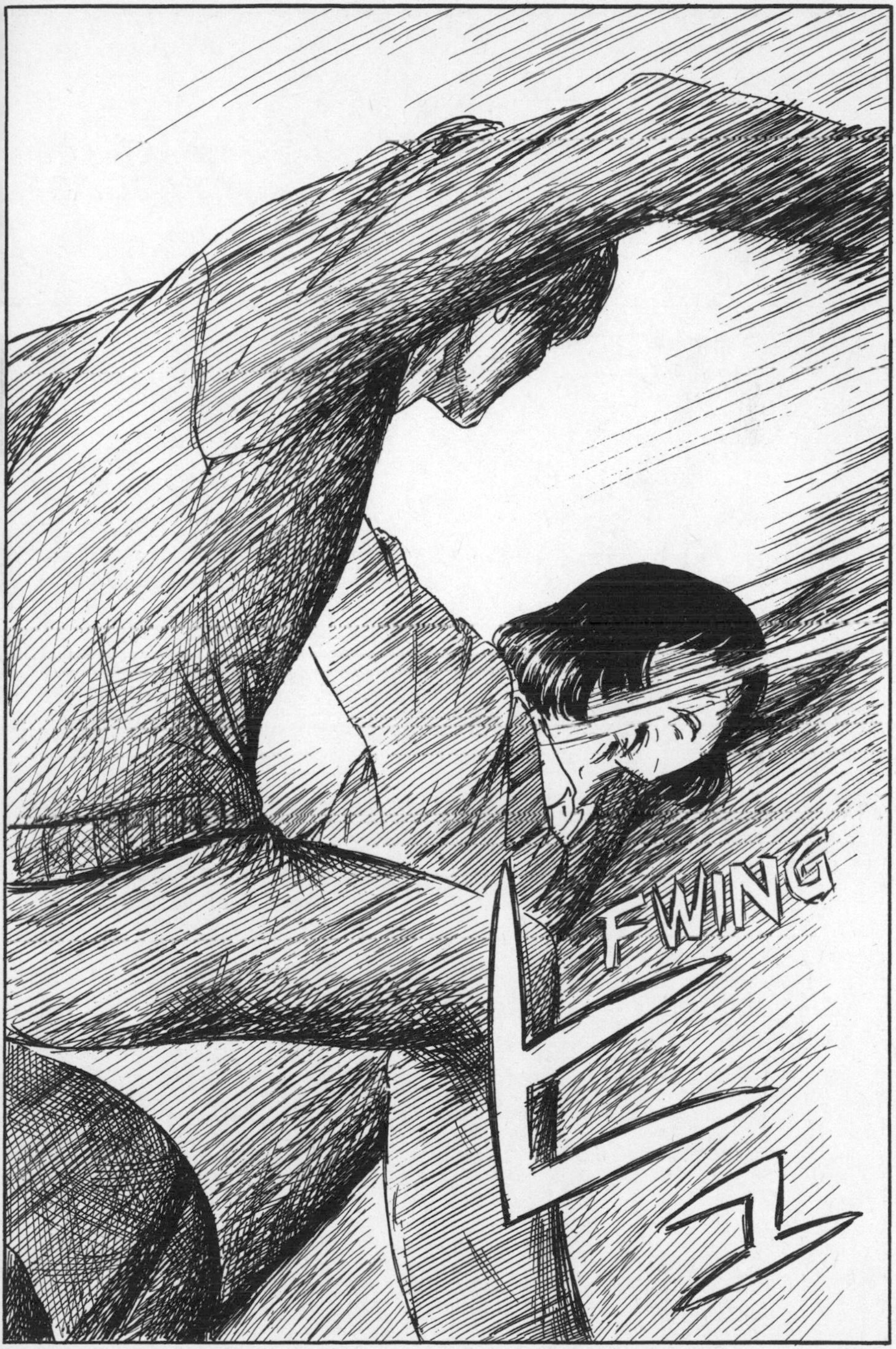
FWING
ヒュ

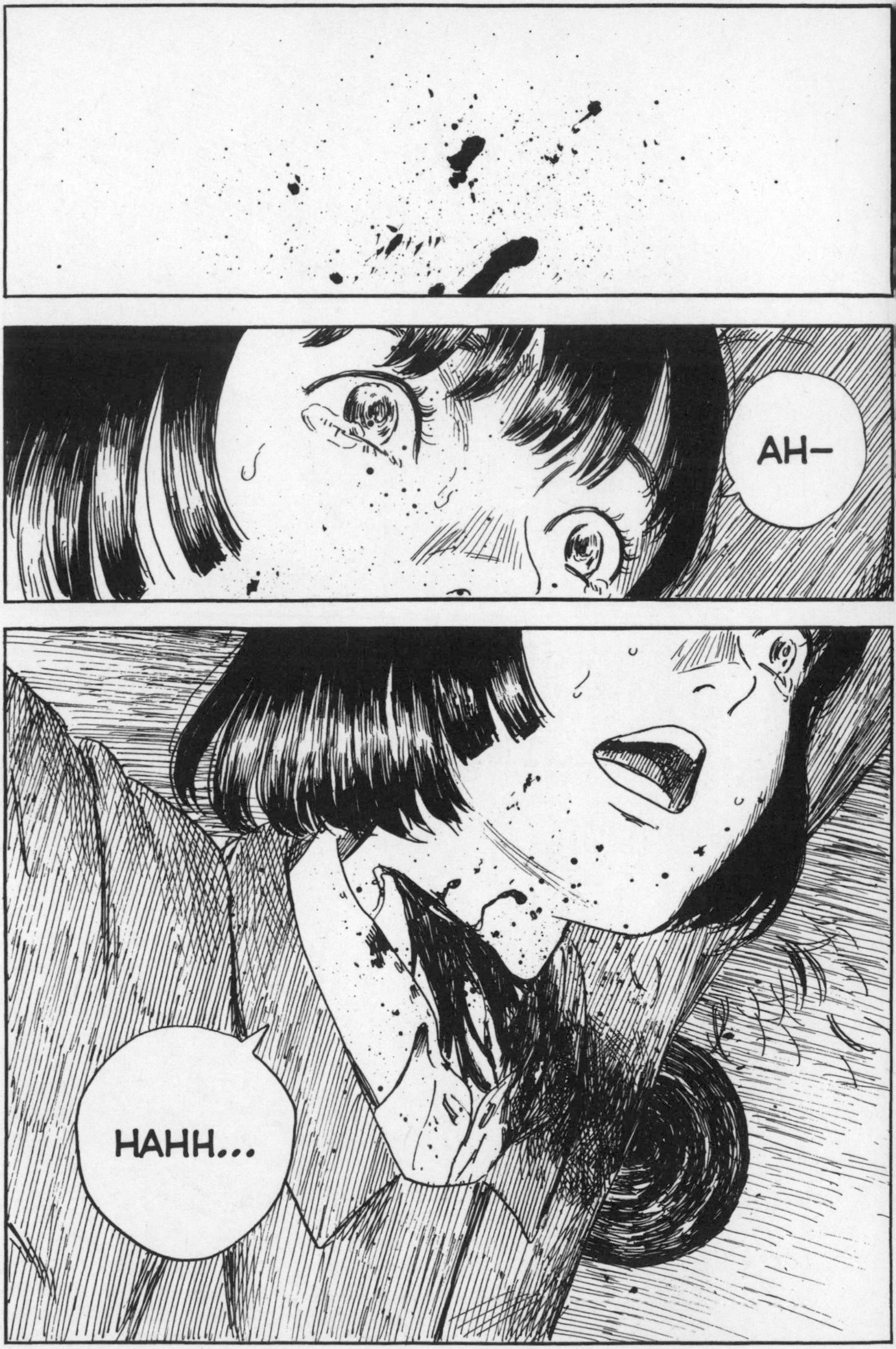
AH–
HAHH...

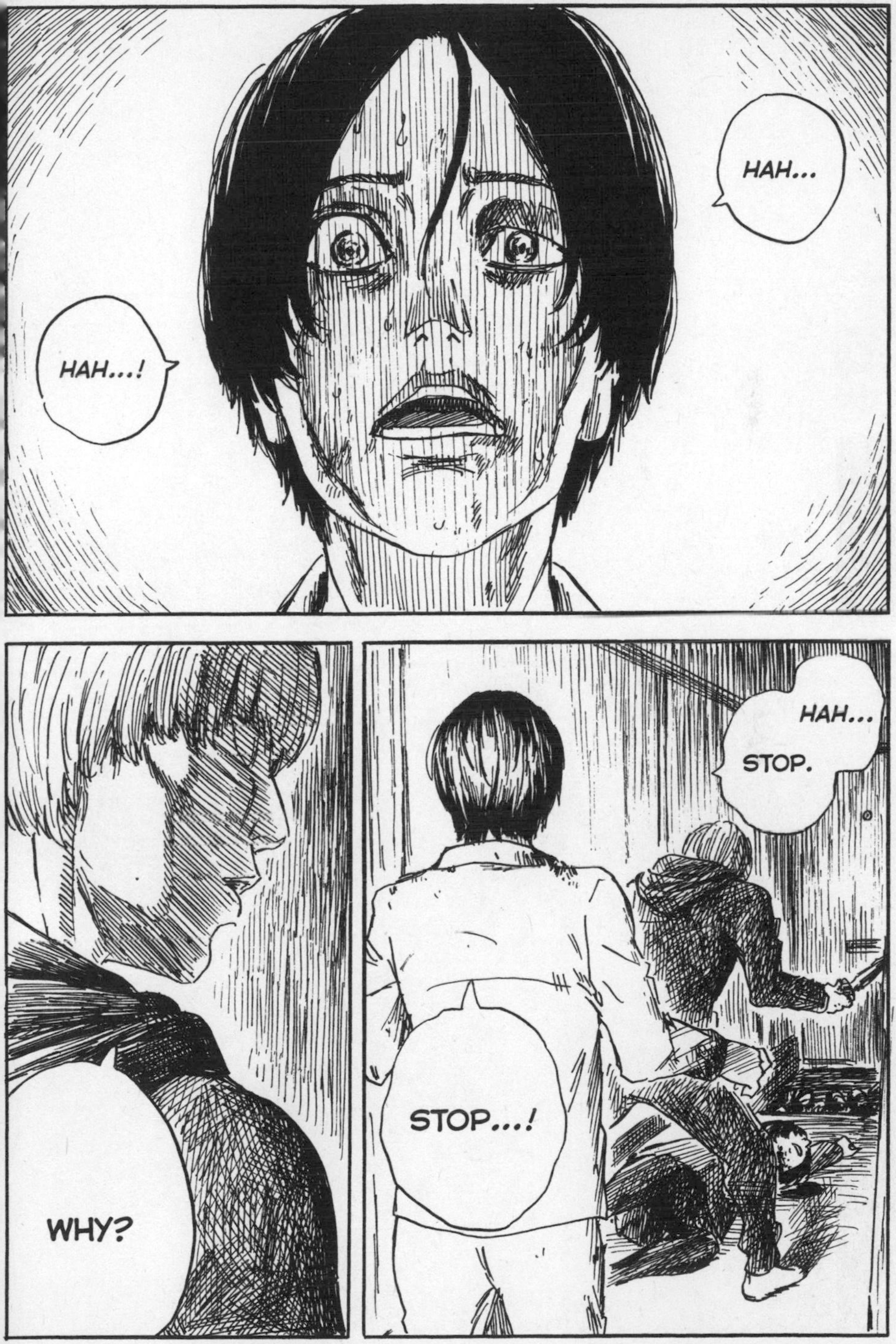
HAH...
HAH...!
HAH... STOP.
STOP...!
WHY?

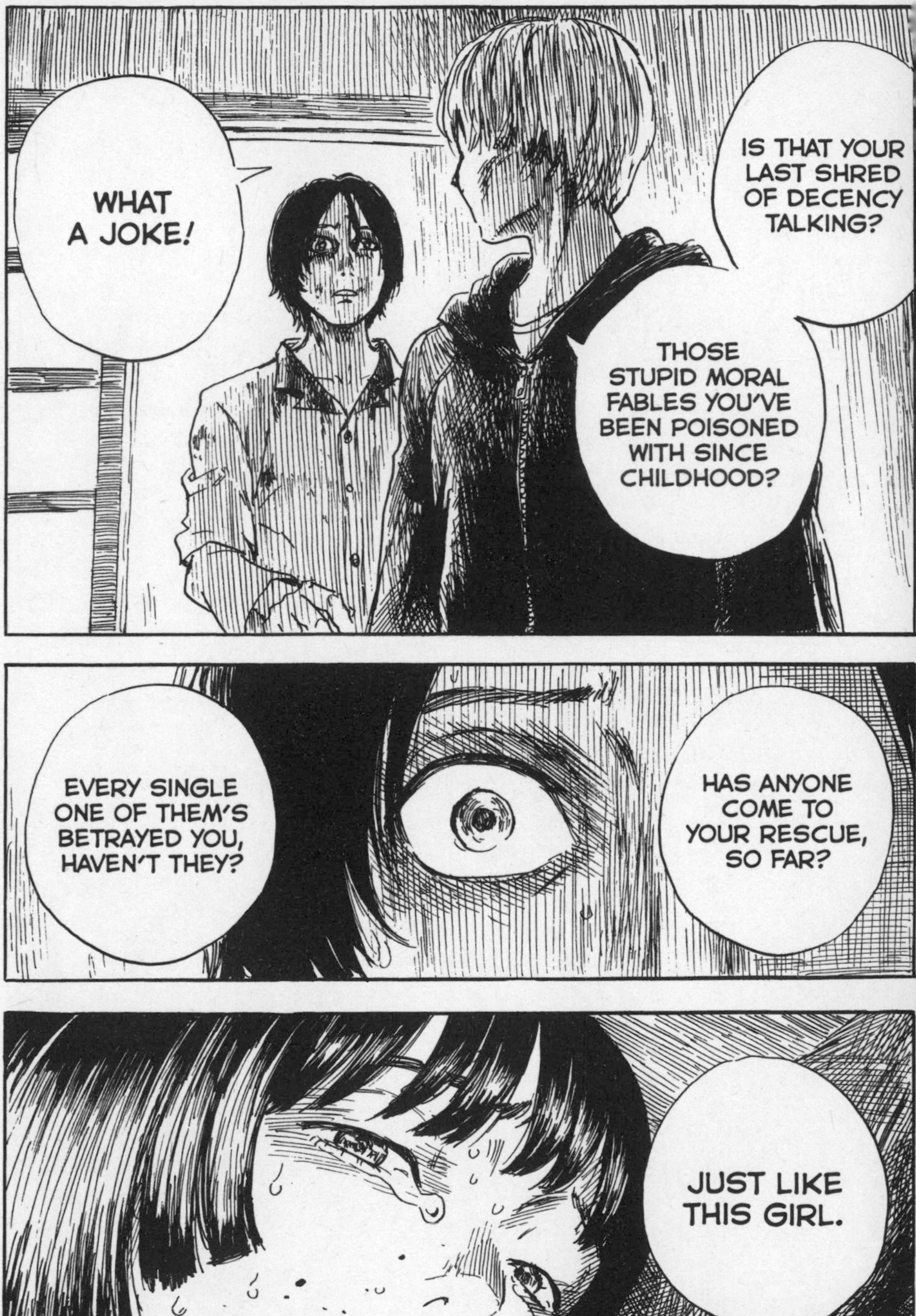
IS THAT YOUR LAST SHRED OF DECENCY TALKING?
THOSE STUPID MORAL FABLES YOU'VE BEEN POISONED WITH SINCE CHILDHOOD?
WHAT A JOKE!
HAS ANYONE COME TO YOUR RESCUE, SO FAR?
EVERY SINGLE ONE OF THEM'S BETRAYED YOU, HAVEN'T THEY?
JUST LIKE THIS GIRL.

LISTEN, YUUKI.
EVERYTHING IN THIS WORLD IS AN ILLUSION.
LIVING, DYING... THERE'S NO MEANING TO ANY OF IT.
YOU'VE ALREADY KILLED.
HAAH
HAAH
YOUR FAMILY, YOUR LOVER...
AND THAT'S GOOD! YOU WERE PERFECTLY RIGHT.

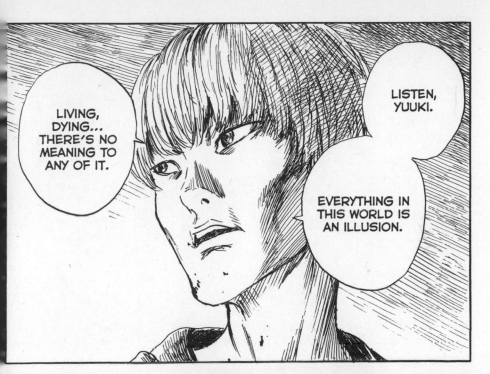

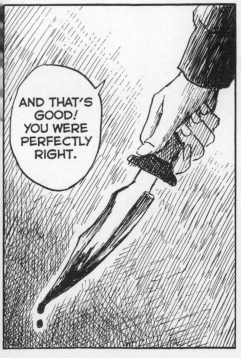

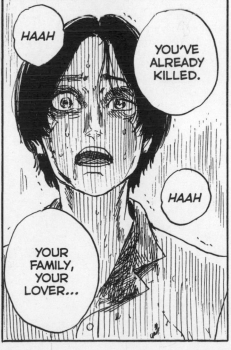

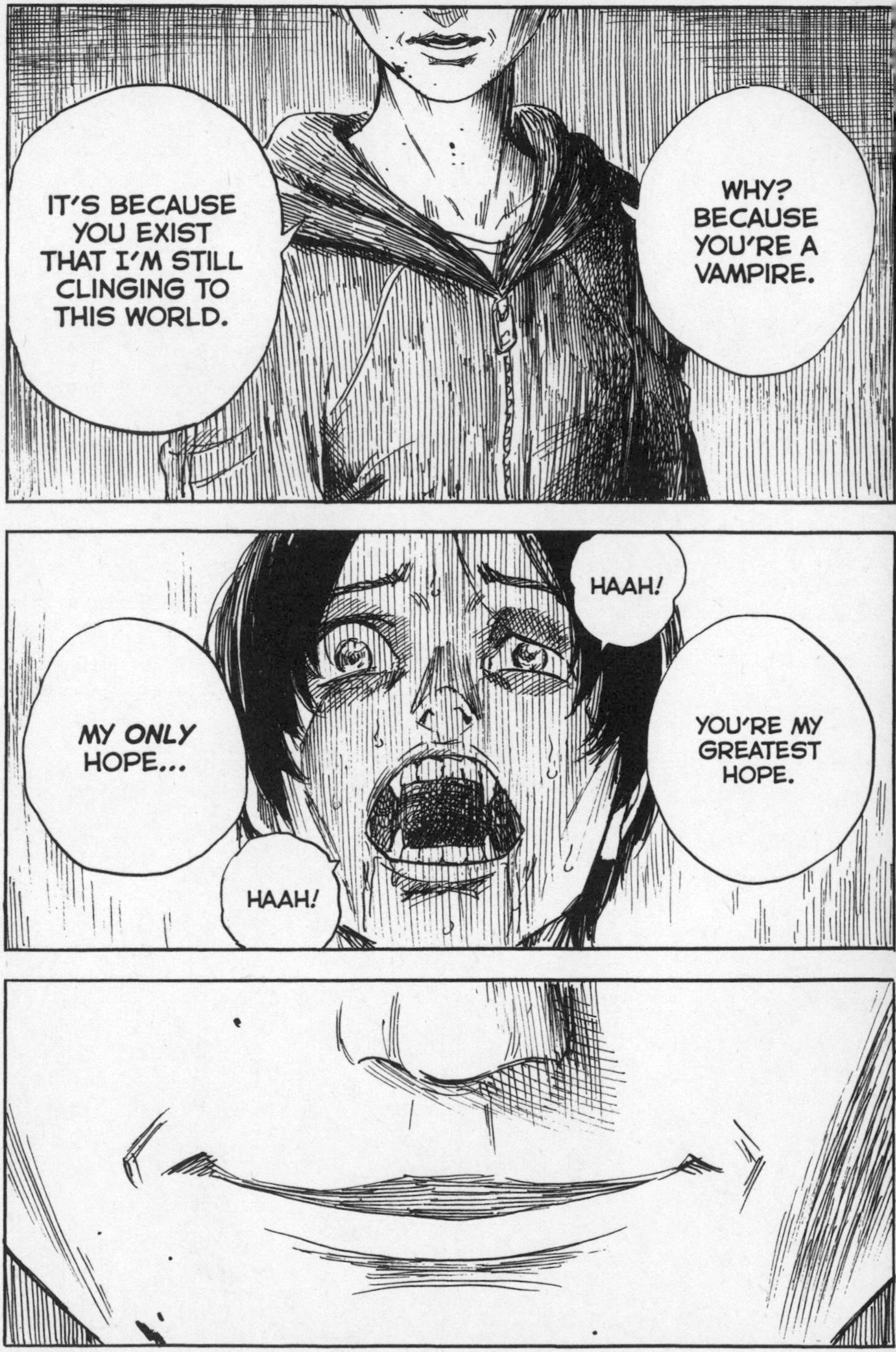
WHY? BECAUSE YOU'RE A VAMPIRE.
IT'S BECAUSE YOU EXIST THAT I'M STILL CLINGING TO THIS WORLD.
HAAH!
YOU'RE MY GREATEST HOPE.
MY ONLY HOPE...
HAAH!

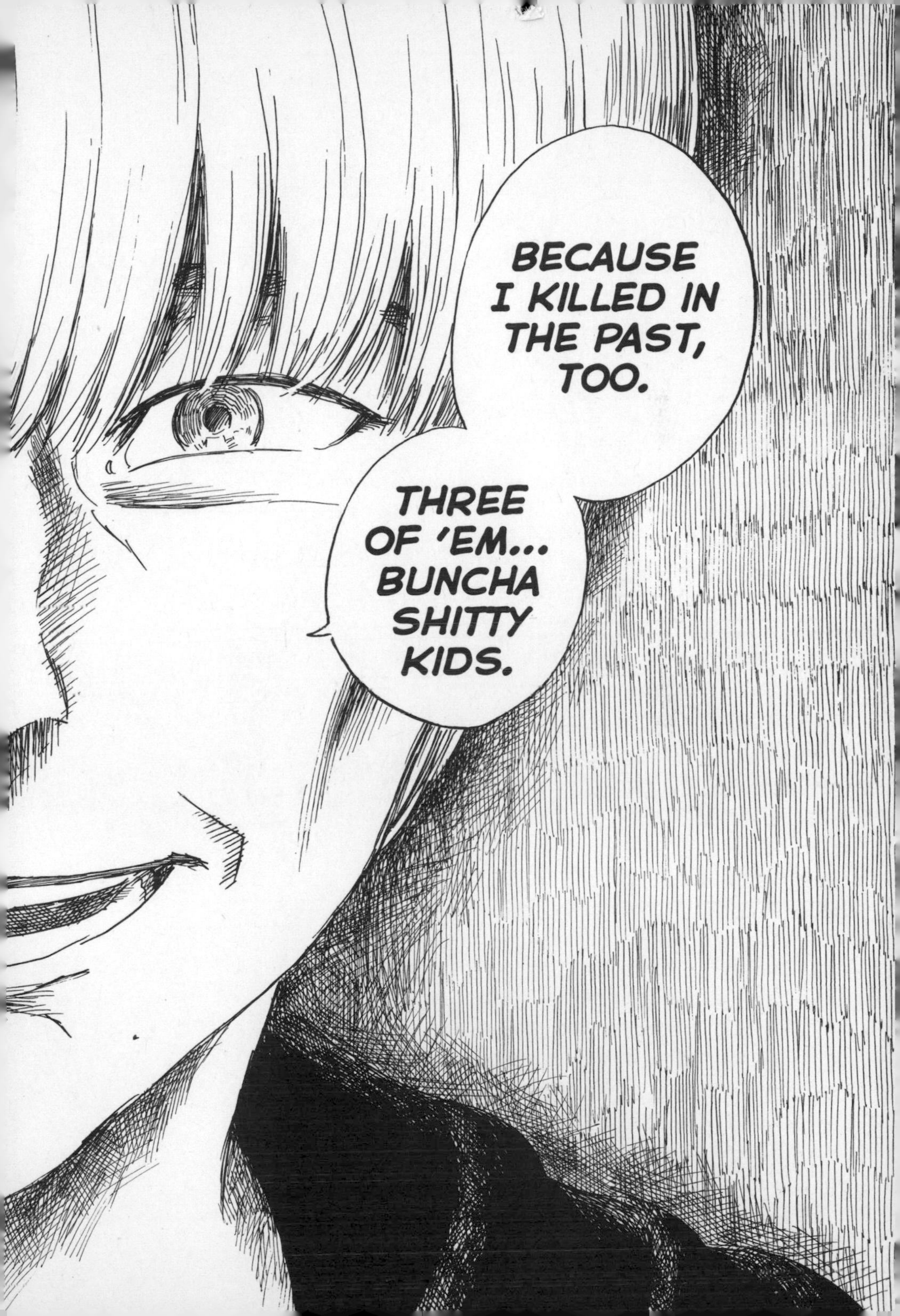
BECAUSE I KILLED IN THE PAST, TOO.
THREE OF 'EM... BUNCHA SHITTY KIDS.

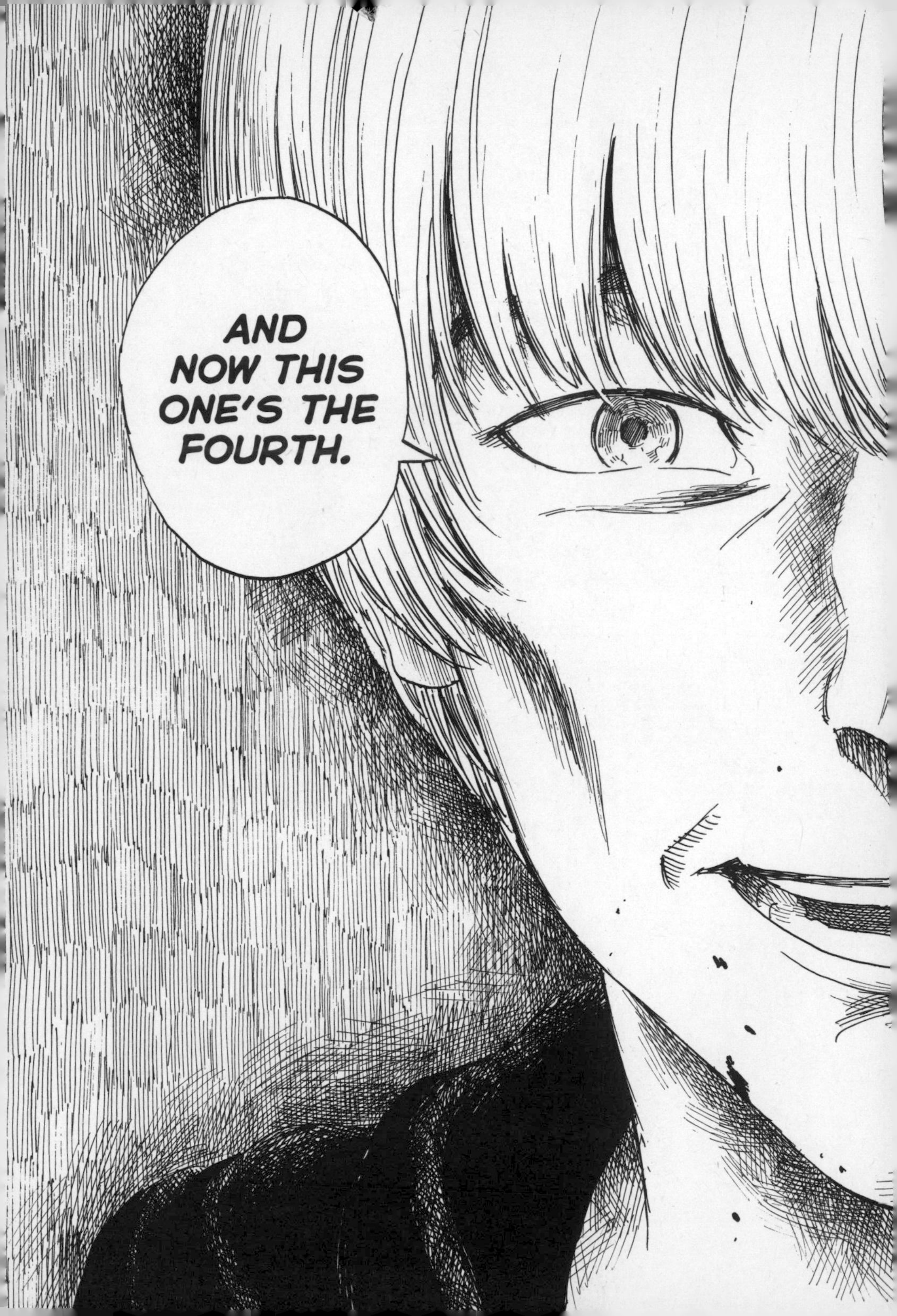
AND NOW THIS ONE'S THE FOURTH.

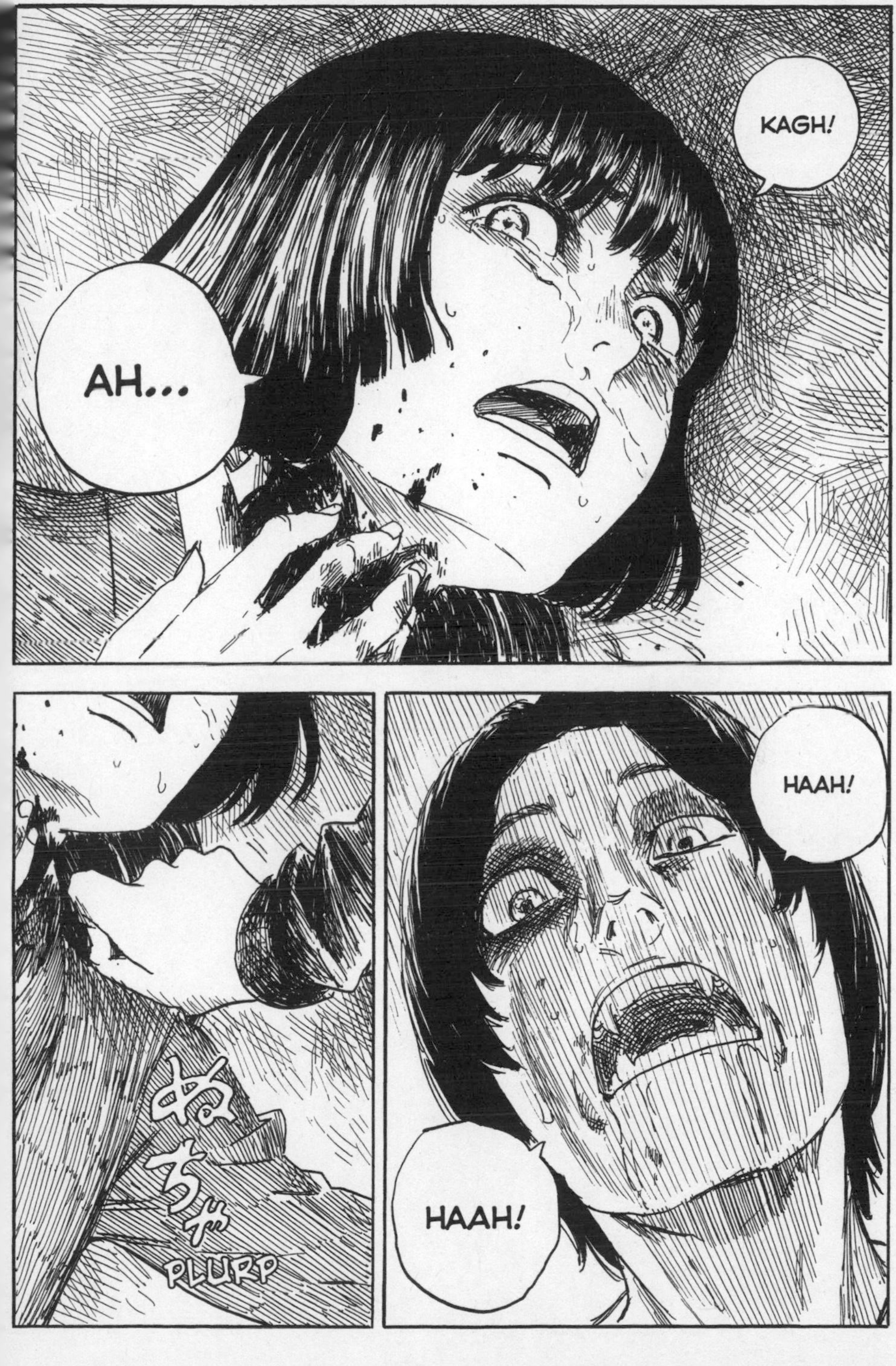
KAGH!
AH...
HAAH!
HAAH!
ぬちゅ
PLURP

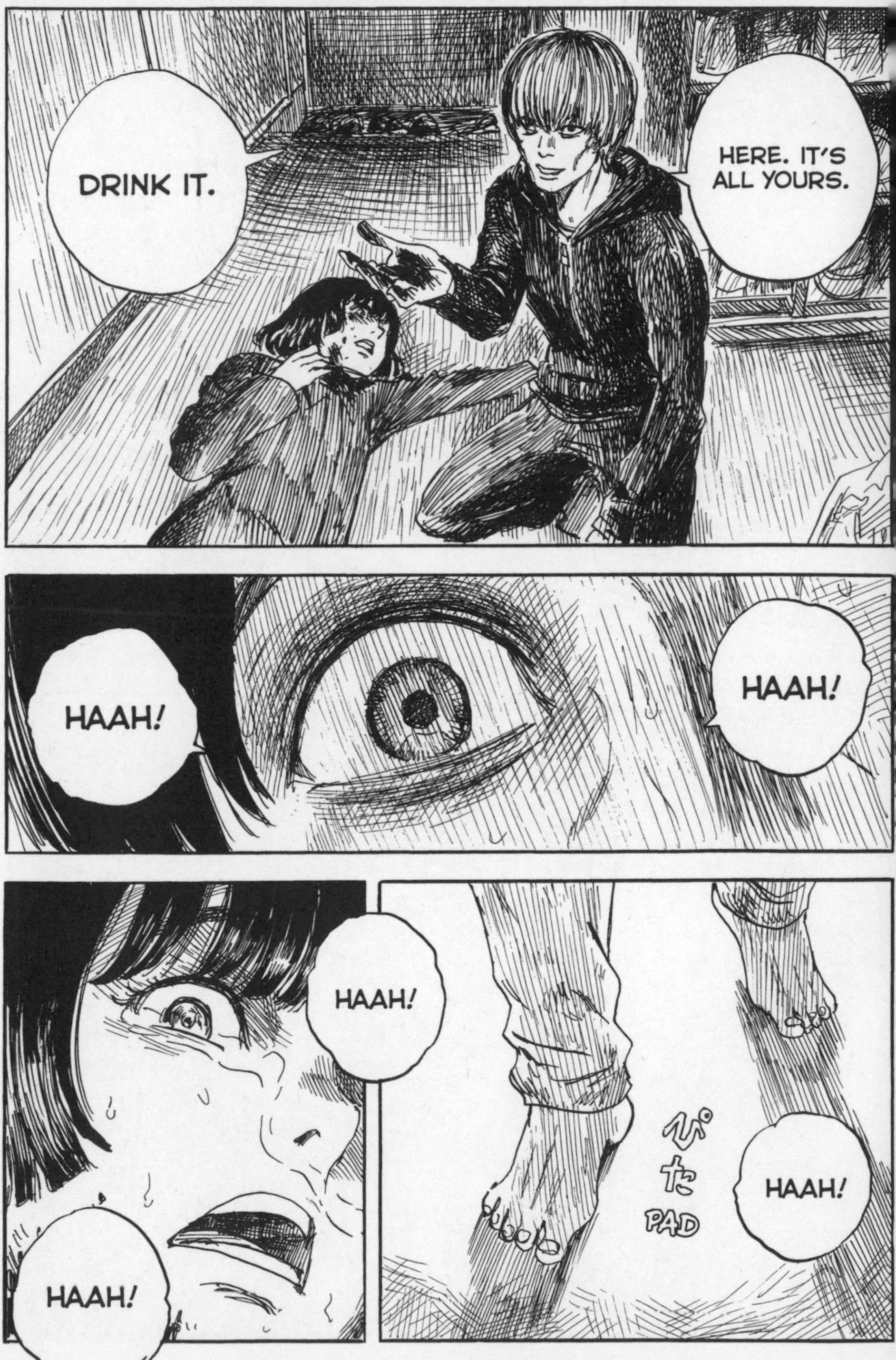
HERE. IT'S ALL YOURS.
DRINK IT.
HAAH!
HAAH!
HAAH!
ぴた
PAD
HAAH!
HAAH!

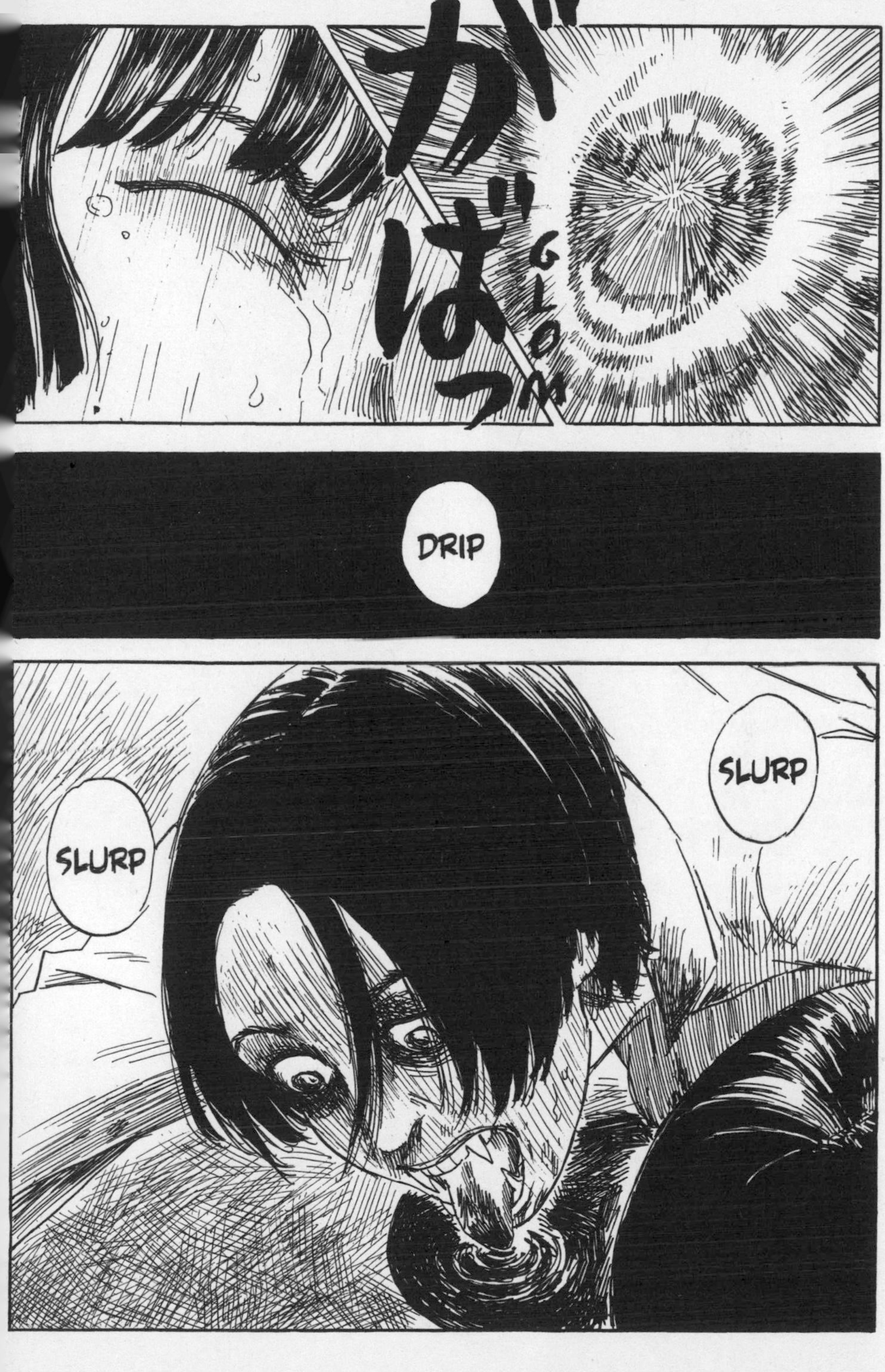
がばっ
GLOM
DRIP
SLURP
SLURP

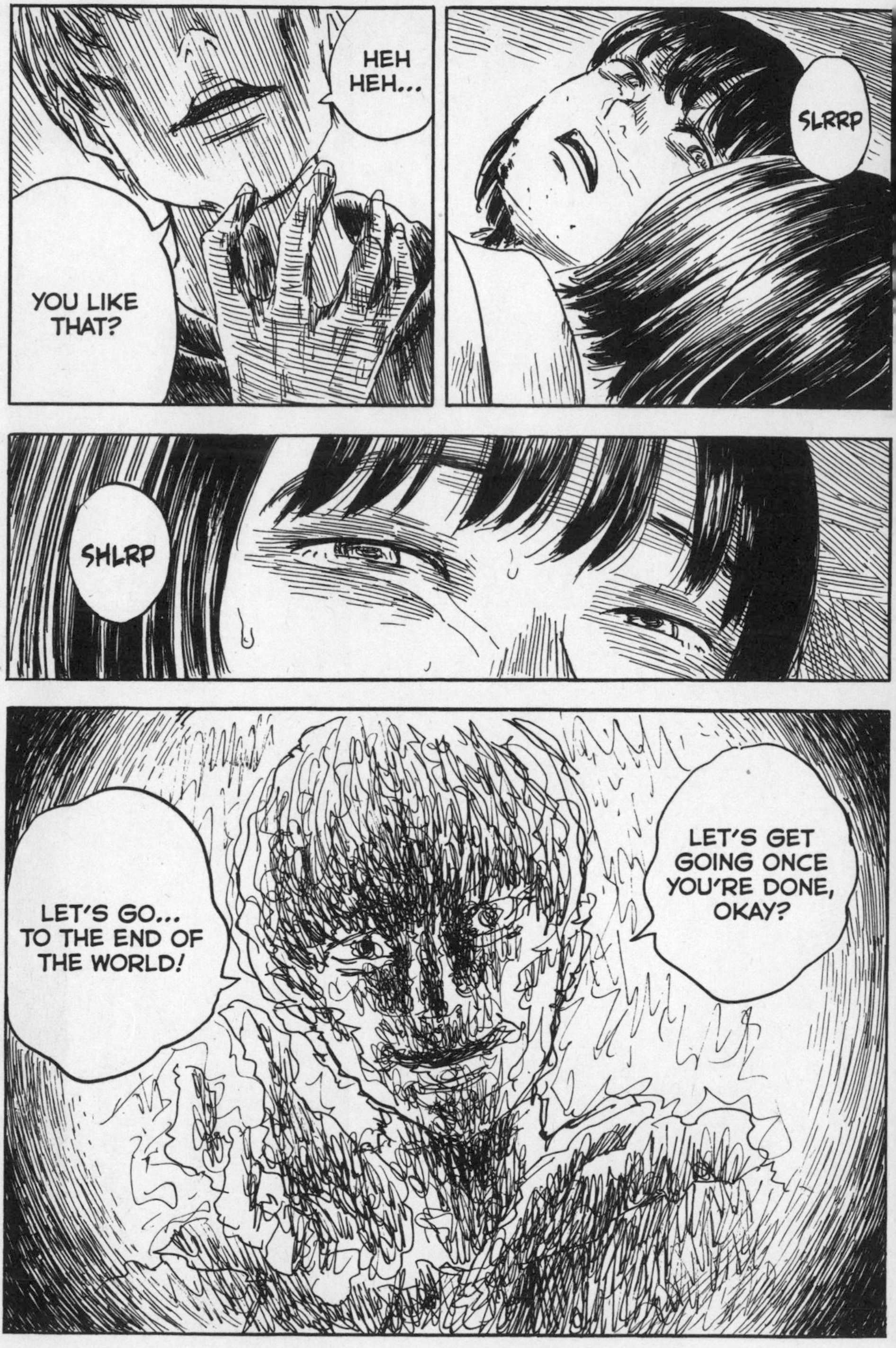
SLRRP
HEH HEH...
YOU LIKE THAT?
SHLRP
LET'S GET GOING ONCE YOU'RE DONE, OKAY?
LET'S GO... TO THE END OF THE WORLD!

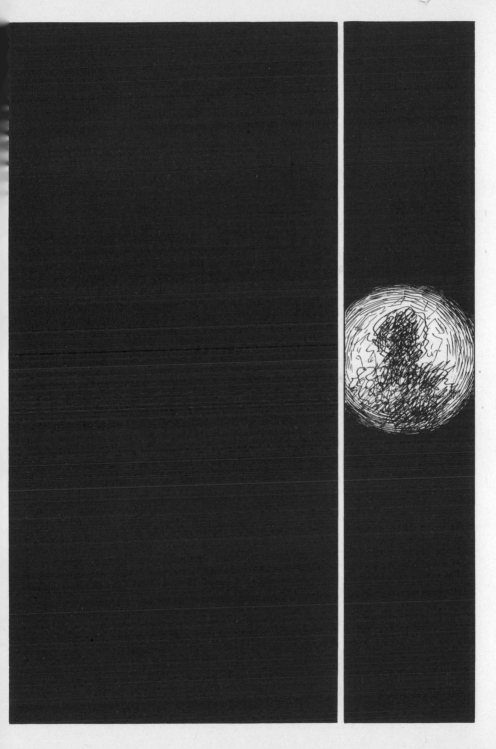

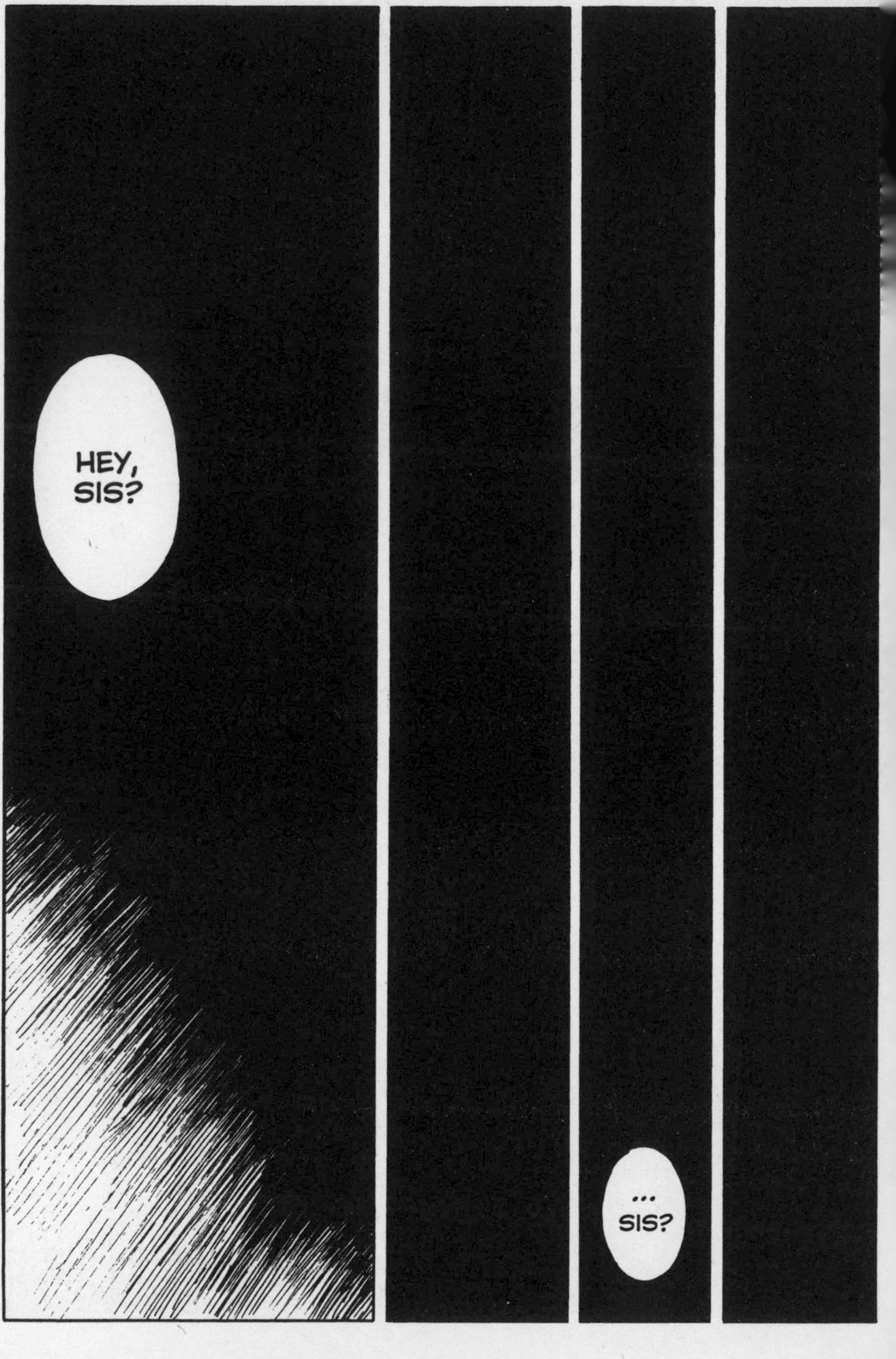
...
SIS?
HEY, SIS?

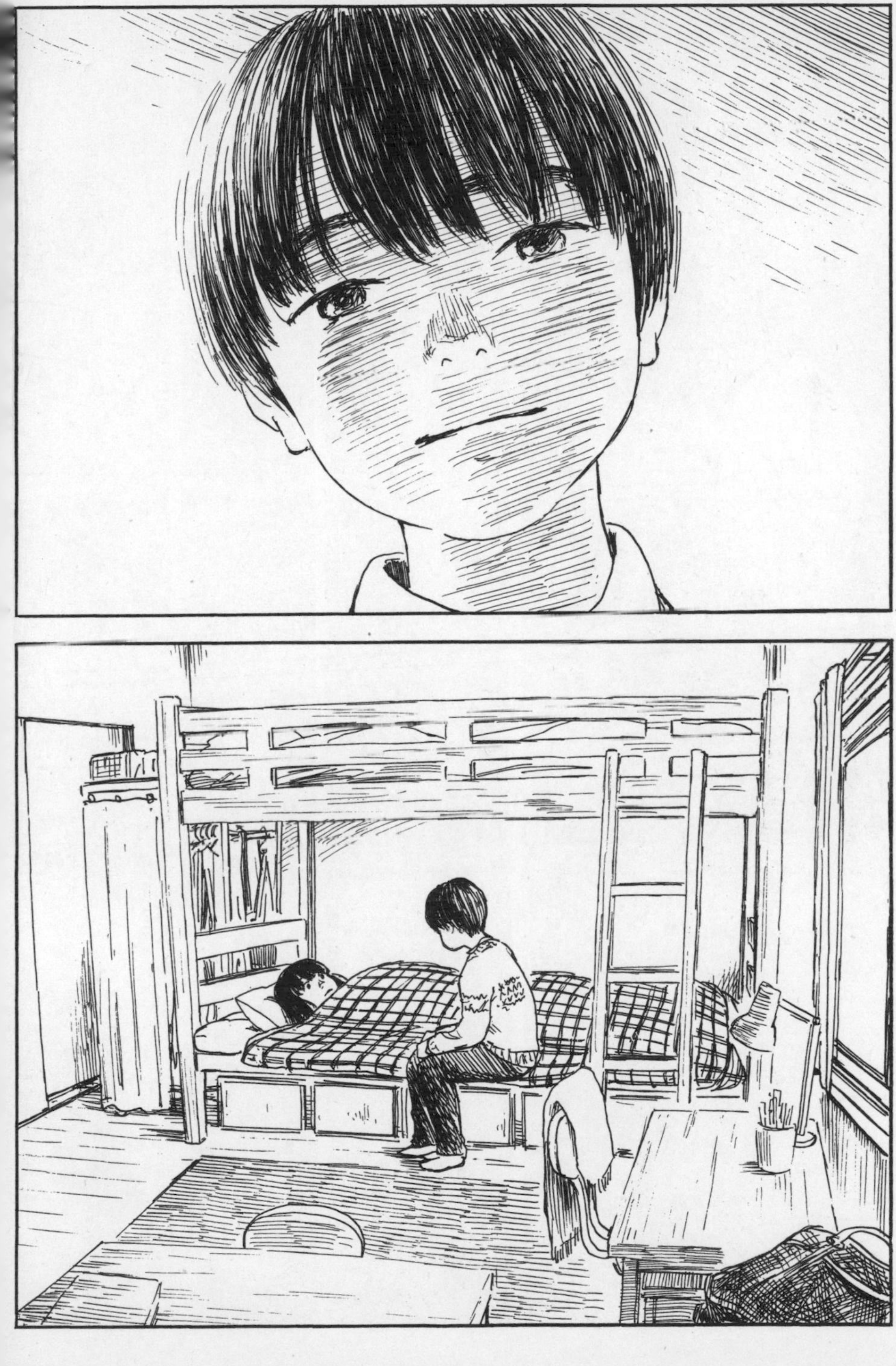

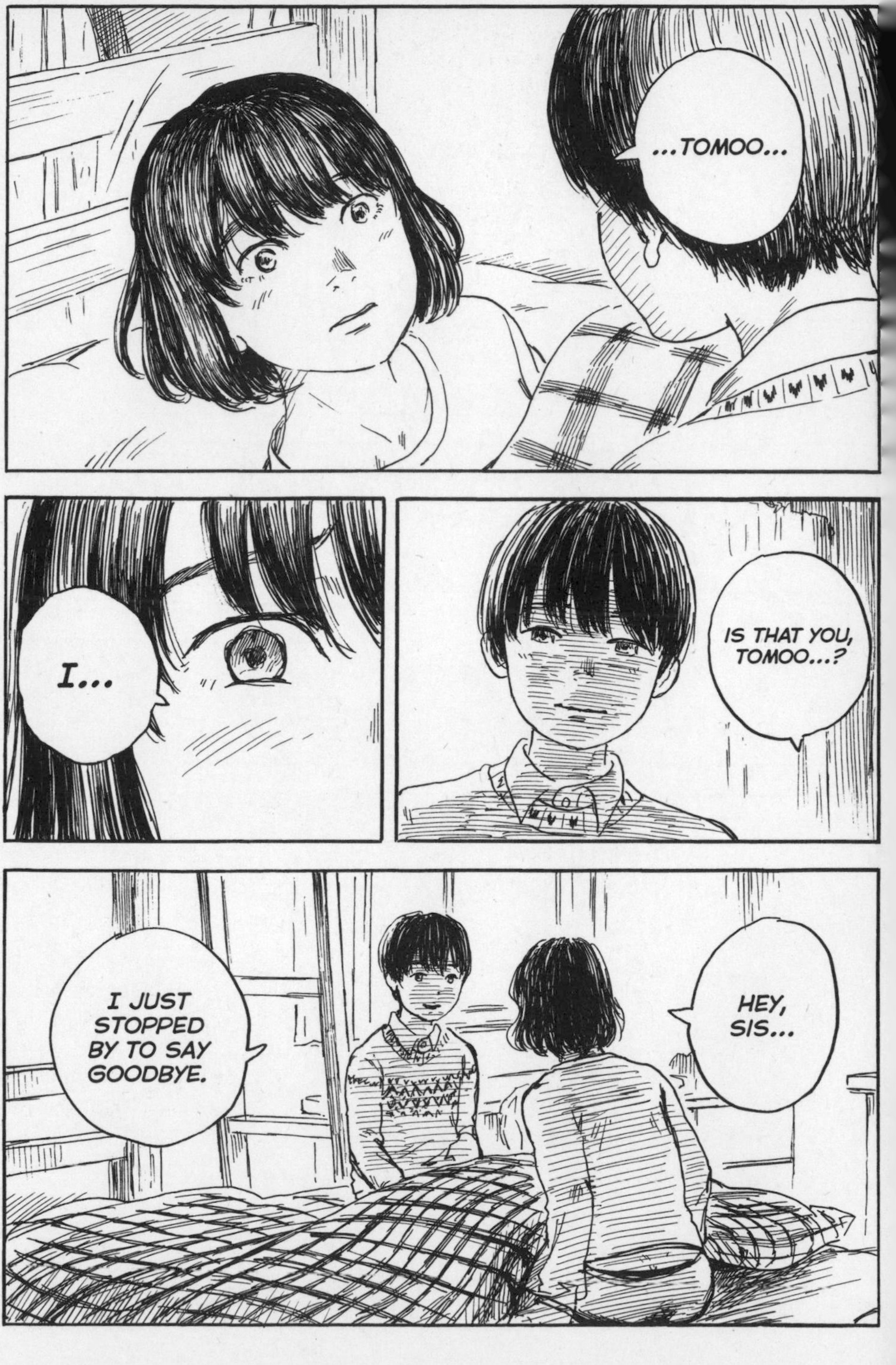
...TOMOO...
IS THAT YOU, TOMOO...?
I...
HEY, SIS...
I JUST STOPPED BY TO SAY GOODBYE.

SO, UM...
...YOU CAN'T COME BACK TO ME AGAIN, OKAY?
TOMOO... WHY?
I FINALLY GOT TO SEE YOU...
...I'VE GOT SO MUCH TO TALK ABOUT...
GOODBYE...
...SIS.

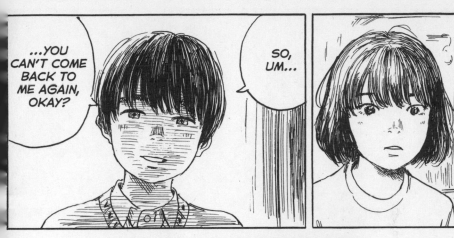

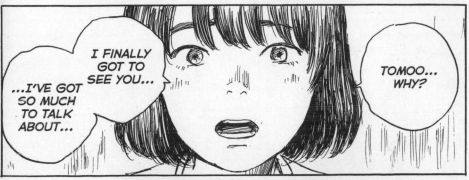

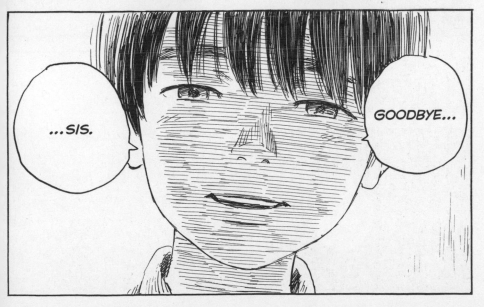

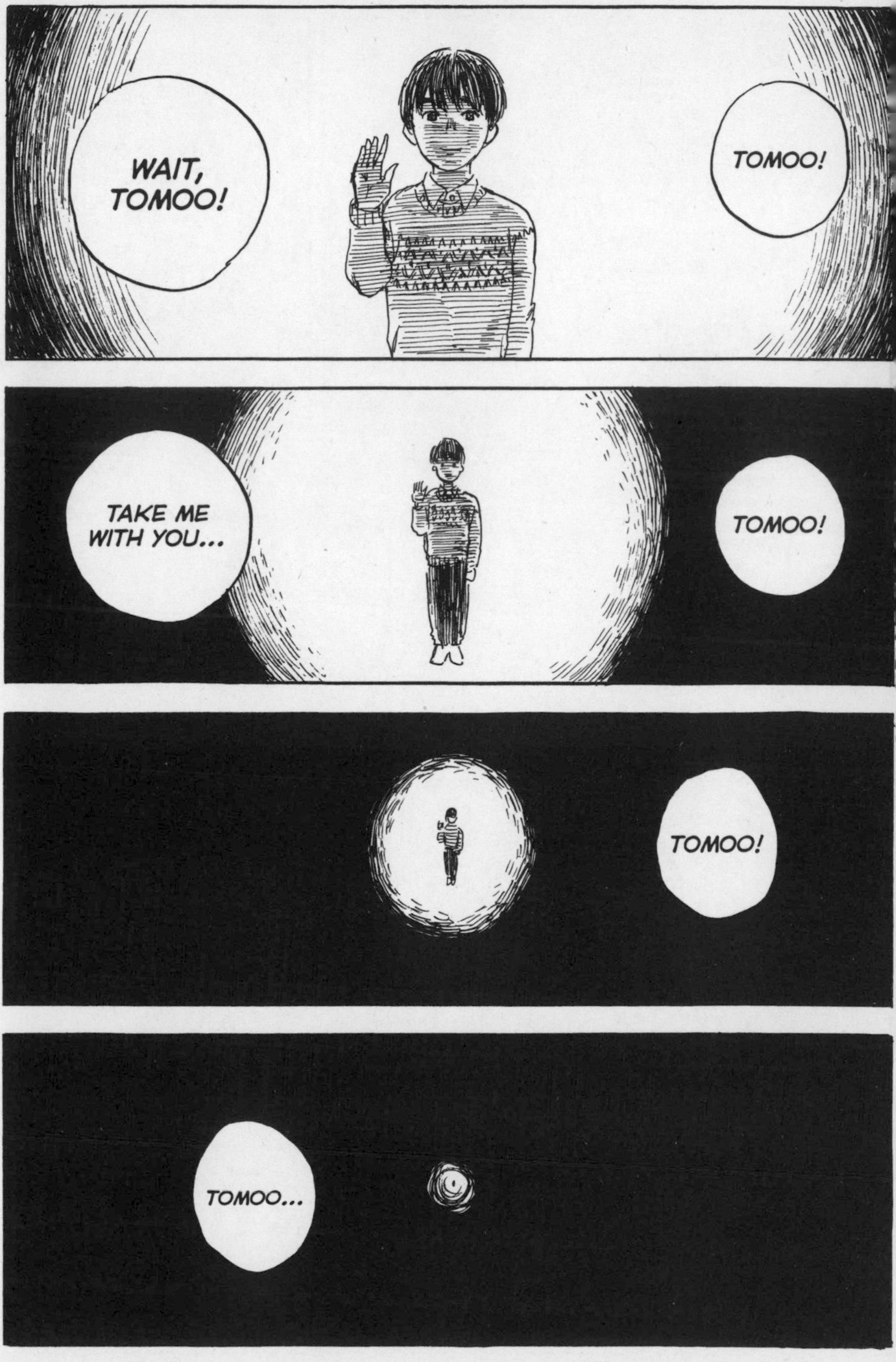
TOMOO!
WAIT, TOMOO!
TOMOO!
TAKE ME WITH YOU...
TOMOO!
TOMOO...

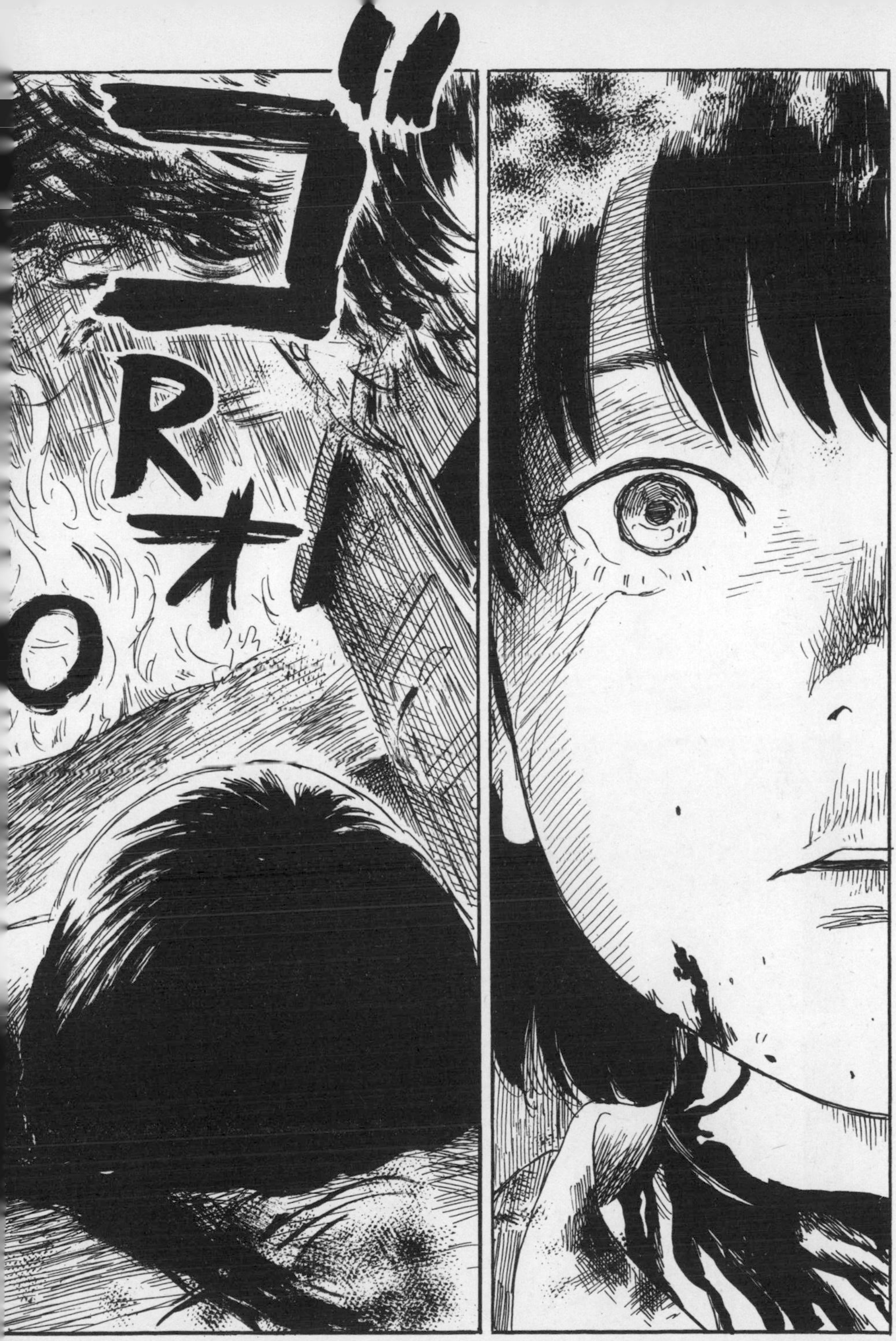
ゴ
R
オ
O

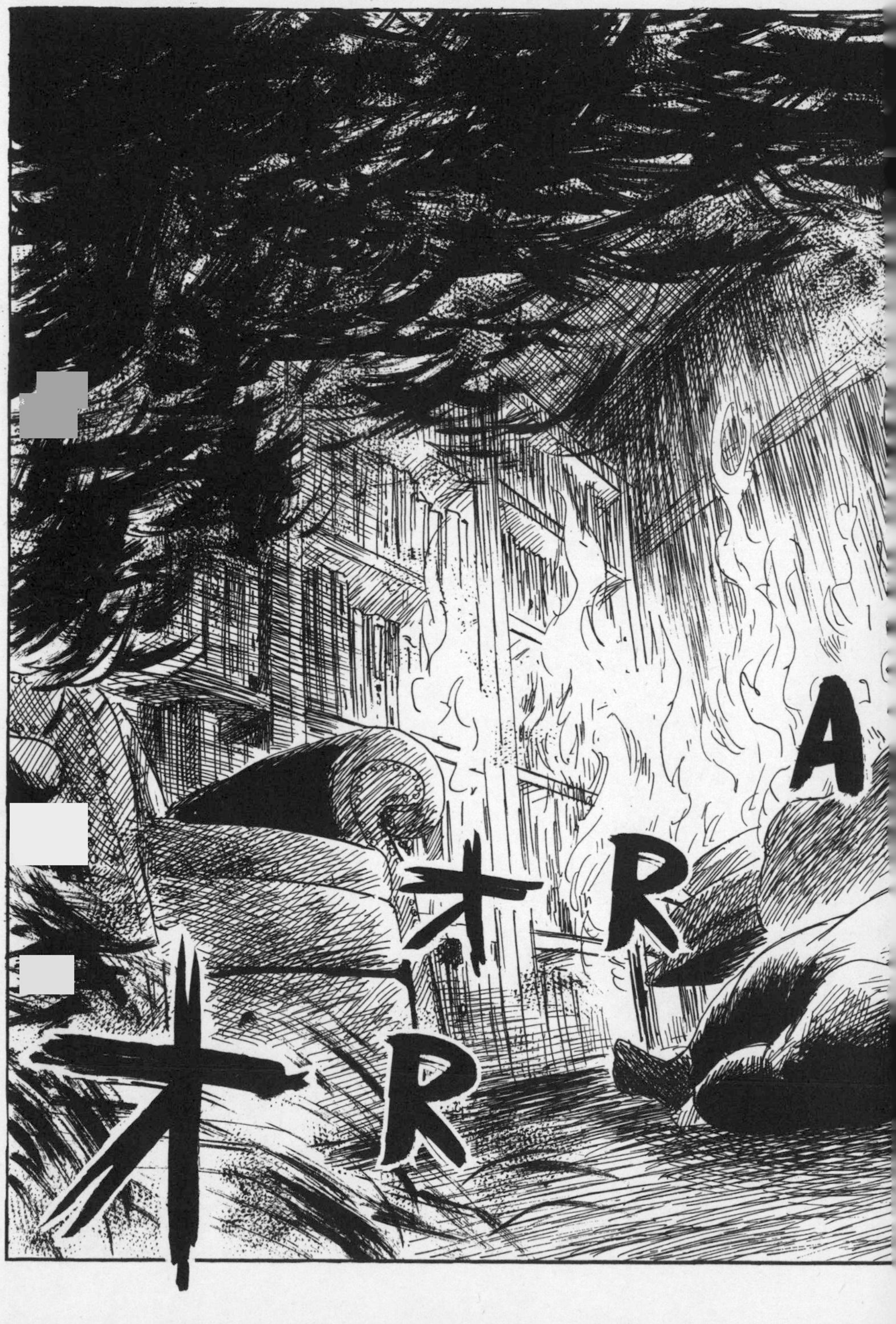
R R A

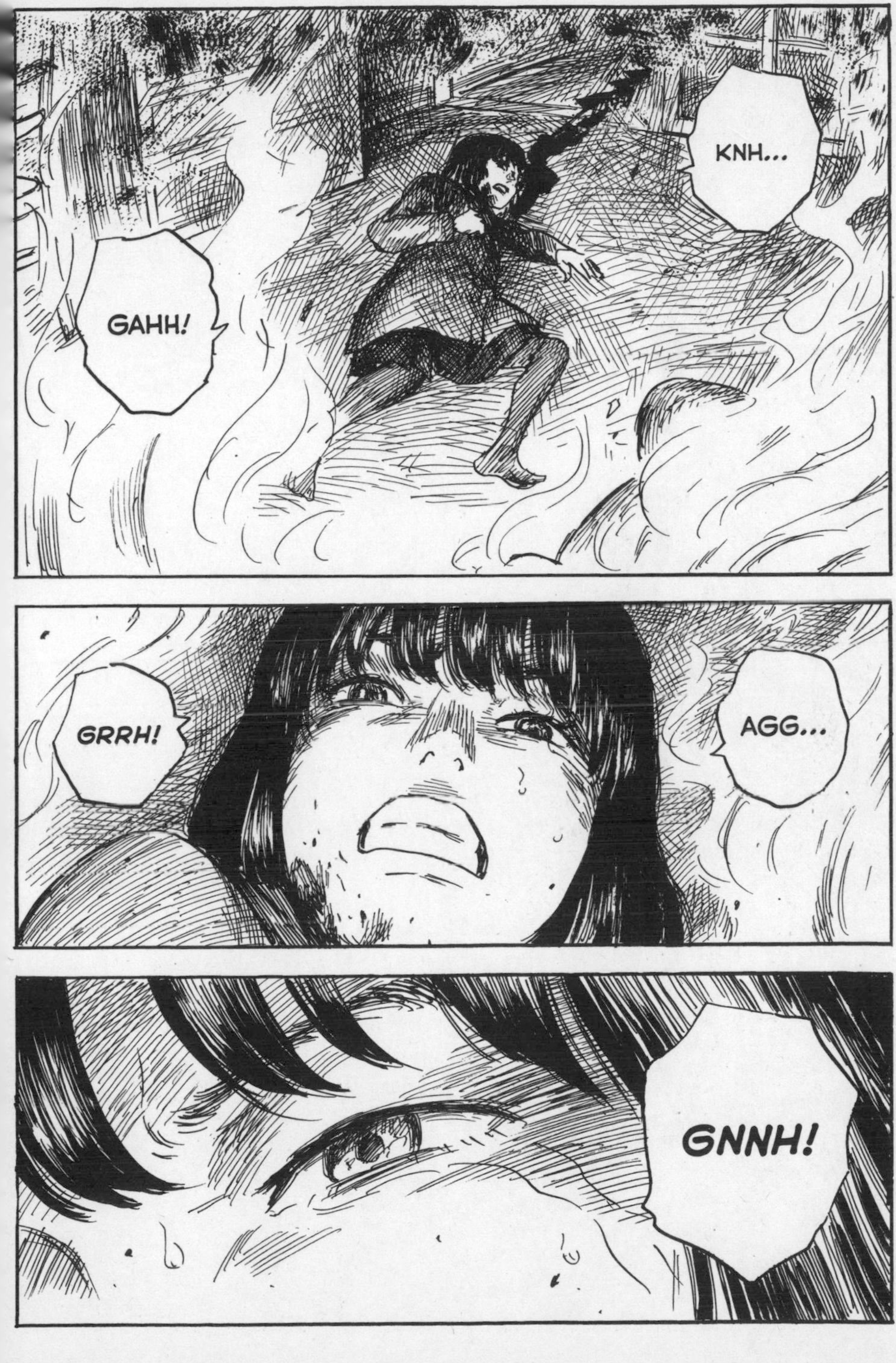
KNH...
GAHH!
AGG...
GRRH!
GNNH!

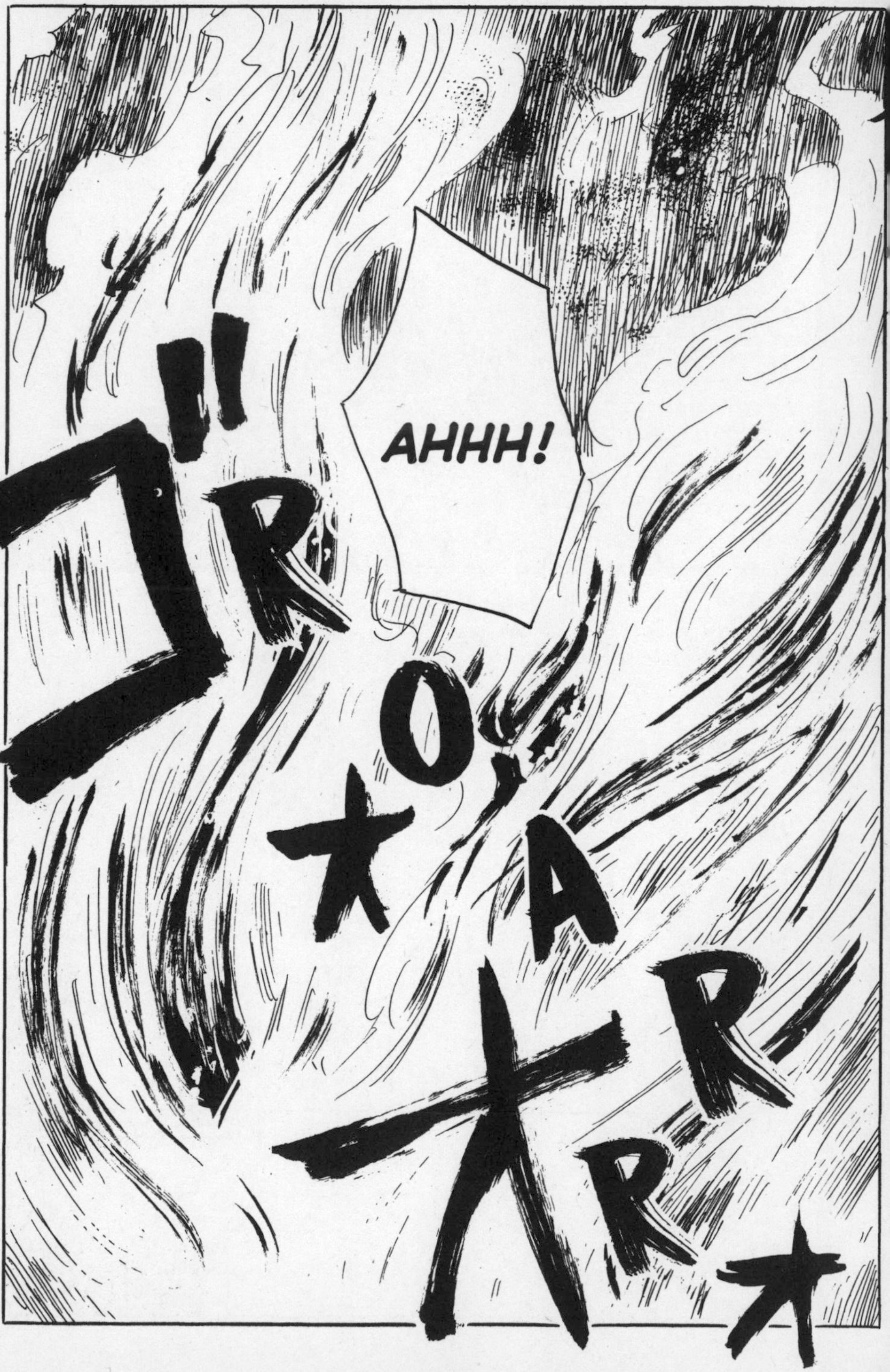
AHHH!
ROARR

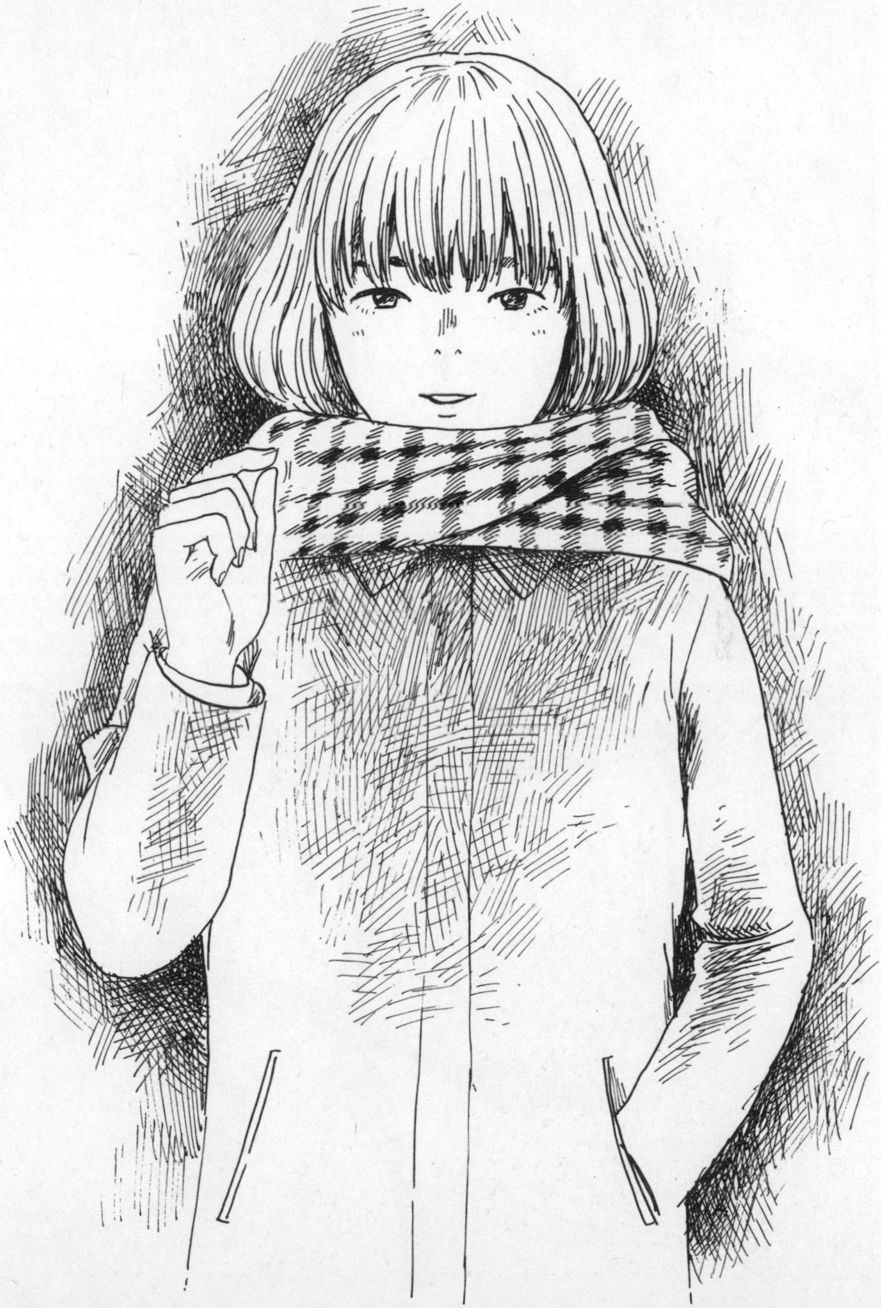

Chapter 24: Escape

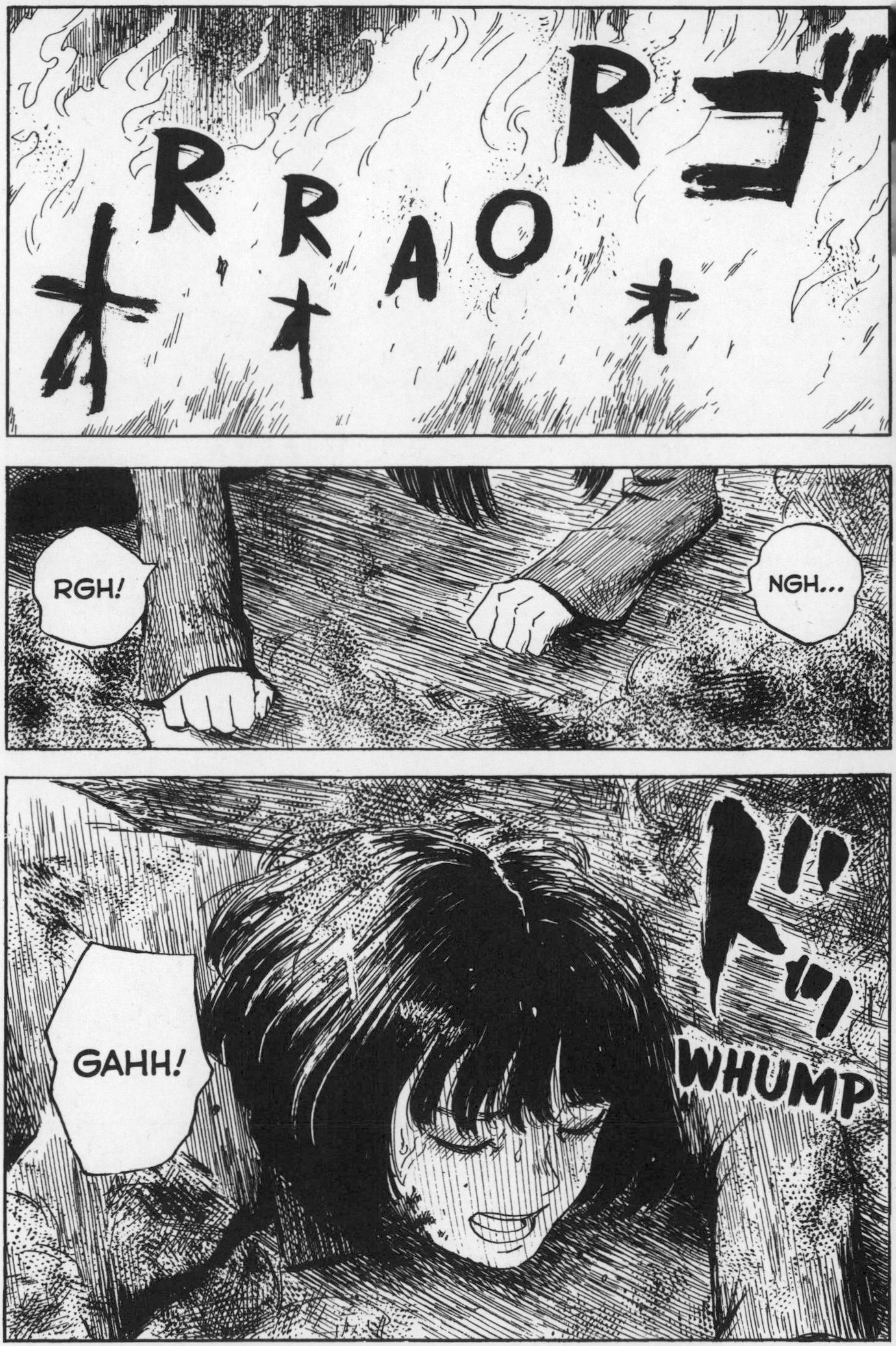
ゴオオオ
RRAOR
NGH...
RGH!
ドッ
WHUMP
GAHH!

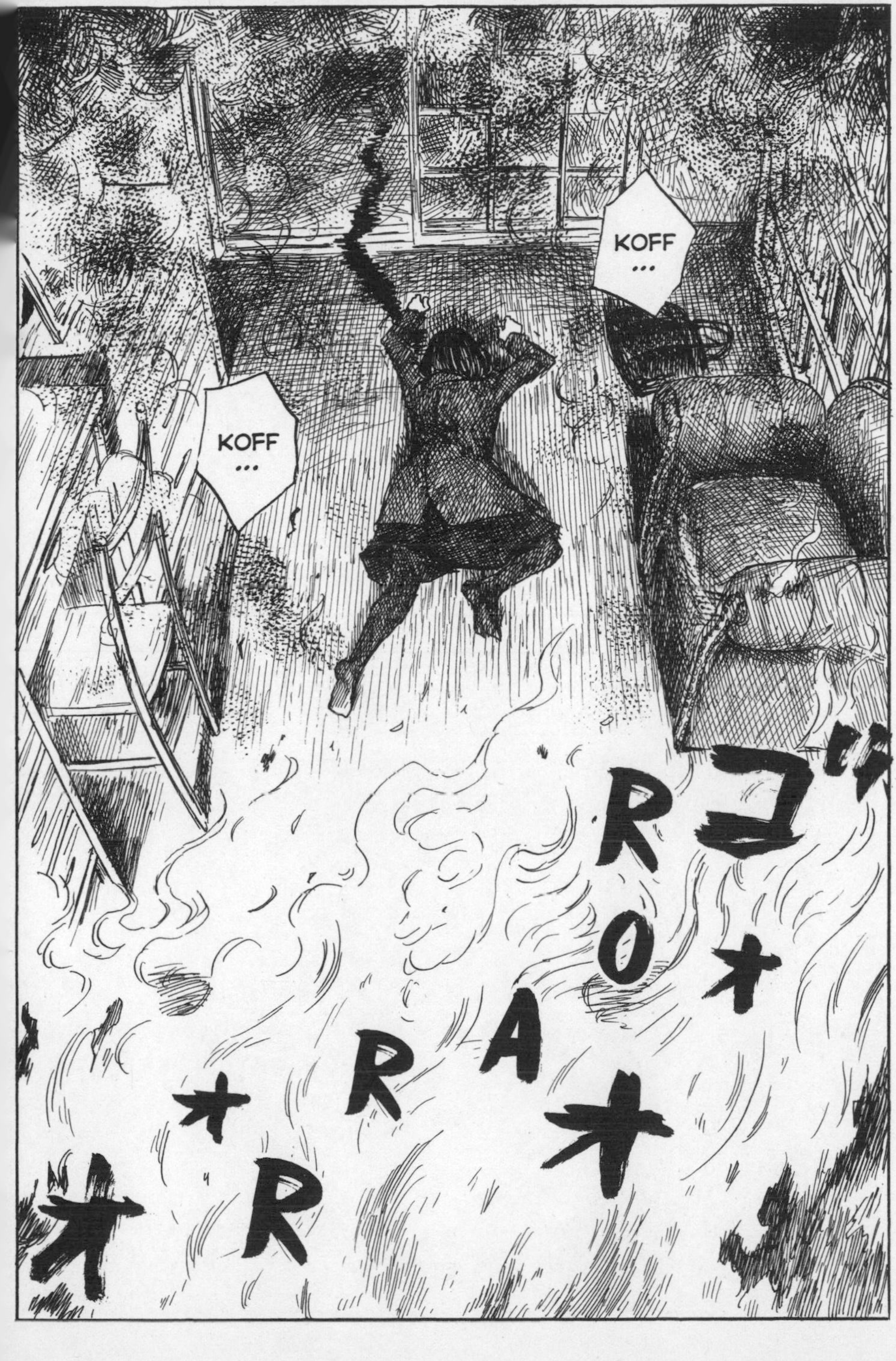
KOFF ...
KOFF ...
ROARR
ゴオオオオ

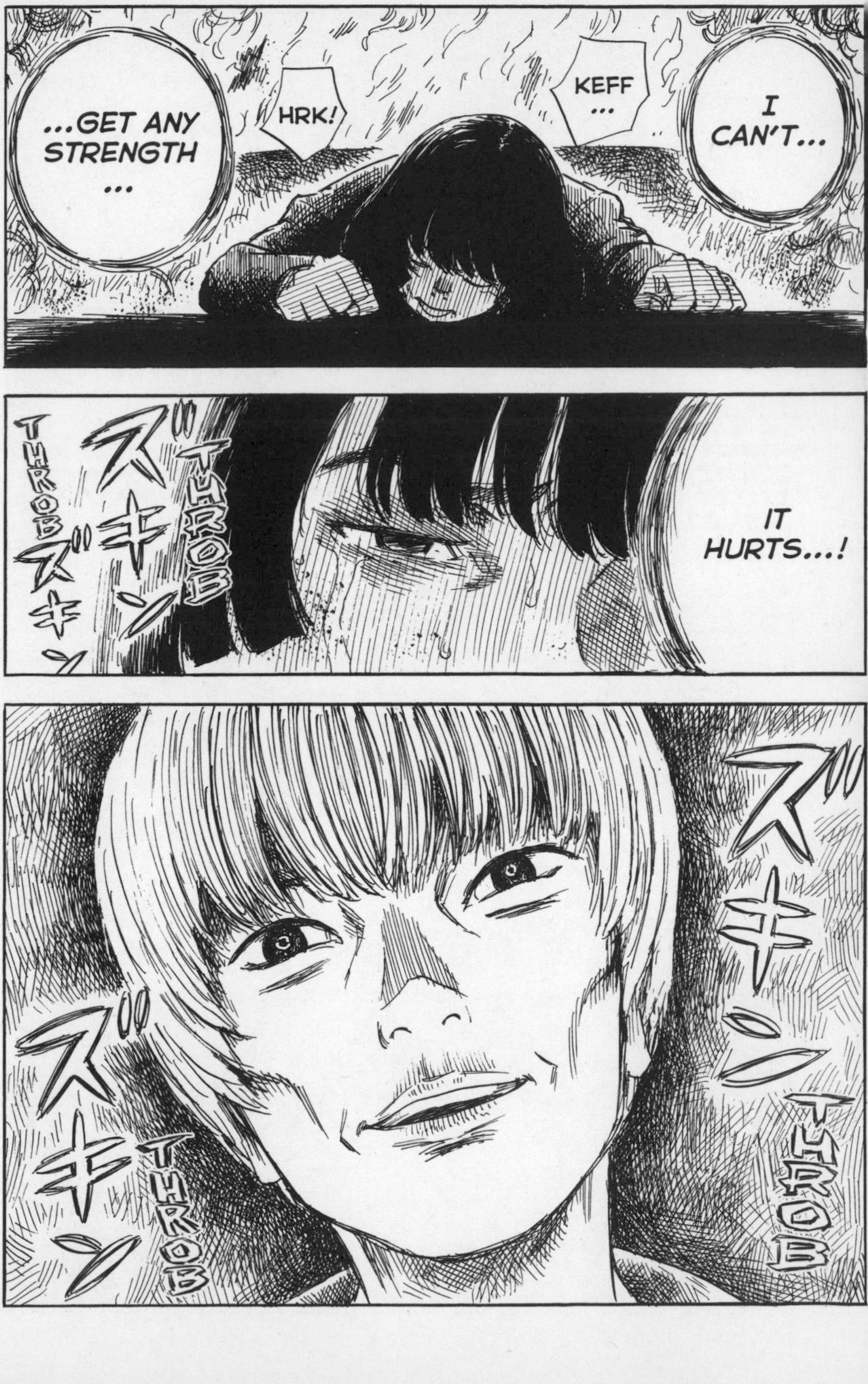
I CAN'T...
KEFF ...
HRK!
...GET ANY STRENGTH ...
IT HURTS...!
ズキン
THROB
ズキン
THROB
ズキン
THROB
ズキン
THROB

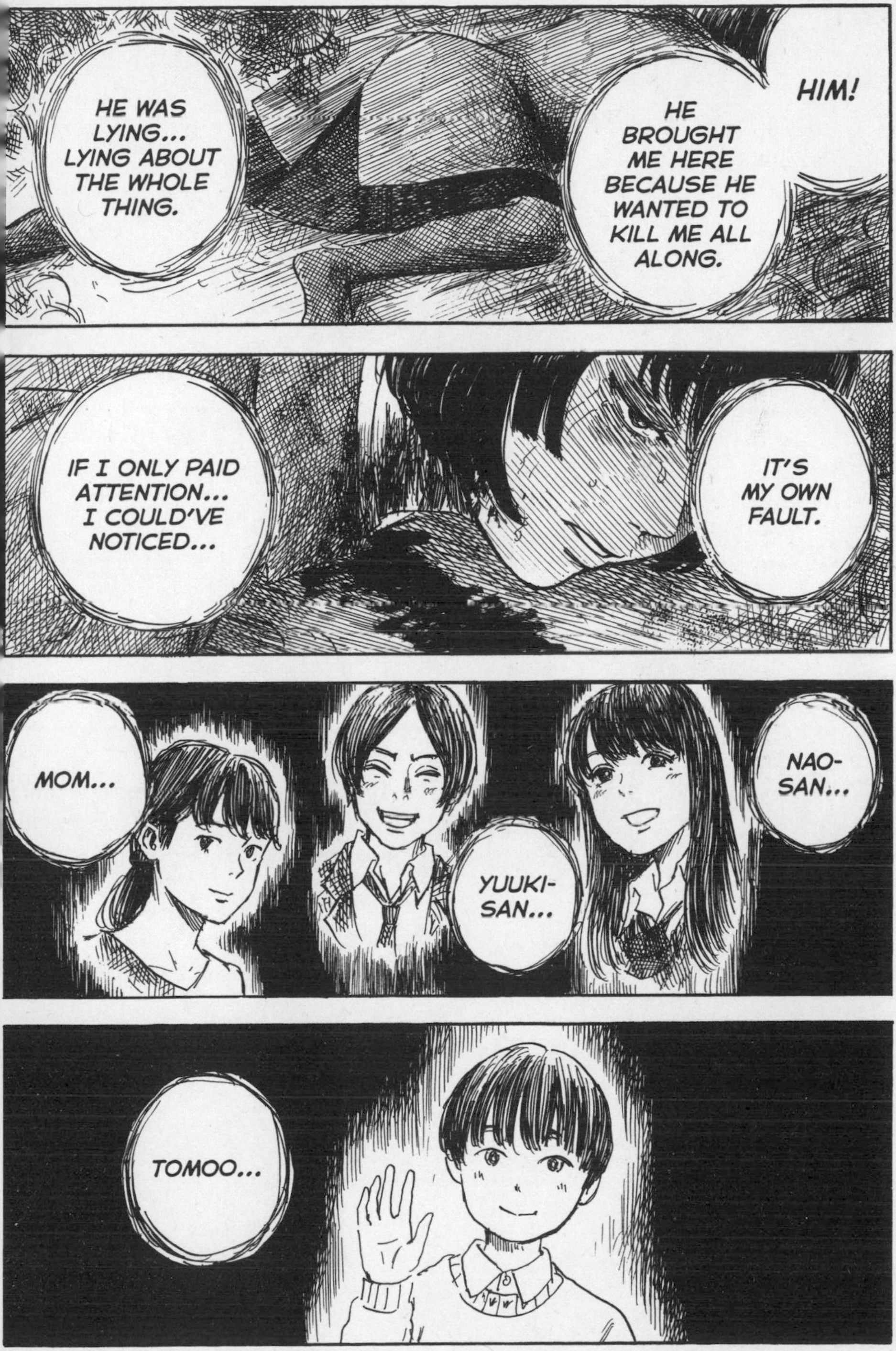
HIM!
HE BROUGHT ME HERE BECAUSE HE WANTED TO KILL ME ALL ALONG.
HE WAS LYING... LYING ABOUT THE WHOLE THING.
IT'S MY OWN FAULT.
IF I ONLY PAID ATTENTION... I COULD'VE NOTICED...
NAO-SAN...
YUUKI-SAN...
MOM...
TOMOO...

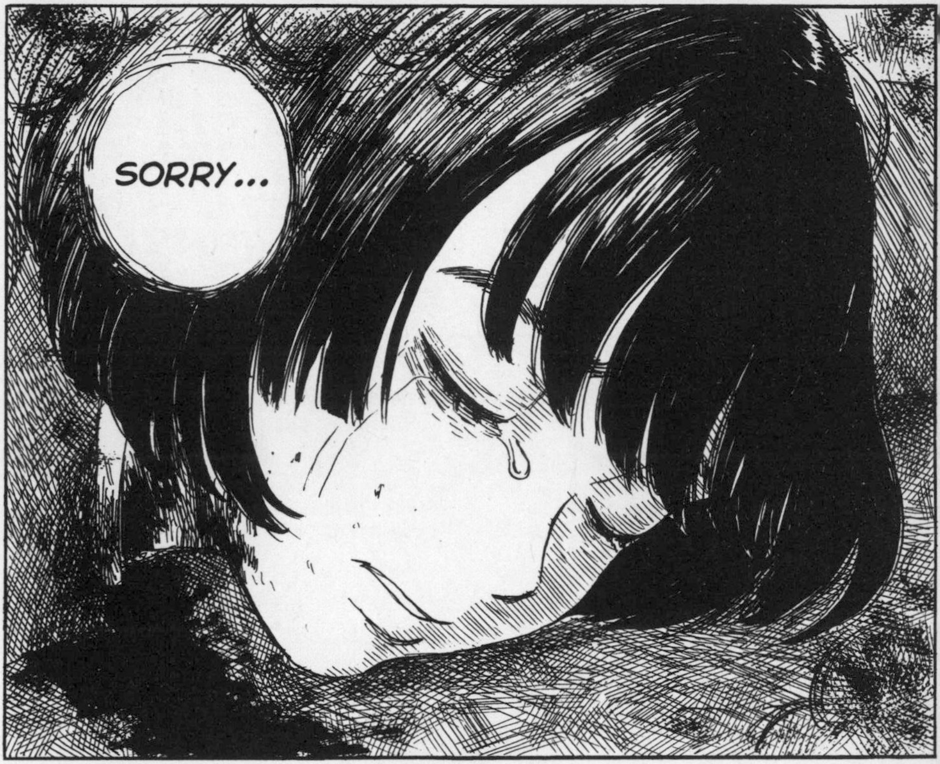
SORRY...

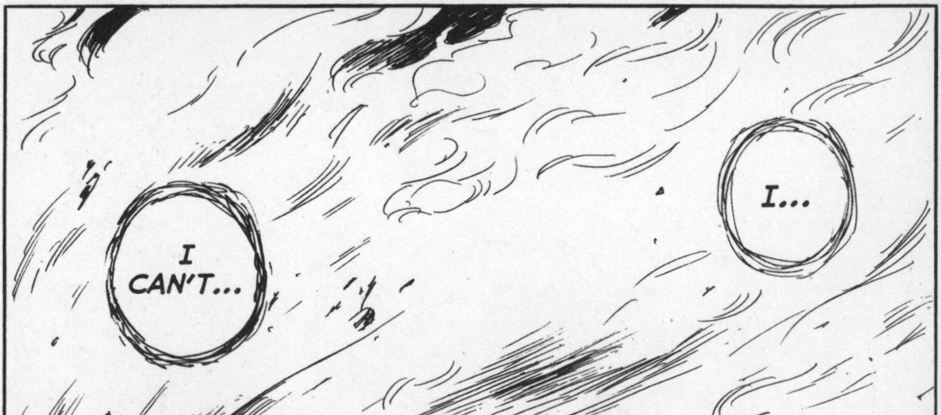
I...
I CAN'T...

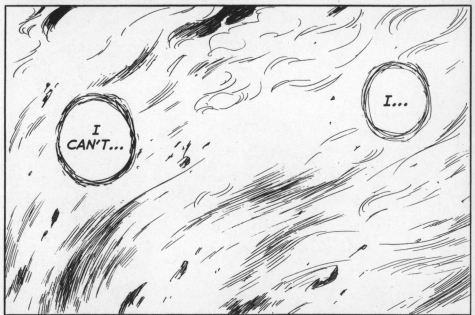

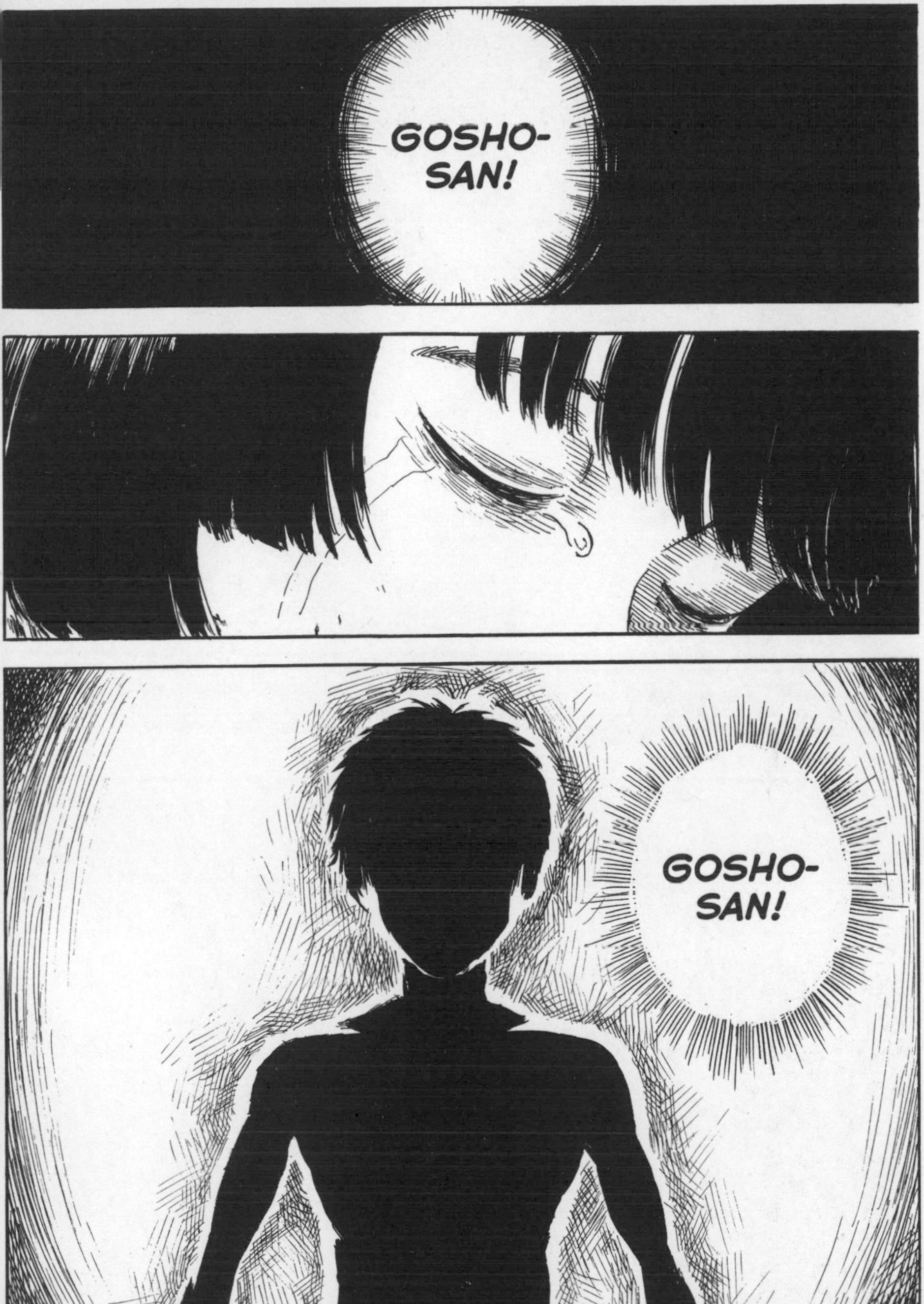
GOSHO-SAN!
GOSHO-SAN!

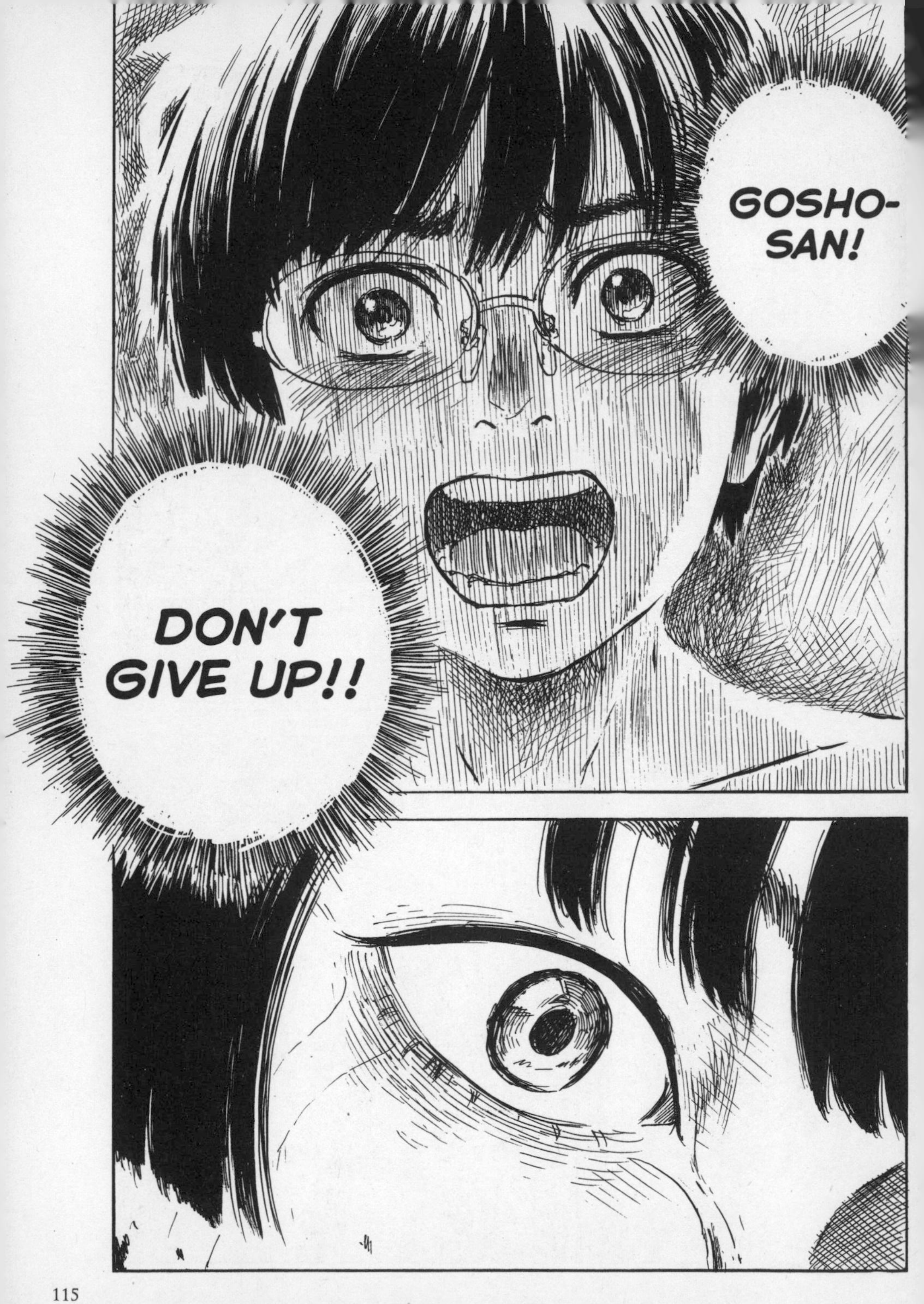
GOSHO-SAN!
DON'T GIVE UP!!

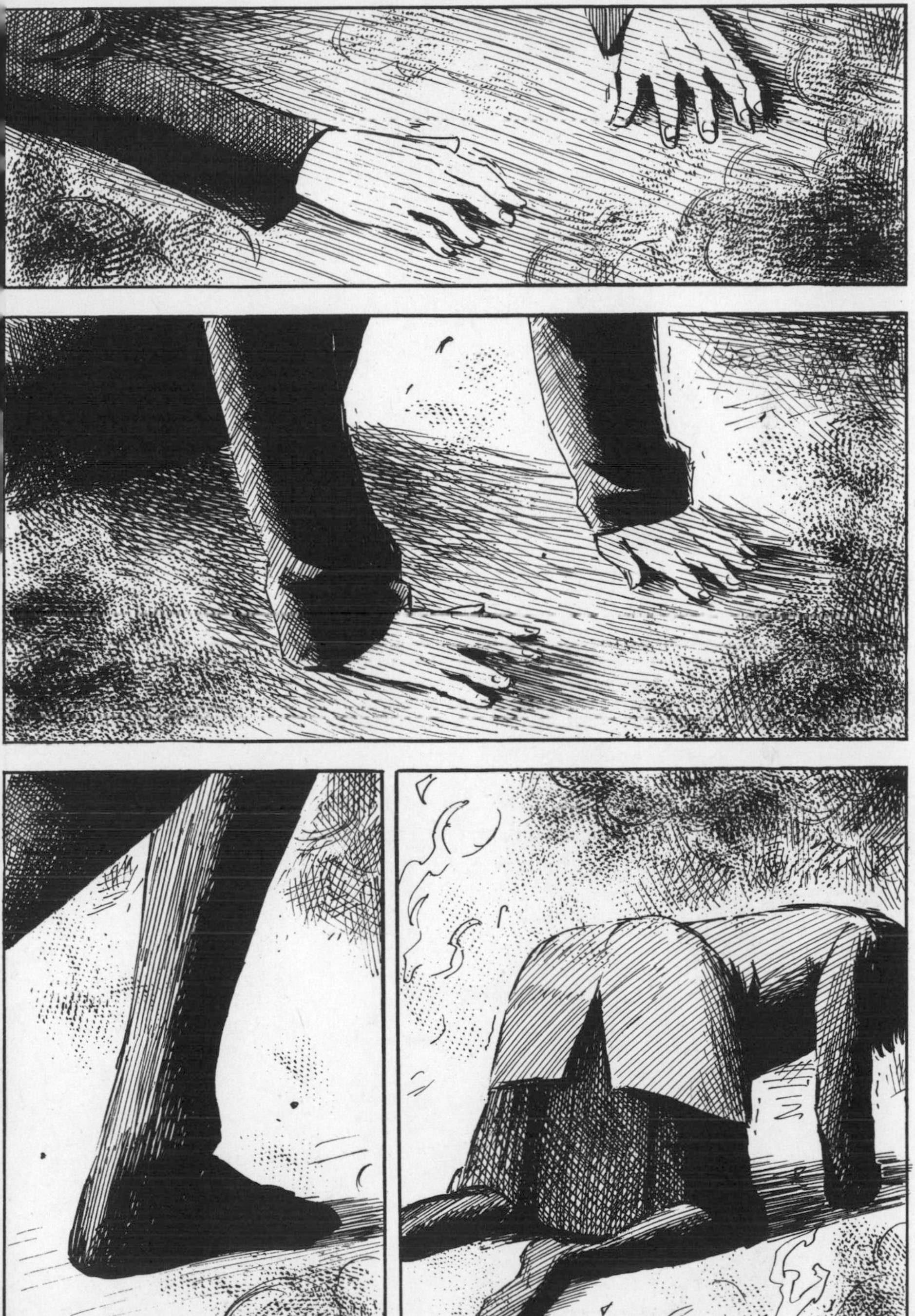

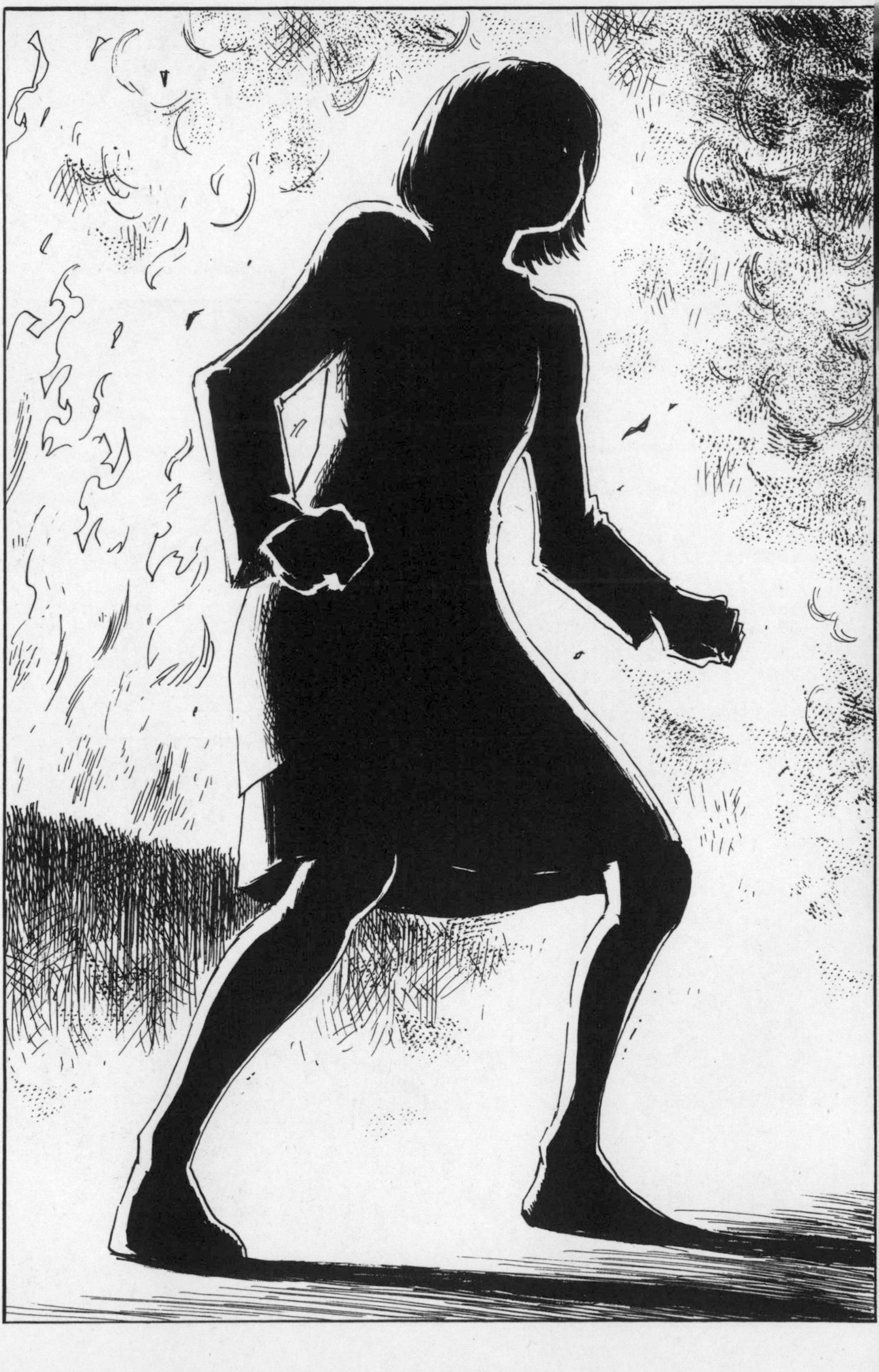

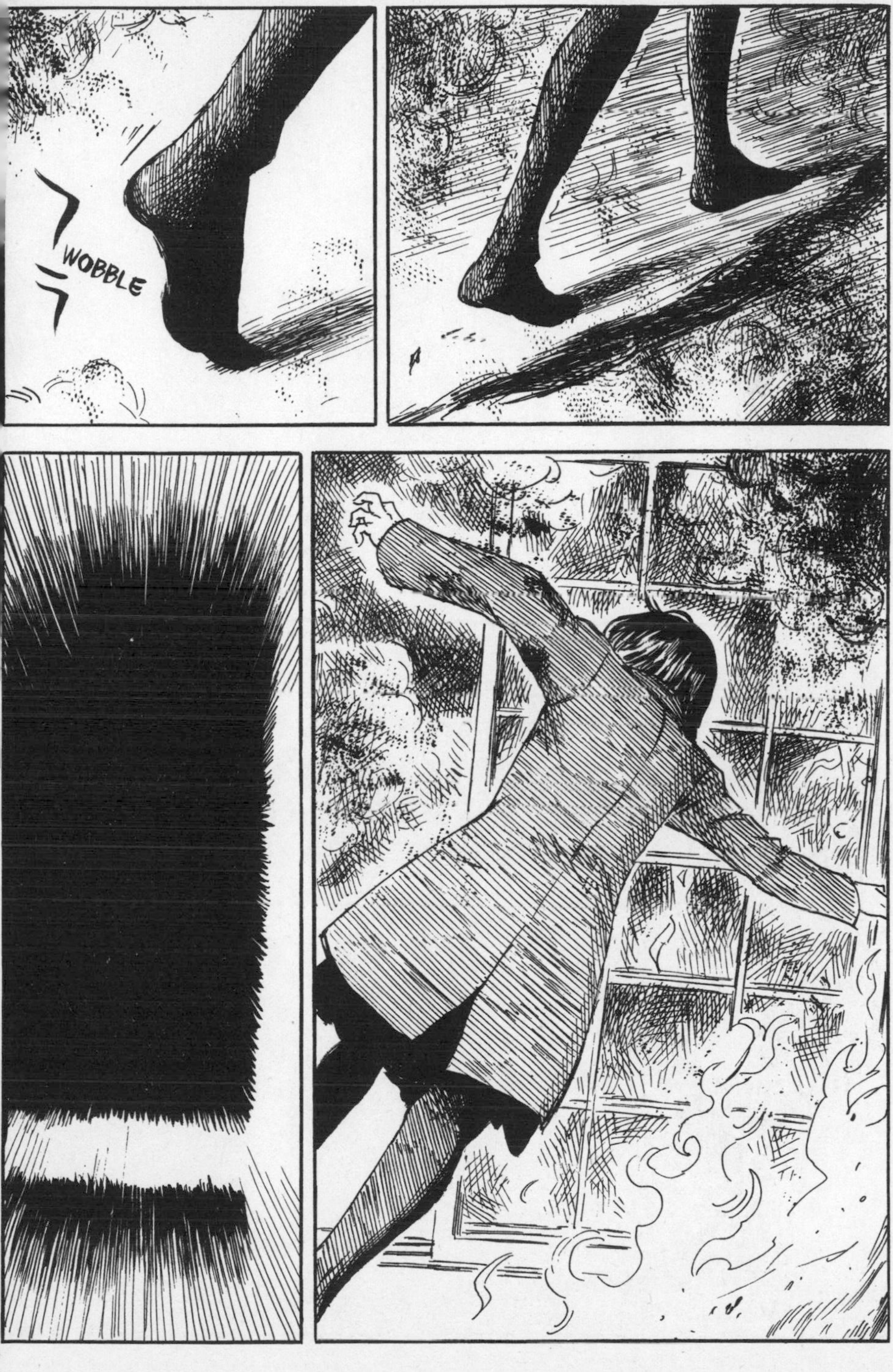
WOBBLE

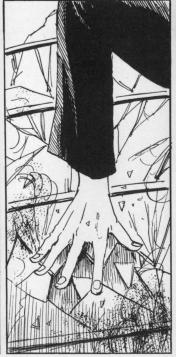

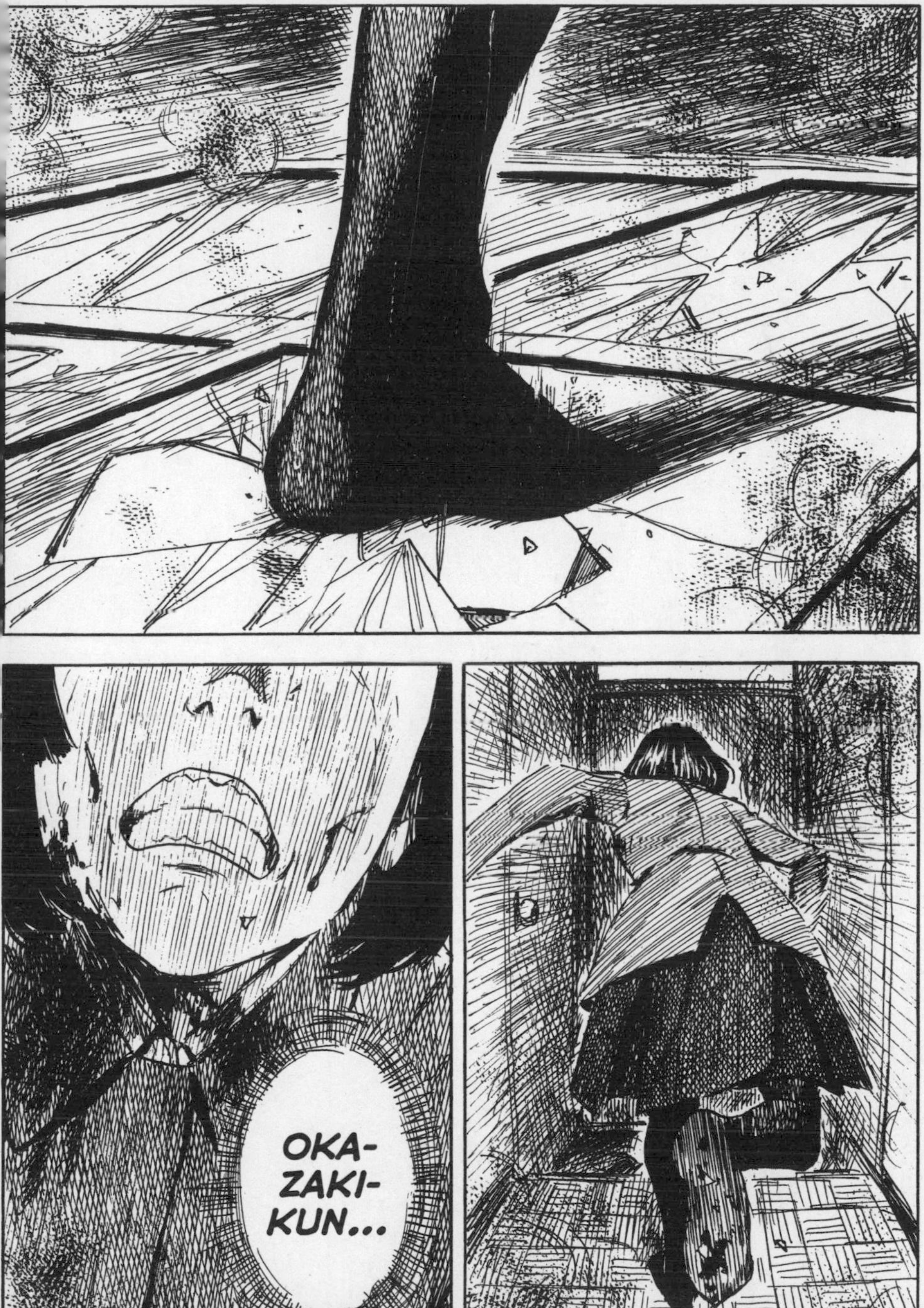
OKA-
ZAKI-
KUN...

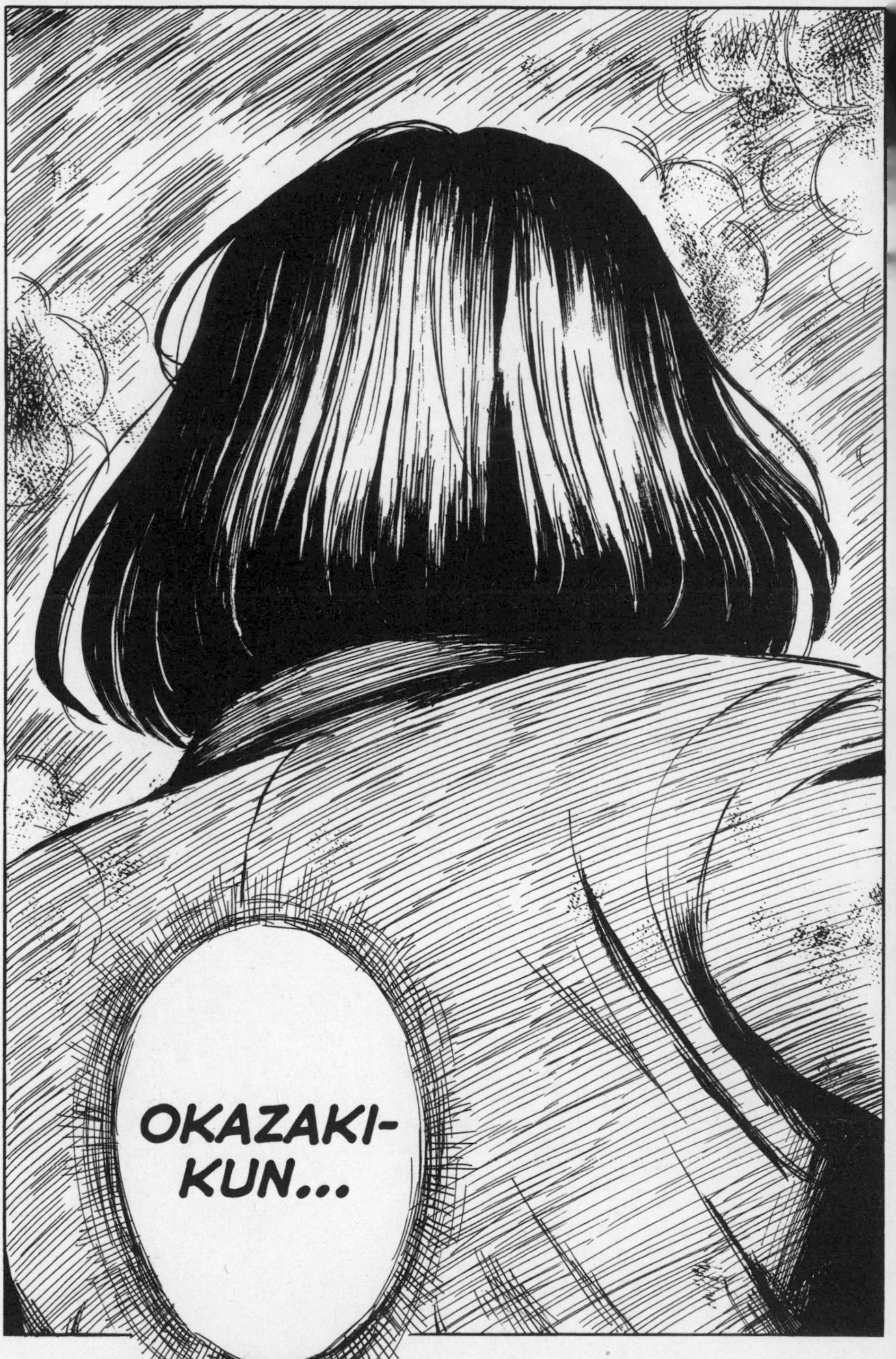
OKAZAKI-KUN...

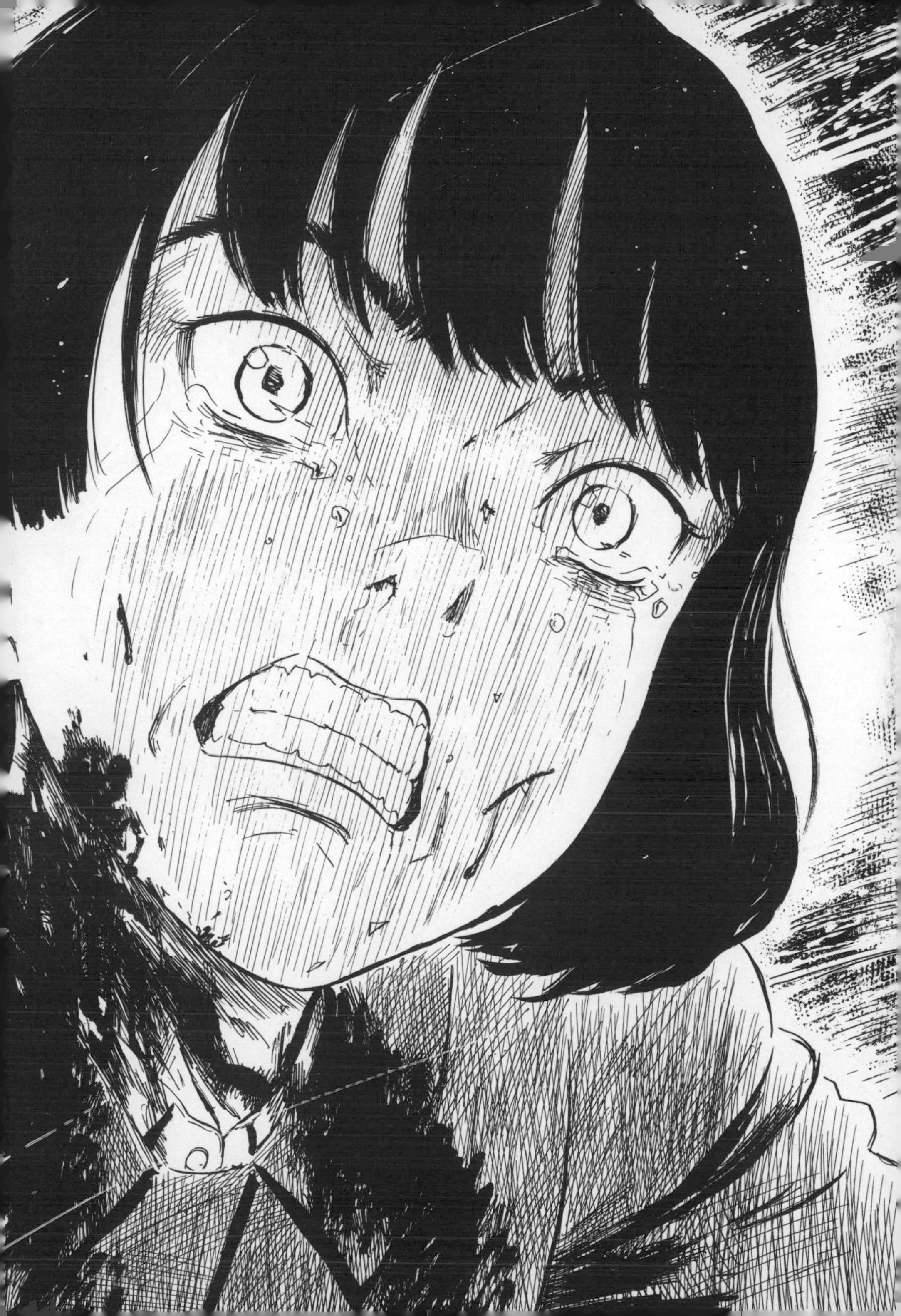

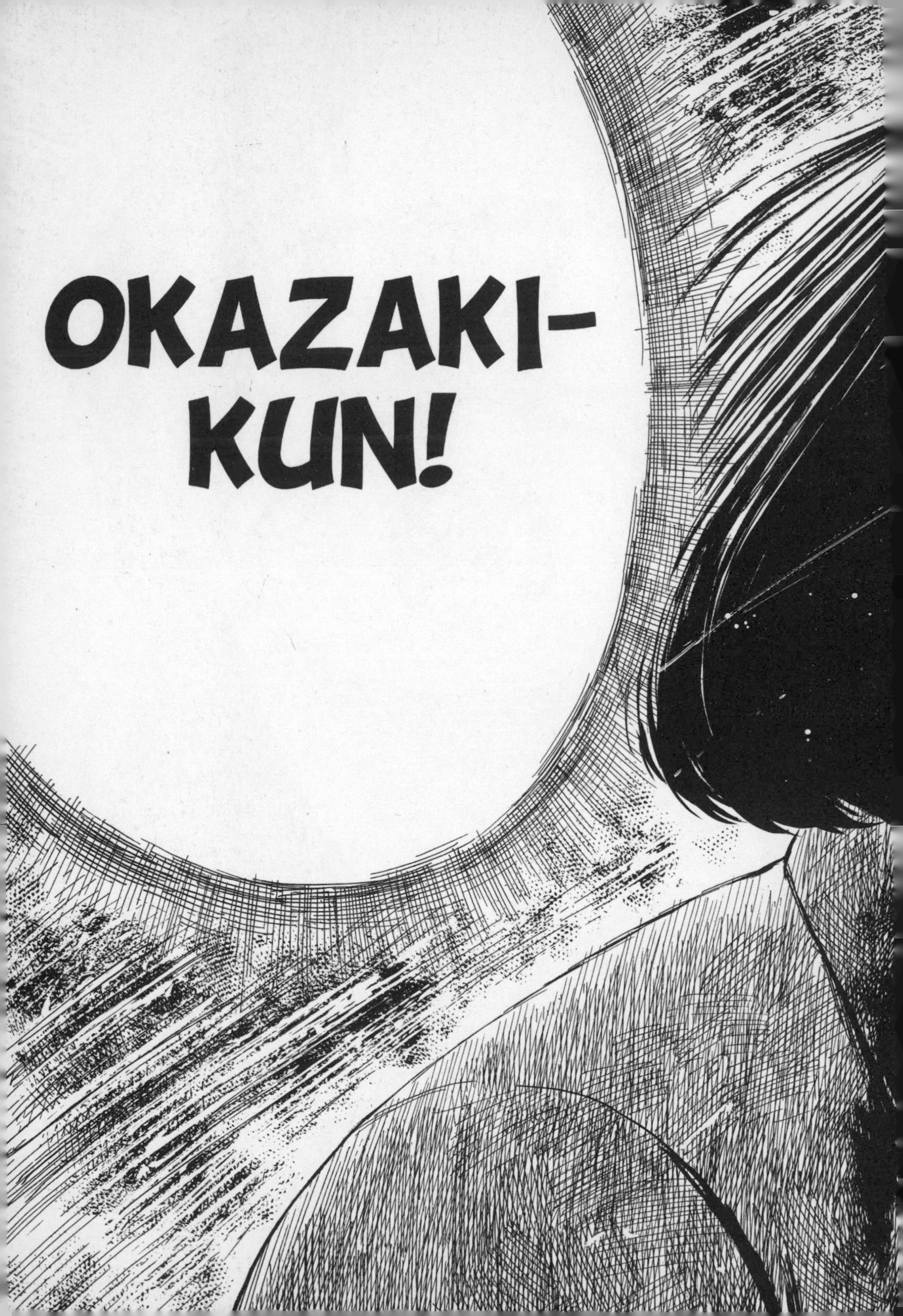
OKAZAKI-KUN!

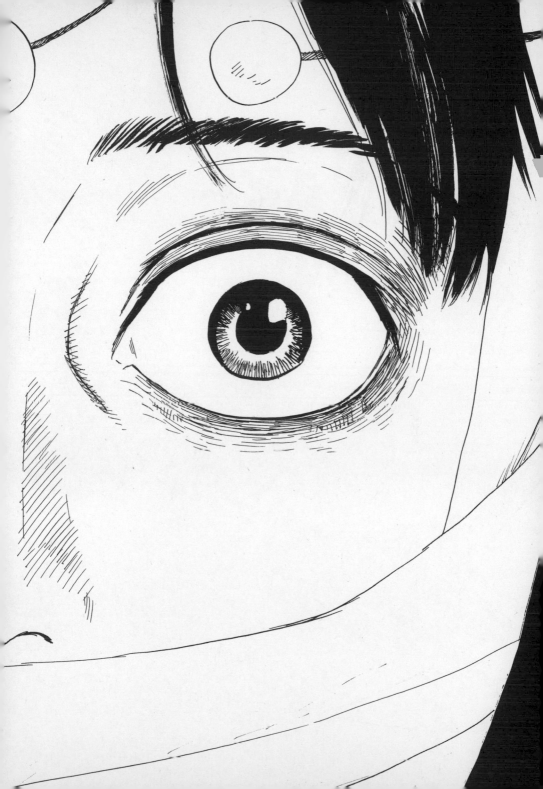

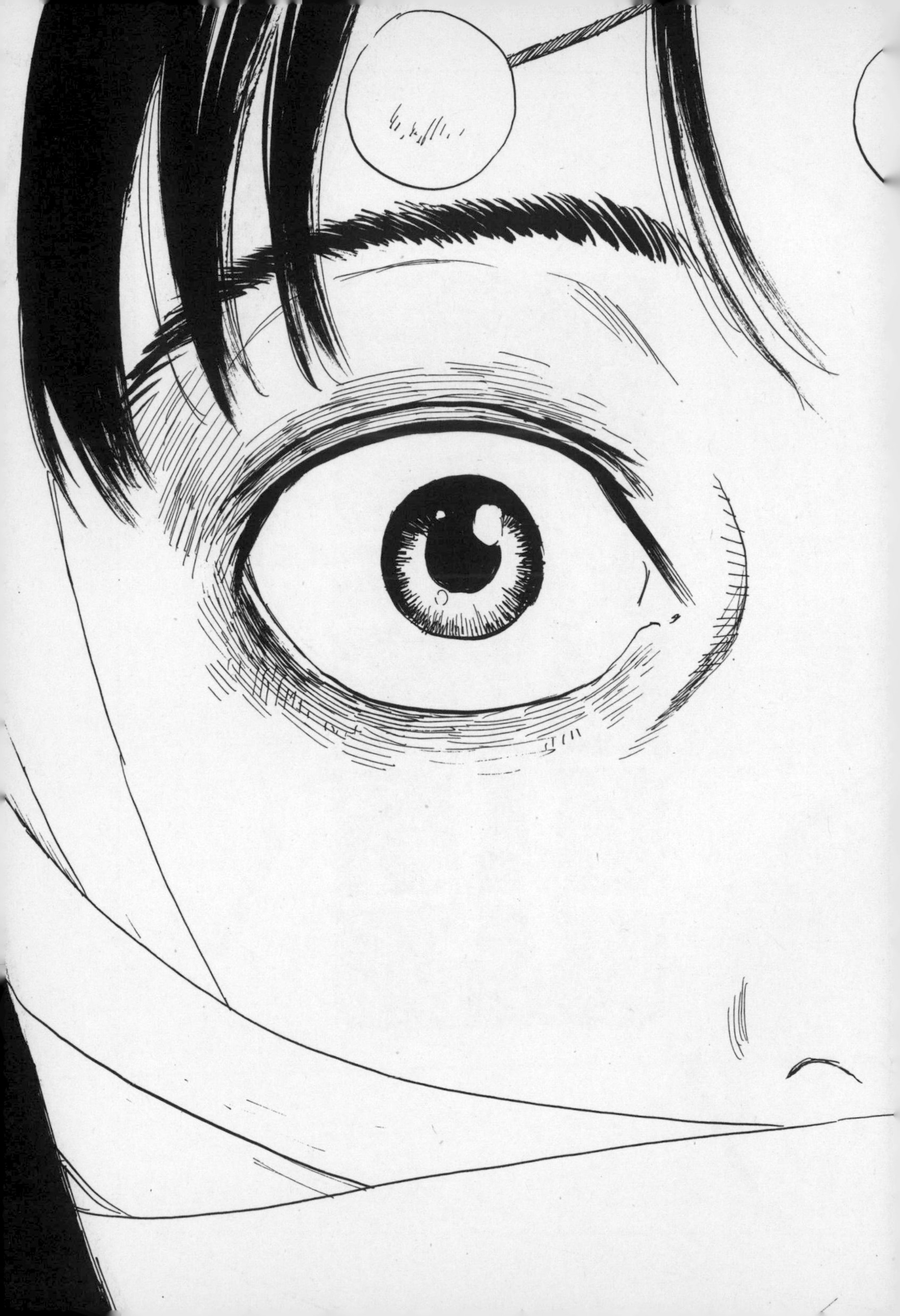

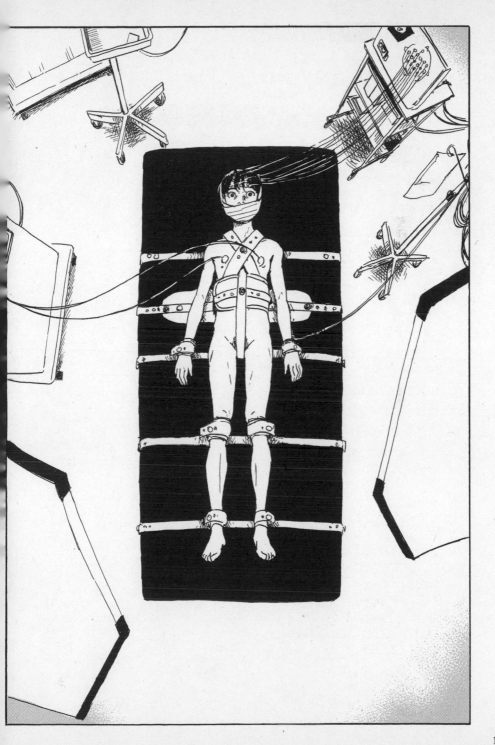

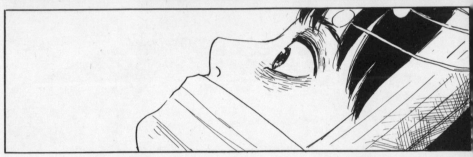

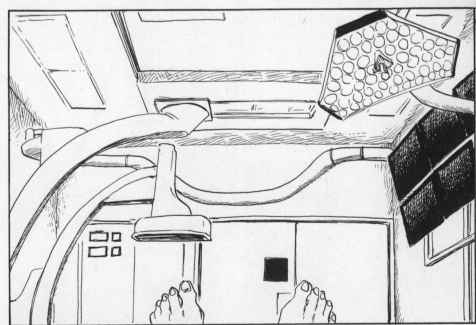

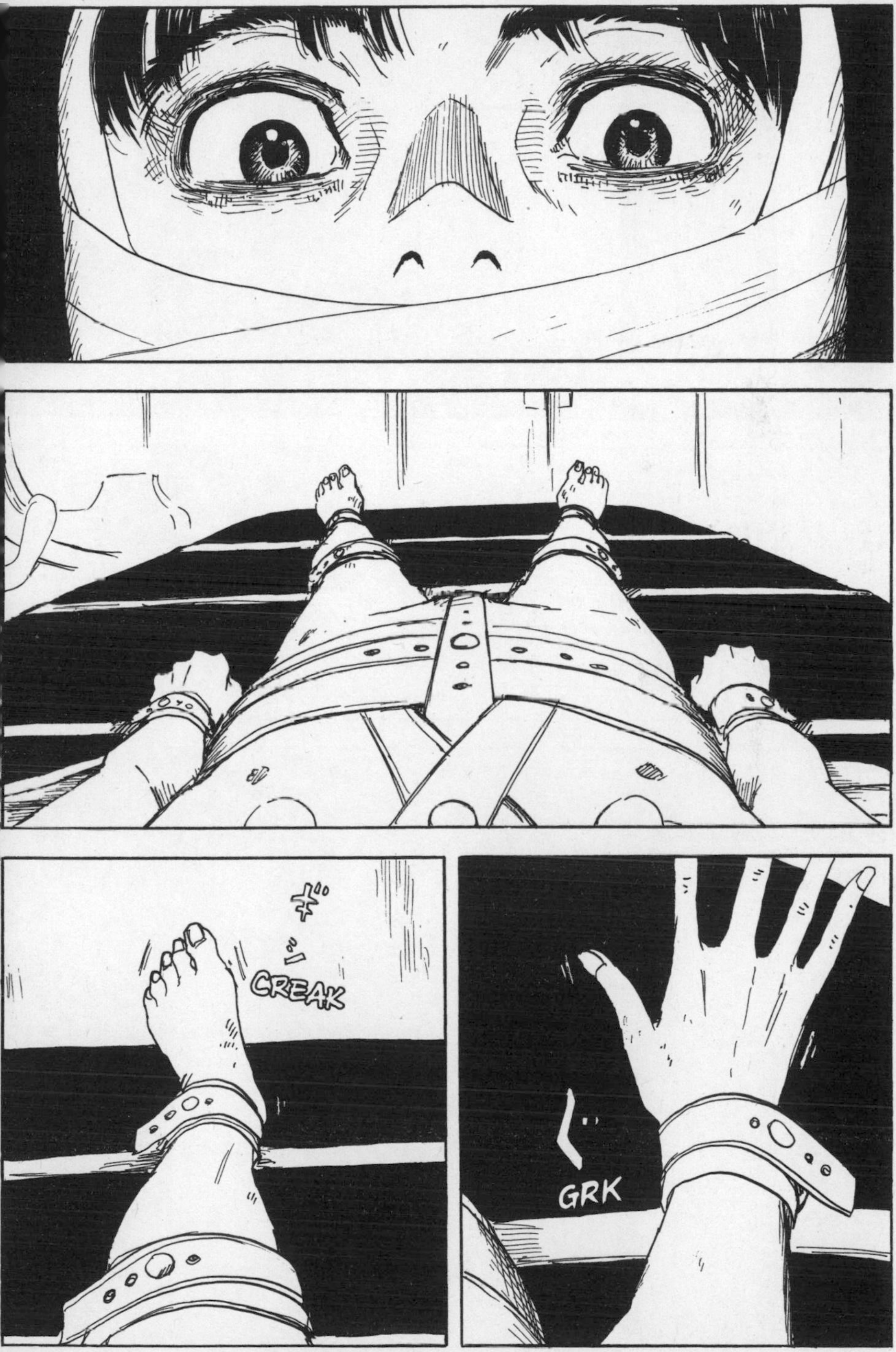
GRK
CREAK

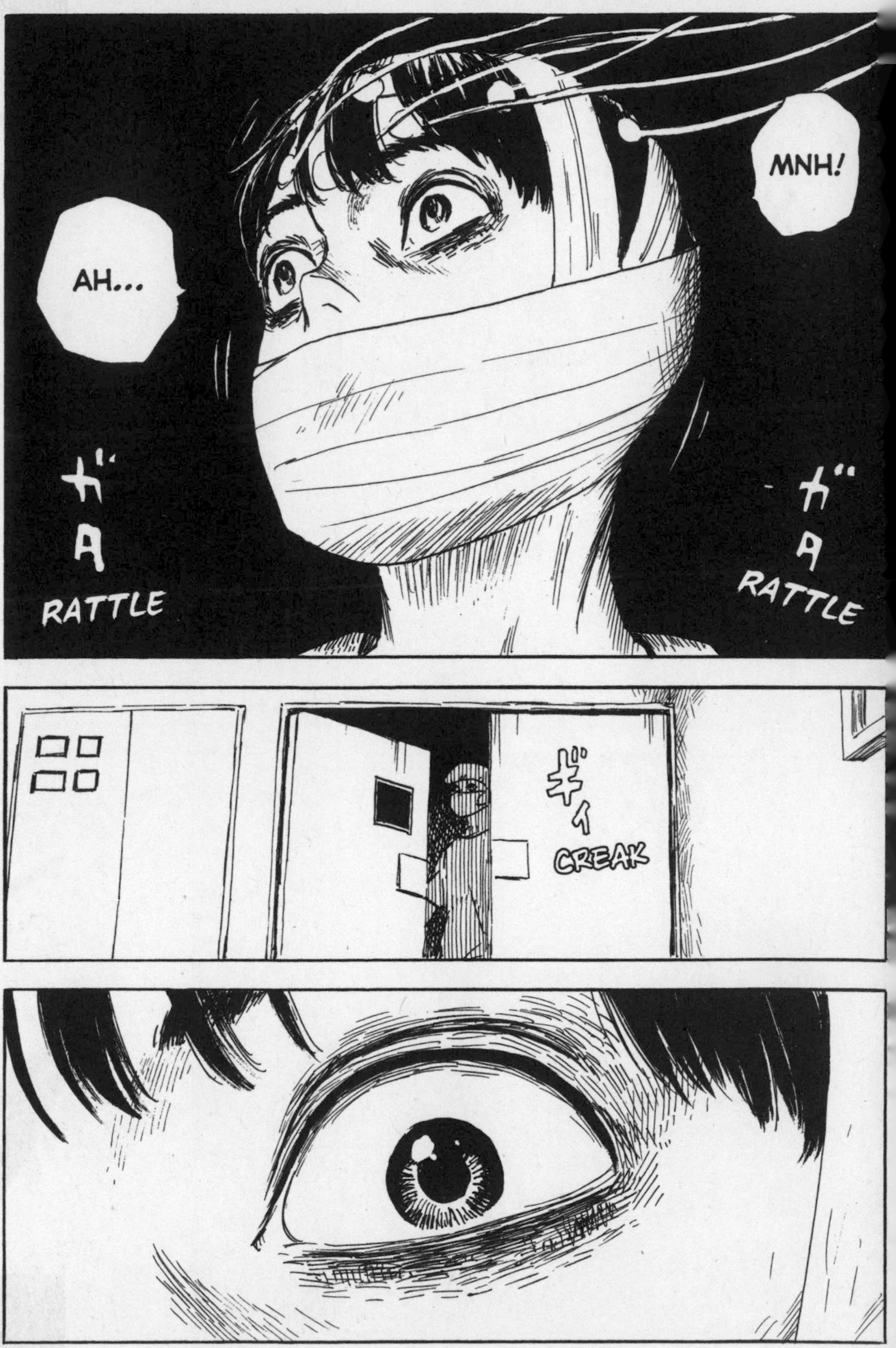
MNH!
AH...
ガタ
RATTLE
ガタ
RATTLE
ギイ
CREAK

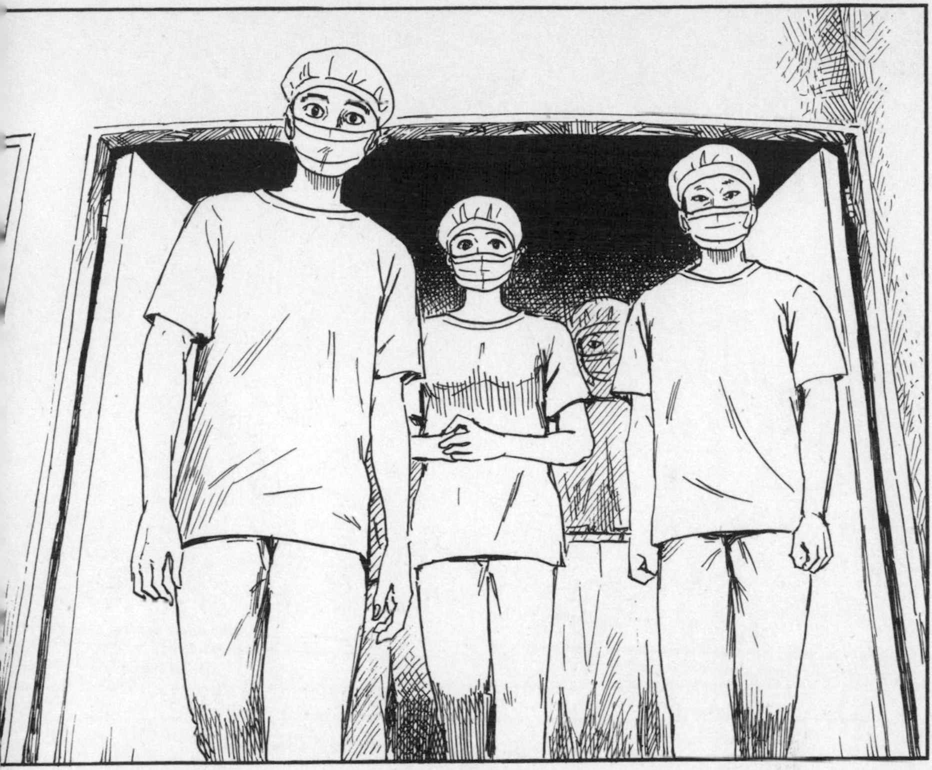

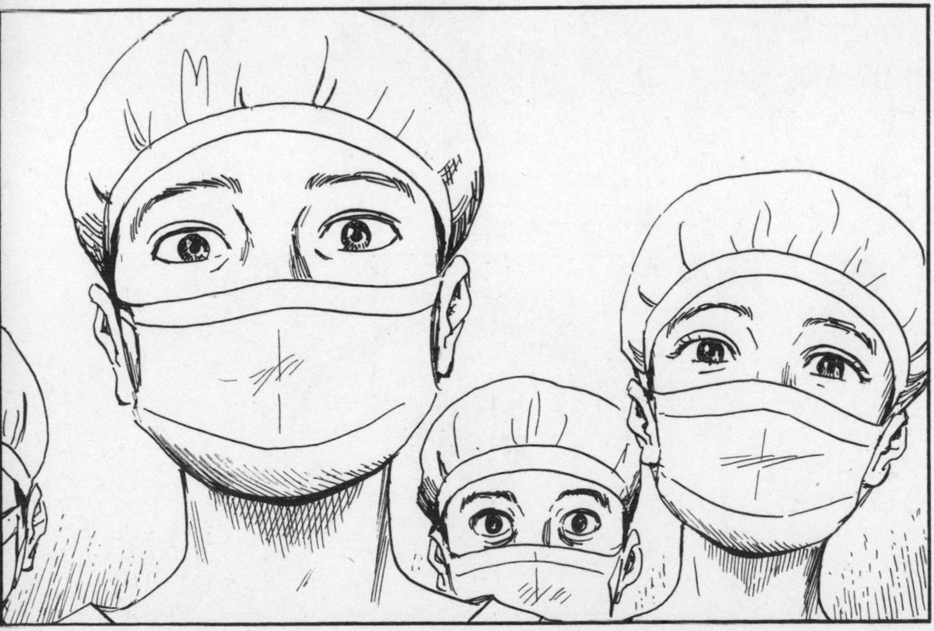

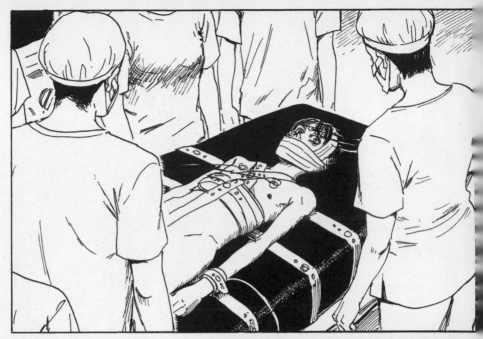

CAN YOU
HEAR ME?

131

TELL ME
WHAT
YOUR
NAME IS.

...OKA-
ZAKI
...

MAKOTO
...

WHERE
AM I?

WHERE'D
YOU TAKE
ME?

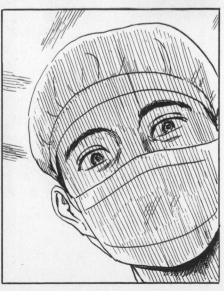

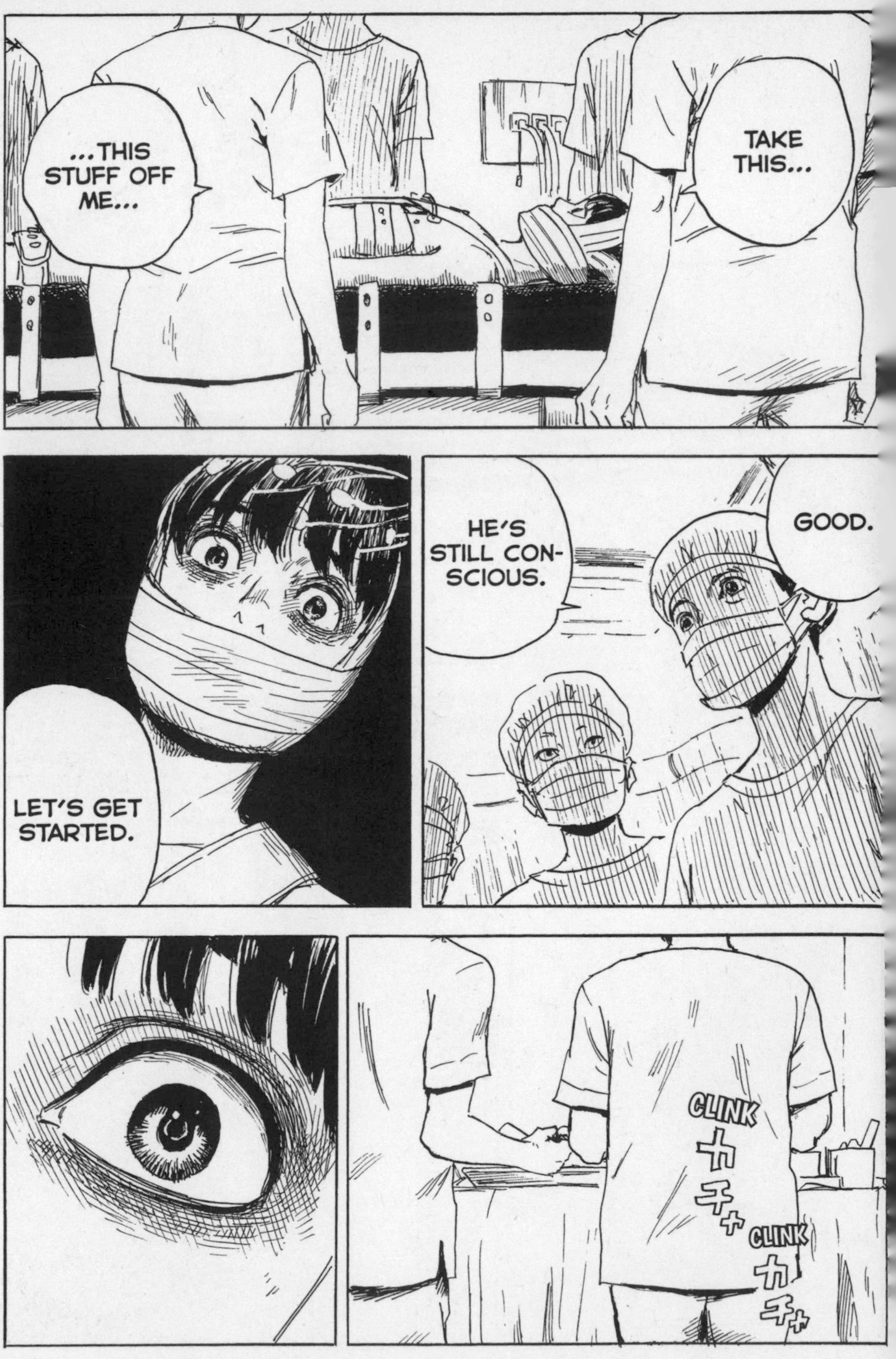
TAKE THIS...
...THIS STUFF OFF ME...
GOOD.
HE'S STILL CONSCIOUS.
LET'S GET STARTED.
CLINK
カチャ
CLINK
カチャ

W-
WAIT...
STOP...
WHY?!
ガタ
RATTLE
ガタ
RATTLE

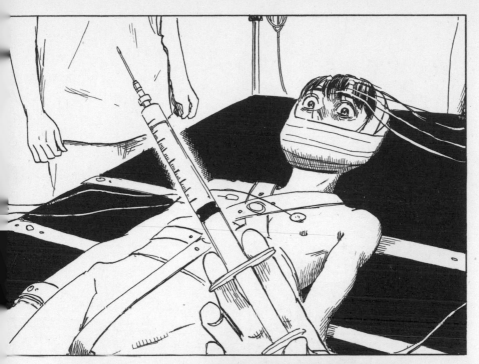

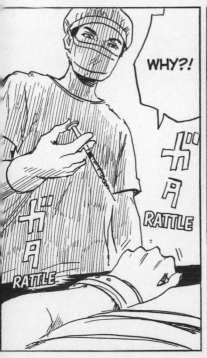

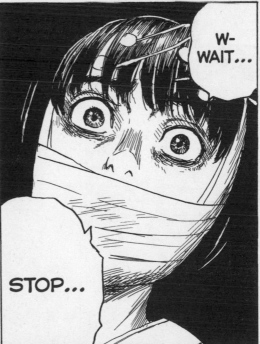

WHAT DID I EVER DO?!
WHY ARE YOU DOING THIS TO ME?!
N-NO!!
HELP ME!!
HELP...

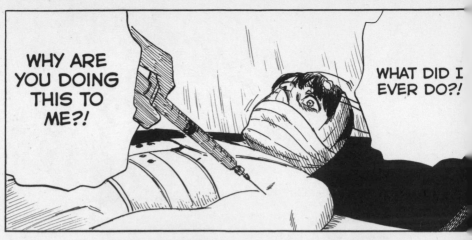

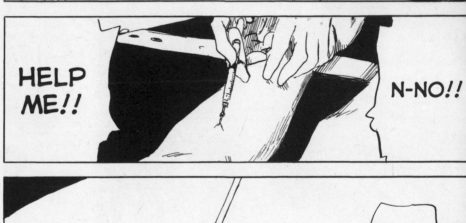

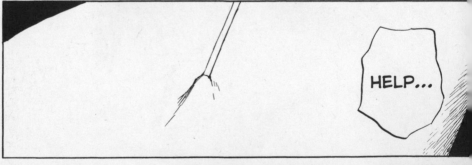

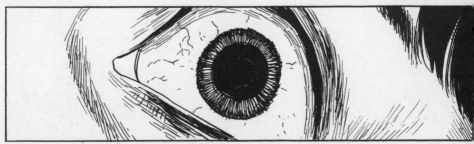

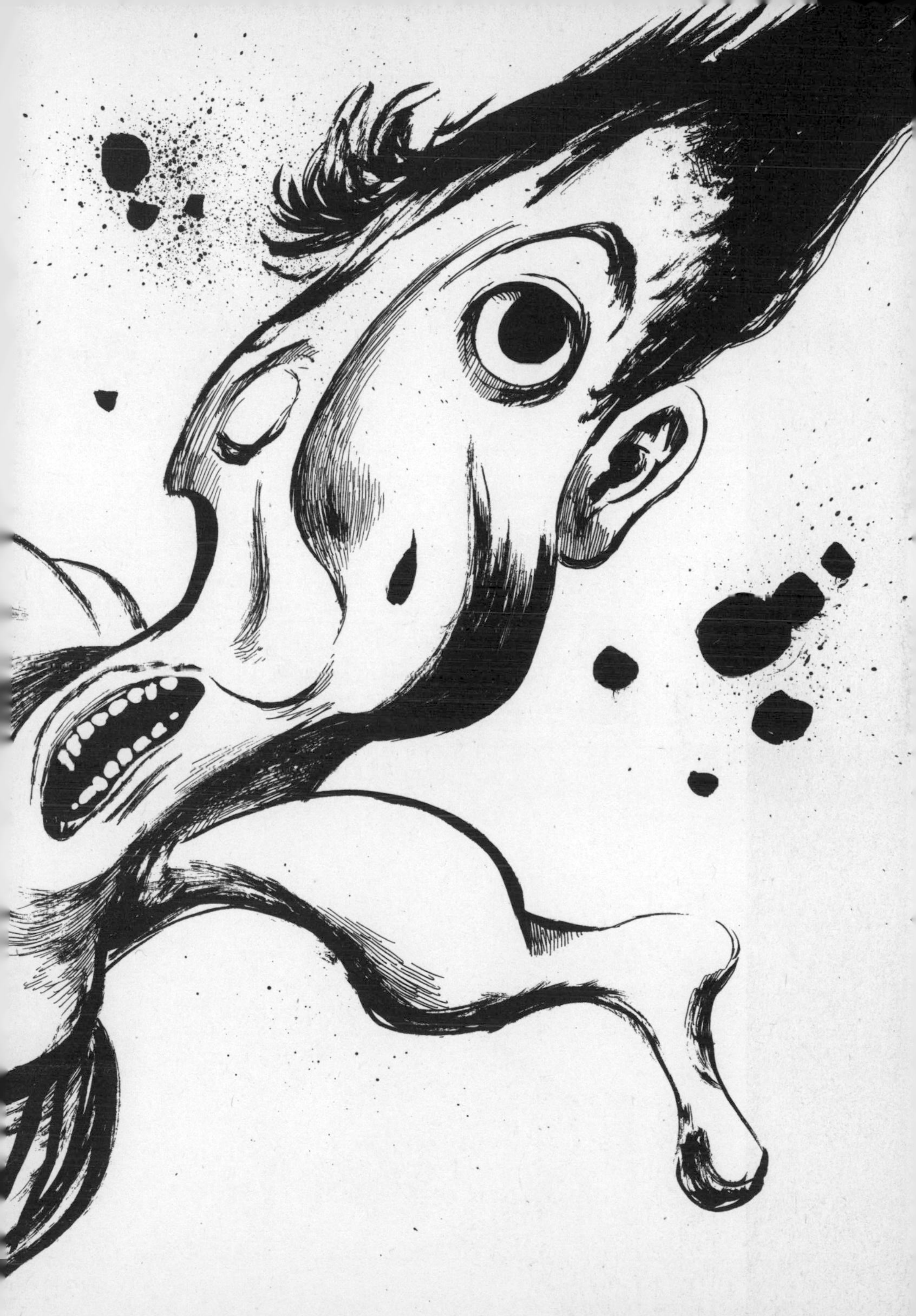

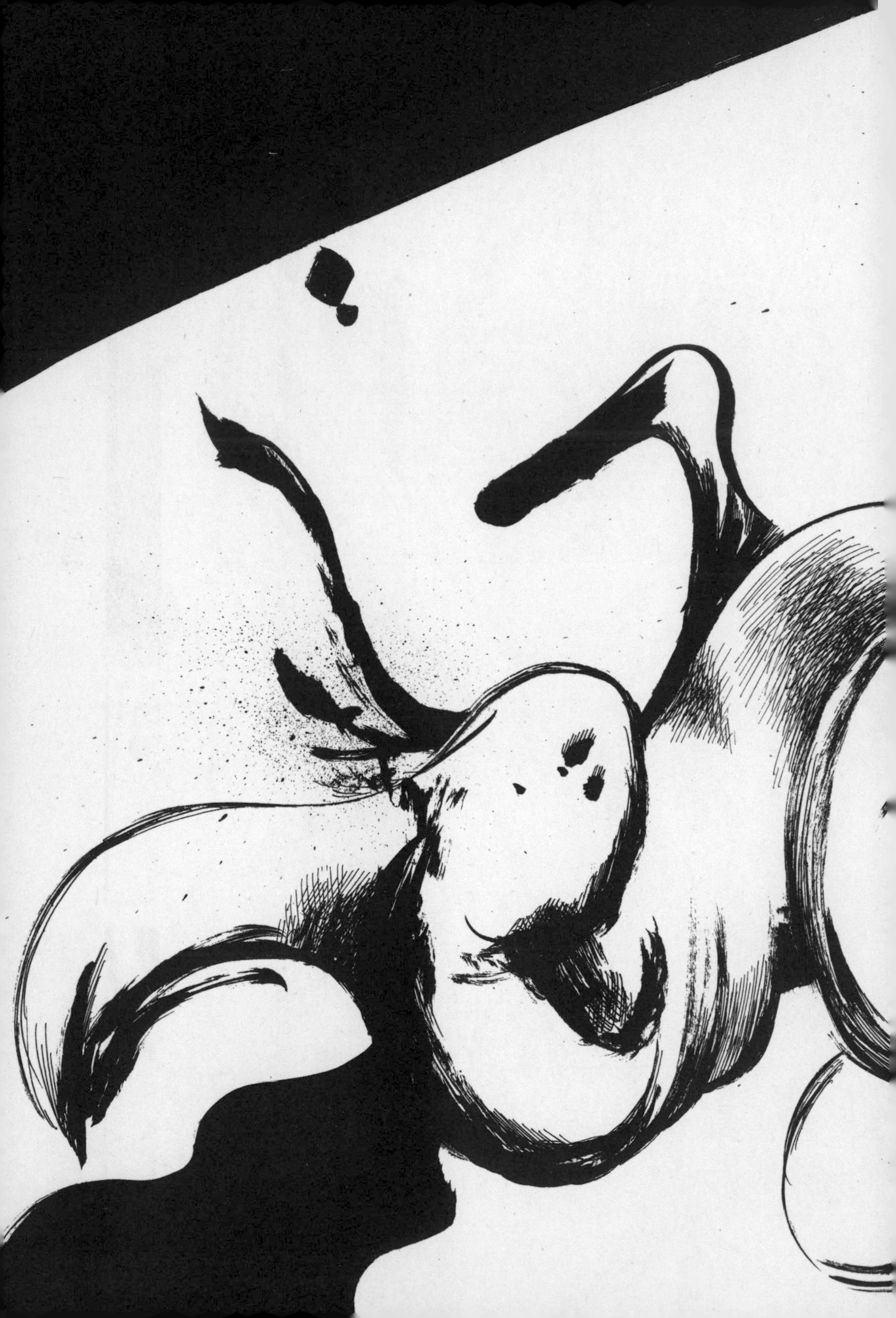

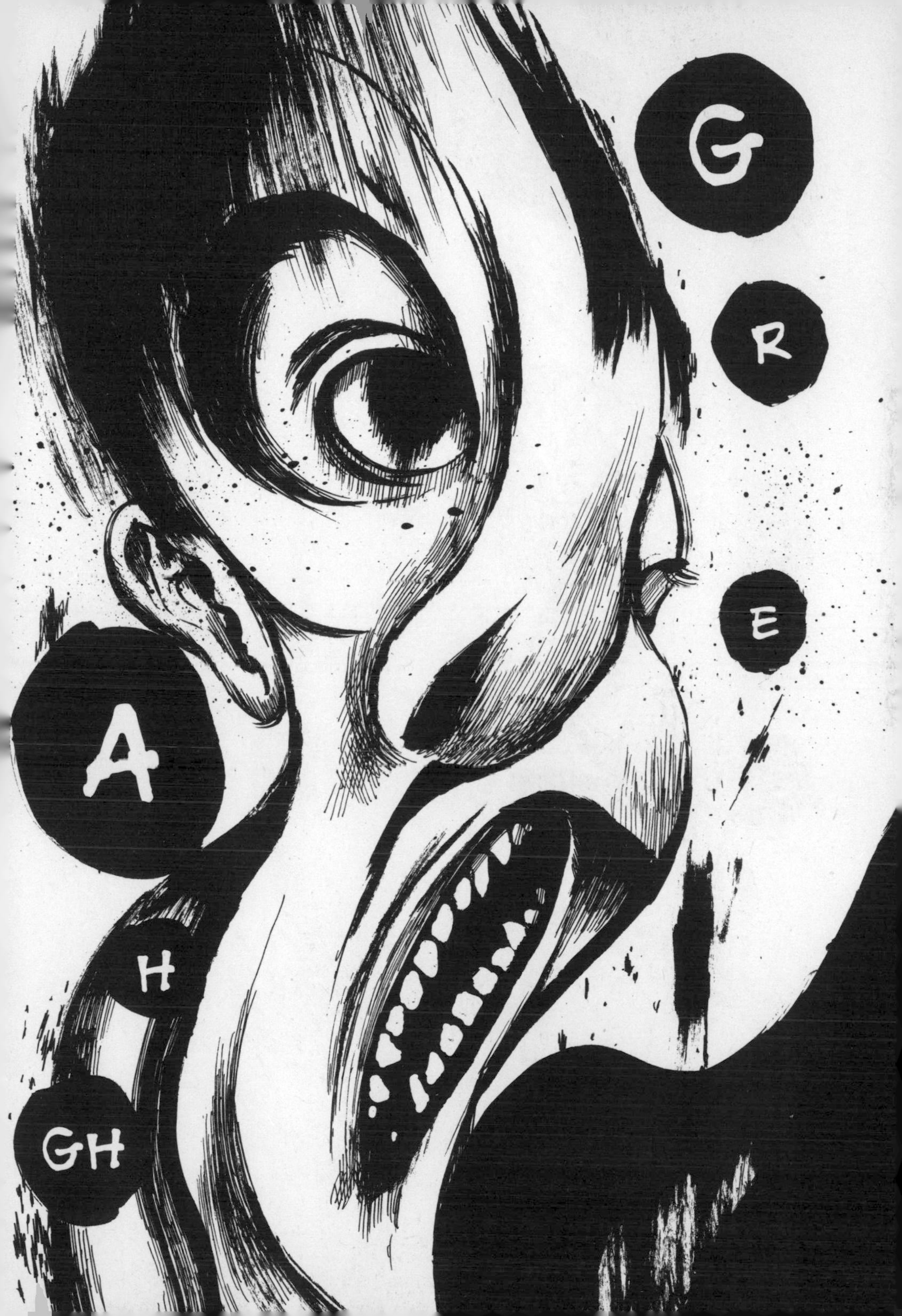
G
R
E
A
H
GH

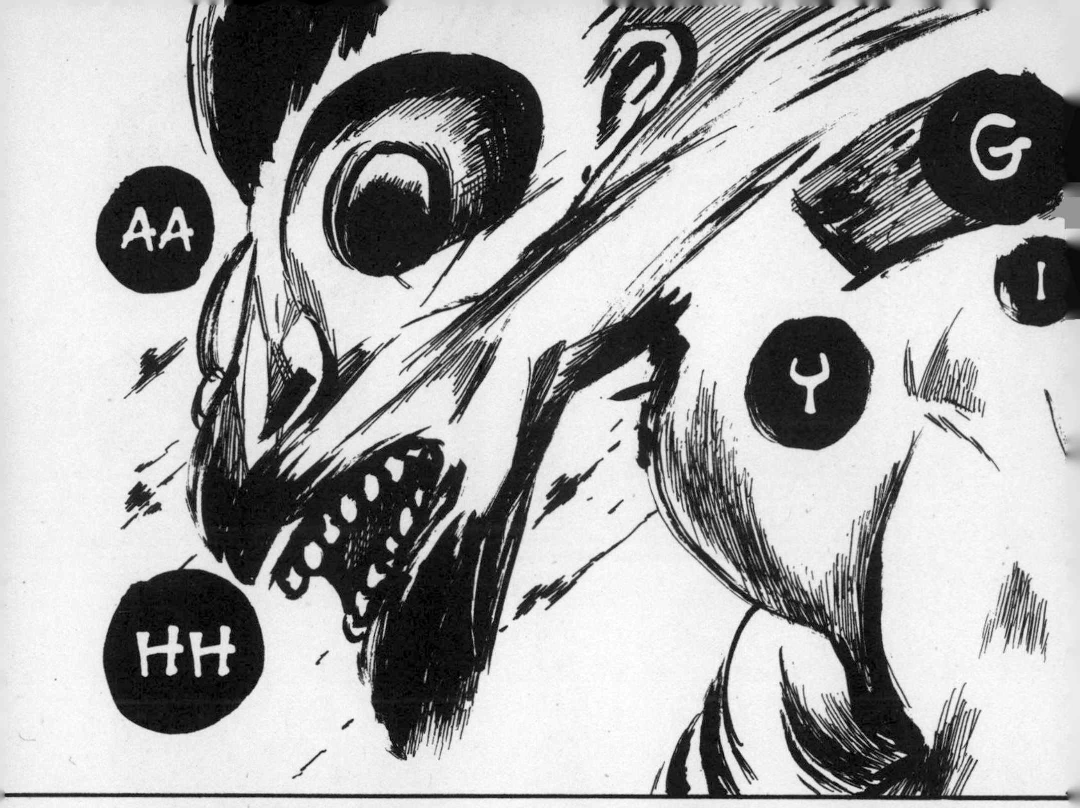
G
I
Y
AA
HH

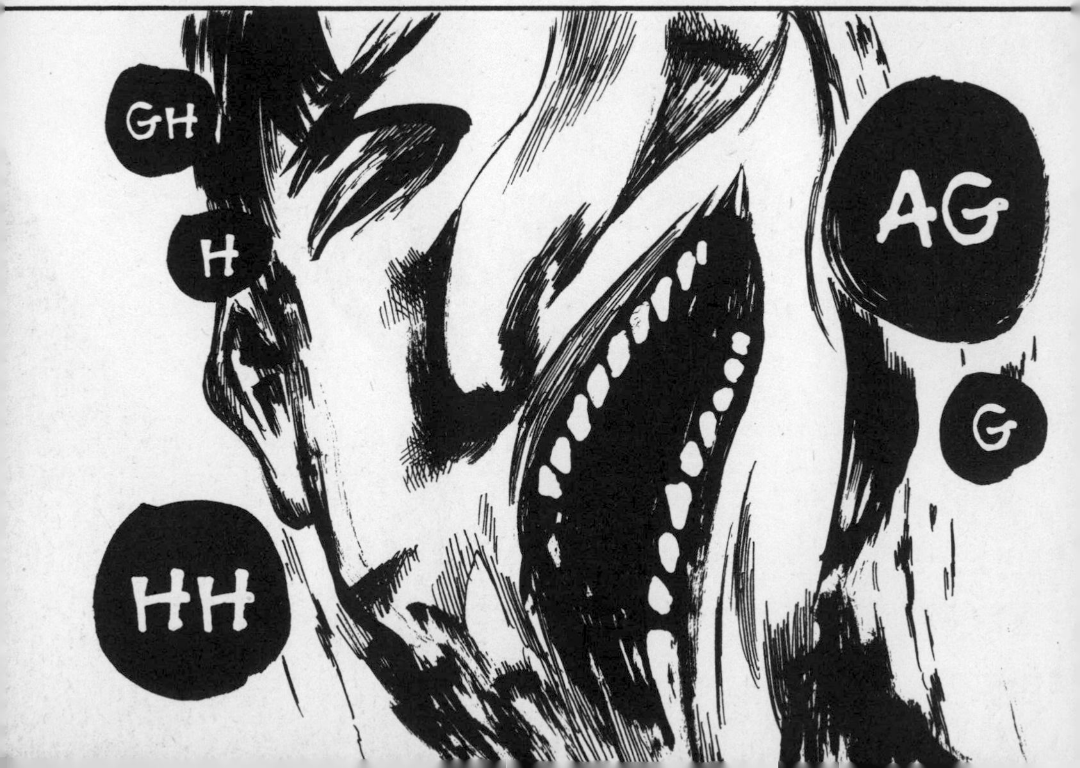
AG
G
GH
H
HH

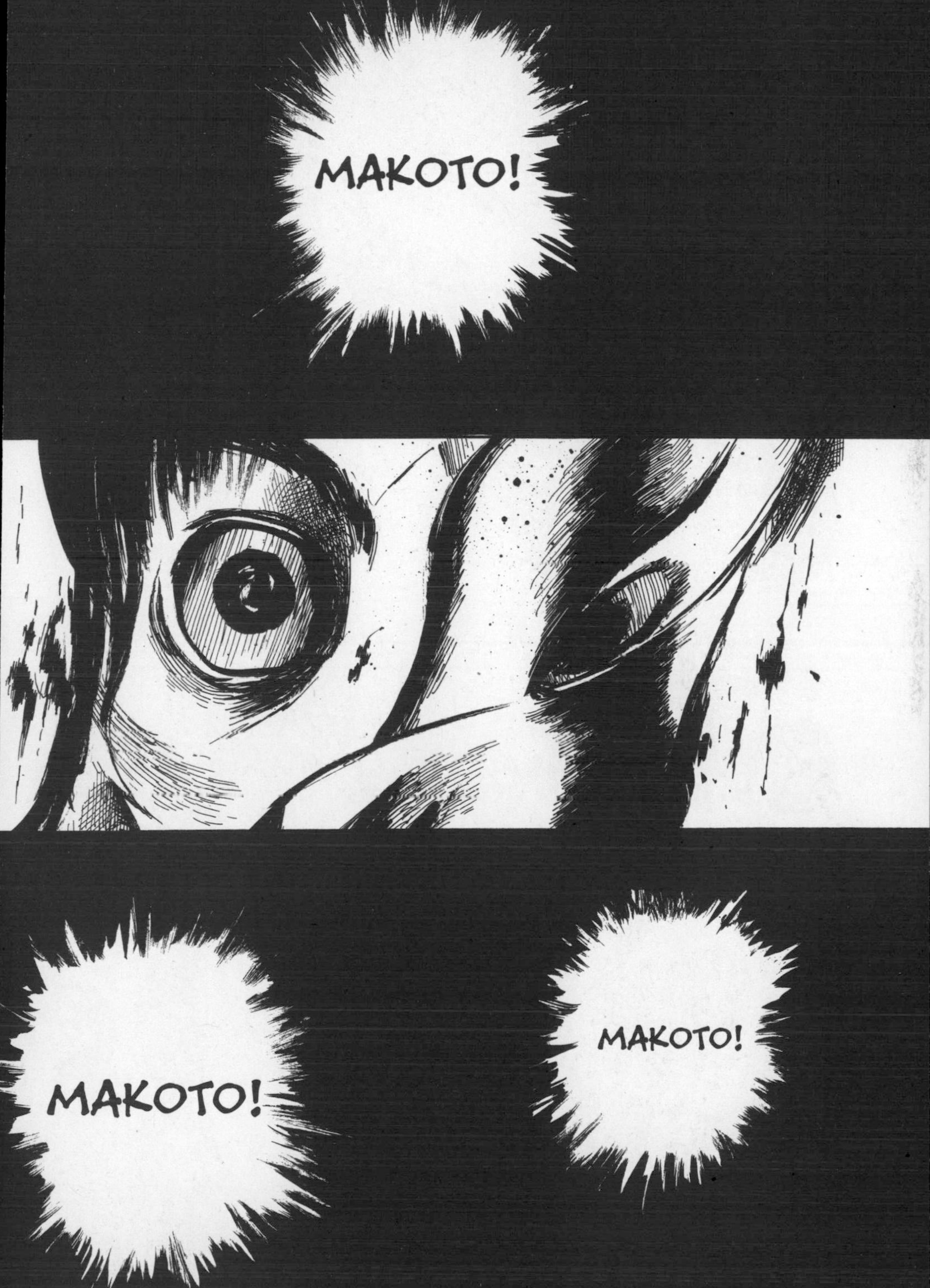
MAKOTO!
MAKOTO!
MAKOTO!

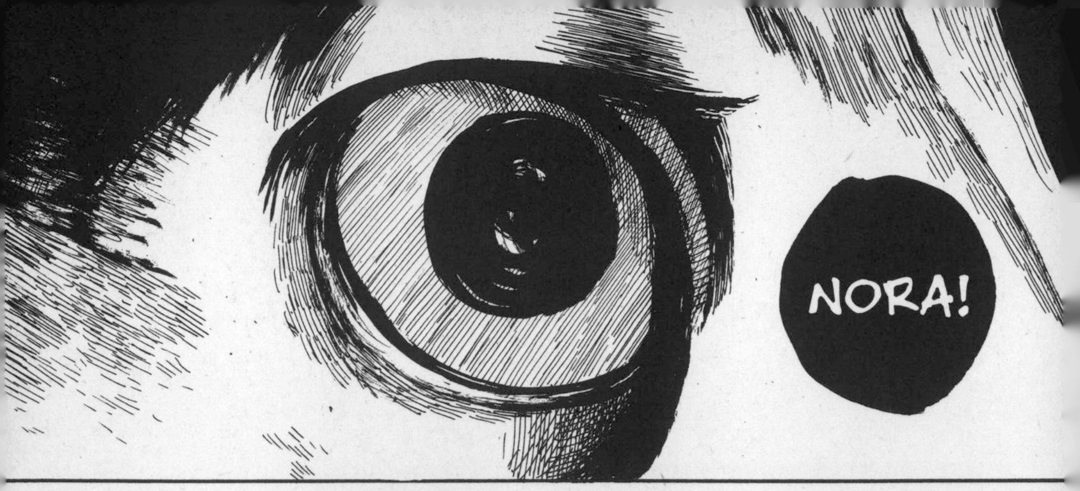
NORA!

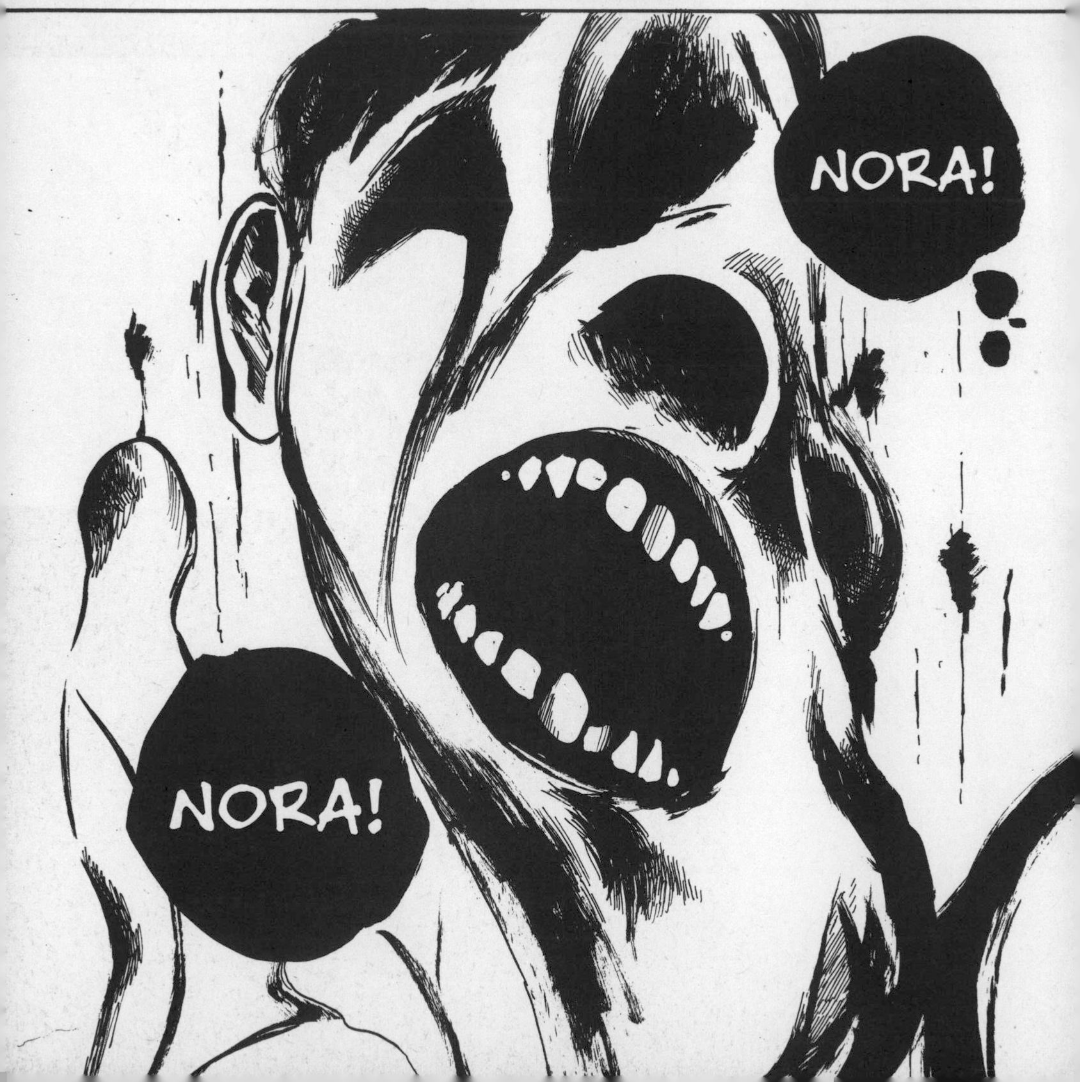
NORA!
NORA!

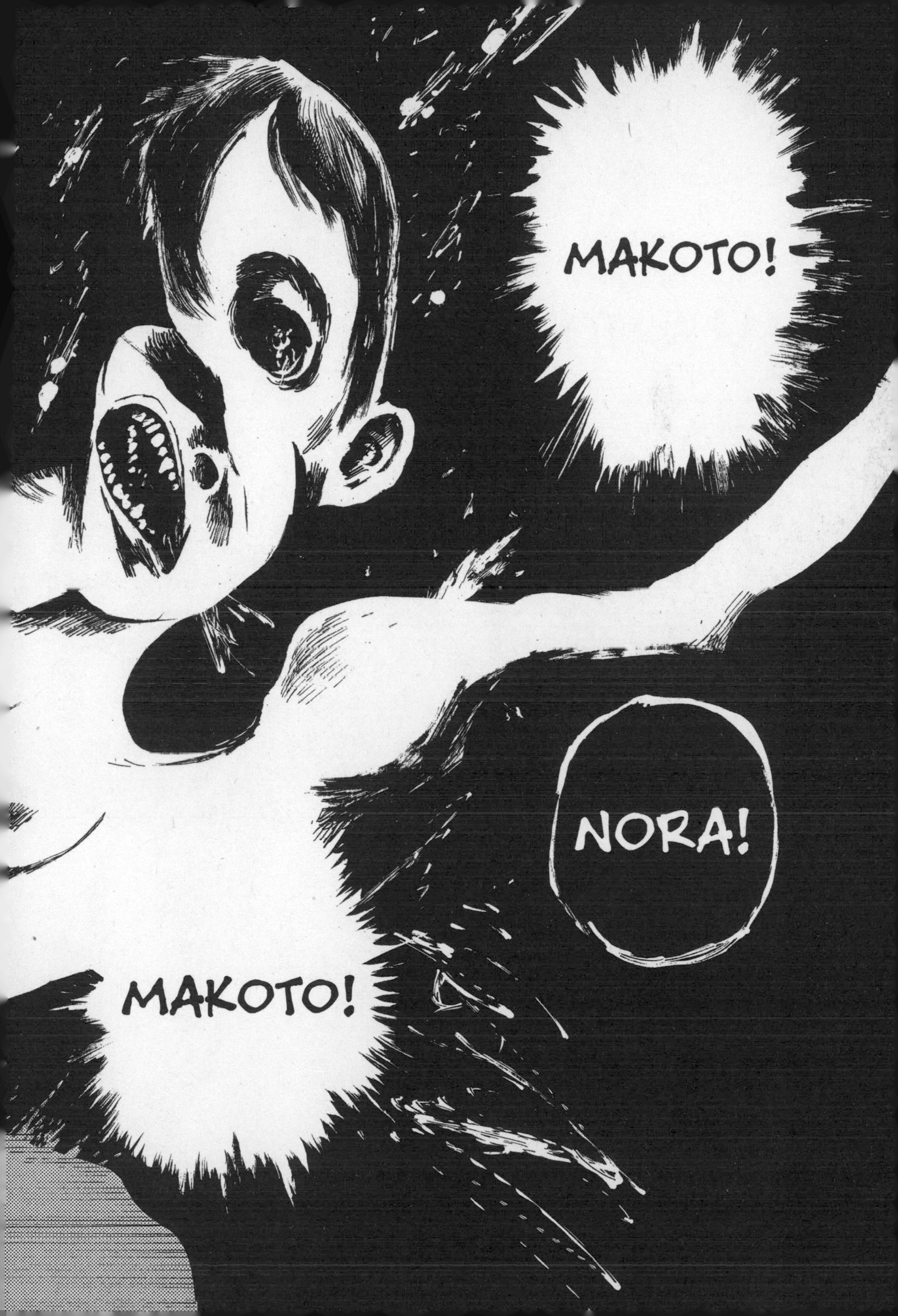
MAKOTO!
NORA!
MAKOTO!

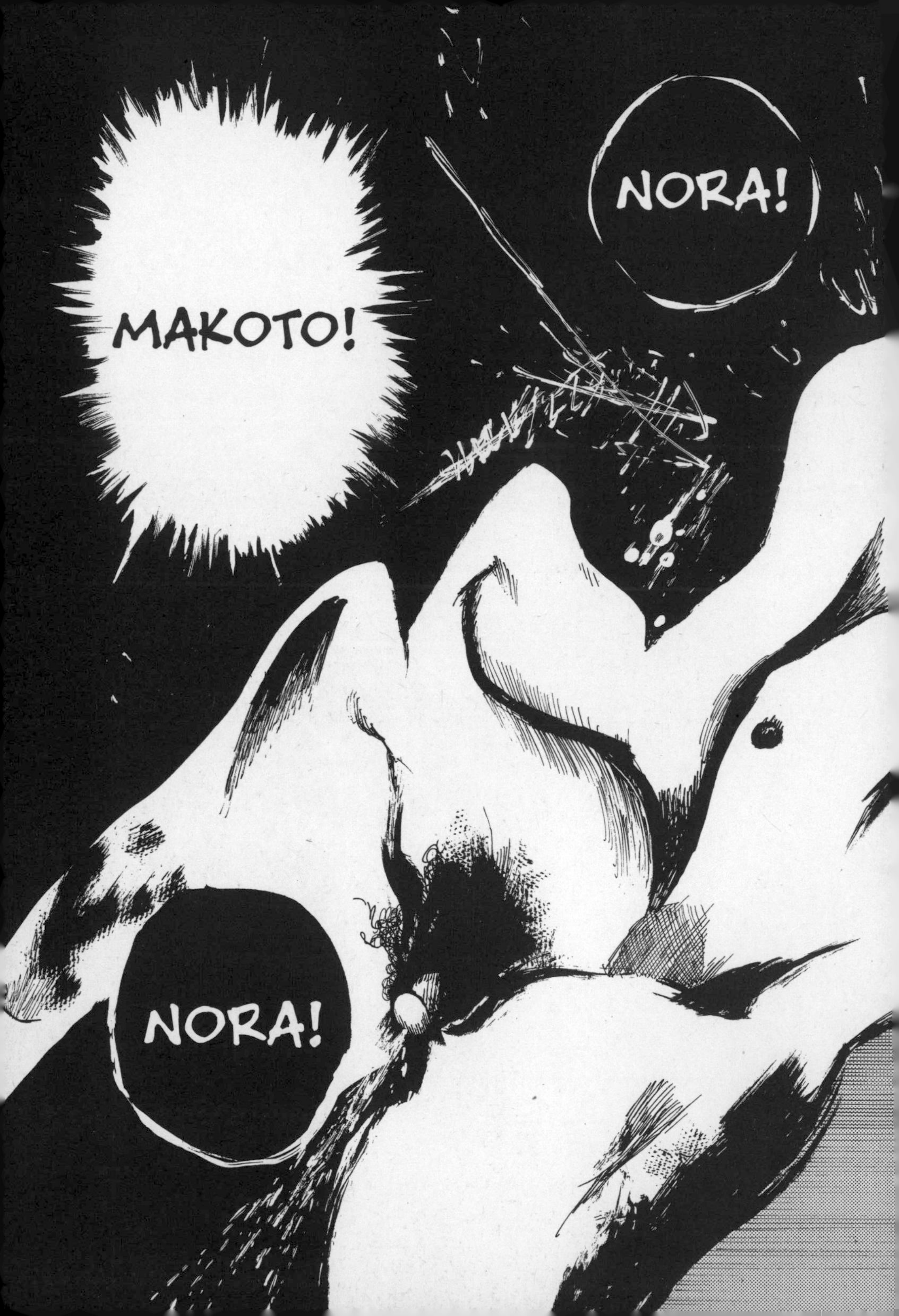
NORA!
MAKOTO!
NORA!

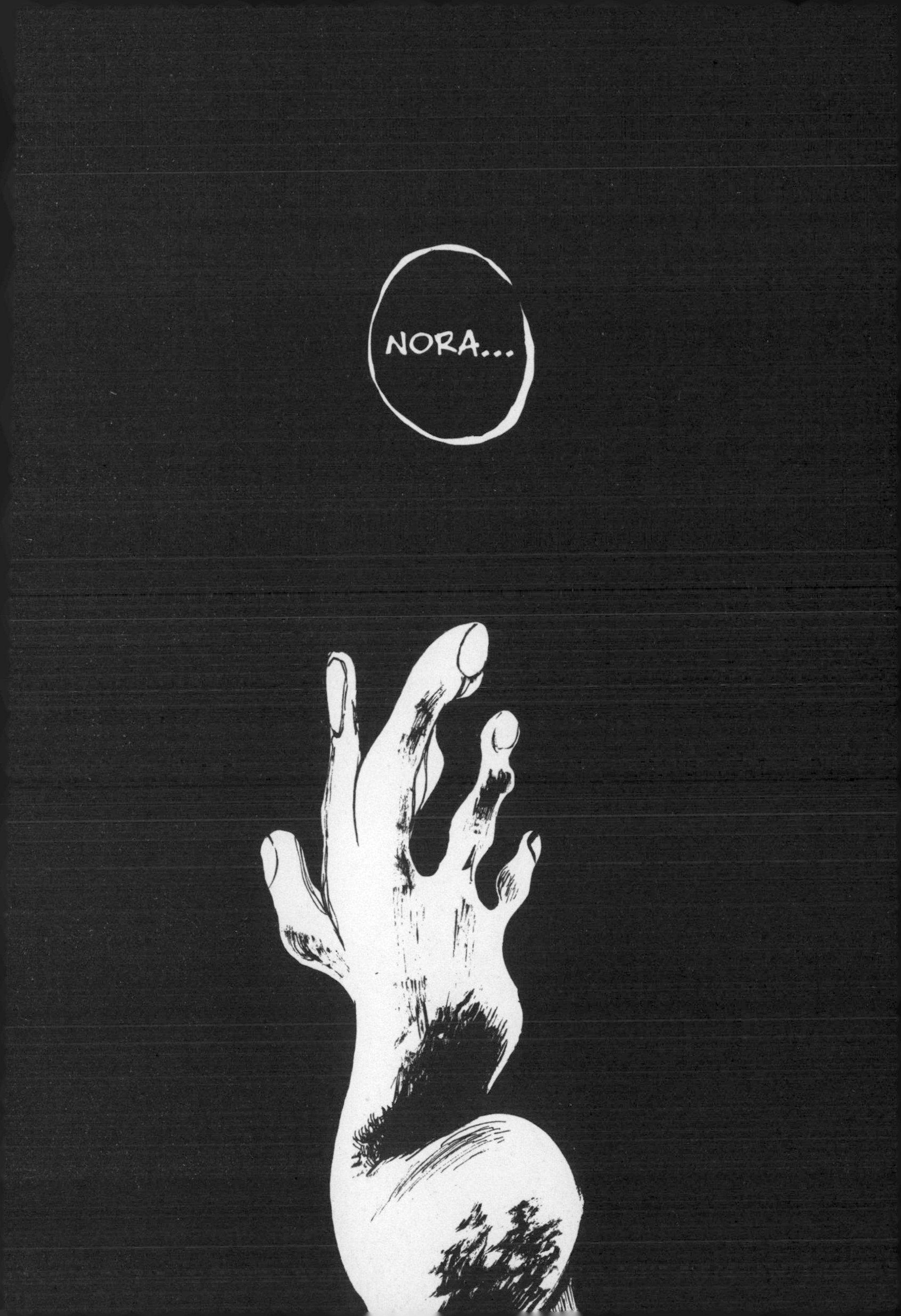
NORA...

Chapter 25: An Old Scar

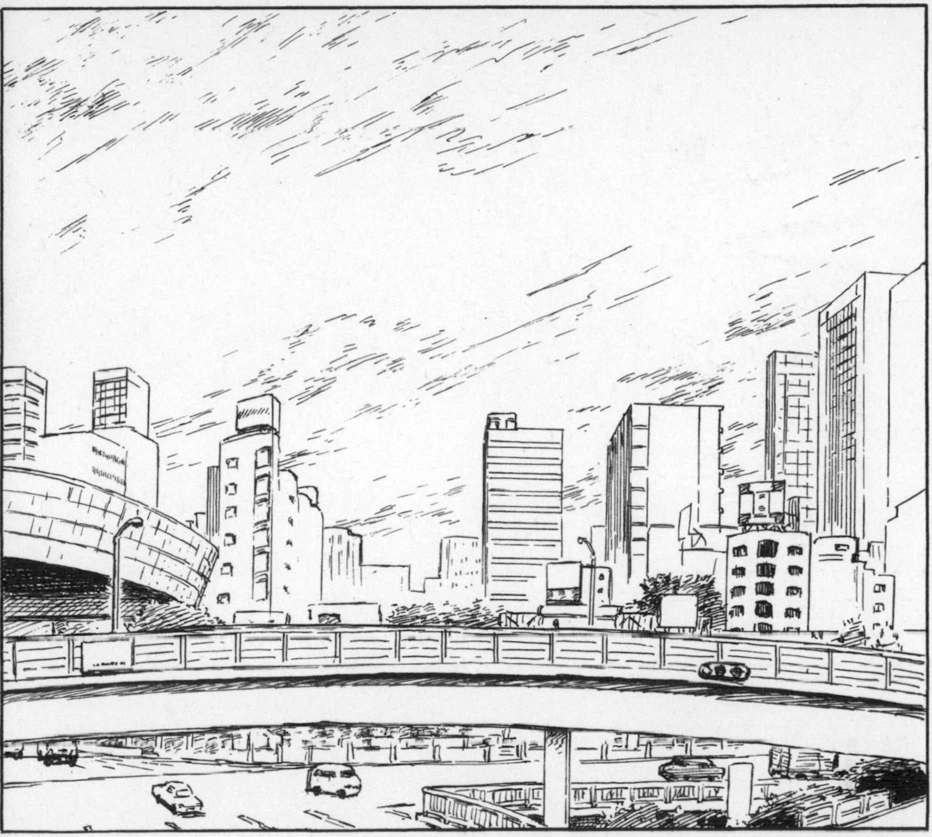

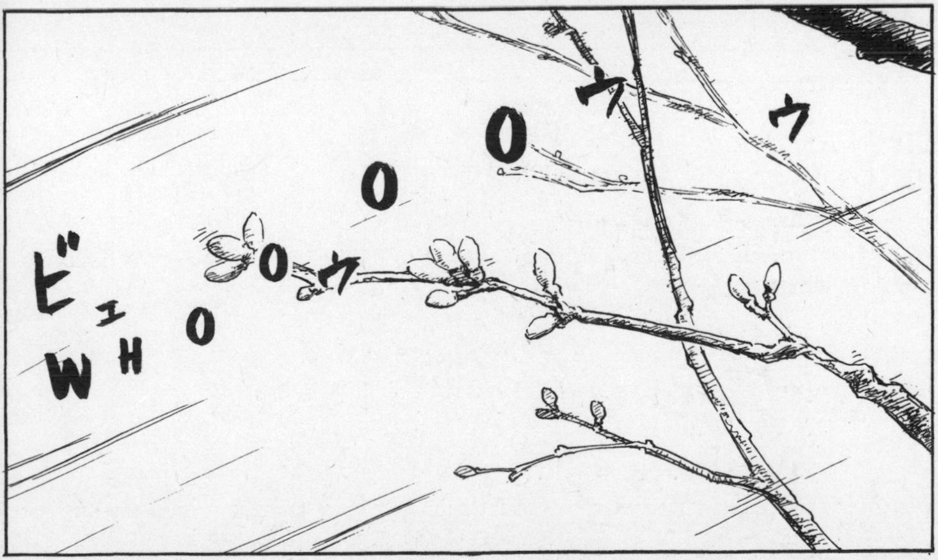
ビュウウウ
WHOOOO

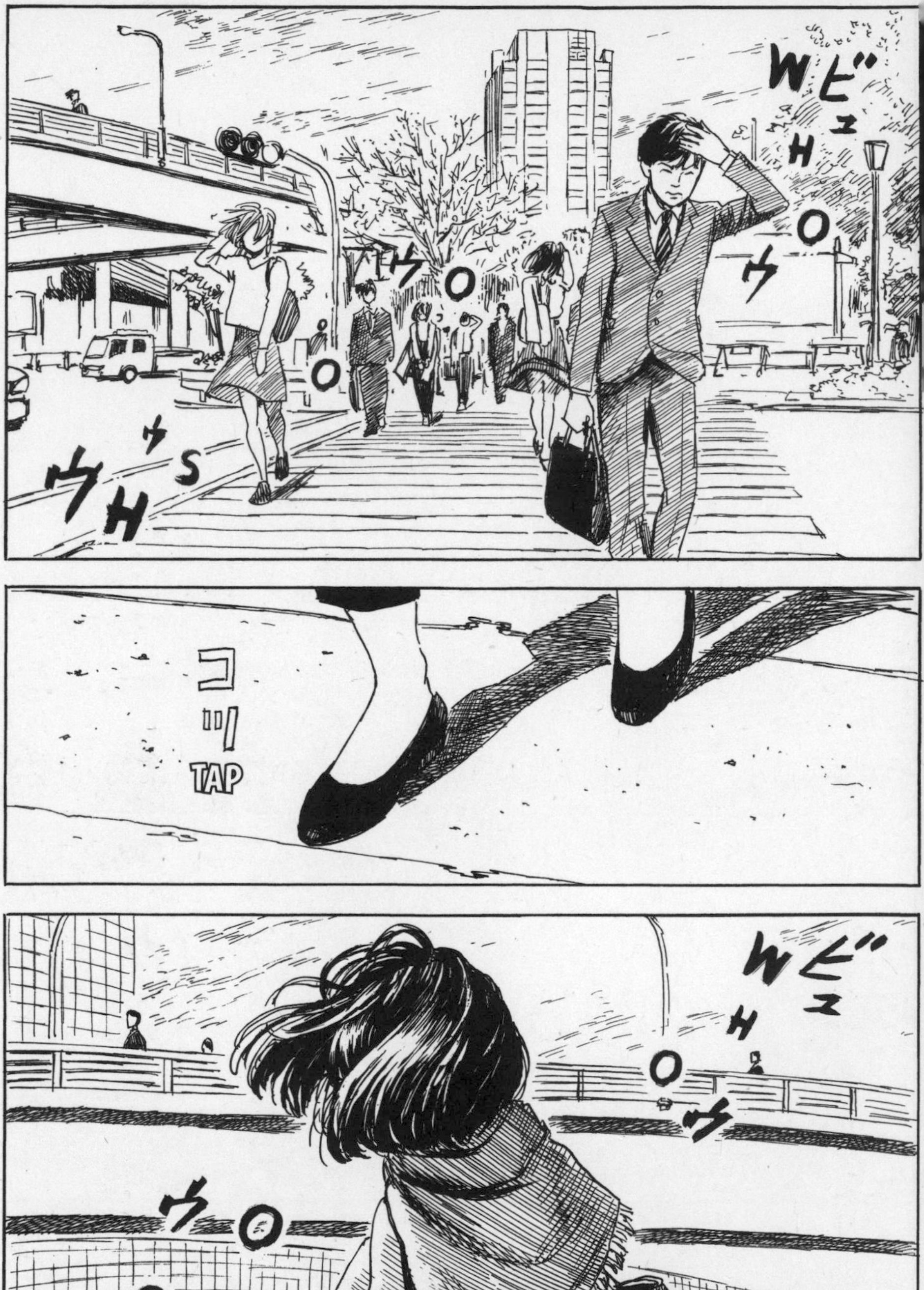

Wビュ
H
O
ウ
ウ
O
O
ウ
S
ウ
H
コッ
TAP
Wビュ
H
O
ウ
ウ
O
O
ウ

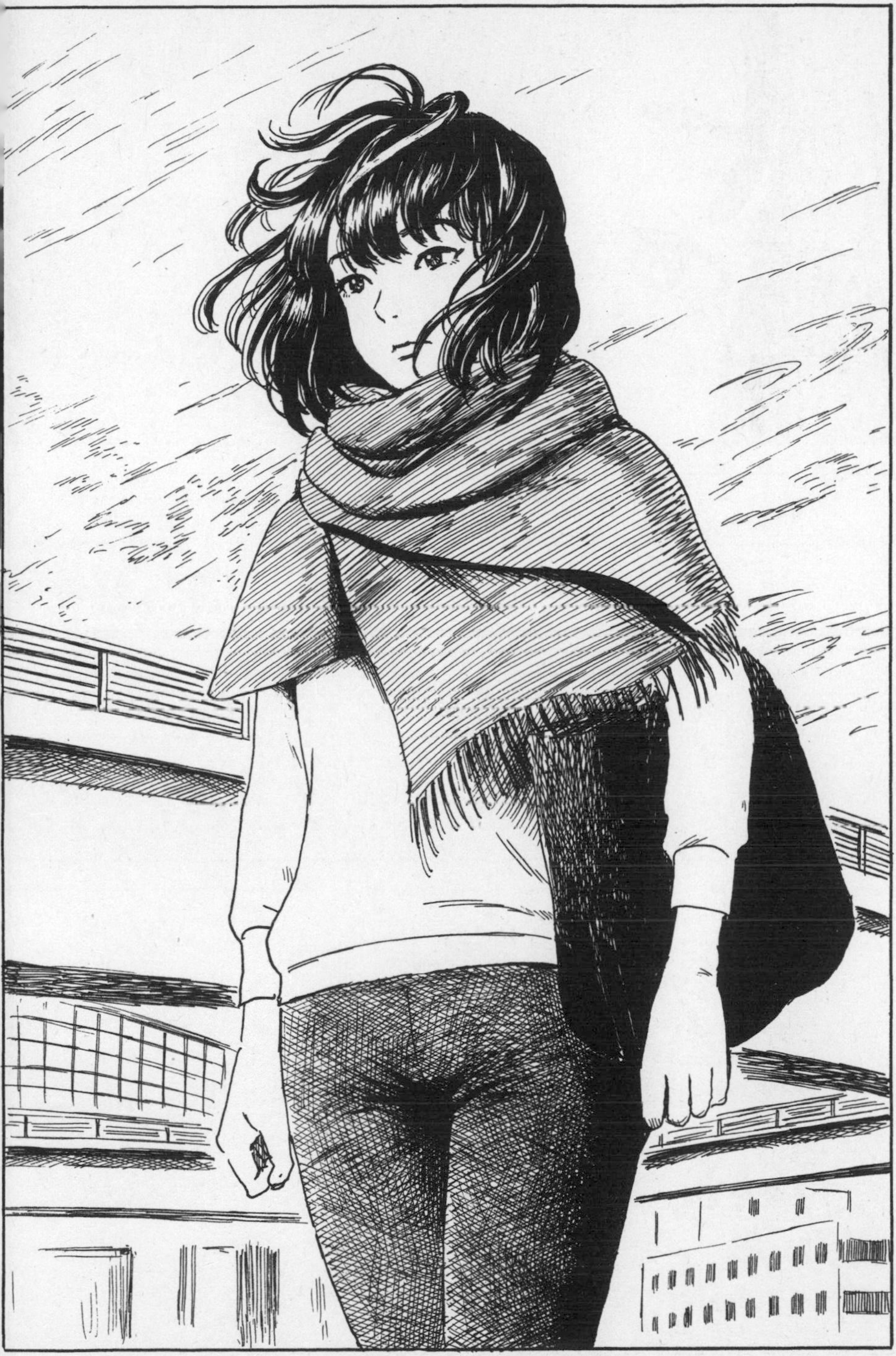

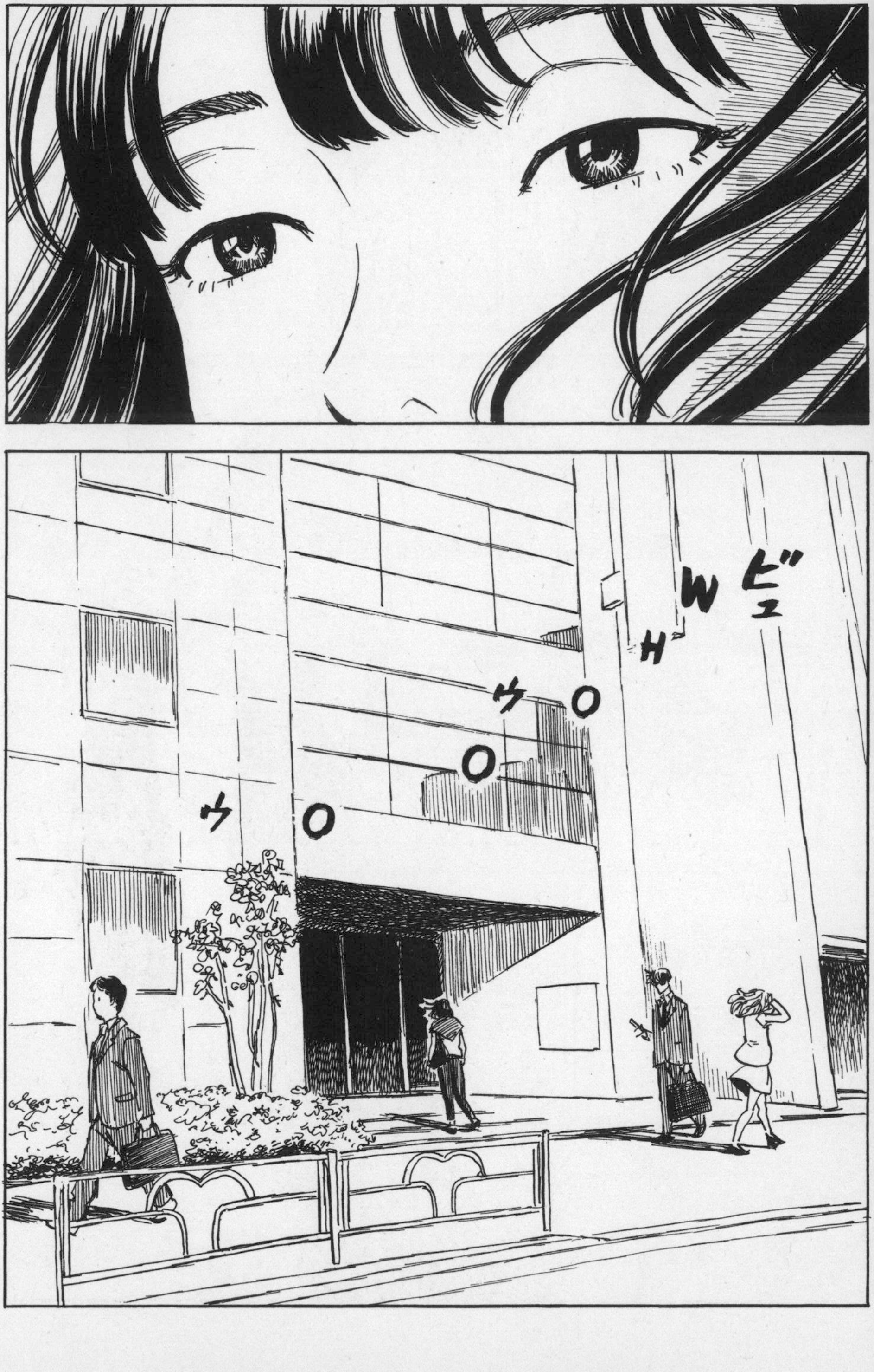

ビュウウ
WHOOO

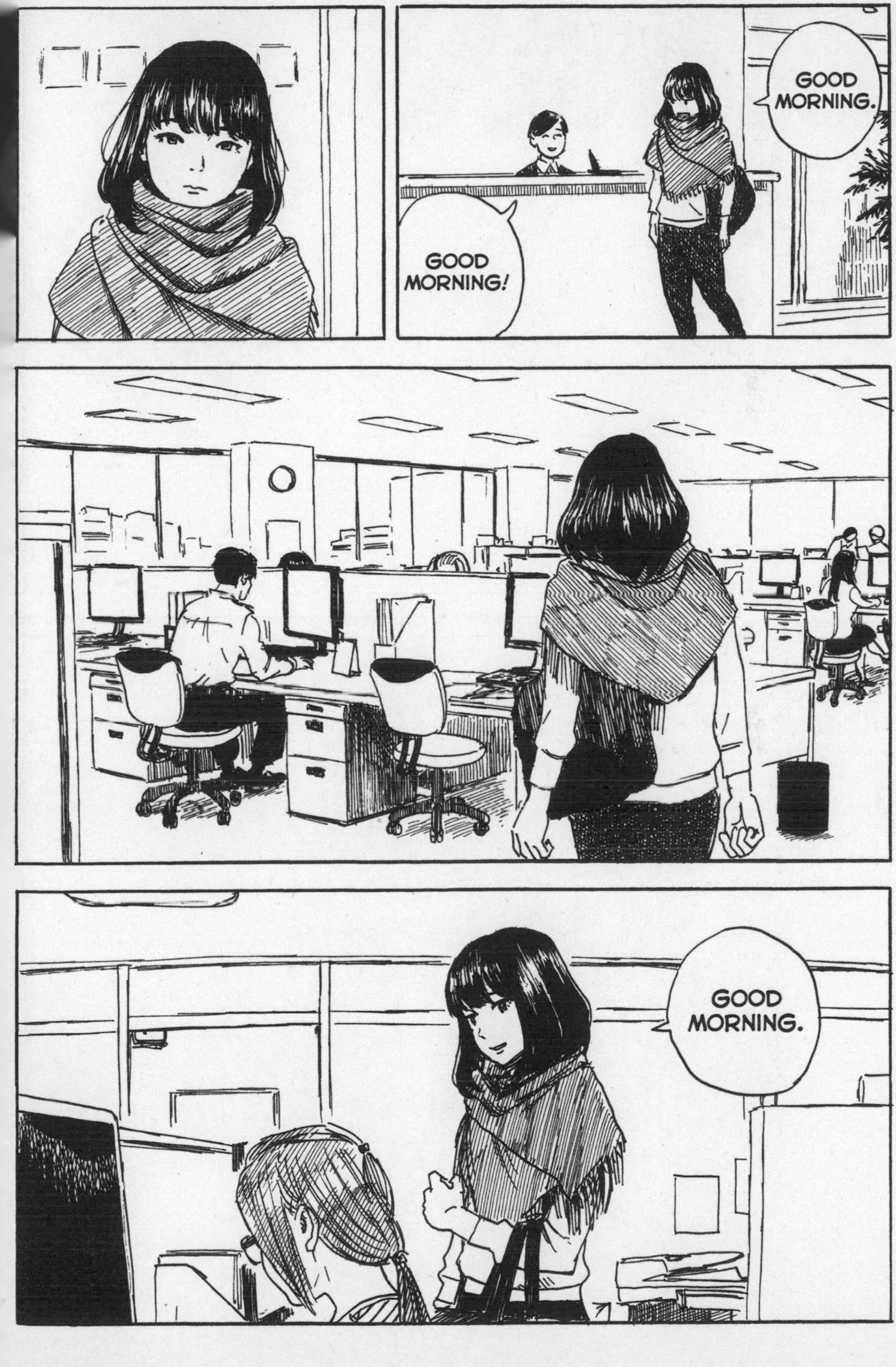
GOOD MORNING.
GOOD MORNING!
GOOD MORNING.

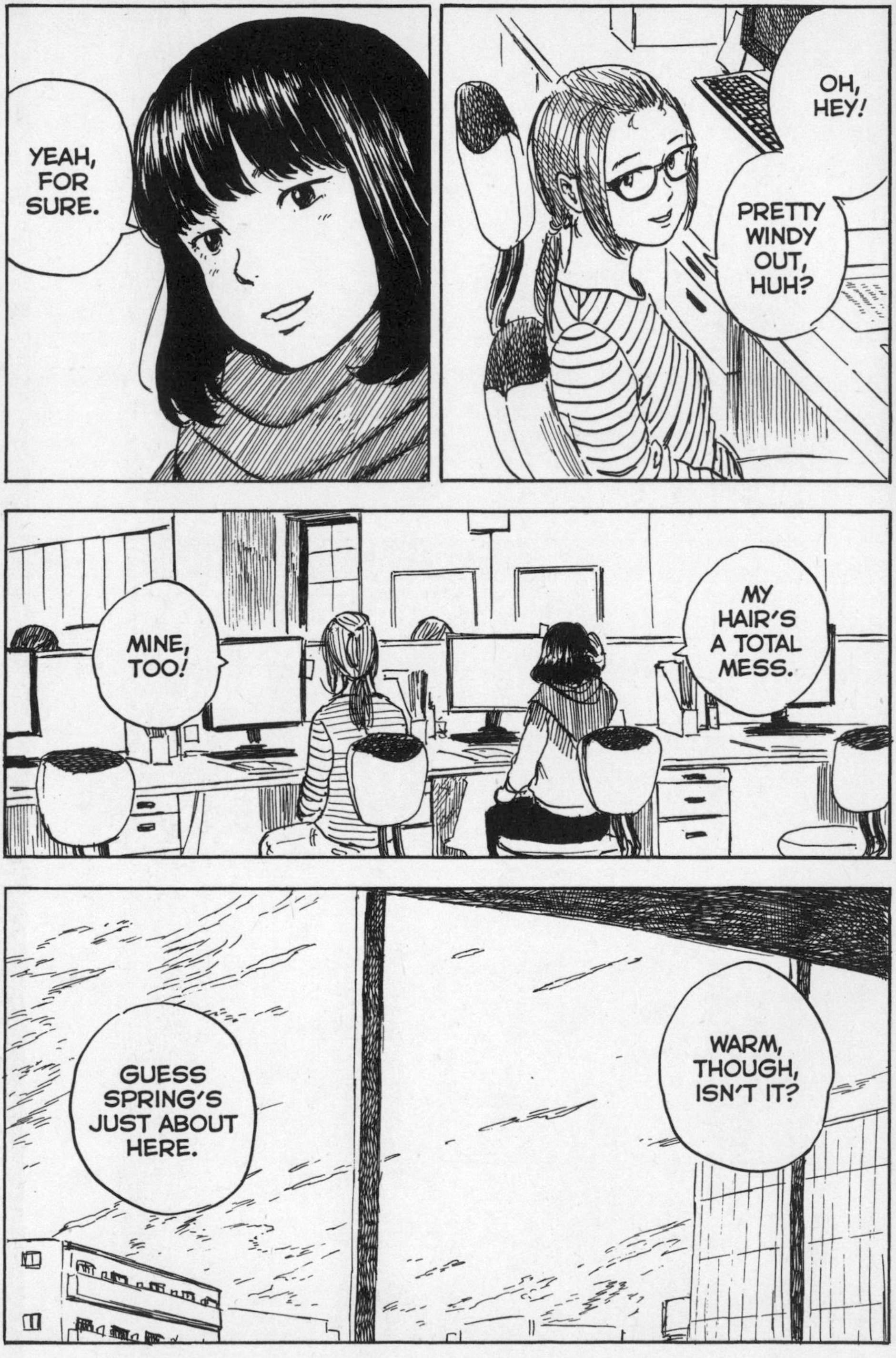
OH, HEY!
PRETTY WINDY OUT, HUH?
YEAH, FOR SURE.
MY HAIR'S A TOTAL MESS.
MINE, TOO!
WARM, THOUGH, ISN'T IT?
GUESS SPRING'S JUST ABOUT HERE.

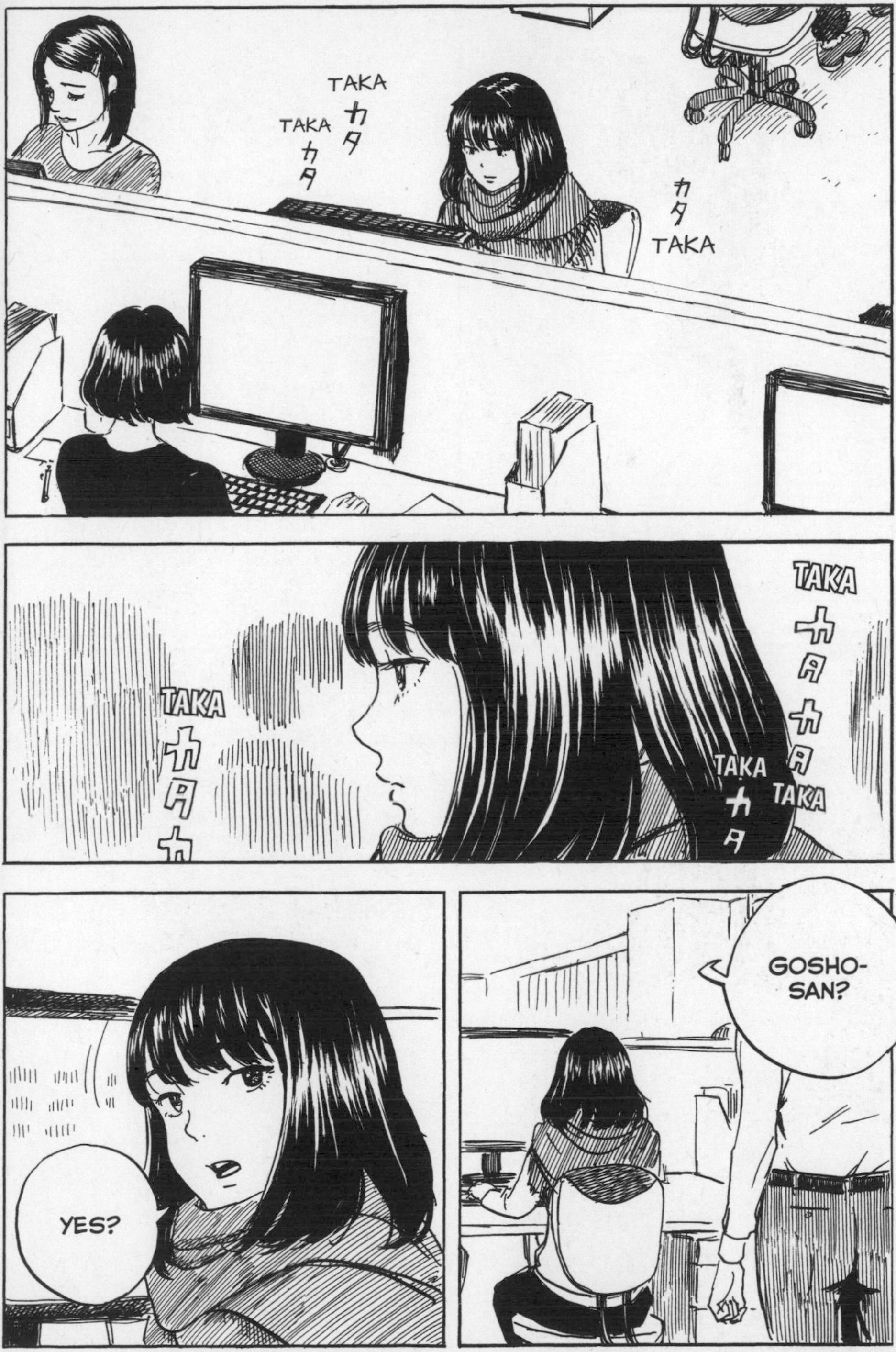
TAKA カタ
TAKA カタ
TAKA カタ
TAKA カタ
TAKA カタ
TAKA カタ
TAKA カタ
TAKA カタ
GOSHO-SAN?
YES?

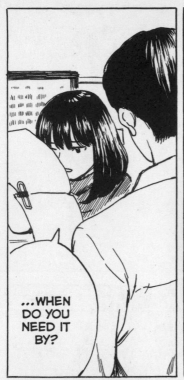

SORRY...
COULD YOU HANDLE THIS FOR ME?
...WHEN DO YOU NEED IT BY?
WELL, UMM...
BY TODAY, IF YOU COULD...
ALL RIGHT.
THAT WON'T BE A PROBLEM.

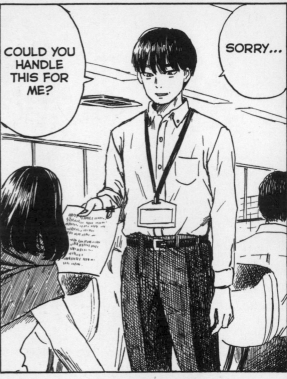

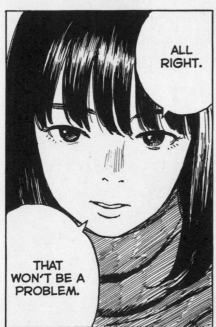

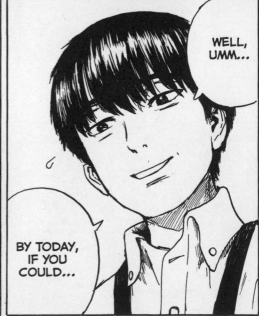

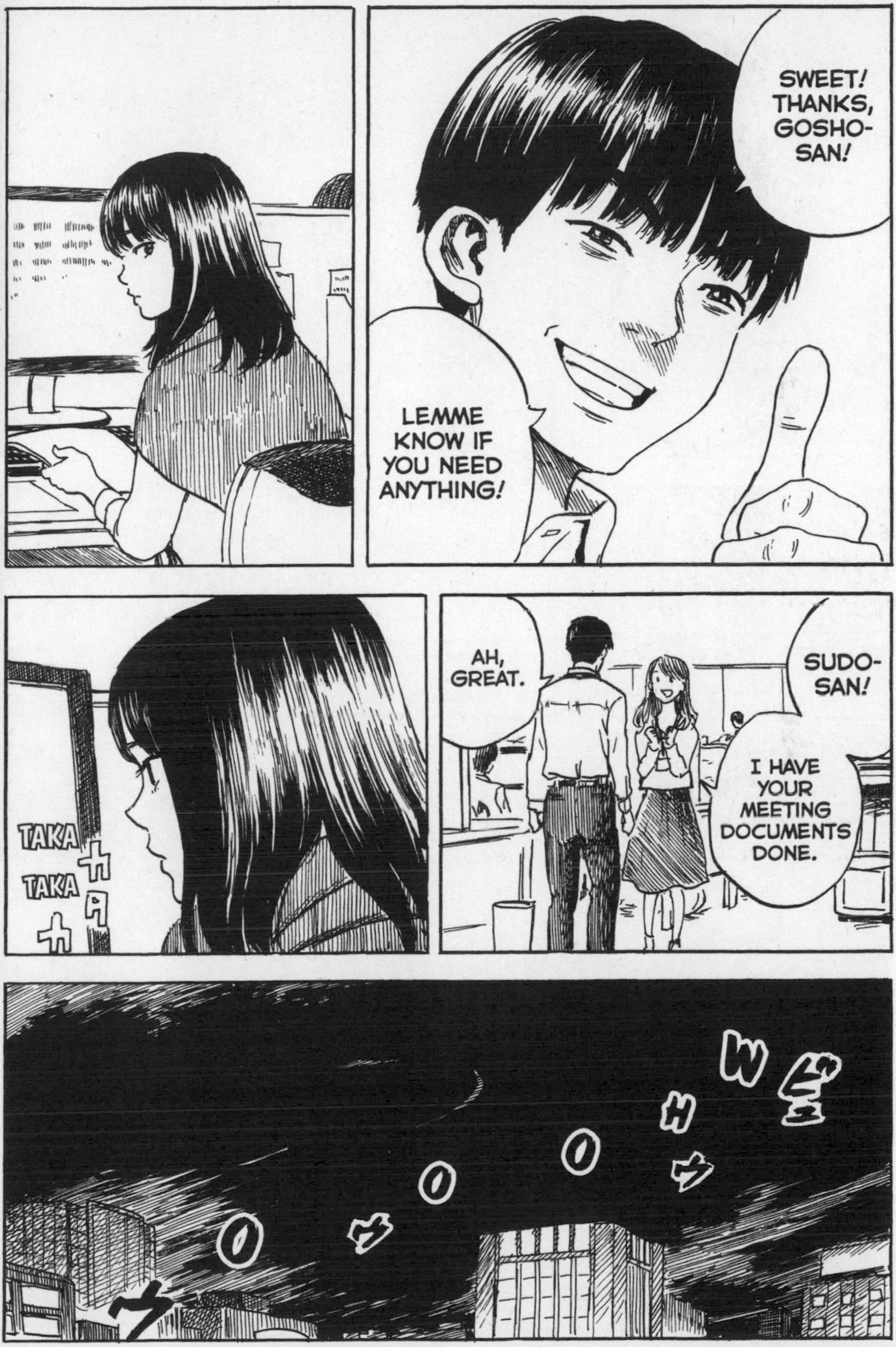
SWEET! THANKS, GOSHO-SAN!
LEMME KNOW IF YOU NEED ANYTHING!
SUDO-SAN!
I HAVE YOUR MEETING DOCUMENTS DONE.
AH, GREAT.
TAKA
TAKA
WHOOOO

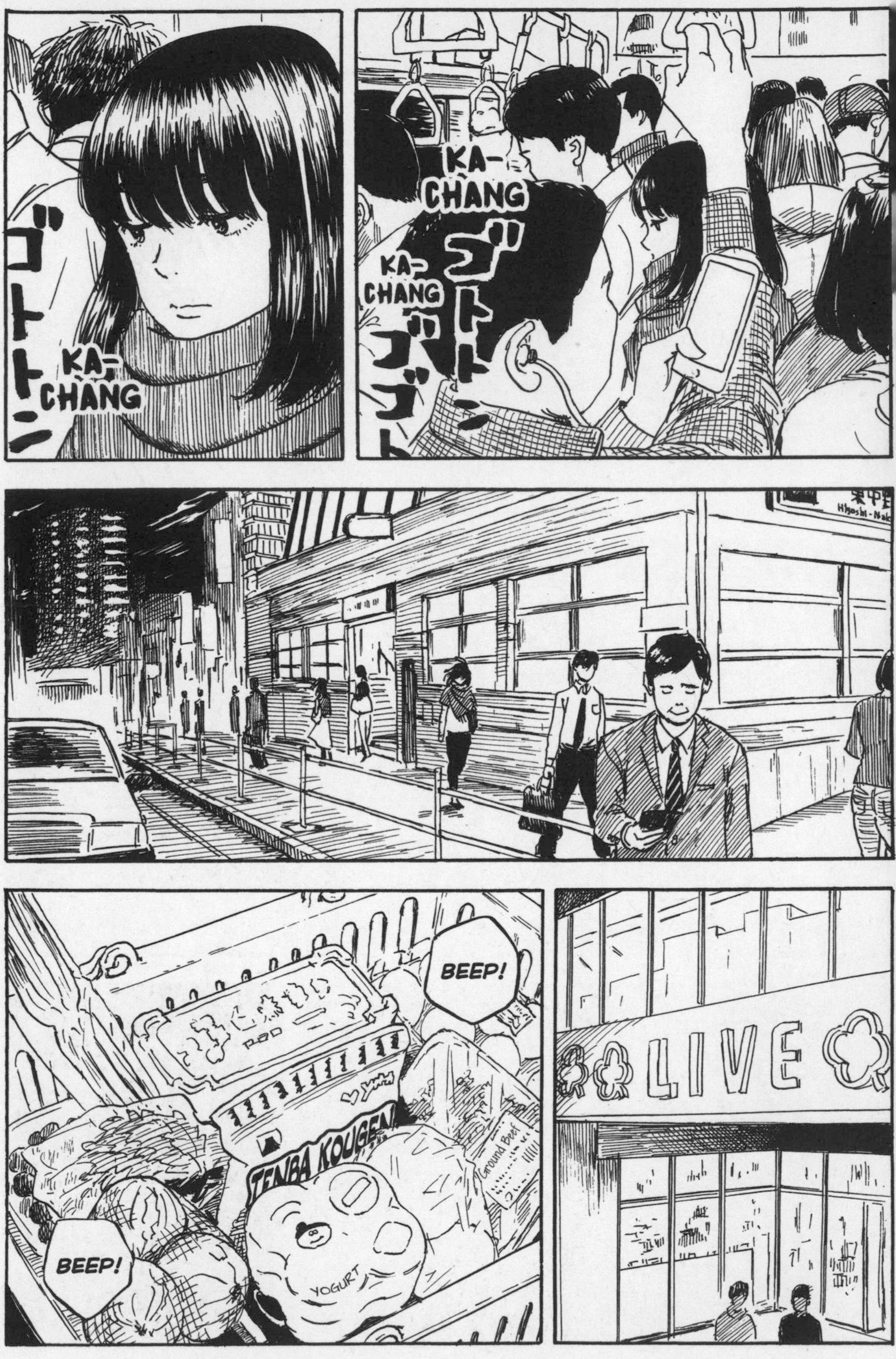

KA-CHANG
ゴトトン
KA-CHANG
ゴトトン
KA-CHANG
LIVE
BEEP!
TENBA KOUGEN
Ground Beef
BEEP!
YOGURT

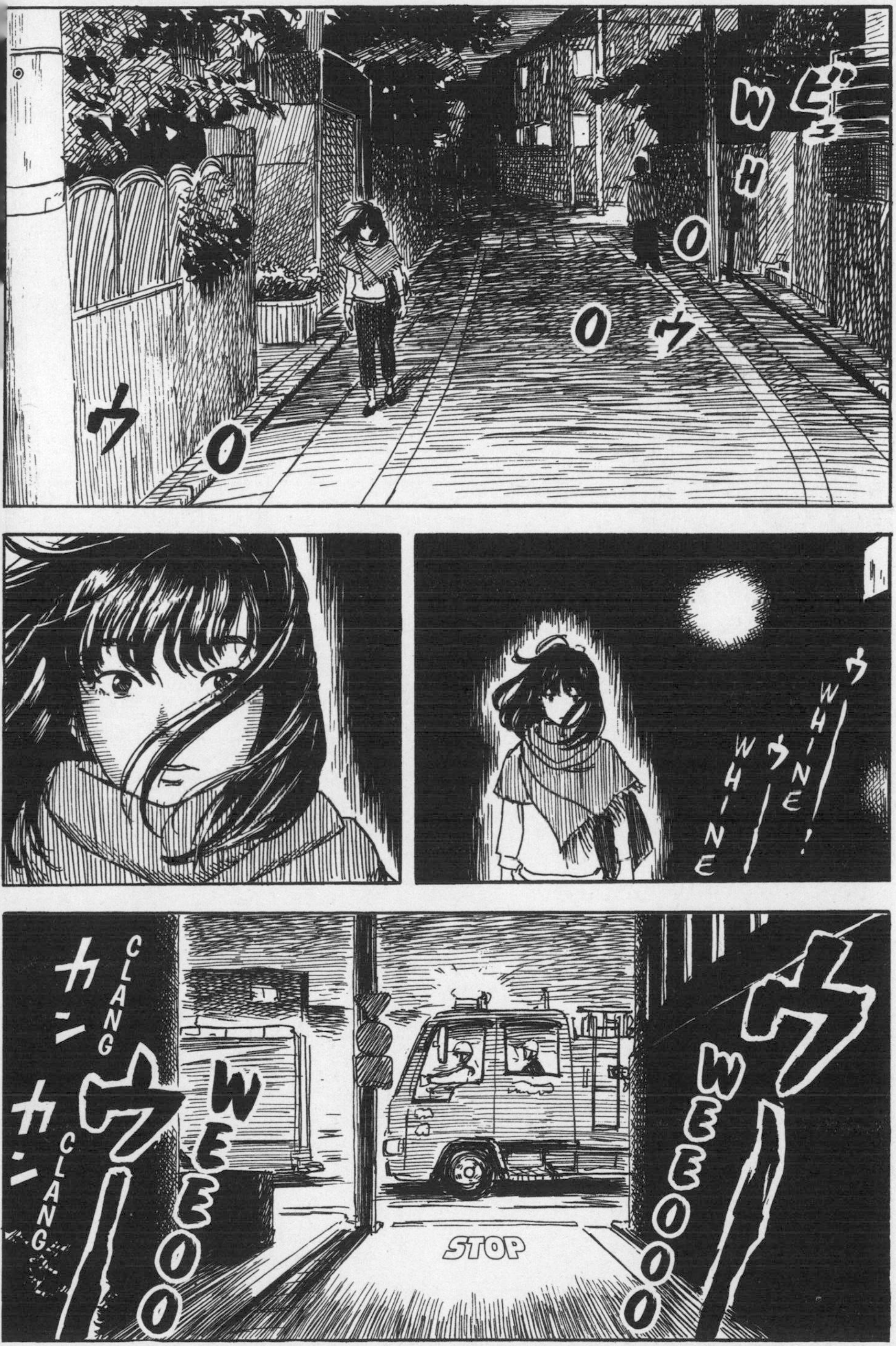
ビュ
WHOOO
ウ
ウ
ウ
WHINE!
ウ
WHINE
ウー
WEEOOOO
ウー
WEEOOO
カン
CLANG
カン
CLANG
STOP

CLANG
WEEOOO
WEEOOO
CLANG
WEEOO
WEEOO

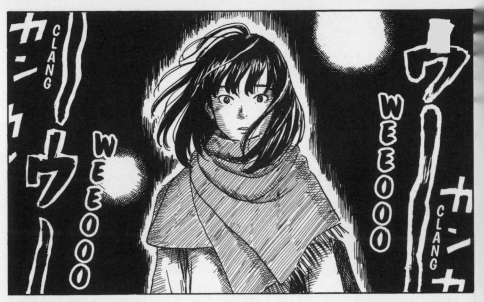

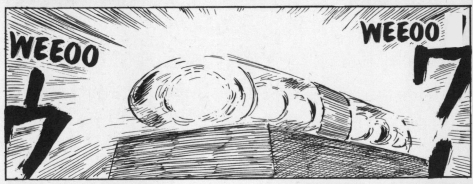

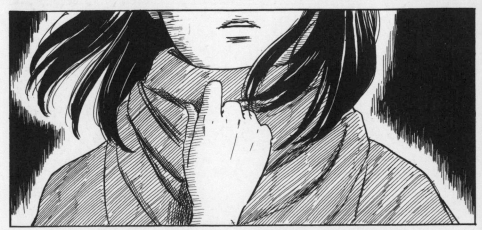

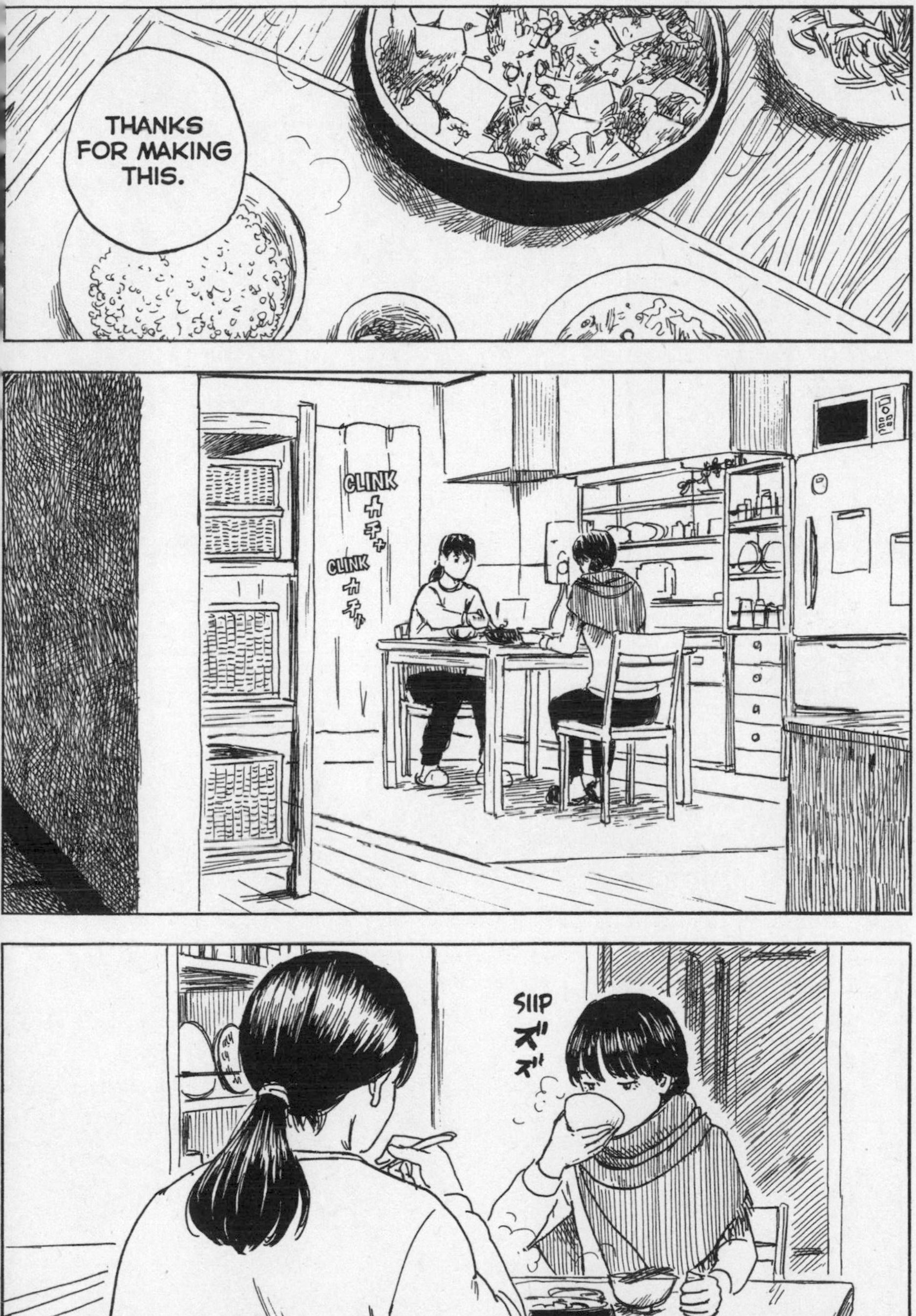
THANKS FOR MAKING THIS.
CLINK
カチャ
CLINK
カチャ
SIIP
ズズ

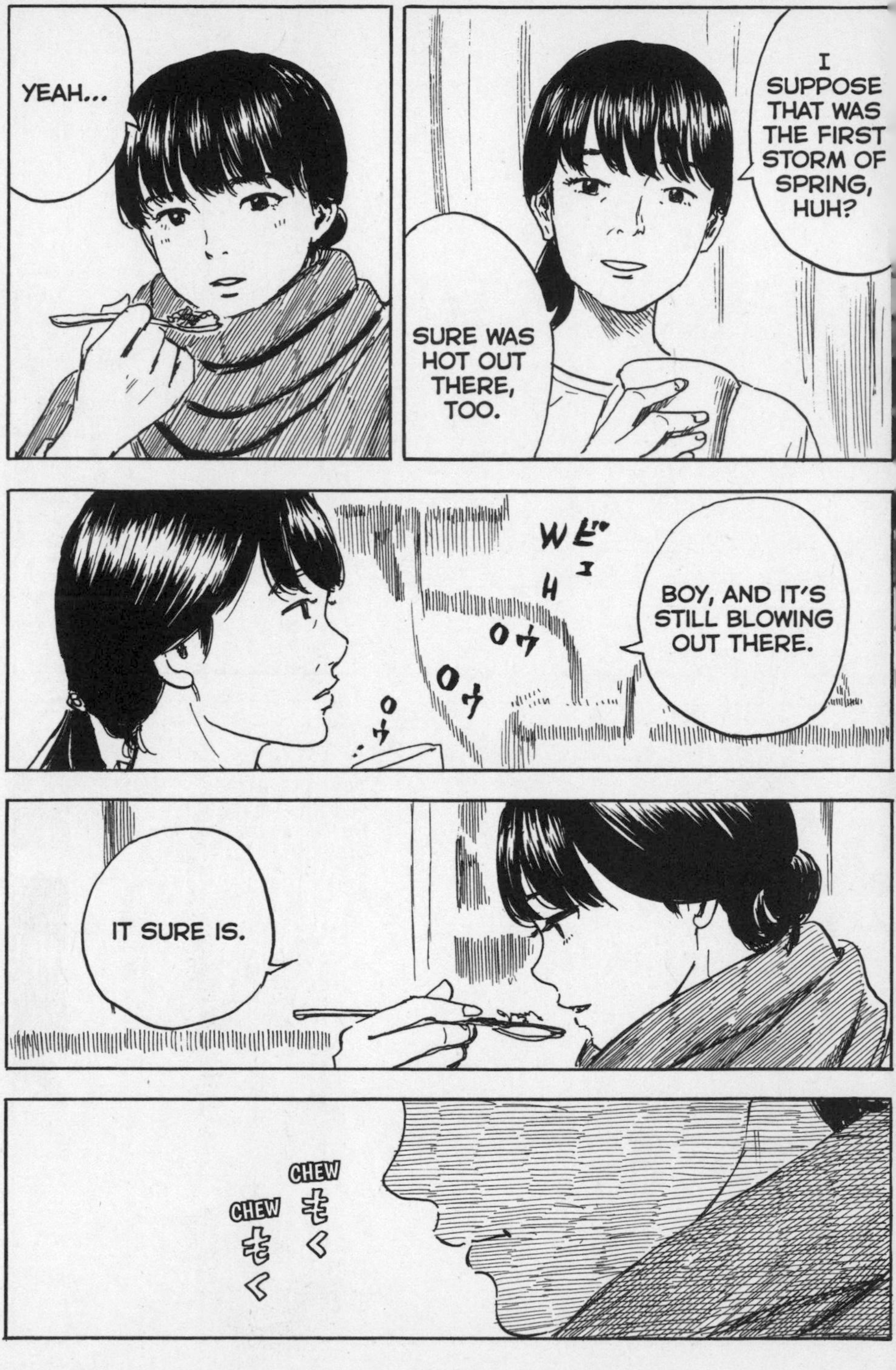
I SUPPOSE THAT WAS THE FIRST STORM OF SPRING, HUH?
SURE WAS HOT OUT THERE, TOO.
YEAH...
BOY, AND IT'S STILL BLOWING OUT THERE.
IT SURE IS.
CHEW もぐ
CHEW もぐ

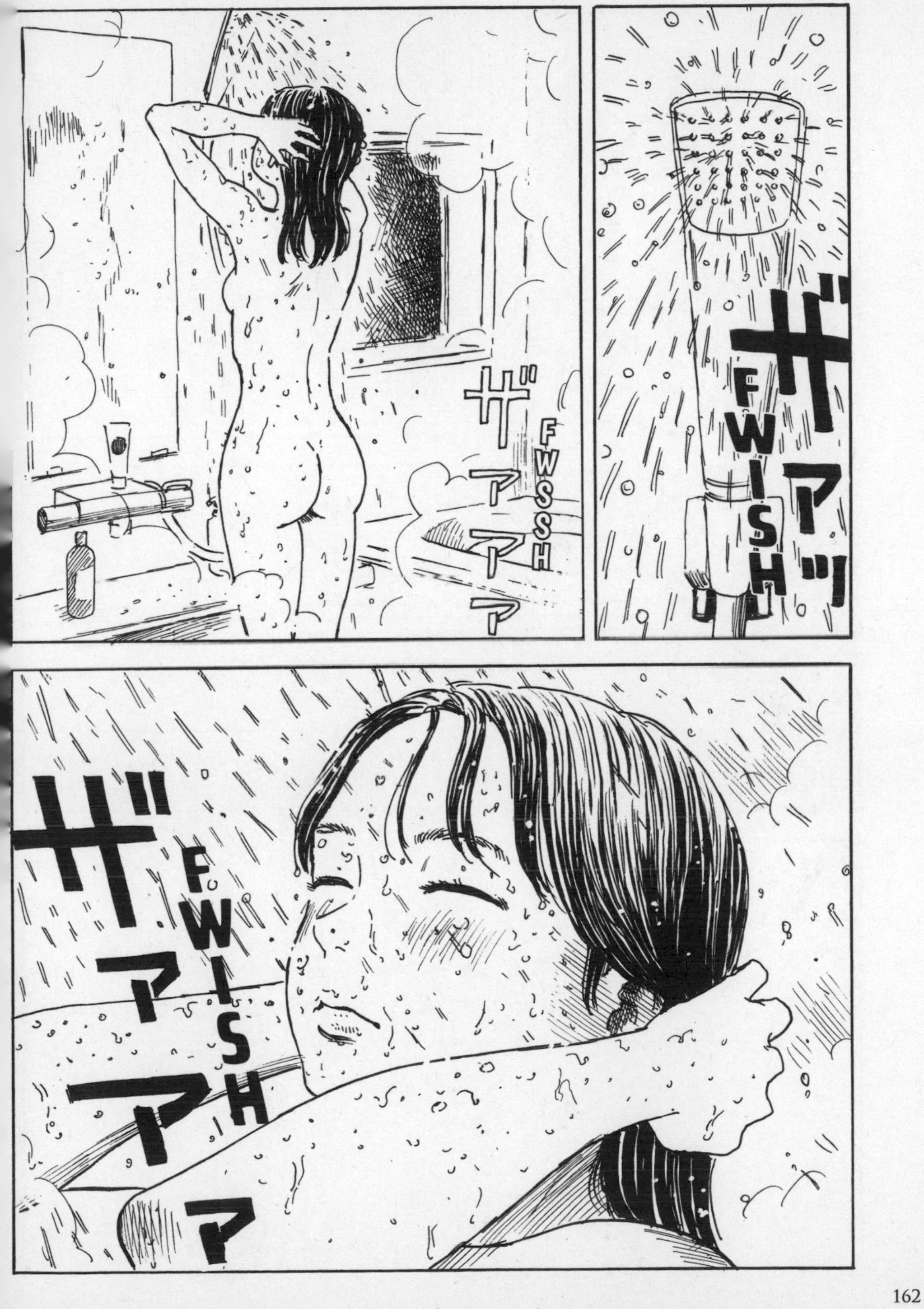
ザアッ
FWISH
ザアアア
FWSSH
ザアアア
FWISH

とた
TUP
とた
TUP
TUP
とた
TUP
とた
ぼふっ
WHUMP

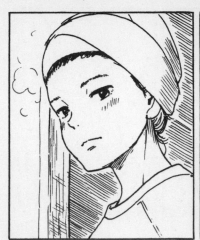

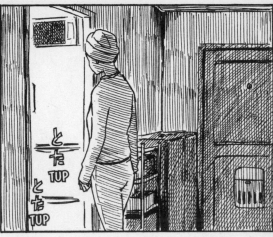

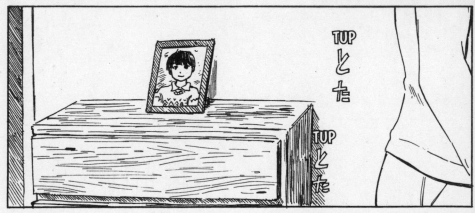

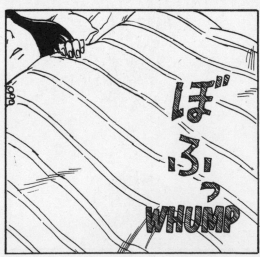

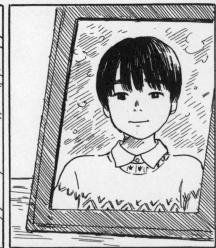

WHOOOO
ビュウウウ…
CLATTER
ガタガタ
CLATTER

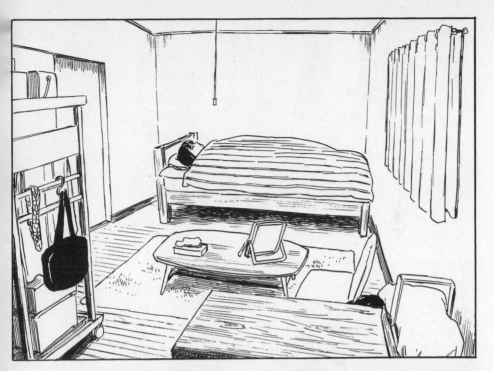

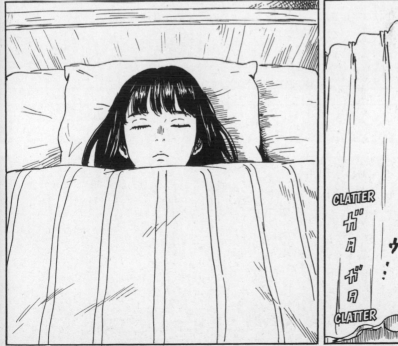

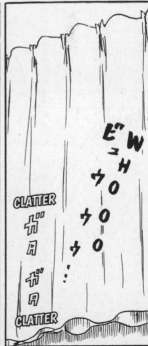

WHOOO
ヒュウウウ
CLATTER
ガタガタ
CLATTER
WHOOO

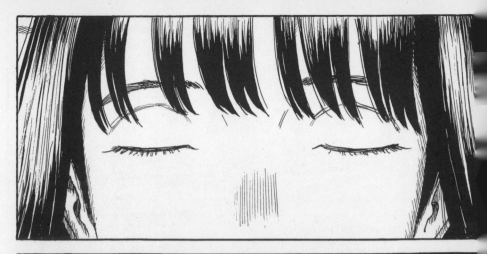

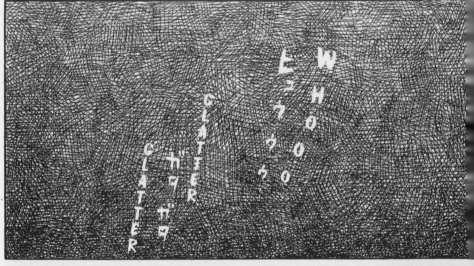

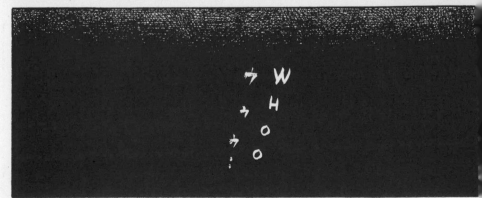

TAKA カタ

TAKA カタ

TAKA カ

YES?

GOSHO-SAN?

TAKA カタ

TAKA カ

TAKA カタ

OH!

THANKS.

IT'S THE LOCATION OF SAMURA-KUN'S FAREWELL PARTY TONIGHT!

HERE...

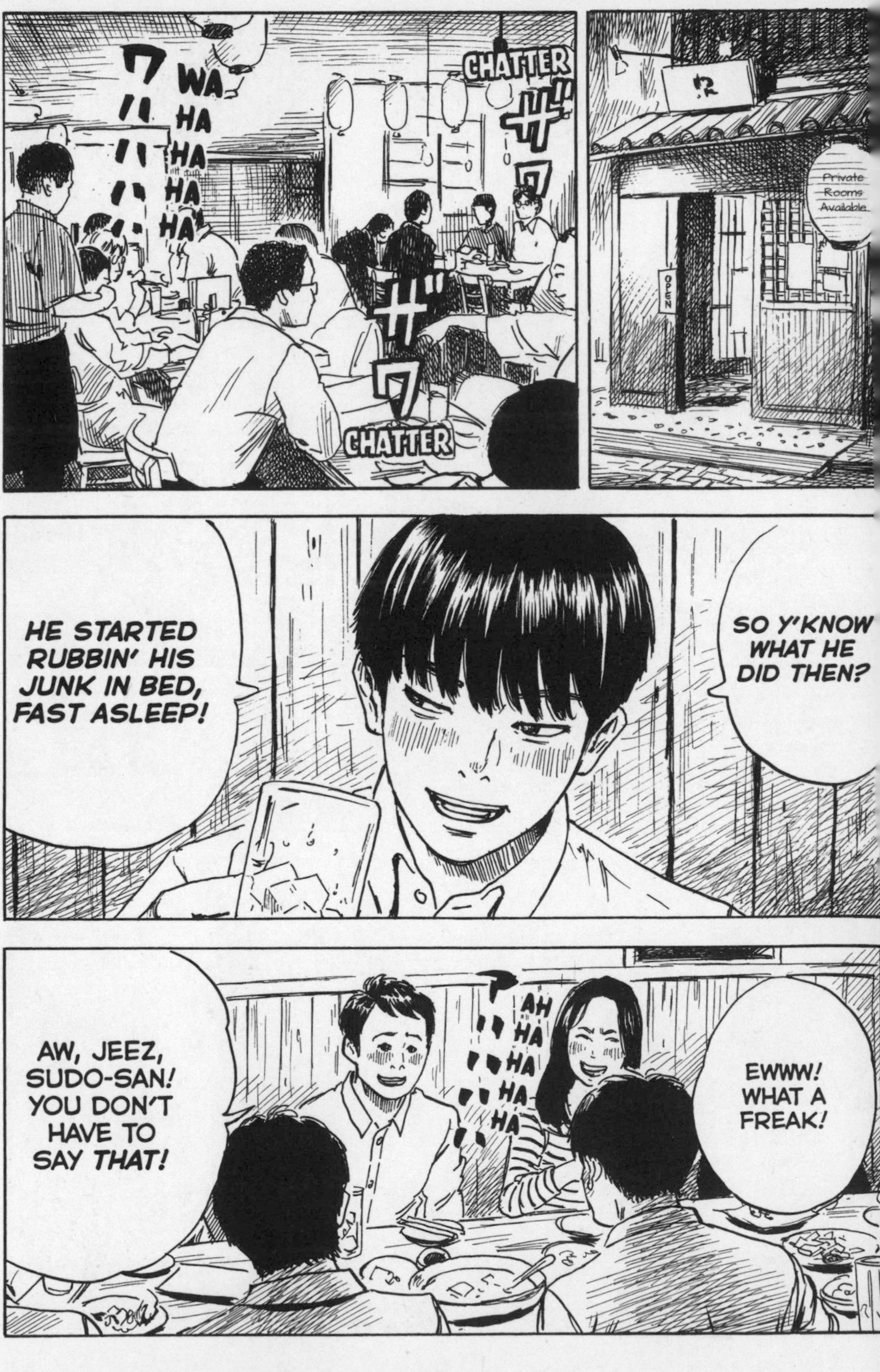
Private Rooms Available
OPEN
WA HA HA HA HA
CHATTER
ザワ
ザワ
CHATTER
SO Y'KNOW WHAT HE DID THEN?
HE STARTED RUBBIN' HIS JUNK IN BED, FAST ASLEEP!
EWWW! WHAT A FREAK!
AH HA HA HA HA HA
AW, JEEZ, SUDO-SAN! YOU DON'T HAVE TO SAY THAT!

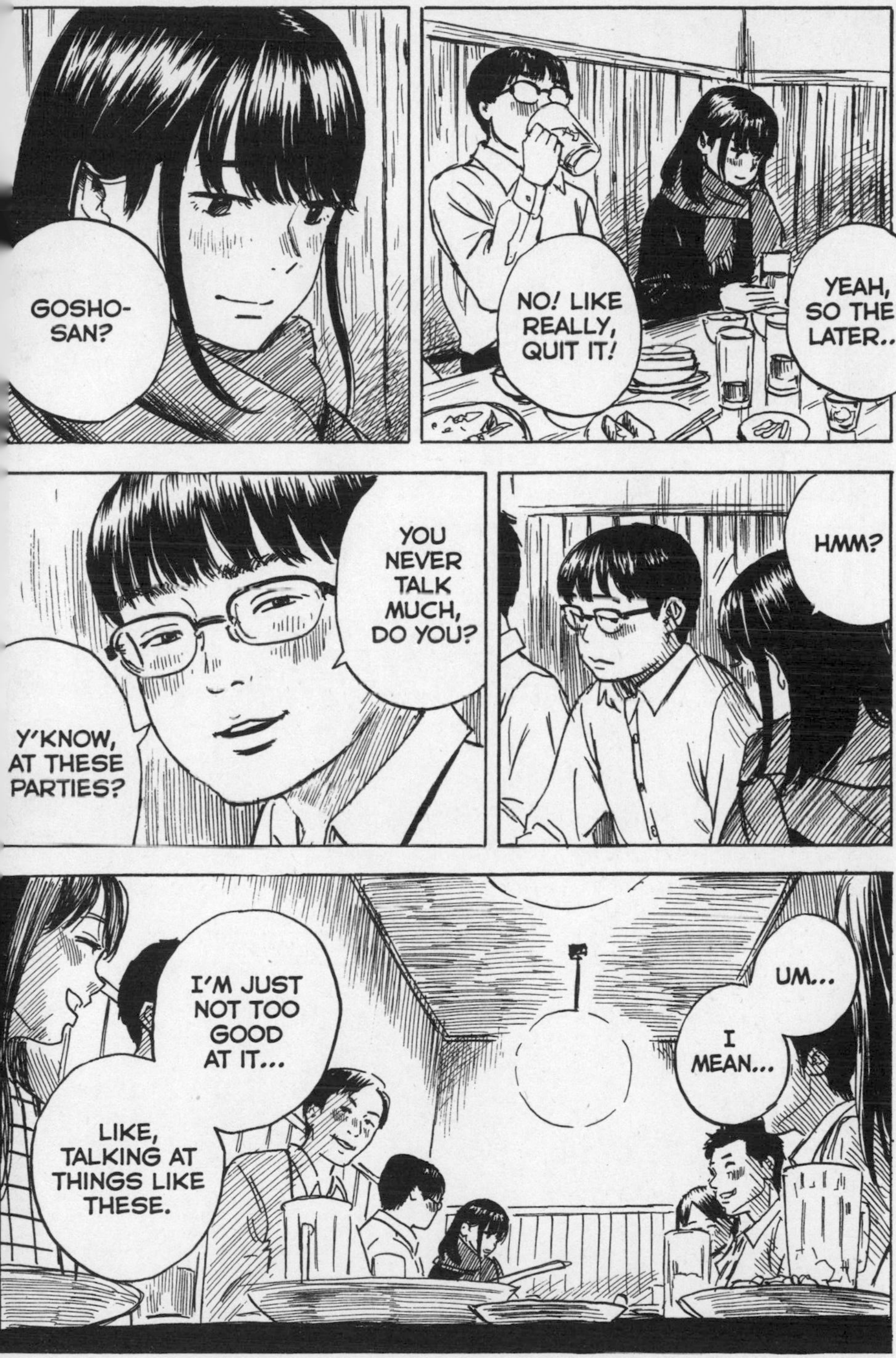
YEAH, SO THEN LATER...
NO! LIKE REALLY, QUIT IT!
GOSHO-SAN?
HMM?
YOU NEVER TALK MUCH, DO YOU?
Y'KNOW, AT THESE PARTIES?
UM...
I MEAN...
I'M JUST NOT TOO GOOD AT IT...
LIKE, TALKING AT THINGS LIKE THESE.

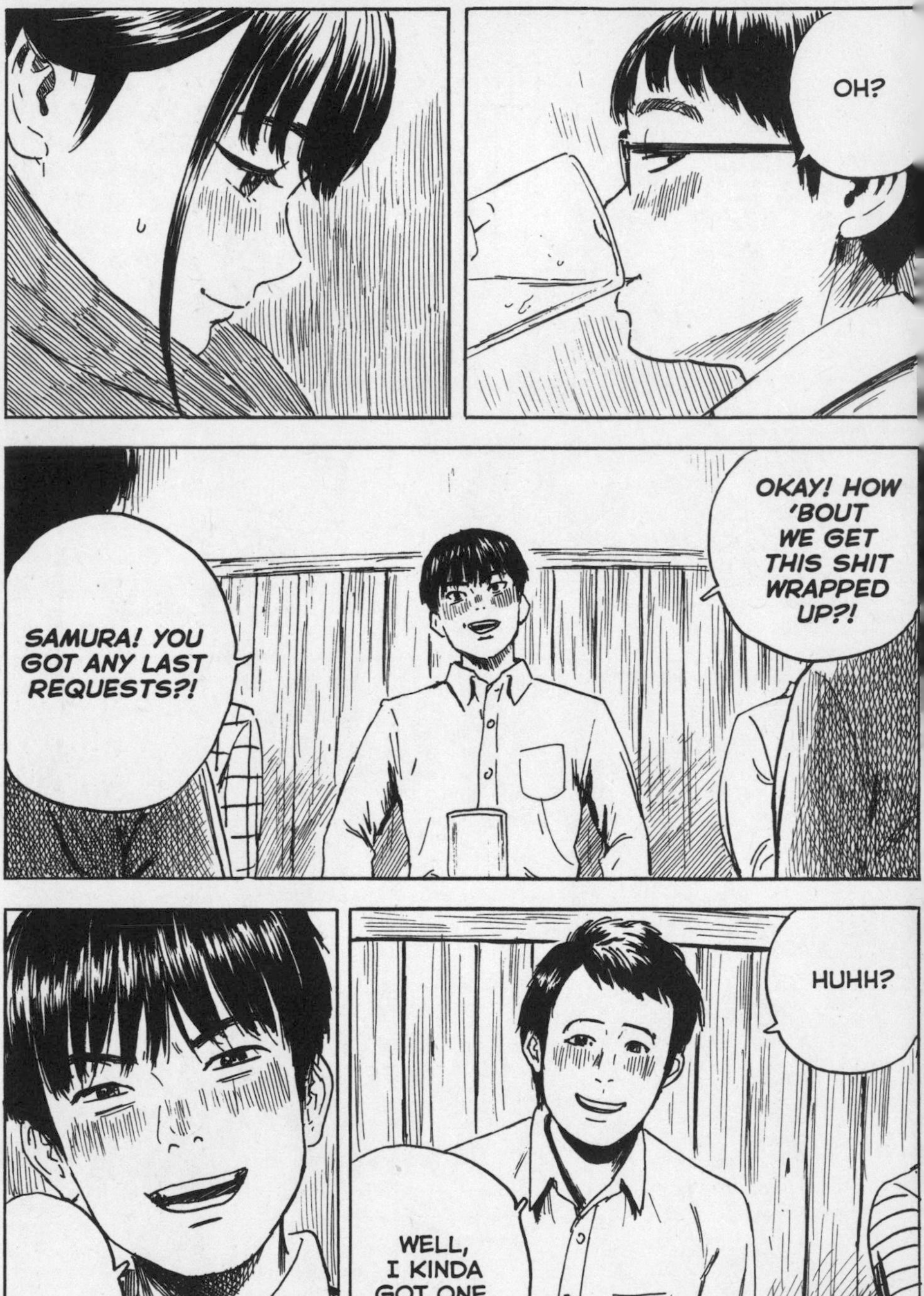
OH?
OKAY! HOW 'BOUT WE GET THIS SHIT WRAPPED UP?!
SAMURA! YOU GOT ANY LAST REQUESTS?!
HUHH?
WELL, I KINDA GOT ONE, ACTUALLY...
SAY IT!

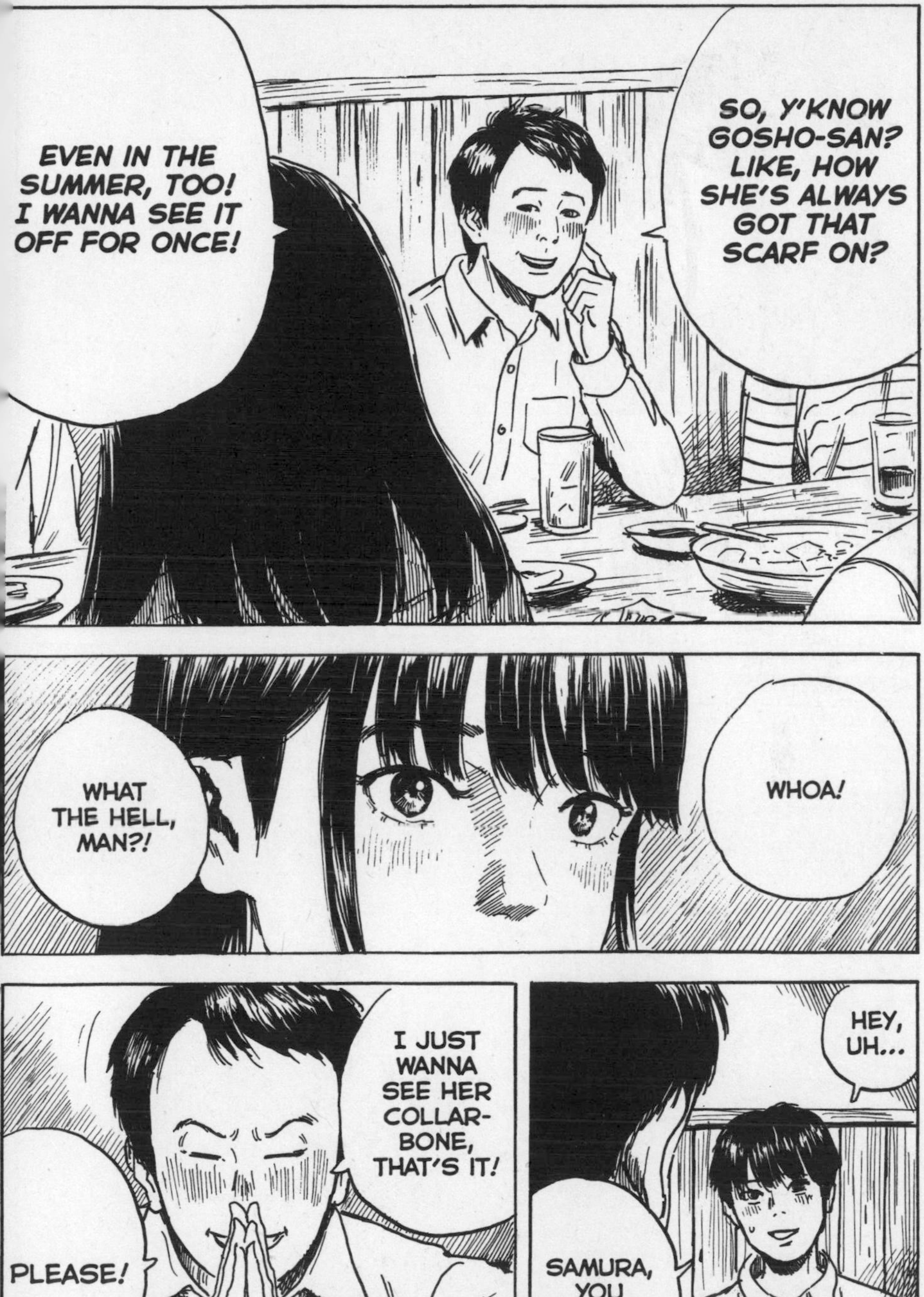
SO, Y'KNOW GOSHO-SAN? LIKE, HOW SHE'S ALWAYS GOT THAT SCARF ON?
EVEN IN THE SUMMER, TOO! I WANNA SEE IT OFF FOR ONCE!
WHOA!
WHAT THE HELL, MAN?!
HEY, UH...
SAMURA, YOU PROBABLY ...
I JUST WANNA SEE HER COLLAR-BONE, THAT'S IT!
PLEASE!

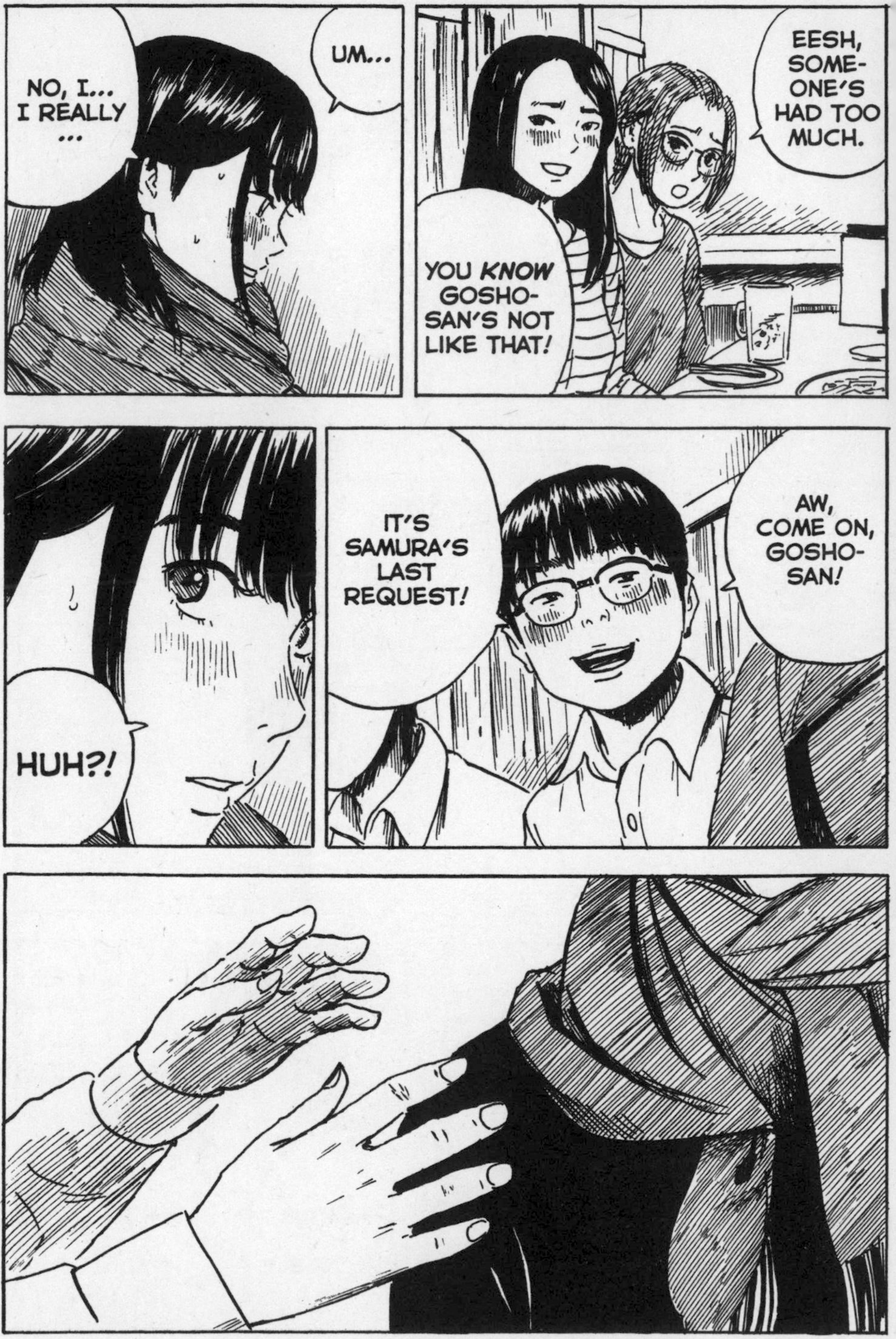
EESH, SOME-ONE'S HAD TOO MUCH.
YOU *KNOW* GOSHO-SAN'S NOT LIKE THAT!
UM...
NO, I... I REALLY ...
AW, COME ON, GOSHO-SAN!
IT'S SAMURA'S LAST REQUEST!
HUH?!

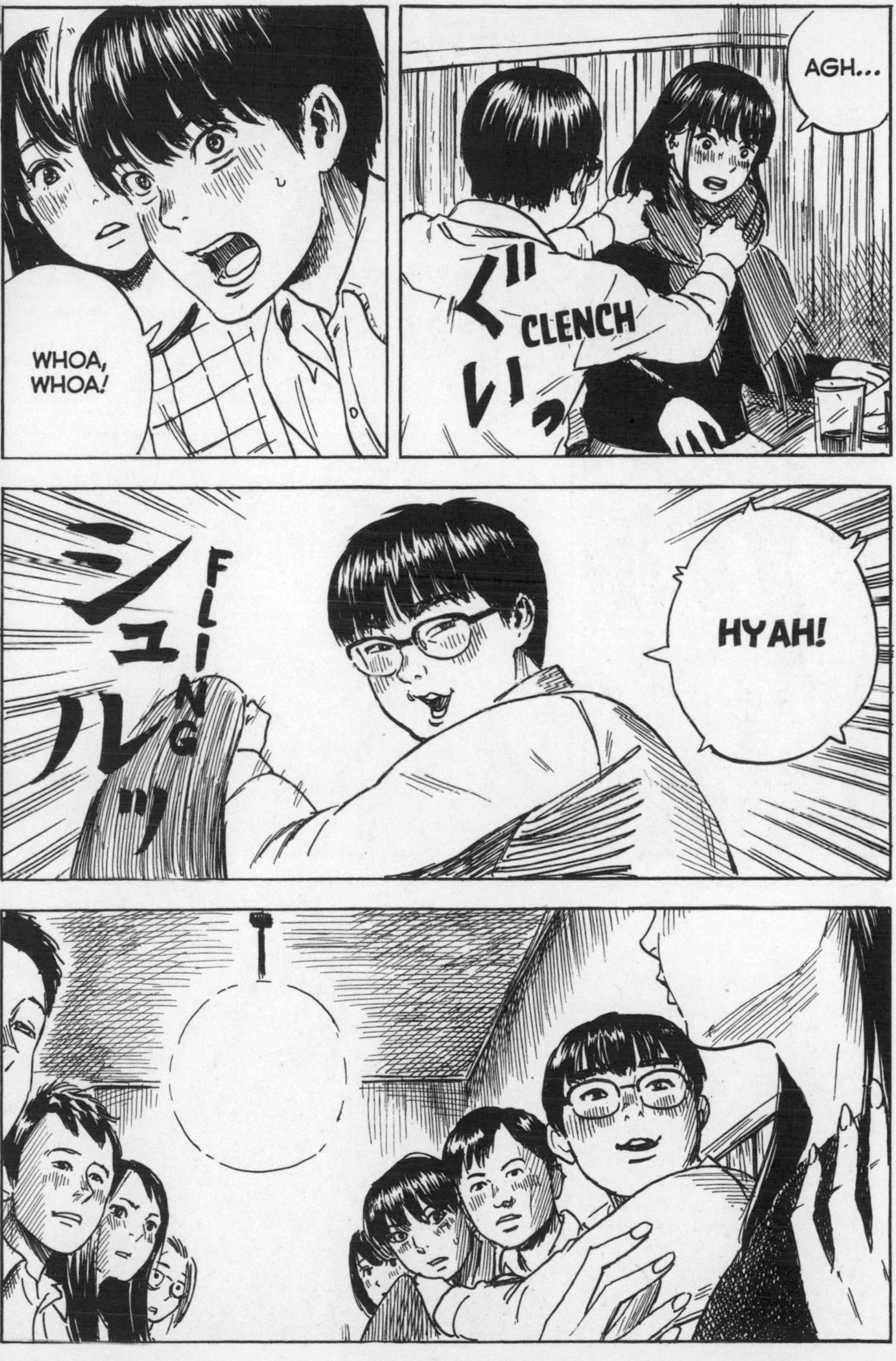
AGH...
ぐいっ
CLENCH
WHOA, WHOA!
HYAH!
シュルッ
FLING

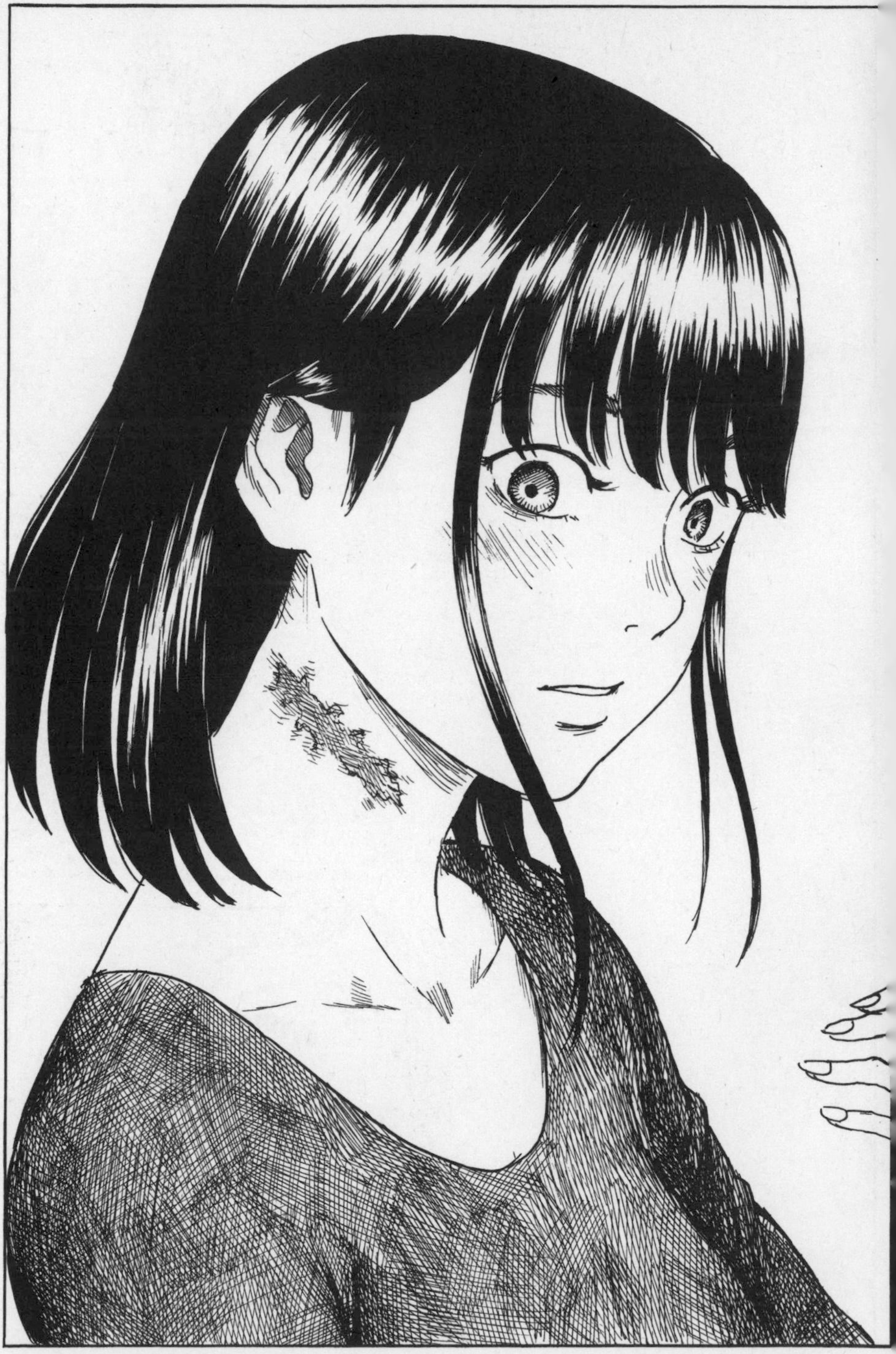

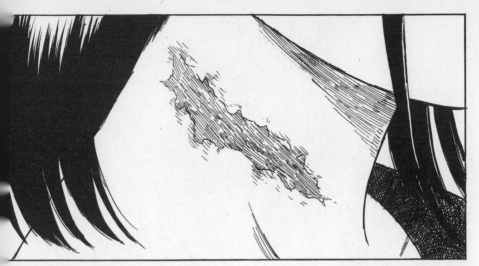

OH...

UM...
SHIT,
I'M SO
SORRY!

I TOTALLY
DIDN'T
KNOW...

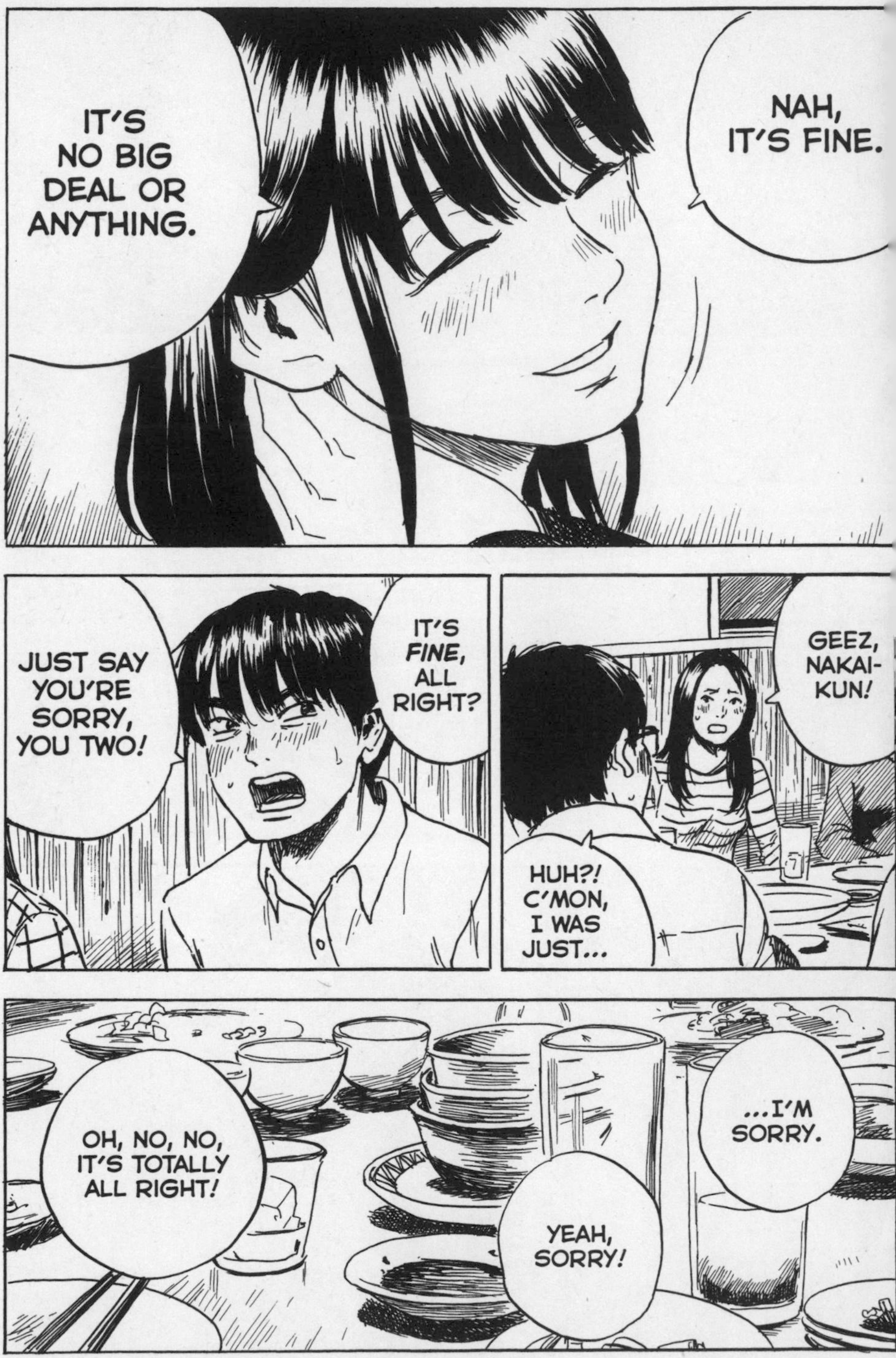
NAH, IT'S FINE.
IT'S NO BIG DEAL OR ANYTHING.
GEEZ, NAKAI-KUN!
HUH?! C'MON, I WAS JUST...
IT'S *FINE*, ALL RIGHT?
JUST SAY YOU'RE SORRY, YOU TWO!
...I'M SORRY.
YEAH, SORRY!
OH, NO, NO, IT'S TOTALLY ALL RIGHT!

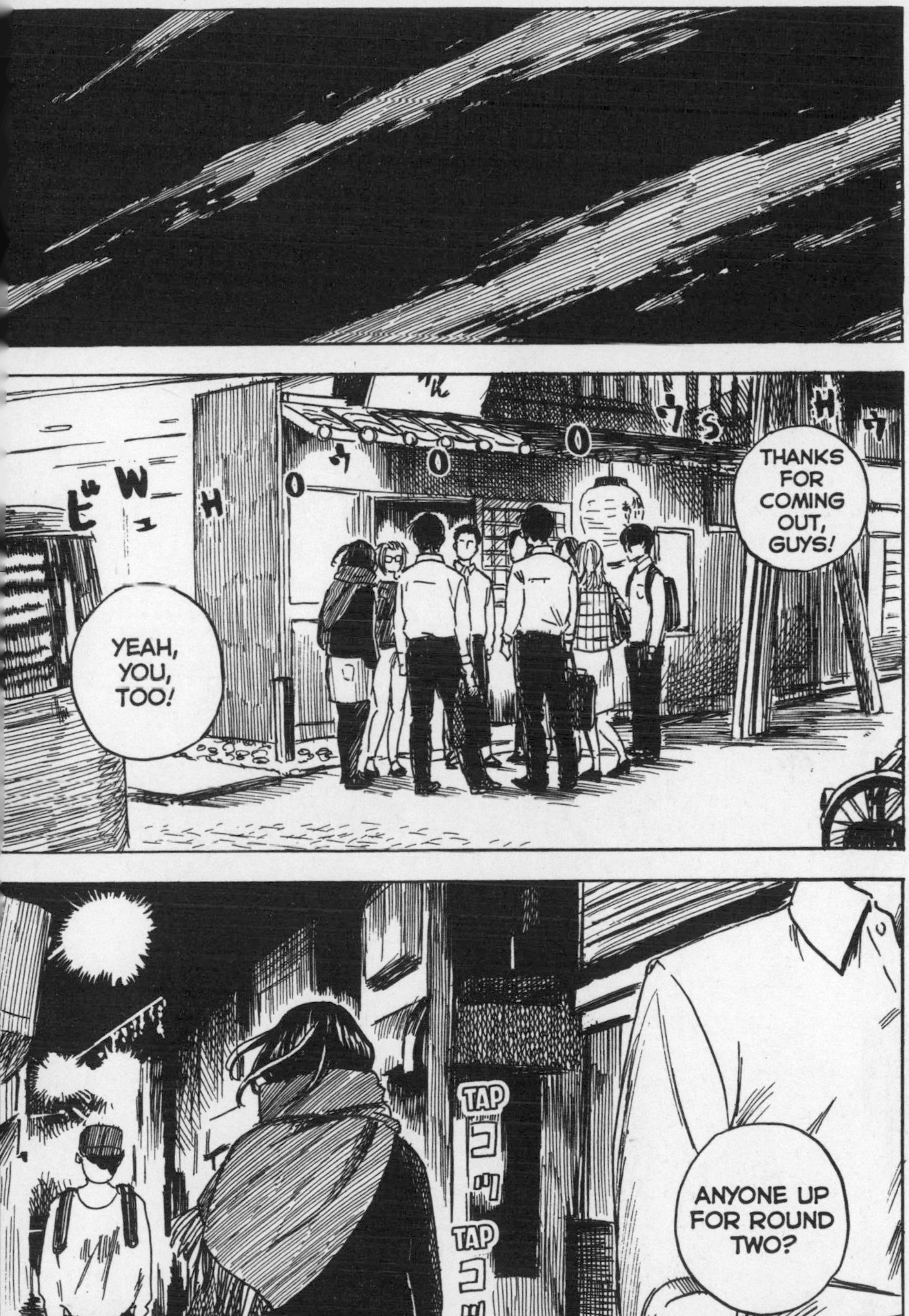
THANKS FOR COMING OUT, GUYS!
YEAH, YOU, TOO!
ANYONE UP FOR ROUND TWO?
TAP
TAP

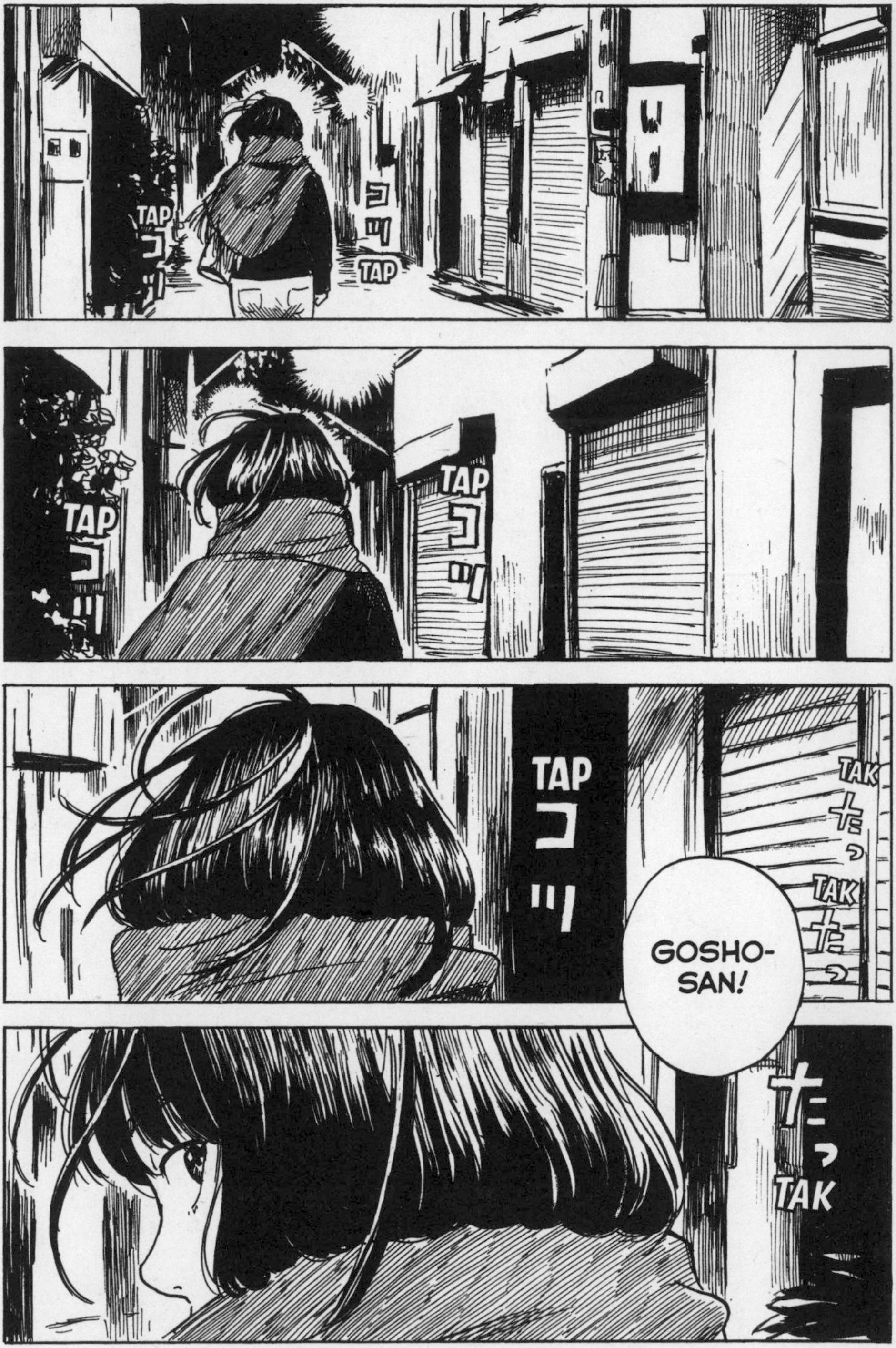
コツ TAP
TAP コツ
TAP コツ
TAP コツ
TAK たっ TAK たっ
GOSHO-SAN!
TAP コツ
たっ TAK

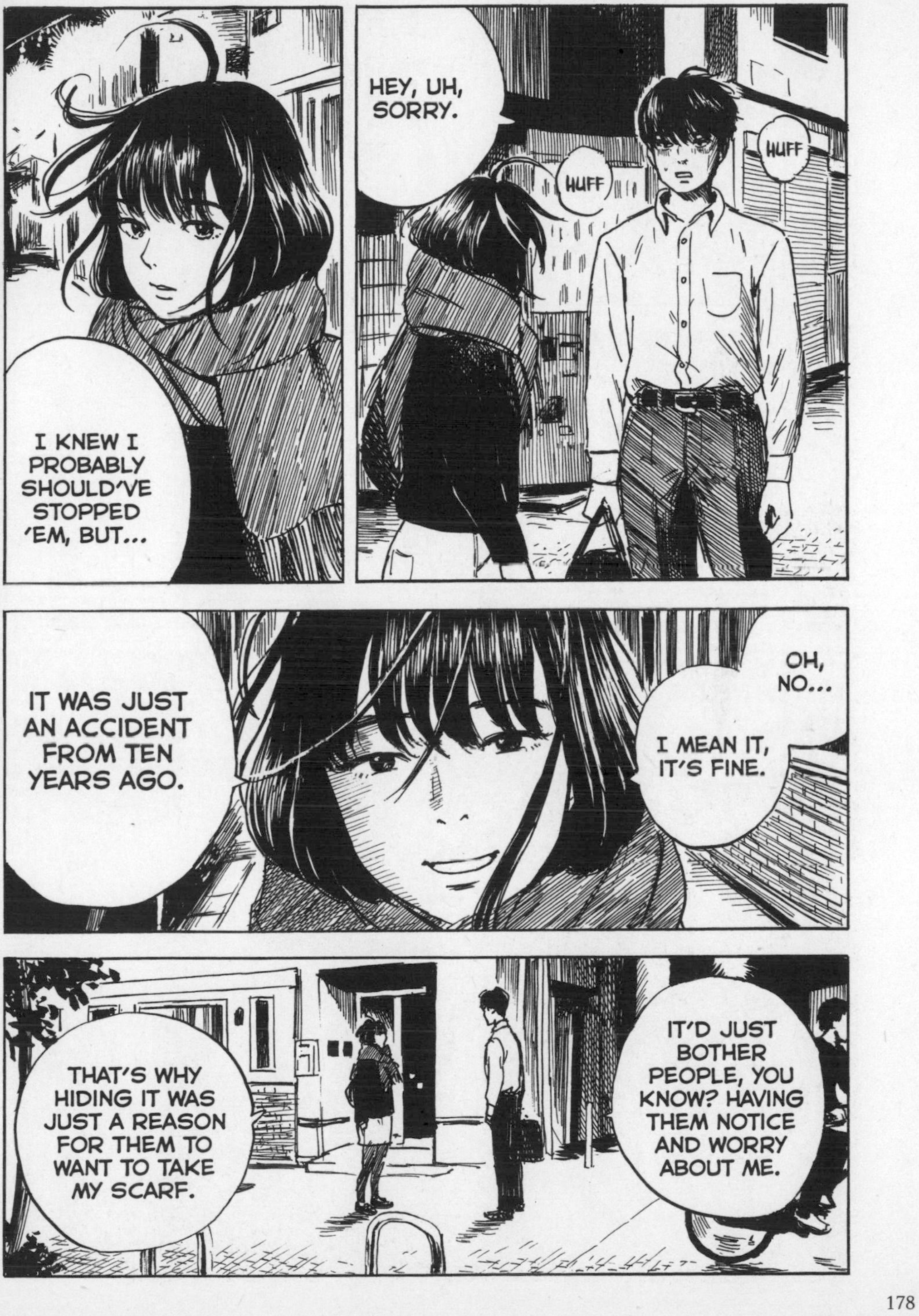
HEY, UH, SORRY.
HUFF
HUFF
I KNEW I PROBABLY SHOULD'VE STOPPED 'EM, BUT...
OH, NO...
I MEAN IT, IT'S FINE.
IT WAS JUST AN ACCIDENT FROM TEN YEARS AGO.
IT'D JUST BOTHER PEOPLE, YOU KNOW? HAVING THEM NOTICE AND WORRY ABOUT ME.
THAT'S WHY HIDING IT WAS JUST A REASON FOR THEM TO WANT TO TAKE MY SCARF.

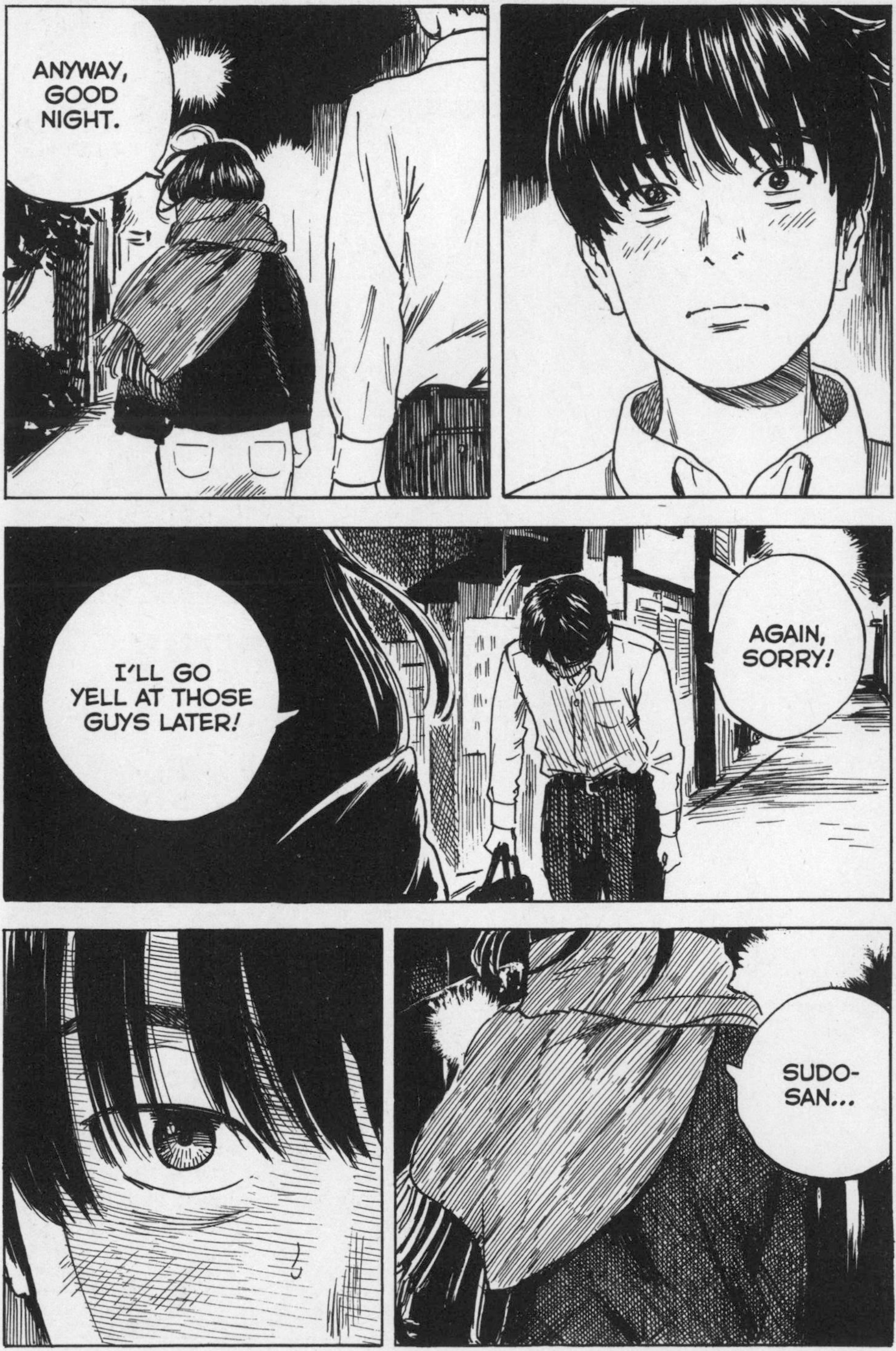
ANYWAY, GOOD NIGHT.
AGAIN, SORRY!
I'LL GO YELL AT THOSE GUYS LATER!
SUDO-SAN...

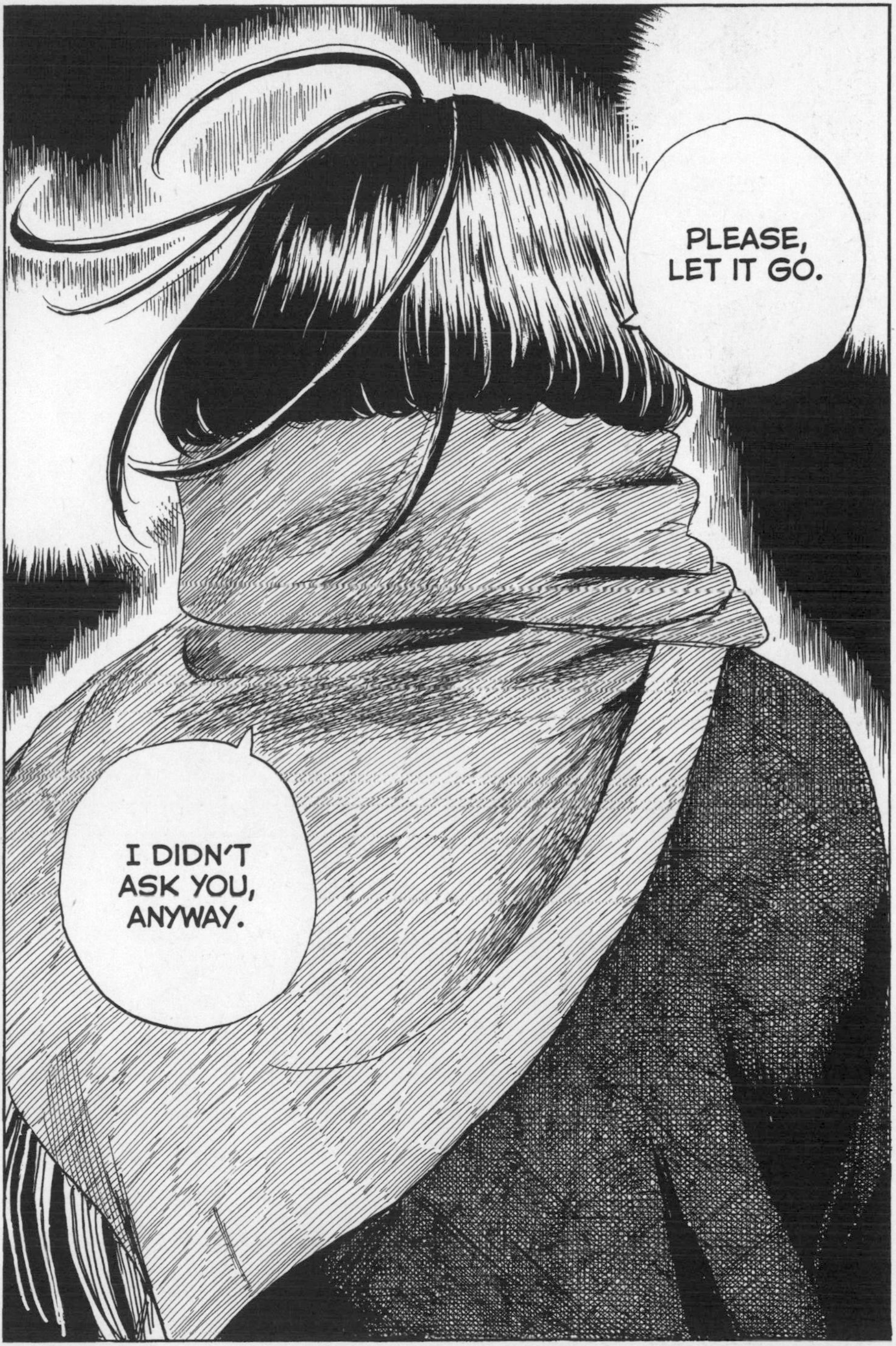
PLEASE, LET IT GO.
I DIDN'T ASK YOU, ANYWAY.

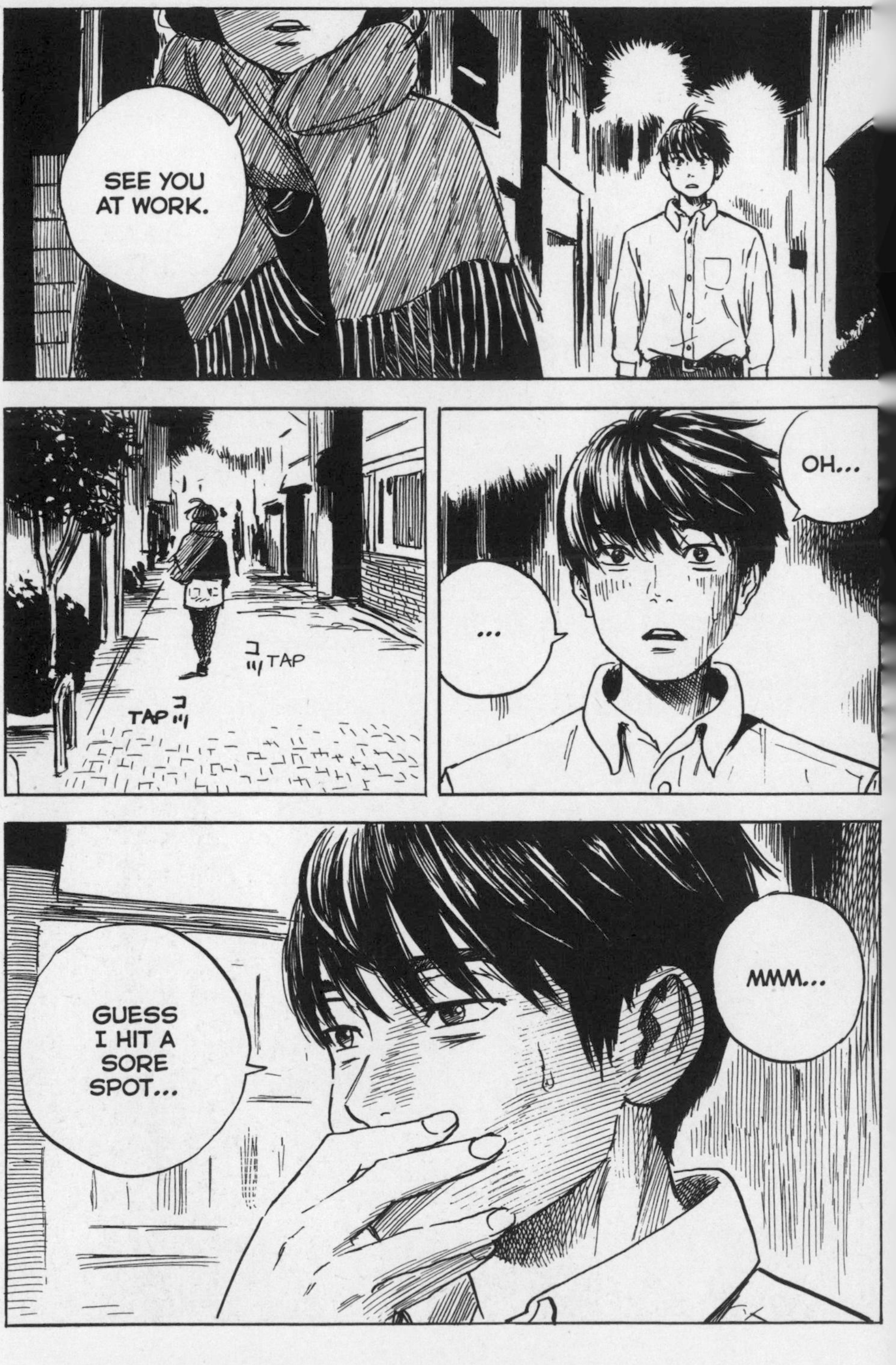
SEE YOU AT WORK.
OH...
...
TAP
TAP
MMM...
GUESS I HIT A SORE SPOT...

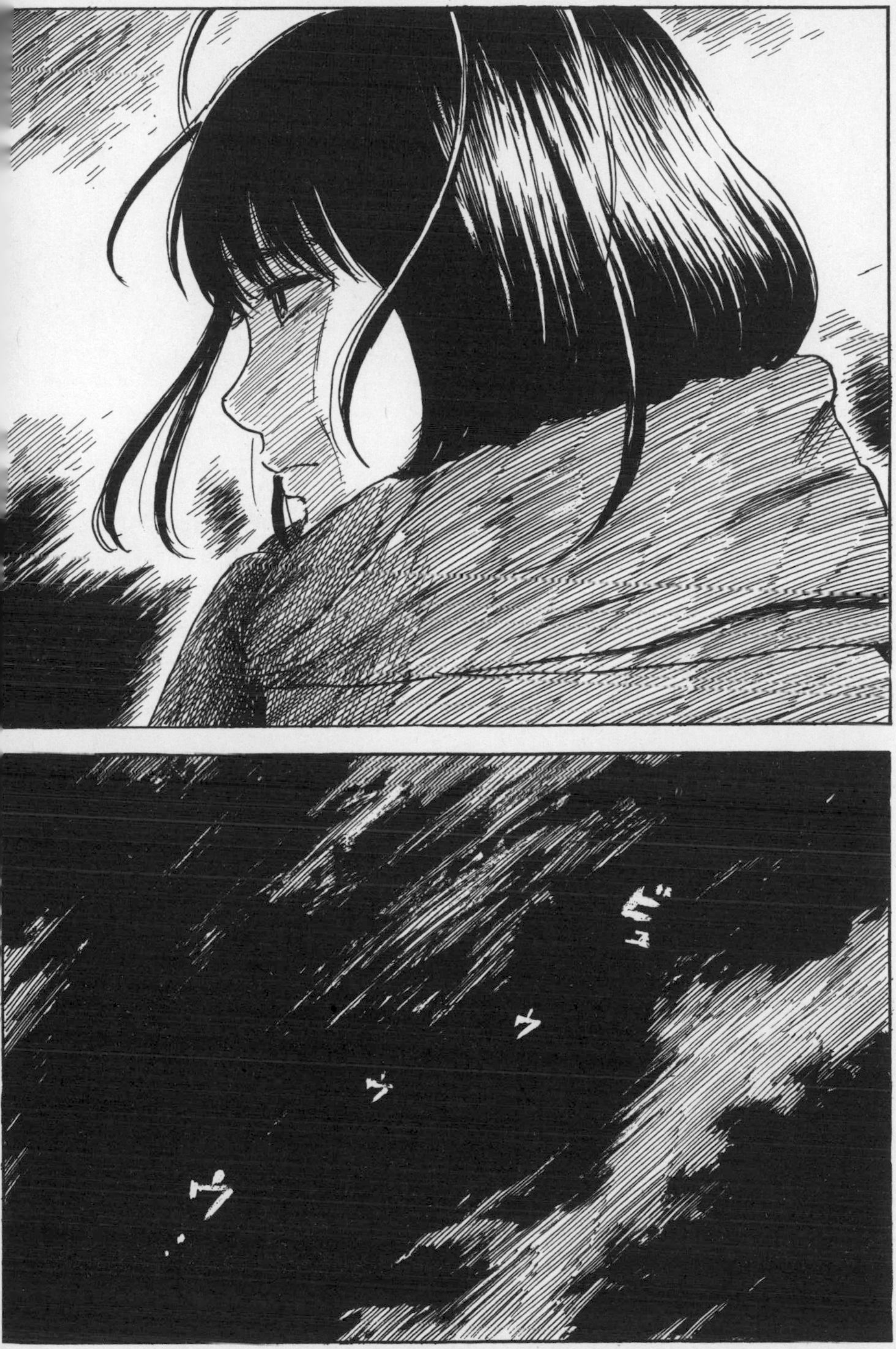

CONTINUED IN #6

HAPPINESS

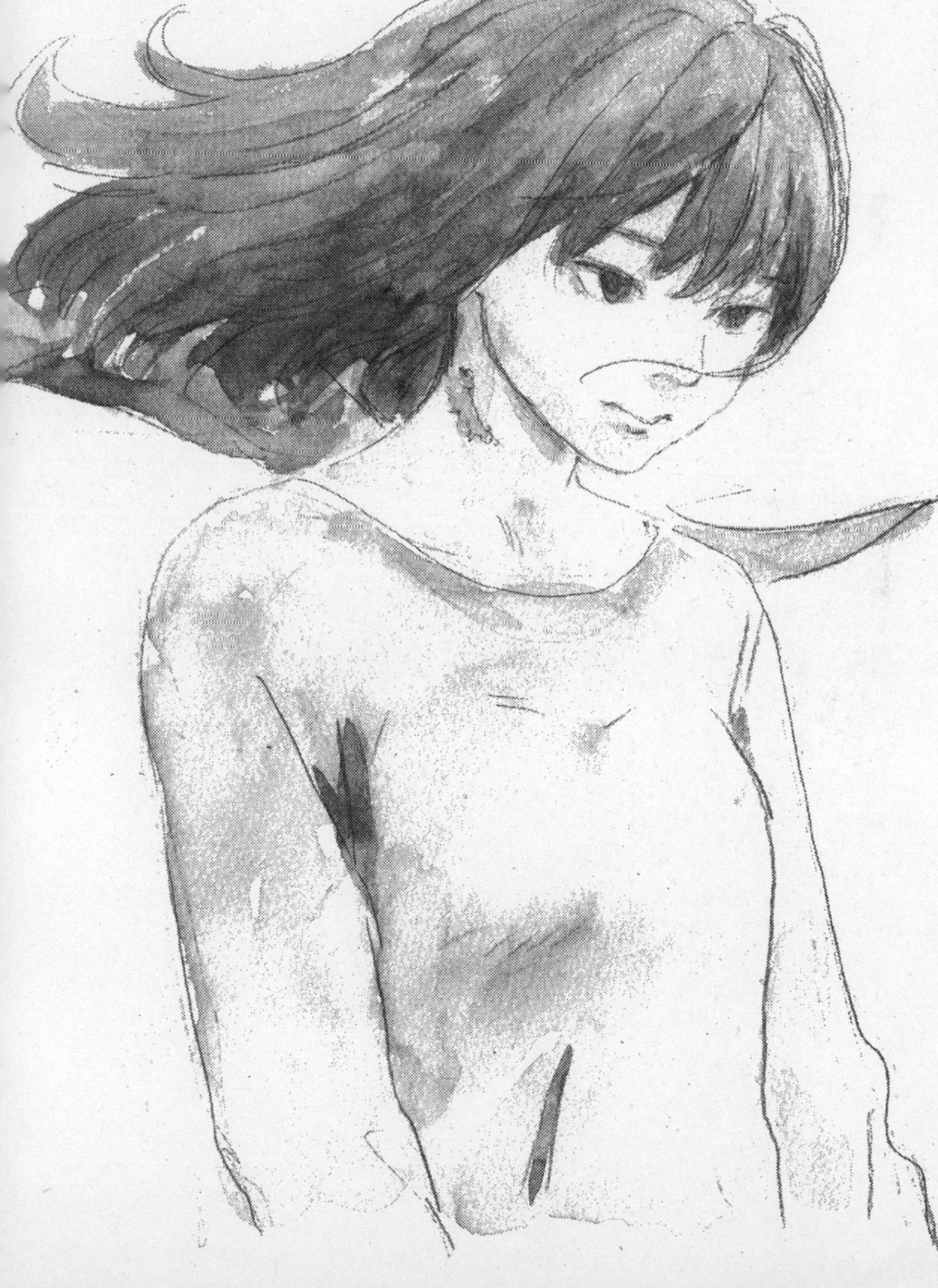

HAPPINESS NEXT VOLUME

VOLUME 6
COMING SOON

Gosho lives her quiet life, keeping her past carefully
hidden. But the smell of blood is once more on the
wind, and the captive Okazaki stirs...!

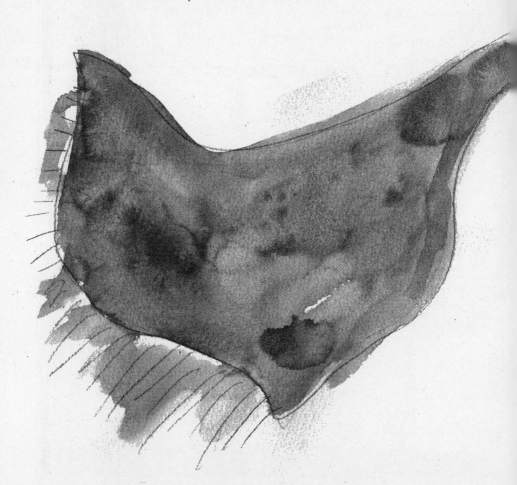

BONUS MANGA

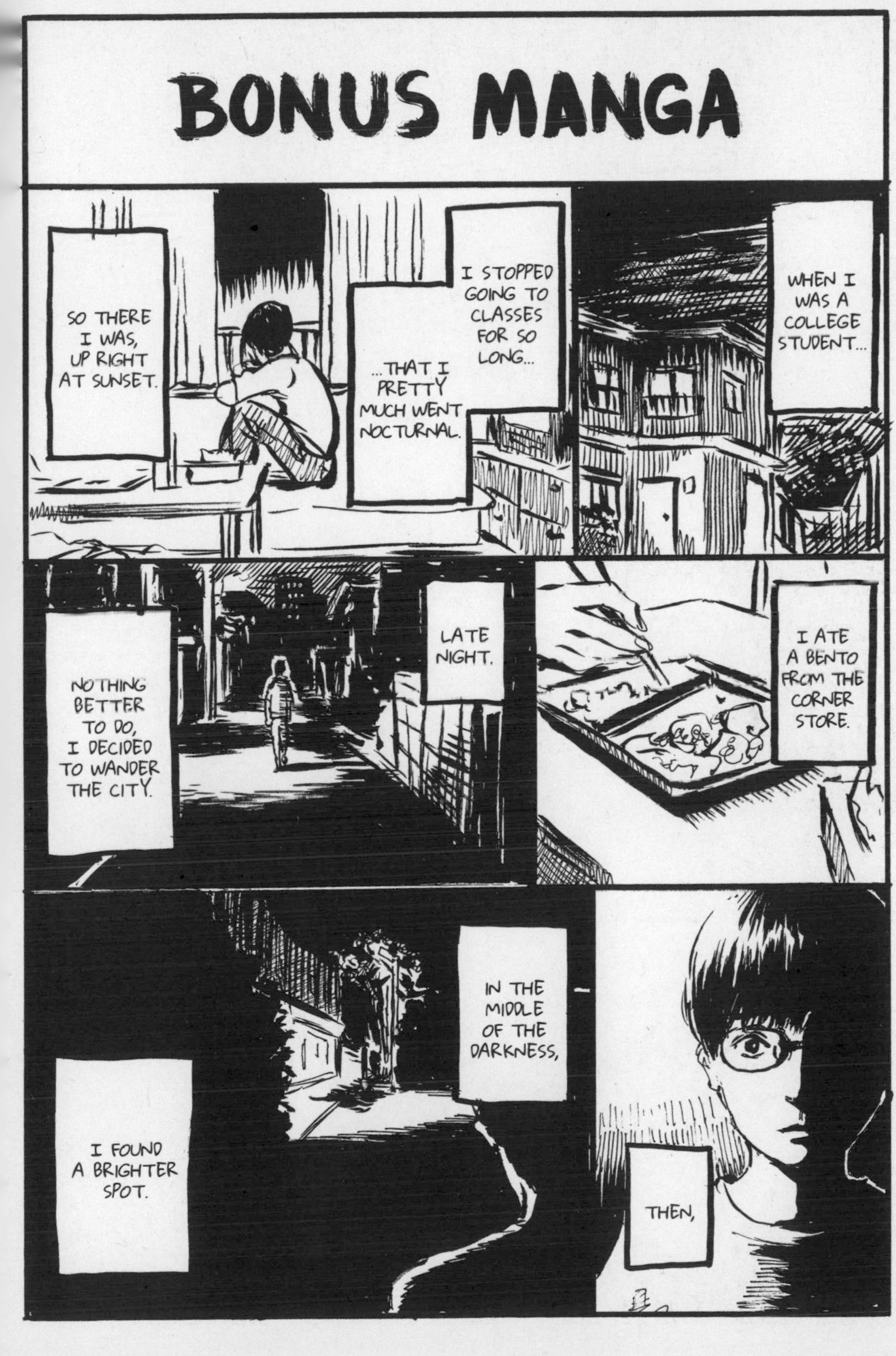
WHEN I WAS A COLLEGE STUDENT...
I STOPPED GOING TO CLASSES FOR SO LONG...
...THAT I PRETTY MUCH WENT NOCTURNAL.
SO THERE I WAS, UP RIGHT AT SUNSET.
I ATE A BENTO FROM THE CORNER STORE.
LATE NIGHT.
NOTHING BETTER TO DO, I DECIDED TO WANDER THE CITY.
THEN,
IN THE MIDDLE OF THE DARKNESS,
I FOUND A BRIGHTER SPOT.

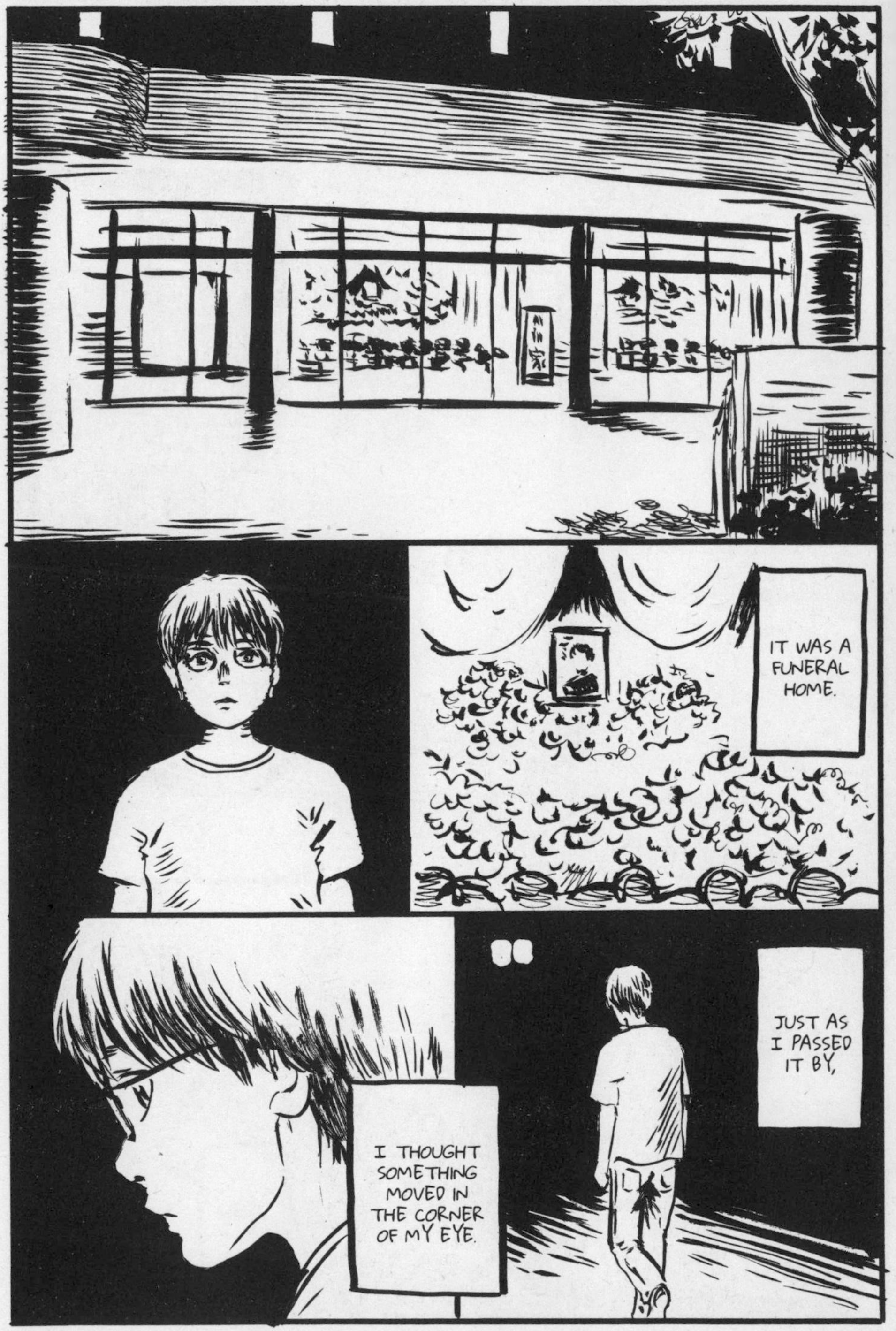
IT WAS A FUNERAL HOME.
JUST AS I PASSED IT BY,
I THOUGHT SOMETHING MOVED IN THE CORNER OF MY EYE.

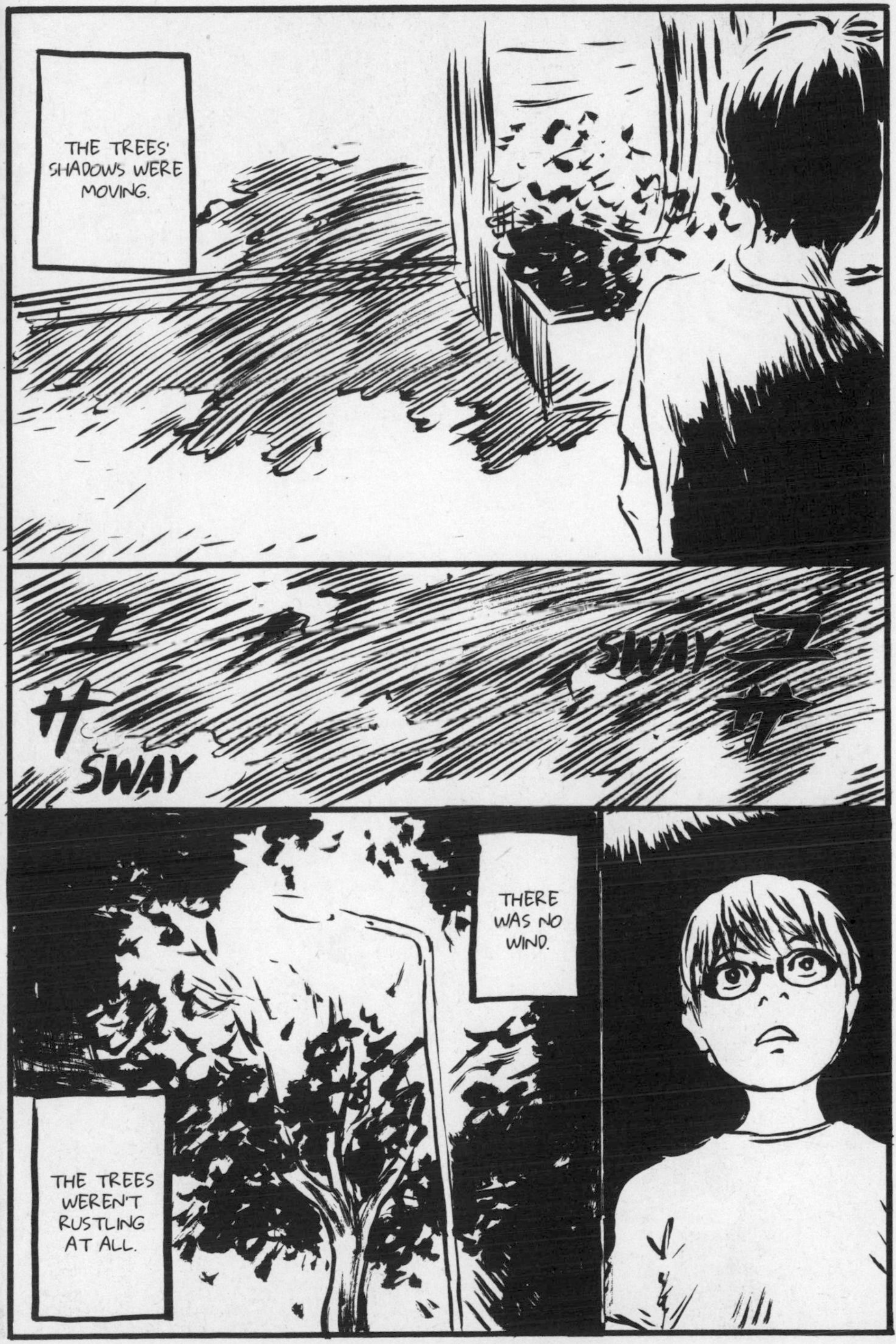
THE TREES' SHADOWS WERE MOVING.
ユサ
SWAY
ユサ
SWAY
THERE WAS NO WIND.
THE TREES WEREN'T RUSTLING AT ALL.

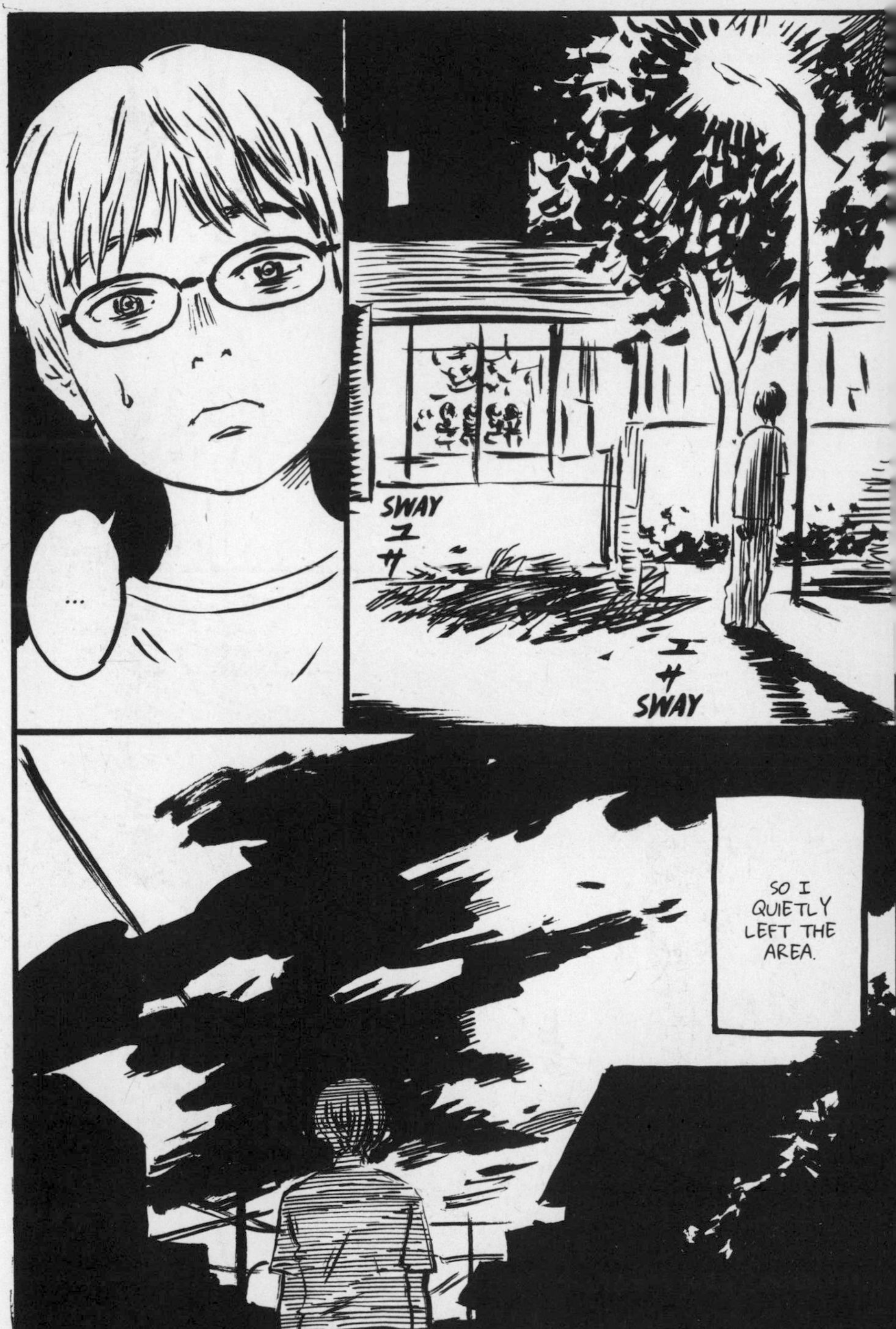
SWAY ユサ
ユサ SWAY
...
SO I QUIETLY LEFT THE AREA.

THE END

"I'm pleasantly
surprised to find
modern shojo using
cross-dressing as a
dramatic device to deliver
social commentary...
Recommended."

-Otaku USA
Magazine

The prince in his dark days

By Hico Yamanaka

A drunkard for a father, a household of poverty... For 17-year-old Atsuko, misfortune is all she knows and believes in. Until one day, a chance encounter with Itaru-the wealthy heir of a huge corporation-changes everything. The two look identical, uncannily so. When Itaru curiously goes missing, Atsuko is roped into being his stand-in. There, in his shoes, Atsuko must parade like a prince in a palace. She encounters many new experiences, but at what cost...?

Based on the critically acclaimed classic horror manga

The first new *Parasyte* manga in over 20 years!

NEO
ParaSytε f

BY ASUMIKO NAKAMURA, EMA TOYAMA, MIKI RINNO, LALAKO KOJIMA, KAORI YUKI, BANKO KUZE, YUUKI OBATA, KASHIO, YUI KUROE, ASIA WATANABE, MIKIMAKI, HIKARU SURUGA, HAJIME SHINJO, RENJURO KINDAICHI, AND YURI NARUSHIMA

A collection of chilling new *Parasyte* stories from Japan's top shojo artists!

Parasites: shape-shifting aliens whose only purpose is to assimilate with and consume the human race... but do these monsters have a different side? A parasite becomes a prince to save his romance-obsessed female host from a dangerous stalker. Another hosts a cooking show, in which the real monsters are revealed. These and 13 more stories, from some of the greatest shojo manga artists alive today, together make up a chilling, funny, and entertaining tribute to one of manga's horror classics!

Happiness volume 5 is a work of fiction. Names, characters, places, and incidents are the products of the author's imagination or are used fictitiously. Any resemblance to actual events, locales, or persons, living or dead, is entirely coincidental.

A Kodansha Comics Trade Paperback Original.

Published in the United States by Kodansha Comics, an imprint of Kodansha USA Publishing, LLC, New York.

Publication rights for this English edition arranged through Kodansha Ltd., Tokyo.

First published in Japan in 2017 by Kodansha Ltd., Tokyo, as *Hapinesu* volume 5.

ISBN 978-1-63236-433-3

Printed in the United States of America.

www.kodanshacomics.com

9 8 7 6 5 4 3 2 1

Translator: Kevin Gifford
Lettering: David Yoo
Editing: Paul Starr
Kodansha Comics edition cover design by Phil Balsman